$3.00

Inierior: 3.00

Ag...

0   25   50   75

R. Tisza

Szeged

botica

K A B A

J V O D I N A

ROMANIA

ovi Sad

remska
Mitrovica

Iron Gates

BELGRADE

R. Sava

Mladenovac

R. Greater Morava

Bor

R. Danube

Valjevo

Ba

Rava Gora

Kragujevac

Čačak   R. Western Morava

Užice   Požega

Kraljevo

Zlatibor

grad

R. Drina

SERBIA

Niš

Dimitrovgrad

R. Southern Morava

Sofia

BULGARIA

Nova
Varoš

R. Ibar

Novi Pazar

R. Lim

Trepča

Žabljak

R. Durmitor   R. Tara

Bijelo
Polje

Kosovska
Mitrovica

Priština

NTENEGRO

R. Piva

Kolašin

Peć

KOSOVO
METOHIJA

šić

Titograd

Cetinje

Kotor

L. Shkodër

Bar

Shkodër

Skopje

MACEDONIA

R. Vardar

ALBANIA

Prilep

Durrës   Tirana

L. Ochrid

L. Prespa

G R

3/94

DJILAS

THE PROGRESS OF A REVOLUTIONARY

DJILAS

THE PROGRESS OF
A REVOLUTIONARY

STEPHEN CLISSOLD

Introduction by Hugh Seton-Watson

UNIVERSE BOOKS
New York

Published in the United States of America in 1983
by Universe Books
381 Park Avenue South, New York, N.Y. 10016

© 1983 The Estate of Stephen Clissold
Introduction © 1983 Hugh Seton-Watson
Map by Sue Lawes

83 84 85 86 87/10 9 8 7 6 5 4 3 2 1

Printed in Great Britain

Library of Congress Cataloging in Publication Data

Clissold, Stephen.
  Djilas, the progress of a revolutionary.

  Bibliography: p.
  Includes index.
  1. Djilas, Milovan, 1911–   2. Statesmen—
Yugoslavia—Biography.   3. Authors, Serbian—20th
century—Biography.   4. Yugoslavia—History—1918–1945.
5. Yugoslavia—History—1945–   I. Title.
DR1305.D56C57 1983   949.7'023'0924 [B] 83–4906
ISBN 0–87663–431–5

We are grateful to the following for permission to reprint copyright material:

Associated Book Publishers for *The Unperfect Society* by Milovan Djilas,
  published by Methuen & Co Ltd
Campbell Thompson & McLaughlin Ltd for *The Embattled Mountain* by F.W. Deakin
Granada Publishing Limited for *Conversations with Stalin* by Milovan Djilas
The Guardian for an interview with Milovan Djilas published on 14 September 1968
Harcourt Brace Jovanovich, Inc., for excerpts from *Conversations with Stalin* and
  Memoirs of a Revolutionary, both by Milovan Djilas; excerpts from *Parts of a Lifetime*
  (copyright © 1975 by Milovan Djilas), *The Unperfect Society* (copyright © 1969 by Harcourt
  Brace Jovanovich, Inc.) and *Wartime* (copyright © 1977 by Harcourt Brace Jovanovich, Inc.),
  all by Milovan Djilas, are abridged and reprinted by permission of the publisher
William Heinemann Ltd for *The Triumphant Heretic: Tito's Struggle against Stalin*
  by E. Halperin
Secker and Warburg Ltd for *Wartime* by Milovan Djilas

All page numbers refer to English editions of works quoted

Contents

Introduction

THE subject of this book, Milovan Djilas, is one of the most interesting figures in the political history of our troubled age. He was born in Montenegro in 1913, in a society which in some ways resembled the Scottish Highlands before the 'Forty-Five', but which had also been for centuries a frontier outpost of Christendom against the formidable Ottoman Empire. It was a land of heroism and cruelty, of clan feuds and fierce personal loyalties, a land – as the title of one of Djilas's own books later put it – 'without justice'. One of the passions of the Montenegrin people, as also of other small endangered peoples of modern times, including the Scottish Highlanders, was the passion for learning. Young Djilas was one of many who, in the 1930s, went from Montenegro to the University of Belgrade, on the southern edge of the Central European plain, the meeting-place not only of the great Danube and Sava rivers, but also of the main trends of modern European culture. Djilas was able to read massively, to talk half the night in cafés, and to write poetry and political journalism. He was soon affected by the sympathy for Communist revolution, and the admiration for unknown and distant Russia, which gripped so many Serbs of his generation. But he went further than this, became an active organiser of the underground Communist Party, was twice arrested, and the second time tortured and then sentenced to a term in prison. When war broke out in 1939 he was at liberty, and supported the Comintern line of theoretical neutrality and practical preference for the Hitlerian side, though this could not be and was not much to his liking. When Yugoslavia was invaded and dismembered in 1941, and Hitler then attacked the Soviet Union, he was from the beginning a leader of the Communist armed rising, at first in his Montenegrin homeland and then in the different regions to which the 'long march' of Tito's army led. He was engaged at different times in battle, in night marches, in administration of liberated regions and in writing news bulletins and propaganda for press and broadcasting (through the wireless contact with the Comintern in the USSR and the 'Free Yugoslavia' radio station operating somewhere in Russia). He also had diplomatic duties, including conversations in 1943 with German army representatives on exchange of prisoners, conversations with British missions, and an official journey to Moscow in April to June 1944. When Belgrade was liberated by the Soviet army in October 1944 he returned to the capital as a leading member of the Party Politbureau and editor of the main party newspaper *Borba*.

In the post-war regime Djilas was one of Marshal Tito's three closest and most influential advisers: the others were Kardelj, who was responsible for constitutional planning and problems, and was also a sort of 'overlord' for the north-western, most advanced, republic of Slovenia; and Ranković, responsible for public order including the security police. Whereas his two fellow-hierarchs and his less powerful comrades from wartime had departmental and administrative tasks of a practical and more or less precise nature, Djilas was in charge of propaganda, and was a kind of cultural overlord. He spent his time not so much in organising others as in writing and in thinking. He produced a flow of articles and some short books. The gibe made against him later by his colleagues, that while they did the hard work of administration, he had a comfortable life reflecting in his study, was unfair but understandable. It is the conventional reproach, made in western societies no less than in 'socialist' states, against writers and thinkers by bureaucrats (not excluding academic bureaucrats) who pride themselves that they are 'too busy to do any thinking'.

Djilas thought a good deal, and observed what was going on around him, what was happening to his fellow-revolutionaries turned bureaucrats, what had happened to such people in the Soviet Union, which he visited again in April 1945 and in January-February 1948, and what was happening outside the 'socialist camp'. He was also directly concerned in the negotiations between Yugoslavia and the USSR whose break-down led to the Cominform's formal public excommunication of Yugoslavia in June 1948. After this his thoughts took a still more radical turn. He began to see not only that Stalin was unjust towards Yugoslavia, but that the bullying attitude, and the impenetrable carapace of self-righteousness, of the Soviet leaders had their roots in the very nature of the Leninist regime. His articles became increasingly critical. For some time he was encouraged to develop his thoughts in the Communist Party's official mouthpiece, the daily *Borba*, was aware of support and sympathy from within the party membership, and was not in any way discouraged by Tito. In all this, the outstanding characteristic of Djilas was his intellectual honesty. He had nothing to gain personally from opposition to the Leninist type of regime, under which, if he had been content to conform, he had an assured brilliant career. He was led to his critical conclusions entirely by honest and fearless thinking. Having convinced himself, he felt bound to express his opinion. There may have been arrogance in this attitude. Certainly it was contrary to the Leninist ethos of utter subordination to the party line. As such it was inevitable that the leaders of the Party should in the end condemn it. But a western democratic observer must feel a combination of admiration for the courage with astonishment at the independence of mind, unparallelled in the history of Leninist regimes.

In the end resentment at his criticisms, perhaps especially from the middle ranks of the party *apparat*, led to a crisis. Tito decided that Djilas had gone too far; a special meeting of the Central Committee was held in January 1954; he had to listen to a long series of denunciations, by one former comrade after another, with only one voice defending and one other half-heartedly excusing him; was deprived of his offices and expelled from the party Central Committee; and was in the end forced into a bitterly humiliating confession of his errors.

It is only fair to say that after this the authorities treated him with what, by Leninist standards, must be reckoned remarkable mildness. In the Soviet Union he would have gone to a labour camp, if indeed he had escaped with his life: in Czechoslovakia and Hungary a year or two earlier leading Communists had been put to death for smaller transgressions. The worst thing about his fate in the next years was the enforced separation from almost all his wartime comrades, including those whom he had thought his intimate friends. The party leaders did not wish actively to persecute him, but were determined to exclude him from Yugoslav public life. But he himself was not prepared to be silent. As his thoughts led him to ever more radical conclusions, he insisted on publishing them; and as he could not do this in Yugoslavia, he arranged for publication abroad of his highly controversial short work, *The New Class*, which essentially applied a Marxist analysis to the society that had grown up under Communist Party rule. This was too much for Tito. Djilas was sent to prison from December 1956 until January 1961, in the same prison in Sremska Mitrovica where he had served his sentence under the pre-war regime. He was then released for over a year, but would not abandon the struggle. When he arranged for publication abroad of his *Conversations with Stalin*, most embarrassing to Tito in view of his improved relations with the Soviet Union, he was sent back to prison, from April 1962 until December 1966. Throughout these years he kept up his literary output. In prison he had only lavatory paper to write on, but this at least was not prevented. Since his second release he has continued. His chief published works have been volumes of mixed history, autobiography and reflection. He remains fearless and unbowed, talking to compatriots or foreigners who visit him and putting his reflections in writing. A man of action and a man of ideas, he has played a leading role in his country's history, and he has had his part in shaping political thought in 'West' and 'East'. Whether in his seventies he will reappear in active politics must be an open question. Yugoslavia faces difficult years, but so does the rest of Europe, and not only Europe.

The career of Djilas seems to me exceptional and significant in two respects. We see in him an outstanding politician who continued to think for himself after victory, and pursued his thoughts to their conclusion regardless of all political expediency. His other striking characteristic is his quite extraordinary honesty. This emerges most clearly in his autobiographical works, in which the bare realities of the national and civil war appear, the sufferings and the courage, but also the brutalities and injustices which he and his companions committed, without question-begging self-exculpation. These are rare qualities at any time or place, and especially perhaps in this century.

The author of this book, my friend the late Stephen Clissold, was unusually qualified to present this story to the English-reading public. Many years spent in Yugoslavia, in peace and in war, including a period as a liaison officer with the Partisans, had given him an excellent knowledge of the country, its people, language, culture and history. No revolutionary himself, he had the sympathetic understanding needed to penetrate the revolutionary mind, and the gentle but untiring persistence to explore it. Familiarity with all the literary works of Djilas and with the wider historical literature on Yugoslavia in several languages, reinforced by personal experience, have enabled him to produce a work which can be confidently recommended to all who wish to probe below the surface of today's Europe.

Hugh Seton-Watson

CHAPTER ONE

A Montenegrin Boyhood

d. 1945.

MILOVAN DJILAS was born on 12 June 1911 at Podbišće, on the borders of what was then the tiny independent Kingdom of Montenegro. His father, a frontier officer of hardy peasant stock, had built his house on virgin land cleared from the forest and nearly one hour's walk from the village itself. It was a plain, two-storeyed stone building, only half finished, standing on a bluff between the Tara and Štitara rivers. His mother hid herself in the woods for the birth, for it was accounted shameful for a child to be born within the walls of a still unfinished house. Milovan was the second of her three sons; four daughters were also to be born to her, but that was considered a matter of less account.

The Djilas family was an offshoot of the Vojnovići, one of the clans which made up the population of Montenegro. Their forebears were Serbs of the Orthodox faith who had sought refuge amongst the crags of Crna Gora (the Black Mountain or Montenegro, as it was called in the Venetian dialect) when the Turks destroyed the mediaeval Serbian Empire in the fourteenth century and pushed on over the Balkan Peninsula towards the heart of Europe. Though the Sultan's armies more than once penetrated to Cetinje, their mountain capital, and plundered it, the Montenegrins never acknowledged his suzerainty. Warfare against the enemy of their faith and against each other became their way of life, the pride and the curse of the whole race. Heroism and manly honour were held to be the supreme, almost the sole, virtues.

The Djilasi could not pride themselves on a particularly illustrious descent. Their surname, like many others in Montenegro, probably stemmed from a nickname derived from the verb *djilasnuti*, 'to make a great leap'. Did it commemorate, as Milovan's father liked to boast, an ancestor who had gained fame by leaping across a chasm, or some such feat? Milovan was inclined to attribute a more prosaic origin to it relating to a determined widow – old Djisna, whose existence not even his father could deny – who 'leapt at' a certain miller she was set on remarrying. In any case, the name stuck, and in the person of Marko Djilas, an uncle of Milovan's grandfather, won celebrity of a sort. Marko lived most of his life as an outlaw. He had made one or two attempts to settle down, once when he hired himself out to a well-to-do peasant whose Turkish landlord he then killed, and later, entering the

1

service of the famous Prince-Bishop Petrović-Njegoš whose displeasure he soon incurred by murdering two Turkish emissaries committed to his charge. An outlaw once more, Marko was eventually lured from his cavern hide-out and shot by a chieftain acting, it was commonly suspected, under the orders of Danilo II, the Prince-Bishop's successor.

Marko left no sons to avenge him. That duty devolved on his nephew Aleksa, Milovan's grandfather. Aleksa discharged a blunderbuss in the face of the murderer and then stabbed him to the heart, but was himself in turn later betrayed and slain. His son, Milovan's father, then eighteen months old, narrowly escaped the same fate. The orphaned family fled for their lives and lived in dire poverty until the new ruler, Prince Nikola, who was anxious to pacify his vendetta-ridden country, ordered that a place should be found in the officer cadet school for one of Aleksa's surviving sons. Milovan's father, on whom the choice fell, could not, however, free himself from the thought of revenge. The royal dynasty itself was sacrosanct but those related to it by marriage might be considered fair game. He was tormented by the suspicion that some of those amongst whom he found himself at Cetinje were stained with his father's blood. He seems to have meditated some coup for which he was arrested, held in fetters and eventually pardoned by the ruler, who also gave him and his brothers land near the frontier town of Kolašin. This virtually amounted to exile; but at least it betokened a reconciliation of sorts and assured the Djilas family a means of livelihood.

As Milovan and his brothers grew older they secretly resented their father's decision to accept reconciliation. Yet the old clan system, with its ways and values more suited to a Homeric age than to the twentieth century, was breaking down, especially in areas of mixed and recently resettled population like their own. They themselves hardly knew where they belonged. Their mother was Montenegrin only by adoption, for her family, which could never bring itself to look with favour on her marriage, had come from Serbia and felt different and culturally superior to the more primitive folk amongst whom they lived. The boys nevertheless felt Montenegrin enough to adopt the traditional ethic of pride and rebelliousness, though it was directed less against the father to whom they were bound by deep affection than against the prevailing social order, which they resented as corrupt and restrictive, a 'Land without Justice', in the phrase which Milovan later adopted as the title for his boyhood reminiscences. They had been born into a race where violence was endemic, inevitable; personal and inter-tribal blood-feuds sharpened the struggle of faith against faith, one region against another, and whole communities against those set in authority over them. 'Generation after generation, the bloody chain was not broken. The inherited fear and hatred of feuding clans was stronger than the fear and hatred of the enemy,' Milovan recalled. 'It seems to me that I was born with blood in my eyes. My first sight was of blood. My first words were blood and bathed in blood.'[1]

When Milovan was one year old, Montenegro joined Serbia, Greece and Bulgaria in declaring war on Turkey. His father was amongst those charged to incite border clashes to provide pretexts for the opening of hostilities. Fortune favoured the Allies, and the Montenegrins overran the neighbouring Sandžak province. The fighting was fierce, for although the Ottoman empire was in decay and rapidly defeated, the 'Turks' who lived in the conquered territory were for the most part of the same race and tongue as the Montenegrins and Serbians – Slavs who had accepted Islam. These Moslems were bitterly hated by their Orthodox kinsmen who pillaged them without mercy. Turkish rugs and carpets made their appearance in Captain Djilas's house.

The First Balkan War ended in victory. It was succeeded the following year by the Second Balkan War when Bulgaria, dissatisfied with her gains, turned on her Allies but was worsted. In August 1914, before the Balkan countries had time to settle down after two successive wars, the Austrian Archduke Franz Ferdinand was assassinated in Sarajevo and the convulsion of the First World War began. His assailants were young Serbs from Bosnia, resentful that their homeland, with its mixed population of Orthodox, Catholic and Moslem Slavs, should have exchanged servitude to the Turks only for annexation by Austria-Hungary. They wished to see it joined instead to the Kingdom of Serbia, as many Montenegrins wished their small state to seek union with the Serbs in a common South Slav state. At first the Serbian army was able to repulse the Austrian advance, but towards the end of the year it was forced to give ground and retire southwards, yielding up the territory coveted by the Bulgarians, and to make the painful retreat through the mountains of Albania to the sea. Montenegro had been quick to declare war in solidarity with Serbia, but despite some initial successes in Bosnia-Hercegovina, it failed to prevent the enemy from penetrating to the capital where King Nikola and his government were forced to capitulate. But on the north-western flank the Montenegrins held back the Austrians and prevented them from cutting off the Serbian retreat through Albania. Then came the order from Cetinje to lay down their arms. Wounded in their martial pride and resentful that their heroic resistance had been in vain, the Montenegrin forces sullenly complied. They felt betrayed by their leaders; some also blamed the Serbs for not letting them join in the withdrawal to the coast.

Stragglers from the Serbian army began to pass through Pobišće and the neighbouring villages. Captain Djilas was away with his unit and made only a rare appearance, but his house offered what food and shelter it could, though to Milovan it seemed that 'our people pitied the Serbians more than they helped them.' He was now four and a half, and some memories of those terrible days were to remain vividly alive. Christmas came – it was the Orthodox Christmas of January 1915, celebrated a fortnight later than in the West. But instead of going out into the woods, as was the custom, to bring home the Yule-log, the family found itself spectators, participants almost, in a bloody battle raging all around them. 'There was a ceaseless thunder and flashing on all sides,' Milovan recalls. 'The cannon never stopped, as if they could feel no fatigue. And whenever a howitzer went off the mountain bellowed from its womb. The thick white beds of snow could not soften that blow.'[2] Montenegro was fighting its last and most glorious battle as an independent state. Its unconquered army was forced to lay down its arms.

For the next three years, whilst the fighting raged on other sectors of the world-wide front, Montenegro lay under enemy occupation. The Austrians, at least to begin with, did not indulge in senseless looting and slaughter. Their troops were orderly and the authorities treated the Montenegrins correctly, sometimes even with a certain sympathy, for there were amongst them men of the same Slav tongue and blood, some of whom already shared the dream of Slav brotherhood. The Croats were the most numerous of Austria-Hungary's South Slav subjects and made good soldiers; one of those who served briefly on the Serbian front was a certain NCO called Josip Broz whom the world was later to hear more of under his conspiratorial name of Tito. But however correct the enemy occupation, the Montenegrins could not long remain docile under it. Incidents occurred and reprisals were taken. Men took to the woods, as they had always done in the age-long struggle against the Turks. Were they patriots or brigands? It was often hard to say. They called themselves guerrillas and could count on the peasants supplying them with food and shelter. To betray one who had sought hospitality was an unforgivable crime. Sooner or later, every informer must expect short shrift, and so must those who needlessly fraternised with the enemy. Terrible cases occurred. In a neighbouring village, an Austrian sergeant attacked a girl and was killed by her brother; the boy was then bayonetted and the whole village burned down. A widow suspected of betraying a guerrilla had her tongue torn out before being killed. A young woman known to have slept with Austrian officers was stripped naked and crucified at a cross-roads. The land had lost its liberty but could still take a terrible revenge – for 'revenge is its greatest delight and glory' – on its faithless sons and daughters.

There were also those who knew how to turn the occupation to account for the settling of old scores, adding fuel to the flames which consumed the nation's vital energies. Rival clans, still intent on pursuing their blood-feuds, did not scruple to draw in the Austrians, as they had once drawn in the Turks, to further their ends. Vendettas would then be fought out under the banners of 'restoring law and order' or of assisting the guerrilla patriots. It was to be the same, on a vaster and fiercer scale, during the occupation and civil strife of the Second World War. This was a lesson, though not one in the school curriculum, which was not lost on little Milovan, now attending his first class.

Milovan began his schooling at the then unusually early age of six. 'I was such a bad child that my mother could not stand me,' he declares, and she was relieved to see him away from home and out of mischief. She must have noticed that he was of more than average intelligence and liveliness. A favourite game, which he would play with his elder brother Aleksa, a pale, thin serious lad, was to carry a burning ember out of the house, place unexploded bullets on it, and then rush off out of range of the lethal fireworks which followed. Once Aleksa wounded his brother whilst playing with his father's pistol. No wonder the harassed mother, on whom the whole labour of the household devolved, was eager to get the boys off her hands and into the care and discipline of school.

Milovan was a quick learner. He had inherited his father's exuberant imagination and fondness for words. He particularly loved the old ballads, still handed down, added to, and occasionally recited by some bard or *guslar* to the monotonous drone of a one-stringed fiddle. The ballads enshrined both beauty and wisdom, and Milovan quickly got them by rote and was not averse to showing off a little by reciting them to the peasants.

It was a hard childhood which left few happy memories. Father, to their great joy, returned safe from the fighting; but before long he was fetched away to internment. His eldest son, who worshipped him, was inconsolable. Mother took his absence more stoically. A woman of few words and simple, strongly held moral convictions, she devoted herself unstintingly to her husband and children. The latter she would beat without emotion when they deserved it, but she spared no pains to smooth their path in life, even when she saw it leading them in directions she neither approved nor understood. Her sons opted to become 'intellectuals'; she did not learn to read or write a little until she was sixty. But even when times were hardest the mother could pride herself on always providing enough for the children to keep body and soul together, though their fare was sometimes no more than freshly gathered nettles boiled with a sprinkling of flour and sour silk.

Despite poverty and the vicissitudes of war, the family grew. Milivoje, a younger brother, and four sisters were born. Grandmother died aged ninety-three. Uncle Mirko fell ill and died at the age of sixty, full of grief, of rage even, at leaving behind no male progeny. He concentrated his affection on Milovan, whom he would get to sit by his bedside and recite some passage from the folk-epics. As death approached, he was consumed more and more by the dominating Montenegrin passion. 'Remember, it is your sacred duty to avenge me!' he exhorted his nephew. Revenge – but against whom? Uncle Mirko seemed to have no particular enemies. It was life itself which he believed had wronged him, and the dying man yearned to be avenged on the whole human condition. Milovan promised; the atavistic passion was not to be resisted. 'Vengeance – this is a breath of life one shares from the cradle with one's fellow clansmen, in both good fortune and bad, vengeance from eternity. Vengeance was the debt we paid for the love and sacrifice our forebears and fellow clansmen bore for us,' he wrote.[3]

When he was ten, Milovan spent the summer months tending the cattle in the hill pastures. For all his curiosity and animal spirits, the boy loved the solitude of his native mountains. Life, with its emotions and questionings, seemed enhanced by their pure and changeless beauty. There everything gained in intensity, became more unashamedly *itself*; the nights darker and more impenetrable, the mornings more gleaming.

The mountains were unchanging, but not so the social and political conditions under which those sheltering in their valleys lived. The war was over, leaving a trail of ferocity, conflicting ambitions and half-realised dreams. As the Austrians withdrew, the Montenegrins felt free to indulge their dominating passion. They plundered and harried the laggards to their hearts' content. Even women and children joined in. If there was little honour to be had by so doing, there were many old scores to be settled, and the innocent must be made to pay the debts incurred by the guilty. Probably the vengeance would have been greater had not so many of the potential avengers themselves fallen victim to an epidemic of Spanish influenza. In Podbišće there were hardly enough able-bodied folk left to bury the dead. But the Djilas family were spared. Captain Nikola returned home, gaunt and grey but still nimble as an old wolf. Milovan noted that his mother seemed 'petrified with joy' and, ashamed to be seen so demonstrative, rushed off to the woods to give vent to her glad tears.

The advocates of union with Serbia now had things their own way. Those who could not reconcile themselves to the new order, or simply preferred the lawless anarchy to which enemy occupation had accustomed them, took to the woods. A new generation of outlaws, of guerrillas, was born. Captain Nikola Djilas was himself no enthusiastic supporter of unification. Though he had little reason to love the old deposed king, he felt that union with Serbia belittled Montenegro, which had ceased to be an independent state. It also seemed likely to blight his own personal prospects. What future was there for peasant-officers like himself in an army dominated by Serbian professionals? He served for a time, it is true, as gendarmerie commandant at Kolašin, the local market town, but found little satisfaction in his duties. He knew it could only be a matter of time before he and his like would be pensioned off by the new government.

It was probably around this time that Milovan first heard serious talk of the Communists. The Yugoslav Communist Party, recently formed from the fusion of various left-wing groups, had made an unexpectedly good showing at the elections to the Constituent Assembly, for which it had secured fifty-nine mandates. The Party's success, and the capacity it was already showing for stirring up trouble, caused alarm and resulted in the enactment of repressive legislation. The Communist militants, particularly some youthful hot-heads, retaliated by organising an unsuccessful *attentat* against Alexander, the Prince Regent, and then by murdering the Minister of the Interior responsible for the anti-Communist measures. This provoked the government to act still more harshly against them, banning the Party and all revolutionary propaganda and agitation. Communism became identified in the popular mind with opposition to authoritarian, centralised government.

In the autumn of 1921 Milovan was sent with his elder brother to attend high school at Kolašin. They boarded in the house of an aunt, about one hour's walk from the town. The family, which consisted of three daughters and a son, was very poor but aspired to better itself. Cousin Ilija was already a teacher in a near-by village. He was a supporter of the Democrat Party and of unification with Serbia, and an enemy of the Communists. Ilija was not unkind to his young cousins, though Milovan, with a schoolboy's cockiness, provoked him by boasting that he had become a Communist! The grown-ups laughed at him; what could this precocious youngster know of such things? Very little indeed, except that he had a *kum* or godfather, a young peasant called Mihailo, who claimed to be a Communist 'because he loved justice – like Christ!' Mihailo, a gentle soul, soon landed in jail where his Communist pretensions wilted. Milovan felt sorry but uneasy when he learned of his *kum*'s defection. Whatever it might be exactly, Communism seemed to him to be a creed for which one should be ready to sacrifice oneself. Ilija had a friend who sometimes paid them a visit and appeared to be a 'real' Communist. He was a medical student and had been sent to prison for his beliefs. A hearty fellow, he prided himself on behaving like a man of the people. 'He kissed all the grandmothers, spoke more like a peasant than the peasants, ate with his fingers and belched loudly.' He too laughed good-naturedly when the boys proclaimed that they were Communists like him, but pleased them by observing more seriously that 'every honest man must be one.'

After two years with Aunt Draguna, Milovan moved into Kolašin itself, a market-town of some importance. It was his first taste of town life. Then, for his fourth year of High School, he moved to Berane, where Aleksa was already studying, and remained there for five years finishing his secondary education. Berane was a more sophisticated place than Kolašin. Two languages were in common use, Serbian and Albanian, though it was the Slavs, most of them belonging to the powerful Vasojević tribe, who monopolised almost all the important positions. The suburb of Haremi recalled the days of Turkish suzerainty, when the garrison's women-folk were confined to their own quarters on the far side of the river Lim. At the bottom of the social scale were the gypsies, who lived in a primitive encampment of their own. The two brothers shared a bedroom in a three-roomed house, little better than the gypsy dwellings. It had a thatched roof, white-washed walls, and an outside lavatory. Water had to be fetched from a neighbour's well. Food – beans, potatoes, flour and cheese – was brought in from home by pack-horse and cooked by the widow who owned the house. Aleksa, no longer a weedy boy, had grown into a muscular young man who was beginning to take an interest in clothes and girls. Though they had many a sharp scrap together the brothers were very close, sharing the same bed and all the intimacies of their lives. Aleksa, increasingly frustrated and restless at school and resentful of all authority, longed to make his way in the world, and without seeking his father's permission he suddenly left Berane for Belgrade. His place was taken by the younger brother Milivoje, with whom Milovan lived on similar terms of intimacy and conflict, though not quite so close.

In the freer environment of Belgrade, Aleksa quickly finished his schooling and returned the following year with stirring tales of the great city and of the political demonstrations in which he had himself taken part. His hatred for the gendarmes, from whose strong-arm methods he had already suffered, and for the authorities in general, was more burning than ever and communicated itself to Milovan whom he found recovering from a bout of typhus. Aleksa had developed politically and was now an avowed revolutionary. Milovan too was taking the same path. 'We developed politically at a different pace,' he recalls, 'but in the same direction.' Family solidarity reinforced political ties. In time, all seven brothers and sisters came to consider themselves Communists.

Persecution had driven the Yugoslav Communist Party to the wings of the political arena. The centre of the stage was occupied by the country's two largest national groups – the dominant Serbs and the Croats, represented by their charismatic peasant leader, Stjepan Radić. There were also militant Croat, Albanian and Macedonian minorities clamouring for outright secession. The Montenegrins, whilst less concerned with the issue of centralism versus federalism, also had their separatist faction, the 'Greens'. The majority, however, were content enough with the existing structure of the state. Some indeed championed it with the single-minded, though sometimes far from disinterested, ardour peculiar to their race. Amongst these chauvinist fanatics was a certain Puniša Račić, a quarrelsome, swaggering political mercenary who had gained election to the Skupština. He belonged to the Vasojevići, and when not engaged in noisily championing the government's line in that legislature, or lurking in the ante-chambers of patronage-dispensing ministers, was often to be found hanging round the market square and cafes of Berane – a thick-set, swarthy fellow with a clipped moustache and a truculent manner. In the summer of 1928, this man gained sudden notoriety by pulling a gun in the Skupština and shooting dead two Croat deputies and mortally wounding Radić. The Peasant Party leader died a few weeks later, mourned not only throughout his native Croatia but in other parts of the country, Montenegro included, where his open, compelling but volatile personality had won him much sympathy. Radić was no Communist, though he was romantically pro-Russian and had flirted briefly with Moscow's 'Green International', but he seemed to the idealistic Milovan to represent the conscience of the whole nation and to speak with its voice.

Most of Milovan's schoolmates were indifferent or hostile to Communism. A few of the teaching staff professed secret Communist sympathies, though none were disciplined party members or did much to stimulate the revolutionary potential of their gifted pupil. Djilas writes disparagingly of them as weak or flawed individuals incapable of giving their cause the whole-hearted devotion it deserved. There were also Russians in Berane; not Soviet Russians, but refugees from the Revolution who had found asylum and jobs in Yugoslavia. King Alexander Karadjordjević had been educated in Tsarist Russia. A passionate anti-Bolshevik, he opened his country to the White Russian exiles and favoured them with the same energy with which he pursued his own indigenous Communists. Milovan conceived a burning hatred for him and showed little sympathy for the exiles, some of whom were his teachers and gave him a fair knowledge of their language and a love for its literature. The Russian classics in which he steeped himself predisposed his mind, he later declared, to accept the ideals of justice and humanity professed by the Communists.

Was Milovan already an avowed atheist? Most of his schoolmates believed vaguely in God and respected the outward forms and traditions of the Orthodox Church as an indissoluble part of the national heritage handed down throughout the centuries of struggle against Islam. He had himself always possessed a keen sense of right and wrong, and of the cosmic warfare ceaselessly waged between them. But the Church and its ministers seemed to have little connection with this struggle. Its liturgy, with which they were required to familiarise themselves in class, seemed to lack all relevance. His father – except for a time later in life when he became friendly with the village priest, under whose influence he grew a beard, attended church and intoned the responses in a loud voice – had not been a pious man or given his children much of a religious upbringing. The Bible played little part in education, and the place it held in Protestant lands was occupied in Montenegro by *The Mountain Wreath*, the great poems by the Prince-Bishop Petrović Njegoš which enshrined the wisdom of his race and expressed it with force and beauty. Milovan had often mused, in the solitude of the mountains, on the problems of human destiny treated in another great philosophical poem by the Njegoš, *The Light of the Microcosm*. Why, if God exists, is there such suffering in the world? Why are men, if created in His image, so cruel, so blindly selfish?

On the last Christmas of Milovan's schooldays there occurred an event which was to have a profound significance for the country and for the course of his personal life. On 6 January 1929 King Alexander suspended the constitution and took power exclusively into his own hands. Ever since the murder of the Croat leader the previous summer, political passions had been rising to a pitch which made parliamentary government virtually impossible. The old political leaders were at odds with one another and thoroughly discredited. The King believed that a period of stern, highly centralised rule was the only means of keeping the country together. The political turmoil was made worse by the onset of the world economic crisis. Many people, even in Croatia, thought at first that the royal dictatorship might indeed offer the best way out. All political parties were abolished, the ruling cliques lost their power and privileges, and a new generation of placemen made its appearance, responsive to the royal despot in Belgrade, but scarcely an improvement on the old. The press was muzzled and freedom of speech became a dangerous occupation. It was a poor prospect for an apprentice revolutionary and an aspiring writer.

Milovan Djilas wished to become both. If he had to choose between the two – literature or political commitment – he was prepared to opt for the latter. In the first flush of youthful idealism, he also persuaded himself that he must break off his incipient love affairs and keep himself free from emotional attachments for the good of the cause. He thought vaguely that after leaving school he would become a journalist and go to Paris or to Prague where he had heard there was a School of Journalism. Since journalists concern themselves with the contemporary scene, he expected to be concerned (as far as this was possible under the royal dictatorship) with politics. He would become a political writer, a revolutionary writer, and that way might lie the path to fulfilment and literary fame.

Milovan was the only member of his class to proclaim openly that he was for Communism. It was a brave, even foolhardy, gesture to make at a time when the royal dictatorship was stepping up its already severe measures against the Communists. Perhaps it was more adolescent bravado than an act of political defiance. He could not resist the urge to nail his colours to the mast. When Graduation Day arrived, Milovan put on a flaming red tie. He also donned a Russian-style shirt cut to his own design. In this deliberately Tolstoyan guise he had himself photographed and took such a liking to the result that he continued to wear the shirt as both a practical and a suitably symbolic item of attire during his student days in Belgrade.

Captain Nikola Djilas had moved with his younger children to Bijelo Polje where Milovan spent his last summer vacation. Aleksa was doing his military service and was stationed at Cetinje where his brother proposed to break his journey on his way to Belgrade. Aleksa's recalcitrant and stubborn character was already getting him into trouble with the officers. Milovan too was an avowed rebel, but his nature was more complex. He was imaginative and romantic. Already sure of himself, single-minded in his views and intolerant of those of others, eager to throw himself into the struggle between right and wrong and to join the vanguard in the crusade for social justice, he had more contradictory strands in his nature than he perhaps realised. The puritanical strain was strong, but so too was the bohemian. He was naturally pugnacious and would soon learn to be ruthless; but he also had the writer's sensitivity to beauty and the finer shades of human relationships. He favoured clear and uncompromising answers to life's questions and would learn to propagate them with all the assurance of a disciplined dogmatist. But the loud, confident tones could not quite drown the core of moral and intellectual integrity from which would ultimately spring not only doubt and the need for reappraisal, but also the seed of something disturbingly new and irreconcilable with the ready-made ideology which now seemed to offer him an infallible guide through life's adventure.

His material equipment was correspondingly simple. His mother sewed together a sack into which she stuffed his peasant wardrobe – shirts, a sweater, thick woollen socks – together with a tin cup filled with cheese. His father accompanied him as far as Kolašin where he boarded a bus to Podgorica and then another to the old mountain capital where Aleksa was waiting for him. The rest of the journey would be by train – something Milovan had never seen before. At Sarajevo he was told to change, and during the stop-over he hurried out into the town to buy a cheap suit and a city shirt and tie. The young man felt embarrassed by his peasant origins and determined to adopt the urban ways he thought suitable to a revolutionary.

His mental baggage stood in no such need of change. 'Communism was a new idea,' he afterwards recalled. 'It offered youth enthusiasm, a desire for endeavour and sacrifice to achieve the happiness of the human race.' There was also something more; a perfect correspondence between his Montenegrin past and the future he saw opening up before him and all humanity. As he was later to put it: 'The Montenegrin character is rebellious, single-minded, violent and much given to hero-worship. Hence it has a natural affinity with what is popularly taken as Marxism-Leninism. When a Montenegrin rebel meets Marxism-Leninism, the recognition is instantaneous and satisfying. The Montenegrin temperament and the temper of Marxism (and especially Leninism) are a perfect fit.'[4]

CHAPTER TWO

Student Revolutionary

THERE was little about the Yugoslav capital to suggest a revolutionary temper or the ferment of Marxist ideas when Milovan Djilas arrived there early one morning in the August of 1929. Plenty of movement and noise indeed, but it was the bustle of some huge Balkan village trying to turn itself overnight into a western-style city. One-storeyed houses stood cheek by jowl with unfinished offices, ministries and villas. The old Turkish fortress of Kalemegdan still perfunctorily guarded the junction of the Sava and the Danube but seemed to have resigned itself to the role of museum and zoo rather than barracks. Avenues flanked with half-grown trees cut through the old streets to peter out in fields where goats were tethered and sheep grazed.

Djilas – for now that he is away from home he will be generally known by his surname or his party nickname 'Djido' – found himself a room in Balkanska Street. Any notion of going further afield to Paris or Prague was soon abandoned; that was all far too complicated and expensive. He quickly took to the casual student life around him, enrolling at Belgrade University in the Faculty of Yugoslav Literature and spending much of his time in endless discussions on life and politics in the smoke-filled rooms of cheap cafes. It was an easy-going existence. Although Djilas never felt drawn to the heavy drinking, the gambling and womanising in which some of his companions indulged, he did not show himself a particularly industrious student either.

The Dictatorship had effectively stifled all political life. Such Communist organisations as existed in the university had been broken up. The students were restless and sometimes turbulent, but cowed and unorganised. Any professor deemed to be introducing politics into his lectures (apart from the required patriotic and royalist rhetoric) received short shrift. The most popular courses were those given by the left-wing Agrarian, Professor Dragoljub Jovanović, who was sympathetic to the Communists but never identified himself with them. Djilas attended some of his lectures but found them too academic and objective for his taste. Unversed as he still was in Marxist theory, he hungered for its confident assertions, its black-and-white view of a world which otherwise made little sense. Jovanović seemed to him no true revolutionary; he had words of praise for some things in the Soviet

Union, but for others as well in the corrupt capitalist democracies. For the authorities, however, this was already going too far. The professor was suspended, sentenced to a year's imprisonment, and finally banned altogether from the university.

Milovan Djilas was not, in any case, much interested personally in agricultural or any other sort of economics. His passion was for literature. As far as his political development went, the next two years were largely a period of marking time – or rather, of stamping noisily but ineffectively around between street demonstrations and furtive meetings – but at least he was able to make a start as a writer. His first poems, sketches and short stories began to appear in a mimeographed magazine called *Venac (Wreath)* in tribute to the great Njegoš, and then in the more prestigious *Misao (Thought)*. Before long *Politika*, Belgrade's most respected daily, was publishing an occasional story – and paying handsomely for it. The poems were marked by youthful bombast, sombre and enigmatic allusions, and fashionable touches of surrealism; they hardly indicated a major lyrical talent. The sketches and tales were mostly folkloristic, celebrating his native Montenegro and the obscure life and loves of its people.

His new experience in Belgrade also furnished the young writer with some of his themes. One tale gives a moving portrait of 'Mile, the student milkman' spurning amorous enticements and doggedly doing his early morning rounds. Djilas, to earn money for himself and his parents at home, had been forced at times to take on such jobs, though they had not called for such personal sacrifices. Fortune had been kind to him in this respect. Whilst attending his Russian literature classes his interest had been aroused by a fellow-student, a young girl with a pale skin, dark, glowing eyes, and a slender figure. Mitra Mitrović was not strikingly beautiful, but there was a quiet, graceful intensity about her which gave promise of a quick, independent intelligence and an as yet unaroused capacity for emotional and ideological devotion. Mitra came from a small Serbian town where her mother, a woman of exceptional courage and resourcefulness, had struggled to bring up a large family after the death of their father. Mitra had town ways and a more conventional outlook, and Djilas could not resist teasing her about her 'bourgeois prejudices', especially when these stood between him and the physical fulfilment of their love affair. He lectured her on the need to discard them in order to achieve a more complete and ideologically correct commitment to the struggle for social justice. The two first met in the spring of 1931; by autumn the following year they were lovers, treading the same path towards a common revolutionary goal.

Their courtship was interrupted by an incident indicative of the moral earnestness which young Communists often brought at that time to their search for a political creed which was also a way of life. At school Mitra had had an affair with a boy who became a Communist. Seeing that her affections seemed now to be elsewhere engaged, the young man sought out his rival and earnestly deliberated with him what should be done. The revolutionary struggle must on no account suffer through an uncomradely dispute over a girl! Djilas agreed. After much serious talk, they wrote a joint letter informing Mitra that, in the interests of the movement, they had each agreed to end their relationship with her. There was to be neither victor nor vanquished! Mitra appeared to take the matter calmly, but not long after she was seized with a fit of hysteria in class and had to be taken home. Her sister sent for Djilas who sat awkwardly by her bedside torn between affection and loyalty to his comrade. Mitra held his hand and wept silently. She loved him, and he knew that he loved her. One day, when she was well again, she remarked to him suddenly: 'I know you will think I'm very "bourgeois"; but I should like it if we got married!' He raised no objection; there were times when concessions had to be made to the bourgeois conscience.

Djilas was anxious to think and act like a Communist, but he was not one yet, at least in any formal sense. He had not joined the Party. He had not even succeeded in finding it. Official persecution had been so drastic that the organisation in Yugoslavia was thoroughly smashed. Its leaders had been forced into exile and were either in Moscow or Vienna, where what remained of the Central Committee had established itself. Any who returned home ran serious risk of arrest, imprisonment and interrogation under torture. Djaković, the Secretary-General, was caught and then shot 'whilst trying to escape'. His successor, and the Comintern bosses who determined strategy, were so out of touch with Yugoslav reality that they launched the watch-word of 'armed struggle' and insisted on such party members as were still at large adopting an intransigent sectarian line which precluded cooperation with 'bourgeois' opponents of the Dictatorship. Attempts to put these ill-advised directives into practice only played into the hands of the police. Promising middle-ranking leaders were soon serving prison sentences. In Zagreb, for example, Andrija Hebrang, a future Secretary of the Croat Party, was sentenced to twelve years; and the metal-worker Josip Broz-Tito received five for involvement in a so-called 'bomb affair'.

It was difficult in the prevailing atmosphere of clandestinity, caution and suspicion, to discover just who *did* represent the Party. For years it had been riddled with 'factionalism' and weakened by purges and resignations. Some of those whom the authorities still labelled Communist, and continued to persecute, were in fact either disgraced and disgruntled ex-members or dissidents of some kind. The most active and influential figure of this type at Belgrade University was a professor of mathematics, Sima Marković. A Serb – or 'Great Serb' like the bourgeois politicians, his critics declared – Marković had been the Party's Secretary-General but had crossed swords with Stalin himself over the national question. Marković believed nationalism to be an irrelevance which could only distract Marxists from their true concern, which was social revolution. He was accordingly loth to cooperate with the Croat and other nationalists who aimed at the destruction of the bourgeois Yugoslav state. The latter, Moscow had ruled after some initial uncertainty, was a mere creation of the Versailles settlement and the tool of the capitalists. It therefore deserved to be broken up into its component parts; these would then form mini-states which the Soviet Union could the more easily dominate. Marković had been forced to toe the line. Expelled from the Party, he nevertheless still commanded a following in Serbia and continued, at considerable personal risk, with his canvassing and propaganda. Djilas made contact with his supporters without realising how matters stood. When alerted, he dropped them at once, though they offered facilities for printing and distributing illegal material which were beyond the resources of the orthodox Party comrades.

One member of the Central Committee did manage to make his way back and to remain at large for a time in Belgrade. This was a Montenegrin called Petko Miletić, who enjoyed the reputation of a heroic revolutionary fighter. He was a whole-hearted adherent of the Comintern's intransigent line and looked down on the student radicals, even those of peasant origin like Djilas, as unreliable intellectuals half assimilated to the petit-bourgeois class enemy. A quarrelsome, intolerant dogmatist, he had nothing but scorn for the amateurism of the younger revolutionaries and their noisy demonstrations.

'There was a romantic rebelliousness in everything we did,' Djilas recalls. Their Communism was an expression of the restlessness and frustrated idealism to which the dictatorial regime denied any means of orderly political expression. Looking back on those days when mere suspicion of being a Communist could land a man in jail and entail beatings and expulsion from the university, Djilas could write that most of those who became Communists, or thought themselves such, acted 'in the hope of realizing brotherhood and equality, of freeing our people from exploitation, giving them a happier life. . . We felt an inner anguish, dissatisfaction with everything including ourselves.'[1] To be a Communist appealed to youthful idealism and desire for adventure, offering the prospect, however illusory, of escape into a world of purposeful action, comradeship and individual fulfilment in the pursuit of a common social goal. 'I did not know a single man who became a Communist out of ambition or the hope of material gain,' Djilas recalls, writing in the days when things had become very different, the Communist Party was in power, and membership of it a magnet for careerists. But under the dictatorship of King Alexander the very harshness of the repression was to prove a blessing in disguise for the Party, purging it of faint-hearts, dabblers and egotists and forging new, resolute and disciplined cadres.

Nor was it the poorest of the poor, the most underprivileged and downtrodden, who were the first to rally to the revolutionary banners. Extreme poverty and wretchedness inhibit initiative. Many recruits, it is true, came from the 'passive regions' – passive economically, not psychologically – like Montenegro, Bosnia-Hercegovina and the Lika, where the struggle for mere survival was sharpest. But most belonged, as did Milovan Djilas himself, to the more prosperous families in those parts. The calibre of such recruits was above the average; it was the more gifted students who tended to become involved in political activity, though the demands made on their time and energies were at the expense of studies which they often failed to complete. The political struggle came to absorb and dominate them, and Marxist ideology, which at first seemed a liberating force and the key both to action and to an intellectual understanding of the world, finished by blunting the cutting edge of their capacity for independent thought.

If the aims of the youthful radicals were idealistic and grandiose, their methods seemed frequently puerile and crude. The university authorities, bent on preserving what they could of its autonomy, had little enthusiasm for the Dictatorship. But it was against them that the radicals generally directed their fire. Djilas quickly distinguished himself in the organisation of protests and demonstrations. They provided an outlet for his energies and made him feel important.

By the autumn of 1932 each faculty could boast an embryo Communist group, the secretaries of which together comprised a University Committee of which Milovan Djilas was elected secretary. Once he led a deputation to the Rector's office, and finding it locked and empty, broke down the door, smashed the furniture and ransacked the papers. On St Sava's Day, when official celebrations were organised

17

in honour of the university's patron saint, he packed the gallery with his friends and bombarded the podium with missiles; they were only of paper, but they served to disrupt the proceedings. Sometimes forays would be launched outside the university. Such goings-on, Djilas felt, 'helped maintain the fighting spirit at the university and established the Communist image in the public eye. We felt like a secret power, and in the eyes of ordinary people we were indestructible.'[2]

But not in the eyes of the police. Djilas knew that they kept a sharp watch on him now that he was so active in organising student demonstrations. One morning in March, in his third year at the university, the flat which he shared with other leftists was raided and a number of subversive leaflets seized. He was arrested and taken away to the Glavnjača, the old municipal prison. The cells were in the cellars, each lit by a small window looking onto the corridor. The floor was of bare cement, with wooden boards for bunks and a tin bucket to serve as toilet. Number Six was the cell traditionally assigned for political prisoners, though common prisoners were put there too. Georgi Dimitrov, the Bulgarian who later headed the Comintern apparatus in Moscow, and many other well-known Communists had passed through Number Six. Djilas felt proud that he was following in their footsteps. Amongst his cell-mates were one or two lawyers who had been arrested for organising meetings amongst the peasants. One of them was an ex-Communist who had left the Party following disagreements over its narrow, sectarian policies, and was prematurely following the 'popular front' line of joining forces with the non-Communist Opposition. Djilas felt little sympathy for him or his independent tactics.

After a week in detention, Djilas was sent for by Aćimović, the Belgrade police chief who wished to cross-examine him in person. Reports had reached him that the Communists were planning to assassinate some key figure in the regime, probably General Živković whom the King had nominated Prime Minister. Though he would not shrink from violence, nor even from killing a man with his own hands if need arose, Djilas was not personally drawn to assassination, as some of the younger militants had been, either as a way of venting a grudge against society or as good political tactics. Leninist theory in any case deprecated terrorist acts as offering no shortcut to the millennium nor any valid alternative to the mass revolutionary movement. Djilas could truthfully say that he knew absolutely nothing about any plot to murder the Prime Minister or anyone else.

Aćimović believed him. As he had no hard evidence to go on, he decided to let the young trouble-maker off with a warning. The prisoner was told not to dabble any more in clandestine activities or he would soon find himself in prison again, and next time he could not expect such gentle treatment. For a time, Djilas thought it prudent to take the warning to heart.

On vacation, Djilas found that as an educated man, an 'intellectual' and a budding writer, his status amongst the peasants had increased enormously. They listened with respect and credulity to whatever he had to tell them. If they could not always follow his Marxist analysis of the country's political situation or of the causes of their social and economic ills, they were well disposed towards Russia which they believed had somehow found the secret of abundance and prosperity. The most fantastic stories were circulating amongst them – that grain was heaped up high in every Russian village and the peasants had only to help themselves, or that a miraculous machine had been invented where grain was poured in at one end to emerge as bread at the other – with butter on it too. 'I myself never believed such stories,' Djilas assures us somewhat artlessly, 'but I explained everything about Russia as if I had been there.'[3] He had already conceived a boundless admiration for Stalin, for the 'Fatherland of Socialism' and for everything it stood for.

He felt at home amongst the peasants. Though his own life had shifted to the city he never lost touch with them or their problems, and he wrote about them, sometimes with humour, sometimes with emotion, but always with insight and sympathy. With the factory workers it was different. According to Marxism-Leninism they should be in the van of the Revolution, showing the most militant class-consciousness and providing the Party with its finest cadres. In Yugoslavia, an undeveloped country with a still mainly agrarian economy, they were not yet very numerous, and the few there were did not show much revolutionary spirit. It was also extremely difficult to make contact with them. When at last Djilas did manage to come across a more or less organised and Communist-orientated group of workers he found to his consternation that, so far from the proletarian elements, the core of the workers' movement, giving the cue to intellectuals like himself, they had an even more tenuous contact with the Party than he had himself. It fell to him to strengthen its links with the clandestine leadership.

The University Committee now at last had an approved contact with the Central Committee in the person of a Marxist intellectual called Veselin Masleša whom Djilas met from time to time in Belgrade. Zagreb had a still larger coterie of Marxist writers and intellectuals, but they were for the most part of dubious orthodoxy. The outstanding figure amongst them was the dramatist, essayist and novelist Miroslav Krleža, whose long and fruitful career was to be spent in and out of the Party and in constant polemics. Though still a novice in Marxist ideology, Djilas had no hesitation in crossing swords with Krleža and other prominent intellectuals.[4] Was he then in danger of dissipating his energies in the sterile controversies of coffee-house revolutionaries? A call to action saved him from this danger. Early in 1933 the police, who were hot on the trail of Petko Miletić, at last succeeded in arresting the dangerous conspirator. He was held, pending his trial, in a small prison adjacent to the Belgrade District Court. Djilas received a message smuggled out from other imprisoned comrades informing him of this and urging him to organise his rescue.

The difficulties did not appear great. The gendarme on duty at the entrance to the jail was a Montenegrin who was impressed by the knowledge that his prisoner was a compatriot and an important Communist. The other guards seemed slack. Djilas assembled an assault group, procured a pistol, a chloroform-soaked gag and the cooperation of a friendly taxi-driver for the getaway. But the plan went wrong. One of his fellow conspirators fell into the hands of the police and gave away the names of the others. Early one morning the police burst into Djilas's lodgings and arrested him. Instead of the affair ending with Miletić's escape, the would-be rescuer found himself back again in cell Number Six.

CHAPTER THREE

In Jail

On 23 April 1933 Milovan Djilas was sentenced to three years' imprisonment for subversive activity. The Chief of Police had kept his word. The next time the prisoner came into their hands, Aćimović had warned, they would not treat him quite so gently. The Serbian police had inherited from the Turks some of the methods used to punish prisoners or to make them talk, for instance, beating on the soles of the feet with a pizzle until the sharp, cutting pain became unbearable. They had also thought up one or two devices of their own. Sometimes they contented themselves with merely kicking and thrashing. All these different techniques Djilas quickly experienced on his own skin.

The police were persistent if not particularly subtle in their cross-examinations. They wanted names. The defaulting comrade had, under duress, blurted out the name of Djilas; who would he in turn be forced to give away? It came as a shock and disillusionment to him that a working-class man had not stood up to pressure as the proletariat, the cream of the Party, was expected to do. In his own case, he would summon up national pride to reinforce Communist zeal and discipline. The Montenegrins had always been a race of heroes, facing the worst the enemy could do without flinching. Djilas stood up well under the initial torture; but for how long could he continue to hold out? Every man, even the greatest hero, reaches his breaking-point. When they came to arrest him, the search had been only perfunctory and they had not taken away his pocket-knife. He decided to attempt suicide with it. Not that he seriously intended to take his own life; things had not yet reached such a pitch. His idea was was rather to make a suicide attempt serious enough to force the police to suspend interrogation. The comrades would see to it that the news got around, and the authorities were not indifferent to damaging publicity.

Djilas plunged the knife in beneath his left shoulder, not dangerously near the heart, but deeply enough to spread alarm amongst his cell-mates. He was quickly transferred to a clinic and kept there for ten days. The non-Communist opposition took up his case and ventilated it in the press. The news brought his father and Aleksa hurrying up to Belgrade. It also reached and alarmed Mitra who carried out her instructions to see that all his papers, and particularly any addresses, were destroyed. When pronounced fit enough, Djilas left the clinic and was transferred to the new penitentiary which had recently been designated for the incarceration of political prisoners. It was on an island in the River Sava known by its Turkish name of Ada Ciganlija.

Djilas did not feel too daunted by the prospect before him. He had the satisfaction of having survived his first confrontation with the interrogators better than most. To have given ground would have left him branded for life as a weakling, if not a traitor. He had gained in experience, confidence and authority with the Party. His hatred of the system now had a keener personal edge to it. At the penitentiary life should not be too bad. Books and newspapers were allowed, and food could be sent in from outside. He would have time to write and to pursue those Marxist-Leninist studies deemed essential to the formation of every veteran party member. He would meet other comrades, some of them well-known in the revolutionary movement. They would forge a closer comradeship together and re-emerge all the stronger to fight another battle.

Visits from fiancées were not allowed, but Mitra found a way of making sure they would continue seeing each other, at least from a distance. Every Saturday, punctually at noon, a small figure in a red sweater would detach itself from behind the houses which lined the banks of the Sava and stand there waving and staring towards the penitentiary. She knew which was his cell, but all she could make out was the faint outline of hands clutching the bars.

Djilas wrote Mitra a letter begging her to consider herself released from any ties of 'bourgeois loyalty' towards her imprisoned lover. This was the second time he had announced his readiness to sacrifice his personal happiness for the sake of the movement and its prevailing ideology; and for the second time she ignored it. The slender figure continued to appear every Saturday at noon, standing silently on the river bank, signally her faithfulness and perhaps, in the symbolic choice of a bright red sweater, her growing commitment to the cause which she too was coming to make fully her own.

The Party's general approach to emotional and sexual attachments was casual; they were considered of very minor importance compared with obligations towards the Party. Later, and in no small part due to Djilas's own more puritanical leanings, mutual loyalty between a man and the mate of his choice became the norm; but at this time, to expect a woman to consider herself still bound to a man who found himself in prison was looked upon as a mere expression of outmoded bourgeois morality. Or was it simply making a virtue of necessity? Josip Broz-

Tito, also serving a prison sentence, had had to accept the fact that his wife Pelagia Belousova, whom he had brought home from Russia, wished to return there with their infant son. In the Soviet Fatherland they would be well looked after, the Party said. They could not tell him that there too she would find a new partner and make a new life for herself, leaving the little boy to the care of an institution.

Milovan Djilas, a romantic at heart, was secretly glad that his own woman chose to remain faithful to him. He kept her photograph and longed for her with an intensity which he tried to sublimate in his writings. During his time in prison he completed a number of short stories and a novel entitled *Black Hills*, which were largely autobiographical. He hoped that Mitra would one day read them and, finding her sweetheart reflected in them, be drawn more closely still to him. The prison authorities allowed him to send out the finished manuscript of the novel but it has not survived.

Towards the end of 1933 the prisoner was transferred to a penitentiary at Sremska Mitrovica where he was to serve the remaining two and a half years of his sentence. It was there that he came to know many of the Party's leading figures and to accustom himself both to its demanding discipline and to the intrigues and power-struggles within it. There was the Party organisation proper, composed of formally enrolled members. There was also a wider 'collective' embracing all prisoners who were prepared to contribute food and money to the common stock and to recognise the decisions of the elected leadership. Party members were *ipso facto* members of the collective and effectively controlled it. Its aim was to promote solidarity in the face of the authorities and to improve the prisoners' material conditions by organising strikes and other forms of non-cooperation. The authorities, for their part, tried to keep the prisoners passive and disunited by forbidding contact and even communication between the large rooms into which they were divided. The collective, like prisoners of war and political prisoners everywhere, kept themselves busy devising ingenious ways of outwitting and thwarting them. Djilas threw himself into this work with gusto.

Comradeship and unity amongst the prisoners in common hostility towards the authorities, who also represented the 'class enemy' – such was the aim. It reflected the double moral standard in vogue amongst the Communists, particularly when the Party was able to operate in freer and more normal conditions. 'Sentimentality, generosity, friendliness were applicable within our closed Communist circle, and not outside it,' Djilas explains. 'Within this, feelings of love, devotion, unselfishness and sincerity intensified to the point of self-obliteration. The emotional development among Communists played a more important role in the creation of the Communist movement than the revolutionary Marxist ideology. Personal happiness was synonymous with the success of the movement. . . . When he loved and when we hated, when we were awake and when we were asleep, we had one final goal in mind – the destruction of the existing system and the triumph of the Party.'[1] This may have been true of the students and other young revolutionaries prepared to risk their lives in acts of defiance against the Dictatorship, but prison produced a different mentality. The prisoners' sting had been drawn, and there was little they could do to demonstrate their revolutionary fervour. They tended to turn in upon themselves and to squander their energies in factional rivalries and intrigues. Regional, educational and psychological differences made themselves felt, and the hatred and scorn which should have been reserved for the class-enemy and oppressor sometimes vented itself against an uncongenial comrade.

In the closed and unnatural conditions of prison life, the theoretical side of Marxism assumed correspondingly greater importance. Marxism was supposed to enable its devotees to overcome their 'bourgeois' (i.e., their human) weaknesses. It along was held capable of equipping them with the necessary understanding of contemporary society and the historical processes which had produced it, to become true revolutionaries. Few of the youthful enthusiasts who thought of themselves as Communists, even those considered mature enough to be accepted into the Party, really knew what Communism was, and still fewer had attempted to make any systematic study of Marxism. Here in prison they had the opportunity to do so. There were intellectuals and party veterans interned with them who did know about Marxism and had the skill and dedication to impart that knowledge. The prison could become a university for those whom society had hitherto denied such opportunity. Given good will, application, and average intelligence, a man could enter prison an unlettered rebel and leave it a well trained and orthodox Marxist revolutionary. 'The theory strengthened him, purified him and rendered him daring and courageous,' as Djilas put it. In his own case, 'Marxist literature made no impression at all on me until I had made up my mind I was for Communism. Then the literature was for me a world of new ideas which reflected my condition and helped shape my consciousness.'[2] So it was with many of his comrades.

One of those who played a leading part in this indoctrination process was a Marxist intellectual called Ognjen Prica. Djilas felt drawn to him, though their backgrounds were very different, by his stimulating and attractive personality, lively mind and wide European culture. Prica represented the radical leftist tendencies within the Party with which Djilas now felt himself identified. He came from Zagreb, where he had not hesitated to do battle with the formidable Krleža whose views were often at odds with Soviet orthodoxy. Krleža had expressed misgivings about the Moscow trials and the charge that Bukharin, hitherto regarded as a pillar of the revolutionary establishment, had all along been a dangerous imperialist saboteur. Such doubts never troubled Djilas; he and other hard-liners unwaveringly accepted the official line and zealously propagated it. He had become the most steadfast of believers, the most uncritical admirer of Stalin and all his policies and their readiest apologist. The Montenegrin firebrand had a profound contempt for armchair intellectuals and no inhibition about expressing it.

The top-ranking Communist prisoner was Petko Miletić, whose attempted rescue had landed Djilas in prison. As a member of the Central Committee he came with the authority of that distant and almost mystically revered body. He was the first Central Committee member to have been arrested under the Dictatorship and to have escaped execution; an international press campaign on his behalf had probably saved him. His aura was further enhanced by his reputed heroism under torture. It was normal for every prisoner to confess to something under duress; the most he could usually try to do was to 'confess' only what the police already knew. Miletić, the word went round, had resisted even that temptation. His defiance was said to have been simply superhuman. The record of the cross-examination customarily signed by the accused had not even been drawn up in his case; there was absolutely nothing to which he had confessed. With this extraordinary reputation behind him, Miletić set out to win the unconditional allegiance of every Party member in prison.

Not all were willing to concede him the primacy. Miletić was an 'ultra'; he belonged to the radical wing of the Party and soon became its acknowledged leader. But some of the older moderates refused to yield. Neither the Croat Communist leader Hebrang nor Moša Pijade, a Serbian Jew much respected for his caustic tongue and his translation of Marx's *Capital*, had confessed anything under interrogation; but neither had they been tortured, since they were serving long sentences and had been arrested before the introduction of the Dictatorship and its harsh treatment of prisoners. Pijade presented Miletić with his most serious challenge. Their rivalry came to a head in the summer of 1934, after a large batch of prisoners, of which Djilas was one, were transferred for a time to Lepoglava, a penitentiary in Croatia which had once been a well-known monastery and school. Pijade, small and typically Semitic in appearance, was an eccentric, and very popular amongst his fellow prisoners. He was also a talented painter, and had presented one of his pictures to the prison director – in order to ingratiate himself with him, the Miletić faction alleged. Pijade had himself been considered a leftist within the Party, but in contrast to the crude militancy of Miletić and some of the younger generation he now appeared a moderate. He and Djilas were later to fall out, but the younger man enjoyed his company and conversation and found much to learn from him. Perhaps this was one reason why Djilas, a pronounced leftist in sympathy and at first an admirer of Miletić, came to range himself against his fellow Montenegrin, who was the prototype of the revolutionary wholly dominated by the pursuit of personal power.

The issue between moderates and 'ultras' generally boiled down, in the restricted arena of prison life, to the line to be taken towards the authorities. Should it be one of uncompromising confrontation or would it be better to reach some accommodation which, without sacrificing their revolutionary principles or integrity, would result in better living conditions and allow them to concentrate on Marxist study and other forms of Party work? Some months before his term was up Djilas and his comrades returned to Mitrovica where conditions were a good deal worse than those at Lepoglava. On the initiative of the hard-liners, the 'collective' declared a hunger strike. It lasted thirteen days and induced the authorities to grant most of their demands. Djilas was not to enjoy the fruit of this victory for long. By 23 April 1936 his term was up and he left Mitrovica for the customary period of forced residence with his family.

The militants' success seems to have gone to their leader's head. Miletić was rash enough to pick a quarrel with his defence lawyer who happened to be a friend of Pijade. This man revenged himself by obtaining a copy of the report which the interrogators *had* drawn up of his client's interrogation. It was not a particularly incriminating document; Miletić had not betrayed his comrades, but like others he had admitted to a number of things of secondary importance which he hoped were already known to the police. The hero, in short, had in fact been neither more nor less brave than his comrades; his signature on the Minutes of his interrogation was there to prove it. A photo-copy was made and sent to Djilas. This, together with a report sent by Pijade to Tito as Organising Secretary warning him that Miletić was planning to escape, convene a Party congress and get himself elected its leader, was to provide deadly ammunition in the forthcoming struggle for the control of the Yugoslav Communist Party.

CHAPTER FOUR

On the Eve

SEVEN years had passed since Milovan Djilas left his parents' home for Belgrade. For nearly half that time he had remained confined within the closed circle of political prisoners whilst momentous events succeeded each other on the world stage. In Germany Adolf Hitler had come to power and almost at once the Reichstag had been mysteriously burned down and the German Communist Party blamed and banned. It was then that the Bulgarian Communist Dimitrov won acclaim for his spirited defence and was rewarded by Stalin with the Secretaryship of the Comintern, the international apparatus which controlled the Communist Parties of every country, Yugoslavia included. Trials were also staged in the Soviet Union, and good Communists were shocked to learn from them that comrades whom they had revered as leaders of the Revolution had all along been imperialist spies and saboteurs. In France, the following year, popular riots nearly brought down the republic, whose Foreign Minister was later shot down together with King Alexander of Yugoslavia at the start of a state visit. The organisers of the *attentat* were Croat Nationalists; though taught by Marxist-Leninist theory to deprecate such acts of terrorism, the Yugoslav Communists rejoiced at the news almost as much as the Nationalists, although neither expected that things would be much better under the Regency established after the King's death. Society remained as corrupt and unjust as before, and the Dictatorship as oppressive. In Italy, Fascism had become even more aggressive and was beginning the conquest of Abyssinia. In Spain, a left-wing Popular Front government had been voted into office, but its enemies were already plotting its overthrow. In the spring of 1936, when Milovan Djilas regained his semi-freedom, menace loomed over many parts of the world.

Discontent with the Dictatorship had become widespread in Yugoslavia. Some fifty per cent of the electorate voted for the United Opposition organised by the bourgeois political parties, despite strong official pressure to support the government candidates. How could the Communists best exploit this resentment and give it greater revolutionary militancy? Moscow had switched to the 'Popular Front' line. In face of the growing Fascist and Nazi menace Communists throughout the world were now instructed to make common cause with 'progressives' and democrats and to give their support to states like Yugoslavia which stood in the way of Hitler's and Mussolini's expansionist ambitions. But the old Yugoslav Communist Party was so weak and discredited, and its members and sympathisers so well known to the police, that it could do little. What was needed was an entirely new structure, more united and disciplined, with new cadres and a new leadership.

Milovan Djilas realised that in Bijelo Polje he could achieve nothing. In the autumn he was given permission to leave his forced residence and go to Belgrade for medical examination and treatment. The local authorities were probably glad to see the last of him; he was a known trouble-maker, and the three years in prison had clearly done nothing to bring him to his senses. He had in fact been in poor health, and on reaching Belgrade went down with a bout of pleurisy. When he recovered he began to take up the threads of his old life. He was eager to resume his political work, and he enrolled at the university once more, this time in the Faculty of Law. He was without any means of support except for what he could earn from an occasional article and for the money he reluctantly accepted from Mitra.

The Yugoslav Communist Party's contact with Vienna and Moscow had become so tenuous as to be virtually non-existent. By the time Djilas was able to resume work in Belgrade, a new Central Committee had been appointed by the Comintern. Milan Gorkić (Josip Čižinski) remained its Secretary-General, but a new Organising Secretary was nominated – Josip Broz-Tito. Gorkić would stay abroad, but Tito was authorised to make frequent trips to Yugoslavia. In addition to the reorganisation of the Party, a new need had arisen – the recruitment of fighters to assist the hard-pressed Republican Government in the Civil War raging in Spain. At the end of the year Tito was in Split organising the departure of the first volunteers.

Other emissaries from Moscow brought more harm than good to the cause. One fell into the hands of the police with a mass of incriminating papers, and the outcome was a fresh wave of arrests throughout the country resulting in the loss of nearly one third of the Party's estimated three thousand members. By November, what remained of the organisation in Serbia was reeling under these blows. Milovan Djilas was probably the best known Communist still at large in Belgrade. He had reported to the police who kept him under observation but fortunately made no move against him. Mitra was one of those arrested, but she was quickly released following intervention by her family, which had influential connections.

The following spring things began to look up. A Party member whom Djilas had come to know in jail returned to Belgrade after doing his military service and began to reveal a remarkable talent for conspiratorial organisation. His name was Alexander Ranković. Another promising development was the arrival in Croatia of 'a comrade from the Central Committee' who sent a message to Djilas that he wished to see him urgently. Djilas took the train to Zagreb and hurried to the rendezvous. The stranger was a well-dressed, handsome fair-haired man in the prime of life. He spoke clearly and decisively and put shrewd questions on the state of the party in Serbia and its prospects in Bosnia and Macedonia where no organisation as yet existed. He agreed that the tactics of creating an underground organisation – the only type possible under existing conditions – were correct and should be prudently continued. The new 'Popular Front' policy did not mean that the Party should play second fiddle to the bourgeois opposition whose leaders were chary of having anything to do with it. He discussed the possibility of sending men to Spain and also indicated that the Central Committee hoped to be back operating inside Yugoslavia before long. Djilas thought this too risky at present but agreed that the Party would never be effective under its present remote control. Although 'I had a painful feeling that all was not well in the Central Committee,' he recalls, its new Organising Secretary struck him as a man of superior calibre with whom it should be possible to work closely. They arranged to meet again shortly.

The stranger's face seemed vaguely familiar. As he travelled back to Belgrade, Djilas tried to recall where he could have seen it. Then he remembered. Moša Pijade had shown him a portrait which he had painted of a fellow-prisoner; it was that of Josip Broz, known in the Comintern as 'Walter' and amongst his compatriots as 'Tito'. When they next met, Djilas thought it right to tell the new comrade that he knew his identity. 'He attached no significance to this knowledge and smiled cautiously,' Djilas noted. 'There was something beautiful and human in that smile.'[1]

The Organising Secretary did not yet have full control of what was left of the Party in Yugoslavia. He enjoyed Moscow's confidence, but had still to 'prove himself'. Gorkić, as Secretary General, was still in overall command and directing activities for which Tito was not responsible. The recruitment of volunteers for Spain was now given high priority. To facilitate the task, the Central Committee moved from Vienna, where the authorities were cracking down on unwelcome foreigners, to Paris. From there Tito made several further visits to Yugoslavia. In Montenegro, where the appeal for recruits for Spain fell on willing ears, a spectacular scheme was afoot. Though he knew about it, it was not in Tito's hands. The Montenegrins were responding in their hundreds, and to transport them a French merchant ship, *La Corse*, was chartered in Marseilles and sent to the Adriatic.

Volunteers from many parts of Dalmatia and Montenegro made for a rendezvous on the coast near Budva. To keep an operation of such size secret was hardly possible, and at the beginning of March the authorities pounced on the flotilla of small boats which were about to transfer the men to the waiting ship. The organisers, mostly Montenegrin Communists of the older generation, were incompetent and lacked any sense of security. 'They boasted a lot, accomplished little and were more concerned with their own image than with the organization,' observed Djilas, who had been sceptical about the venture from the start.[2] Hundreds were arrested, including the chief organiser, Adolf Muk. To make matters worse, Muk succumbed to police pressure and gave away everything he knew – which was a lot, since he was a member of the Central Committee. Djilas was alarmed and indignant. To be responsible for such a fiasco was sufficiently unforgivable, but to betray one's comrades as well was the basest cowardice and treachery. He denounced Muk's conduct in successive reports to Paris but was disgusted to receive instructions to launch a campaign on the culprit's behalf. The affair was picked up by the international press from a pamphlet printed by the Belgrade students, which he managed to prevent being distributed. Muk himself wrote a secret letter to the Central Committee in which he attempted to justify himself. It was smuggled out to Paris but failed to convince either the comrades there or their Comintern mentors in Moscow. The final blame for the disaster was laid at the door of the Party's Secretary-General. The disgrace was probably the last nail in his coffin. Gorkić was recalled to Moscow, unsuspectingly complied, and disappeared from the scene. The stage was clear for Tito to step into his shoes and consolidate the hold which he had already begun to establish over the Party.

The nucleus of the new Party consisted of four men; the Croat Josip Broz-Tito, the Slovene Edvard Kardelj, the Montenegrin Milovan Djilas, and the Serb Alexander Ranković. This quartet was to constitute the core of the Politburo, and later of the Partisan leadership and of the post-war Communist government, for more than a decade and a half. Tito was indisputably its master, the 'strong man' of Djilas's first impression: his authority was never challenged and his decisions were regarded as final. He was essentially a pragmatist, a political realist, taking careful note of what others had to say and then making up his mind and laying down the course to take. He was the initiator of the policies followed, if seldom of the ideas which inspired them. Within the limits of the orthodox Marxist-Leninist dogmas, which he had assimilated thoroughly if without any particular originality of insight or emphasis, he was open-minded and reasonable; but once a decision had been taken, he was adamant. Retreat threatened loss of prestige and loss of authority, and that must be avoided at all costs.

Tito's will to power was absolute and unremitting, and the path to that power lay through control of the Party with which he identified himself. Later, as leader of the war for national liberation and social revolution, he grew increasingly convinced that the Party represented the aspirations and interests of the peoples of Yugoslavia and that he represented the will of the Party. Nation, Party and leader thus became fused together as one political reality, and personal success was indissolubly bound up with the success of the Party and nation.

Those chosen to work with him had to share the same commitment and could expect a share of the rewards. He demanded unquestioning loyalty from them and reciprocated it generously, whilst preserving always the inmost citadel of detachment which remains inviolate within every great leader. He gave due importance to detail, but was not small-minded; he had a sharp and retentive memory but was not one to harbour scores or dwell on past wrongs; he could forgive mistakes made in good faith, but not weakness or disloyalty to his person or his cause. Altogether he was a man whom Djilas felt he could respect, admire, even come to love.

Kardelj, who gradually assumed the second place in the Party hierarchy, was a schoolmaster whose qualities admirably complemented Tito's. He had an extensive knowledge of Marxism, which he was always adding to by constant reading and which he tended to expound with prolix dogmatism. He was small, careful, deliberate and unimpressive, entirely innocent of any of those charismatic qualities which might have made him dangerous as the great man's second-in-command. He was also persistent, courageous, and far from weak, with an exceptional flair for assimilating the Party line and interpreting the shifting course of events in its light. In the course of time and under the pressure of necessity, he was to become more flexible, almost original, in his thinking. He had been through the Moscow schools and was thoroughly familiar with Soviet ways and aware of the realities of Soviet power. He was unshakeably loyal to Tito and enjoyed the latter's exceptional trust.

Ranković was an organiser, devoid of imagination or humour, serious, observant, suspicious, meticulous in his care for detail and ruthless in the pursuit of his dominant aim – the construction of a disciplined Party on orthodox Communist lines. He was tough, dedicated, unostentatious and aggressive, but always keeping his aggressiveness under tight control and directed to sure and often subtle ends. Ranković, who had been a journeyman tailor, was a Serb from the Šumadija, the Serbian heartland. He lacked the Balkan bluster characteristic of many of his countrymen, and he was to reveal an exceptional dexterity in all branches of intelligence, espionage and security. What was it then that drew this rather sinister individual and Milovan Djilas together? Partly force of circumstances and a common loyalty to the same cause and its leader; partly perhaps the hardness and satisfaction in the crude exercise of power which existed side by side with romantic idealism and enthusiasm in the make-up of the young Montenegrin writer and revolutionary.

The dismissal and disgrace of Gorkić from the post of Secretary General created a momentary leadership vacuum. The fate of the whole Yugoslav Communist Party hung in the balance; it seemed likely that it might be dissolved, as the Polish Communist Party was shortly to be dissolved. The crisis signalled a new opportunity for Petko Miletić, now Tito's most serious rival. Though still in prison, he enjoyed great popularity throughout the country, as he well knew. A campaign for his release was in full swing in the United States, and his prestige stood specially high with the volunteers (for not all had come to grief in the *La Corse* fiasco) who left for Spain and christened one of their batteries in his honour. Djilas, despite certain reservations, continued to admire him, and Ranković was an even keener supporter. But they knew that the Central Committee, though decapitated, was still the source of authority. Miletić, albeit a member of it himself and counting on some supporters in Paris, seemed to be pitting his strength against it. 'All of us in Serbia, Croatia and Slovenia,' writes Djilas, 'took the position we had to stand by the Paris Central Committee and Tito. The Central Committee had not been suspended, even though the Comintern had limited its rights by virtue of having arrested the only person who had veto powers.'[3]

What had induced Djilas and Ranković, the two most influential members of the new leadership emerging in Serbia, to back Tito rather than Miletić? Was it the force of Tito's personality, the intuition that he, and only he, had the strength and wisdom to put the drifting Party on an even keel and set it on the right course, and so must infallibly receive Moscow's endorsement? Or did they sense that their future must lie with the man who was building up a new team and had picked them for key positions in it rather than with Miletić who already had his lieutenants? Whatever their reasons, they gave the absent Tito their loyalty and thereby helped to tilt the balance in his favour. Djilas forwarded the photo-copy of the police report on Miletić to Moscow, whither its subject had made his way after being released from prison. There he disappeared. Tito, one of the few Yugoslav Communists to survive Stalin's purges, later told Djilas that his rival had been arrested by the Soviet Secret Police. It was the first of many challenges which the future master of the Yugoslav Communist Party, in a career spanning the next four decades, successfully beat off.

Between the arrest of Gorkić in the summer of 1937 and the spring of 1938, the Party struggled on inside Yugoslavia as best it could, with no help or directives from the maimed Central Committee. Then, in March, Tito came back for a two or three months' visit, apparently without specific authorisation from the Comintern, to set his seal on the Party's reorganisation. The relationship between the provisional leadership functioning inside Yugoslavia and the still headless Central Committee in Paris remained ambiguous. Tito explained that, whilst the latter remained the senior body, the practical direction of events should rest with the comrades inside Yugoslavia. He was the link between them both and he would go on urging Moscow to permit the two to be merged by the transfer of what remained of the Central Committee to the scene of action inside Yugoslavia. The Comintern was slow to give its consent. The position was not regularised until the beginning of 1939 when Tito was formally nominated Secretary-General.

The first meeting of the Central Committee held at Zagreb under Tito's chairmanship took place in a strained atmosphere. There had been a hitch over the arrangements for his journey back to Yugoslavia and Tito had been obliged to spend three months in Istanbul waiting for a suitable passport. The expert who usually forged such documents had been sent to a concentration camp and it was difficult to find anyone else with the necessary skill. The failure rankled with Tito all the more in that Petko Miletić seemed to have obtained *his* with little difficulty, and he was inclined to blame Djilas whom he seemed to suspect of secretly favouring his rival. Sharp words were exchanged and Djilas, aggrieved and indignant, defended himself with tears in his eyes. Never before had anyone accused him of disloyalty to the Party or its Secretary-General – and so unjustly, too! After the meeting, Tito took him aside and asked him to join him for a walk. It was an unusual invitation, for there was always the danger of being recognised in the street and arrested. 'I was sure he was going to apologise,' Djilas recalls, 'and I began to thaw.' But Tito did not apologise; that was not his custom. He chatted in a relaxed and friendly way about one thing and another until the younger man had been mollified, 'happy as a child whose father understood that he had administered unjust punishment but could not quite admit it.' There were to be other misunderstandings and brushes between the two men, but never – until the final, dreadful break – sufficiently serious to mar a relationship which came indeed to resemble that between a fond but autocratic father and a sometimes wayward son. Djilas's affection was mingled with respect. He and Lola Ribar, the youth leader whom Tito also treated in the same paternal way, took to referring, half in awe, to the Secretary-General as *'Stari'* – 'the Old Man'. The name became current in Tito's intimate circle.

Tito has generally been given the sole credit for the reconstruction of the Yugoslav Communist Party. His contribution – by means of visits, correspondence and the confidence he enjoyed in Moscow – was indeed crucial. But important parts were also played by those inside the country and more closely involved in its grass-roots organisations; by Ranković, who started the systematic infiltration of the Serbian trade unions; by Djilas, at Belgrade university and through his visits to Bosnia, Macedonia and other neglected regions; by Kardelj, who attended the foundation of the Slovene Communist Party in April 1937 (four months before that of the Croatian Communist Party which Tito himself presided over). The independence of the latter parties was indeed only nominal, for each remained under the central control of the Yugoslav Party leadership, but their establishment – agreed in principle three years before, when Tito had no commanding say – was designed to steal the Nationalists' thunder, and in the course of time they did succeed in developing a certain life of their own not always in perfect harmony with Tito's Politburo. The reorganisation and expansion accomplished between 1937 and 1939 was thus the work of many hands besides Tito's.

Nor were these solely organisational changes. New psychological attitudes developed even in the field of personal relations. To the new generation of militants, there *were* no purely personal relations; the sole recognised criterion was the good of the Party, the furtherance of the Revolution. Djilas and Ranković were particularly zealous in propagating the new puritan ethic; Tito less so. Not, indeed, that he was any less persuaded that the interests of the Party must always come first; on the contrary, this had always been, and would remain, his firm conviction. But provided they did not adversely affect the morale and interests of the Party, the conduct of sexual relations seemed to him of little account. No Puritan himself, his energies were as exceptional in this field as they were in politics. In this regard he permitted himself more latitude than was usual with others. Perhaps too he still retained the attitude common in the early years of the Revolution that chastity and marital fidelity were 'bourgeois' concepts. His own experience had not been happy; the desertion of his Russian wife was a deep humiliation. Djilas and Ranković had also had to face crises in their personal lives; but their reactions were different.

In Milovan's case, arrest and imprisonment had abruptly interrupted a relationship which, whatever Communist dogma might hold, had a lyrical and innocent quality about it. In its earlier stages, before Mitra's full conversion to Communism, he had rather callously exhorted her to discard her 'bourgeois' inhibitions; her response had been that of an 'unemancipated' but faithful lover. But later in the course of his three years' imprisonment his revolutionary dogmatism came home to roost. Mitra, in her emotional loneliness and growing commitment to the Party, had had an affair with another man. It ended when he went abroad and her old lover came out of prison. The affair became public knowledge and had to be thrashed out before the old relationship could be resumed. They decided to marry, and in the years of busy revolutionary activity ahead, Milovan and Mitra managed to enjoy several quiet and idyllic interludes amidst the leafy hills of Serbia and by the calm waters of Lake Ohrid. Such precious moments were not to be found in the frenzied swopping of 'free love'; the revolutionary, if he were to have the peace of mind and inner security required for utter devotion to the cause, needed a stable relationship, not binding himself of course to a 'bourgeois' partner, but taking a companion who could share his political activities as well as his bed. Milovan began propagating this new gospel and demanding that others should conform to it too. Alexander Ranković, who had also suffered from the infidelities of his mate, warmly seconded him. Together they instituted a veritable inquisition enjoining strict fidelity between a man and the woman of his choice. A Party Commission was set up with powers to investigate breaches of this code and prescribe appropriate punishment. One incorrigible Don Juan, whose amours were creating havoc amongst the girl-comrades, was even made to pay the supreme penalty. The victim was sent on an 'excursion' with his comrades from which he never returned. 'On the way back he fell off the train "accidentally" and was killed instantly,' Djilas recalls. 'That was the public story – but we knew better.'

A wholly new force, it was clear, was in gestation beneath the surface of public life. The Yugoslav Communists were no more than a handful; an estimated three thousand in the spring of 1939. Their leaders were unknown men; it seemed inconceivable that they would ever carry much weight. Yet here was the embryo of something hard and strong – a new society, its apologists declared, or a new political elite, a new class, as the disillusioned were to find. The Party already lived a life of its own. It had its own ideology, held with the fervour of a religious creed; its own courses for study and indoctrination; its own literature and press; its own code of moral conduct, with the necessary machinery to enforce it. Offenders were disciplined, heretics excommunicated, traitors and rebels expelled and often executed. Heroes and martyrs were revered in an authorised cult. The Party financed itself by means of contributions from members and well-wishers, later by forced levies and confiscations. Though hounded by the authorities, it not only survived but flourished. It was self-supporting and self-contained, yet linked to a powerful protector abroad. Few suspected even its existence, still fewer its formidable potential.

As the months went by and war inexorably approached, Europe had other preoccupations. Austria was absorbed into the Reich, bringing Hitler's armies to the borders of Yugoslavia. At Munich, Czechoslovakia, Yugoslavia's ally, was abandoned to her fate. In Russia, Stalin's purges claimed more and more victims – his own close colleagues, the best generals, leaders of the foreign Communist Parties, including Yugoslavia's. In the summer of 1939 the Soviet Union reached an understanding with Germany, thereby making nonsense of the whole strategy of a Popular Front against Fascism. 'I actually approved of the Soviet Pact, as did most of the leading Communists, with only a few minor misgivings,' Djilas admits. 'We had already trained ourselves to have absolute confidence in the Soviet Union and in the decisions of its Government.'[4] Some of his friends, leftist intellectuals, felt uneasy and cautiously observed that the Pact might have 'negative' as well as 'positive' results. Djilas leapt to its defence. Moscow could do no wrong; given Stalin's infallible wisdom and the provocations of the capitalist powers, it was certain that the Pact would bring only advantage to the Soviet Union and so to the Communist movement in Yugoslavia.

In the same way as Catholic jurists had always argued that war was legitimate in certain circumstances, and distinguished between those that were 'just' and 'unjust', so the Party pundits had now to pronounce whether the impending conflict was an 'imperialist' or an 'anti-Fascist' war. Was it to be supported or opposed, welcomed or denounced? They admitted little difference between the Western democracies and the Fascist states but lumped them all together under the label of 'capitalists' and 'imperialists'. If the latter chose to fall out amongst themselves, that was only to be expected and all to the good. The Party would stand aloof; if anything, its sympathies would lie with Germany, since it was now allied to the Soviet Union. Public opinion, it is true, did not see things this way, though most Yugoslavs fervently hoped that their country would manage to stay neutral. Even the students, well disposed in general towards the Soviet Union, were confused and dismayed, and many sympathised openly with the democracies. The tension mounted. How would the Party analyse the situation and react to it? Tito was abroad; Kardelj away in Slovenia. Djilas held earnest discussions with the Regional Committee for Serbia, which decided to postpone any categorical statement. He was so excited that he could not sleep. The next day – the eve of Britain's declaration of war on Germany – he went to the university to address a student meeting.

'I suddenly felt a change taking place within me,' he writes, 'something bright and cheerful, as if I was being relieved of a burden. All things surrounding me grew light, playful and soft. The street was like a river, its vehicles appeared to be rushing by like toys, and the pedestrians were unhappy ants drowning in the river.'[5] Doubts and hesitations vanished and he faced the students with confidence; the war was 'imperialistic' and the pact between Hitler and Stalin a statesmanlike contribution to peace and the advancement of Socialism.

Djilas had been bold to the point of rashness. Not only had he ignored the Regional Committee's prudent decision to wait, but the Central Committee had not yet taken its stand. It had not even met to consider it. No lead came from Moscow. Not until the middle of September, when Europe had been at war for ten days, did the Central Committee manage to meet in Zagreb. Djilas took a train and found Kardelj and Lola Ribar waiting on the station platform.

'"Just" or "unjust"?' he asked impatiently as the train drew in.

'Unjust, of course!'[6]

It was a great relief that the comrades had independently come to the same conclusion. But not all of them; some of the Croat Communist leaders in particular were wavering, fearing that the Party's stand might lose it public sympathy. They were overruled. Djilas developed the new official thesis in a paper which the Central Committee approved, almost without change, and sent to Moscow. In Zagreb, he was not known to the police and he had been able to sit comfortably in a fashionable cafe composing it. Tito told him later that the paper had been well received and that he was proud of the resolute and 'correct' stand the Yugoslav Communists had taken. It was to remain, with only minor changes, the official party line on the war until June 1941 when the Germans invaded the Soviet Union. Then the war naturally became 'anti-Fascist' and therefore 'just'.

If public opinion was shocked by the Pact, alarm and indignation deepened with the speedy partition of Poland between Germany and the Soviet Union. There was fellow-feeling amongst the Yugoslavs for the Poles as brother Slavs, though their harsh right-wing government had forfeited the sympathy of the left. Was not the speedy disintegration of Poland's army and state, the Communists argued, convincing proof of a corrupt and unjust social structure? Few might be glad to see an extension of German power as the result of Hitler's invasion, but Stalin, by reincorporating the 'liberated' Ukrainians and Byelorussians, had checked him by a clever counter-move. 'We Communists were thrilled by the partition of Poland,' Djilas freely admits. They were less enthusiastic over the Russians' invasion of Finland the following year and with the slow progress made by the Red Army against its small foe. The Party commissioned a booklet on the subject which Djilas edited. The claim that the invaders' eventual success represented a 'triumph for revolutionary war against Capitalism' was hard to swallow. The public found it difficult to reconcile the Soviet Union's action with its vaunted image as the leading 'anti-imperialist' power, and even some Party members harboured misgivings. The sceptical Krleža was openly critical. 'I have a mind to go off to the Finnish Front myself to fight!' he announced in the Corso Cafe, adding: 'For the Finns, of course!'[7]

Djilas did not feel personally too worried by the Soviet attack on Finland, though he could not show quite the same enthusiasm for it as for the partition of Poland and the incorporation of the Baltic countries. He shared with the other comrades in the Party leadership an unquestioning devotion to the 'first land of Socialism' and its leader. 'We thought of Stalin,' he recalls, 'as the sole heir to Lenin and the sole representative of the only kind of Communism we recognised. Devotion to Stalin was for us the same as devotion to Lenin, the Revolution and Communism.'[8]

In October, when the war had been raging in Europe for more than thirteen months, Tito convened a conference of Party representatives to take stock of the situation. It met in the greatest secrecy in a Zagreb suburb and was attended by over one hundred delegates from all parts of the country. Djilas was commissioned to present a paper on the nationalities problem. Just before the outbreak of war the bickering Serb and Croat politicans had been induced to sink their differences to the extent of reaching an agreement of sorts giving the Croats a measure of autonomy under their own Ban or Governor. This *Sporazum*, as it was called, satisfied the nationalists on neither side and was also contemptuously dismissed by the Communists. Another problem which aroused strong feelings was that of Macedonia, historic home of contention between Serbs, Bulgars and Greeks. The delegate from that area demanded that the Party should press for the expulsion of Serbian gendarmes from Macedonia and exchanged heated words on the subject with Djilas. Tito had to intervene to pacify them.[9] Six months later, when the Bulgarians joined in the Axis invasion and dismemberment of Yugoslavia, the same delegate transferred the local Communist Party organisations in Macedonia from Tito's jurisdiction to that of the Bulgarian Communists. The nationalities problem posed by disaffected Macedonians, Croats, Albanians and others was to remain Yugoslavia's Achilles heel, and the Communists, whatever Djilas might claim, would not find it easy to provide the answer.

Ten days after the end of the clandestine Party conference in Zagreb, Mussolini ordered the Italian forces massed in Albania to attack Greece. They were repulsed, and had to be saved from ignominious defeat by German intervention. Hitler sent his armies into Rumania and then into Bulgaria, putting increasing pressure on Yugoslavia. On 25 March 1941 Prince Paul's government yielded and signed Yugoslavia's adhesion to the Axis Tripartite Pact. Two days later, amidst scenes of wild patriotic fervour in Belgrade, the government was overthrown, the Regency ended, and King Peter declared of age. The Communist Party played no part in the coup and knew nothing in advance about it but was quick to turn the popular enthusiasm to account. Party activists harangued the crowds. Djilas dashed off a leaflet in patriotic vein calling for democratic reforms and reliance on the Soviet Union. Late at night he addressed a crowd of fifteen thousand people and renewed the call for an alliance with Moscow, the release of all political prisoners, free trade unions, a free press. Mitra, who had also been amongst the day's orators, took the train to Zagreb with another comrade to report to Tito.

The new government set up after the coup under general Simović, though consisting of politicians from the old bourgeois parties, set about doing just what the Communists were vociferously demanding – to negotiate an alliance with the Soviet Union. Prince Paul, though as bitterly hostile to the Bolsheviks as his late cousin King Alexander, had reluctantly brought himself to establish diplomatic relations with them in the hope of bolstering his country against Axis pressure. The presence of a Soviet Legation in Belgrade aroused mixed feelings amongst the Yugoslav Communists. It was Moscow's practice for their diplomats to steer clear of the local Communist Parties as far as possible. Some of its members struck the Yugoslav comrades as poor representatives of the new Socialist society. One of them, a journalist attached to the mission, so scandalised them by his heavy drinking and loose talk that Ranković and Djilas complained to Tito who reported the matter to Moscow and secured the offender's recall. An even more disturbing case was that of an intelligence agent notorious as an inveterate drinker and womaniser. Ranković suspected that he might be a Trotskyist out to make trouble in Moscow for the Yugoslav leaders. Djilas declared that they would have been quite ready to kill him if their suspicions were confirmed. Ranković had him photographed and showed the result to Tito, who recognised him at once. The suspect was Mustafa Golubić, a Yugoslav who held a high position in the Soviet secret service. Tito ordered his zealous lieutenants to leave him alone. The man was on special assignment, he explained, and left matters at that.

Djilas's first meeting with 'Soviet man' also proved rather a disappointment. It took place in the house of Vladimir Ribnikar, the owner of Belgrade's leading daily, *Politika*. Ribnikar was a wealthy man, a sympathiser, but not yet a member, of the Party. Djilas got to know him through Vlada Dedijer, a reporter whose despatches on the Spanish Civil War and readiness to act as a courier between Belgrade and the Central Committee in Paris had brought him to the favourable notice of the Party. Three years younger than Djilas, Dedijer was to become a close friend and collaborator in the field of agit-prop. On 4 April 1941 Djilas and Dedijer met for dinner at the Ribnikars, where they were joined by Tasa Grigoriyev, a Russian newspaperman whom they were later to meet again in the course of the war in his role as a Soviet Intelligence officer. They found Grigoriyev a rather cold and unsympathetic character, but he brought important news. On 6 April the signing of the long-awaited Yugoslav-Soviet Pact would be announced, and the Russian suggested that demonstrations should be organised throughout Belgrade to celebrate the event.

Shortly before 7 a.m. on the morning of 6 April, the agit-prop organisers and the secretaries of the Party's district and cell committees began to gather in the park at Krunska Street where they were to assemble before dispersing to 'mobilise the masses'. They were in high spirits, convinced that one of the Party's main objectives – a Mutual Assistance Pact with the Soviet Union which would compel Hitler to keep his hands off Yugoslavia – was about to be achieved. Their excited talk was interrupted by an unfamiliar and sinister sound – the drone of powerful engines overhead, a siren's shriek, the whine of falling bombs. The planned demonstrations never took place; the Pact was still-born. The German invasion of Yugoslavia had begun.

CHAPTER FIVE

To Fight or Not to Fight?

THE German attack took the whole country by surprise – the government, the High Command, the Communist leadership, the public at large. The coup of 27 March, which overthrew the ministers who had signed the Tripartite Pact and forced the resignation of the Prince Regent, was an act of defiance which Hitler could not forgive. He at once resolved that Yugoslavia must be utterly and mercilessly destroyed. The government of General Simović sought desperately to placate him, and believing that it might succeed, failed to prepare for the worst. It could not hope to beat off an attack for long; but it could at least have done more to put the nation's defences in readiness and work out contingency plans in the hope, however slender, of holding out in some parts of the country until Britain could send help. There seemed to be no plans, no will to resist; only confusion and helplessness deepening to stunned defeatism as the state was overwhelmed and torn apart. The Bulgarians took Macedonia, the Hungarians the rich lands once under the Crown of St Stephen, the Italians Montenegro, most of Dalmatia and that part of Slovenia not wanted by Germany. Hitler and his allies accomplished in a matter of hours what Moscow, until half a dozen years before, had tried and failed to achieve – the disruption and destruction of the bourgeois Yugoslav state.

Djilas, like the other Communist leaders, was bewildered by the suddenness of the attack and the speed and thoroughness of its success. He had realised that sooner or later Hitler might invade and that Yugoslavia would then have no real chance against his war machine; but now that attack had come he felt stunned. What line should the Party take? The pact by which he hoped the Soviet Union would guarantee Yugoslavia's neutrality had come too late. The Party had latterly declared itself in favour of the defence of Yugoslavia; now, suddenly, there was nothing left to defend. Truth to tell, there had been ambivalence, if not downright dishonesty, in that slogan, for Yugoslavia was a bourgeois monarchy which persecuted the Communists and which the Communists were pledged to destroy. The only Yugoslavia they believed to be worth defending was some future, post-revolutionary, Socialist Yugoslavia. Now the old Yugoslavia had

43

been demolished by the Fascists. Would not that make the Communists' task easier, the goal nearer? The 'Old Man', with his extraordinary political insight and his talent for giving lucid expression to what other comrades only vaguely apprehended, would put it all in focus for them. But Tito and other members of the Central Committee were in Zagreb. The immediate problem was what to do now in this ruined city. It was only towards nightfall, when he had managed to collect together a band of dazed and weary comrades on a piece of waste land, that they could improvise some sort of committee meeting and reach a decision. It was agreed that those capable of military service should report to their units and the others leave Belgrade and wait on events. There was nothing they could do amongst the bombs and flames, and the Party must preserve its cadres.

Mitra left to join her mother in Požega. Djilas was moved to see her, usually so calm and controlled, in tears. It seemed to him that she was weeping not only for the burning city but for their life together, likewise about to vanish in the flames of war. She had given her full allegiance now to the Party and knew that she must accept whatever demands it might make on her. They had often had to go their separate ways for a time, following the tasks assigned to them and facing danger on their own. But war would mean longer and more fearful separation; and who could be sure of an eventual reunion, a resumption of the life they had been sharing together?

Djilas, with some other comrades, took the road south to Mladenovac. His plan was to spend the night in a village which was the home of Sreten Žujović, a tall, handsome Serb known amongst his comrades as *Crni* or 'Swarthy'. Žujović had recently returned from Moscow where he had been working for the Comintern. He was one of the few veteran Party members to have survived the purges and to have continued to be politically active under the new Secretary General. A man of enormous dynamism and considerable charisma, he was to remain secretly envious of Tito's pre-eminence as leader of the Party and the Partisan movement.

Djilas soon decided to go back to the capital in the hope of rallying other comrades and salvaging what he could of their agit-prop material. But it was useless; the chaos and horror in the city had deepened, and there was now added danger from patrols of trigger-happy police and 'Chetniks', members of the government-sponsored organisation of irregulars, only too ready to settle accounts with anyone they suspected of being deserters, fifth columnists or Red trouble-makers. He came across 'Tempo', a young Montenegrin active in organising the distribution of the Party's clandestine agit-prop material. Tempo asked for instructions. Go back to Montenegro, Djilas told him, and then decide for yourself. If you find that the Party machine is functioning properly, report to your unit and join up. If there is no sign of any Party activity, start it up yourself. Djilas gave no indication – his own mind was not yet made up – that he too would make for Montenegro. It was impossible, in the deepening chaos, to know what to do for the best.

In retrospect, Djilas could find no better explanation for his impulse to go to Montenegro than that he hoped 'to seek temporary shelter and find out what was going on'. The Communists, like the rest of their fellow citizens, could only wait on events; they had hardly begun to play a part in shaping them. He left Belgrade, travelling by the still partly functioning train through Bosnia and Hercegovina, two days before the Germans entered the crippled capital. He had meant to stop off at Požega to see Mitra but, anxious to lose no time, changed his mind. Other comrades, with whom he did not manage to establish contact, followed suit for much the same reasons. Amongst them was Moša Pijade who, like other political prisoners in Serbia, had been released after the coup of 27 March. As a Jew, as well as probably the best known Communist in the country, his life was in special danger. It was later rumoured that Pijade's idea had been to reach the coast and board a ship which would take him first to Africa and then to England. Tito was angry when the report reached him; Moša was a veteran Party member whose place should be in the front rank in the coming struggle. Pijade indignantly denied that he had ever thought of seeking refuge with the British capitalists. He suspected that Djilas had spread the rumour, and the grievance rankled.

Djilas left the train at Nikšić. His family had hailed from those parts, but as he had never lived there himself he ran little risk of being recognised and denounced. King Peter and his government had flown out of the country from the Nikšić airport a few days before, and shortly afterwards – on 17 April – the Yugoslav High Command surrendered unconditionally. Once again, as when facing the Austrian onslaught in the First World War, the Montenegrins felt that they had been betrayed. They had indeed been outwitted, rather than militarily defeated, by the Italians.

Djilas writes of this brief campaign that 'the Communists had stood up very well in Montenegro, although they did not yet feel it was their war. They believed that the "British imperialists" were using the war to their advantage. Their bitter enemies were in power. But they also knew that the war would soon alter its character and they fought honourably.'[1] The Party leadership must nevertheless bear a share of the blame for Yugoslavia's military *débâcle*. When, at the outbreak of the war in 1939, the government ordered general mobilisation, the Communist leaders instructed their members to ignore the call to the colours since they should take no part in an 'unjust' war nor in a mobilisation manifestly ordered under pressure from the British and French imperialists. By the time the government ordered renewed mobilisation following Mussolini's 1940 attack on Greece, the Party line had been modified, the war seemed less obviously 'imperialistic' in the face of the Fascist danger and the defence of the existing Yugoslav state less to be deprecated. But in Montenegro, most Communists stuck to the old line and largely boycotted the second call-up. For this the instructors sent by the Central Committee were largely to blame, and their deviation cost the Party a serious loss of prestige amongst a population naturally war-like and quick to take up arms against any foreign threat. It was only a few Montenegrin Communists who ignored their leaders' exhortation to boycott the call-up and 'fought honourably'.

The Italians did not abuse their triumph. Though the Blackshirts could not refrain from provocative bluster, the regular army units conducted themselves correctly. The minority of Montenegrins who had always been against the union with Serbia hailed them as liberators, though it was soon to become apparent to all that an independence secured by alien bayonets was worthless. The occupying forces did not even take immediate steps against those suspected of harbouring strong anti-Fascist sentiments, and known Communists were to be seen walking freely in the streets or sitting unconcernedly in the cafes.

Djilas moved on to Danilovgrad where he intended to discuss matters with a comrade whom he knew to be amongst the staunchest of the Montenegrin Communists. Blažo Jovanović had once been a strong supporter of Petko Miletić and Djilas had had a hard job to win him over; now he was loyal to the new leadership and was to prove one of the chief organisers of the Partisan rising in Montenegro. Djilas stayed with him for three or four days and together they worked out plans. Jovanović told him that there was much bitterness against the King and his civilian and military advisers for abandoning their country to the mercy of the Italians. The separatists had little popular backing and were finding it hard to reorganise the gendarmerie with their supporters. The Communists were active in collecting arms from the disbanded soldiers; Djilas himself acquired a couple of rifles in this way. The Party, despite the setbacks and mistakes of the past, still had a strong organisation and the people's fighting spirit and pro-Russian sentiment remained high. The prospects then were good; it only remained to choose the right moment. Even so, Djilas was uncertain and unhappy about his own role. Had he been right to leave Belgrade? What would Tito and the rest think? Would they reproach him for leaving his post without permission? Even though it was under German occupation now and would be more dangerous, he decided to return to the capital. To get an Italian pass was not difficult, and by the last week in April he was back in Belgrade.

Tito remained meanwhile in Zagreb, which had been spared the devastation suffered by Belgrade. The Italians, with the concurrence of Hitler who intended to exploit it economically, had set up a puppet regime ironically styled the 'Independent State of Croatia'. It was headed by Pavelić and his Ustashe exiles who had long been on their payroll. Less fortunate than their comrades in Serbia, the Communists imprisoned in Croatia had not been released at the time of the 27 March coup; they remained at the mercy of the Ustashe, now stonily indifferent to any memory of their former common struggle against Belgrade. Tito, at large and prudently anonymous, wished to remain near the clandestine transmitter installed in a Zagreb villa which kept him in touch with the Comintern. What line would the Russians take now that the government with which they had so lately concluded a Treaty of Friendship no longer had a country to govern? Would they recognise, at least *de facto*, Yugoslavia's violent demise? Four weeks after the Yugoslav capitulation, Vyshinsky informed the Yugoslav Minister in Moscow that his government 'saw no legal justification for the Yugoslav Legation to continue its work in the Soviet Union'. Germany and the Soviet Union were still officially allies, though their mutual hostility could now scarcely be veiled.

At the beginning of May Tito summoned members of his Central Committee to Zagreb for a 'consultation'. One significant absentee was the delegate from Macedonia – 'Šarlo', with whom Djilas had exchanged sharp words the previous autumn – who declined to attend, since he considered that the regional organisation should now come under the Bulgarian Communist Party. Tito was to take up the issue firmly with the Comintern; the secession of the Macedonians would mean a diminution of his authority as Party leader and implied a threatened loss of territory for the future Socialist Yugoslavia. It also set a dangerous precedent. If Macedonians were to cut loose from their Yugoslav connection, what about the Slovenes who now found themselves under Italy? Or the Croats, who had been given their 'independent' state? Or Montenegro, now severed from Serbia? It looked as if there might be precious little left under the aegis of a 'Yugoslav' Party leadership.

The May 'Consultation', which escaped the vigilance of the Ustashe authorities and has received relatively little notice in subsequent historiography, deserves attention for the light thrown on this twilight period between the collapse of the old Yugoslav state and the German invasion of the Soviet Union which was to signal the start of the Partisan movement. Tito's report on the current situation has not survived – or at least not been published – but its gist may be deduced from the lengthy 'Conclusions' subsequently drawn up and published in the party organ *Proleter*. No doubt a shortened version of the report was sent by radio to the Comintern. Djilas, who came from Belgrade for the meeting, allows us an important glimpse behind the scenes.

At this Consultation [he writes] Tito established a new thesis: the possibility of a direct Communist takeover of power, a denial of the need for the revolution to go through two stages, the bourgeois-democratic and the proletarian, which had been the party position until then, following Comintern decisions. Tito also postulated a Communist takeover after the defeat of Germany, to prevent any other party or organization from doing so. Clearly the old machinery of state would be either defunct or compromised by collaboration with the enemy. Tito said that we Communists had to organise ourselves militarily so as to be able to attack our enemies at the time of their defeat, and thus be able to take power.[2]

The Comintern reacted sharply to this unauthorised departure from the party line. 'Bear in mind that at this present stage, what you are concerned with is liberation from Fascist oppression, and not Socialist revolution,' Tito was reminded.[3] He had formulated his thesis as a pragmatist, not as a theoretical deviationist or innovator; and as a pragmatist he had to draw back and toe the line prescribed by Moscow. 'Tito retreated from his position – at least in words,' Djilas records. 'But words later had an important effect on deeds. Some of the Comintern terminology of national struggle entered our own "people's liberation" jargon.'[4]

Djilas goes on to make a further highly significant statement. The speedy collapse of Yugoslavia was attributed in the Consultation's 'Conclusions' to the ruling bourgeoisie which put class before national interests and spawned a treacherous, defeatist Fifth Column. A handful of officers from the old Yugoslav army had, however, refused to surrender and were hiding out in western Serbia, 'threatening to take over after the defeat of the Germans and "save the country" from the

Communists. They were promoting the idea of a Great Serbia and a purge in Bosnia and Dalmatia of all "Turks" and Croats. They were subjecting the peasants to military discipline – those same peasants whom they had shamefully abandoned during the enemy attack. . . . *A decision was made to denounce the officers, to begin an armed struggle against them as well as the Ustashe.* The most important thing was to collect arms and set up military committees, attached to party committees, to be in charge of collecting arms and gathering together fighting units.'[5]

Just who these officers were, and what their aims and tactics might be, we shall consider shortly. One thing is clear; they were not Germans or Italians or avowed Quislings. There is nothing in Djilas's recollections, nor in the published text of the Conclusions which embodied Tito's report and guide-lines, urging immediate armed resistance to the occupying authorities. Arms were to be collected and military preparations made – for action against whom? Against 'the groups of officers hiding in the mountains of Western Serbia' who were also thought to be doing much the same thing – biding their time until the enemy would finally collapse and be forced to withdraw. This was at the beginning of May, scarcely a fortnight after the military defeat and partition of Yugoslavia; there was as yet no talk or thought on either side of any immediate rising against the occupying authorities. The two rival factions were manoeuvring for the mastery of post-war Yugoslavia. The seeds of the conflict between Communist-led 'Partisans' and the 'Chetniks' under the command of Great Serb nationalists were already beginning to germinate. Both foresaw and were planning a merciless Civil War.

The report of recent events, and of the Communists' allegedly outstanding part in them, was clearly coloured to make a favourable impression in Moscow and to strengthen the image of the Party as a patriotic Yugoslav force. The Yugoslav Communists, it was claimed, had done their utmost to prevent Yugoslavia 'from being dragged into the imperialist war on the side of Britain and France' – for such a danger did exist, as 'the followers and agents of Britain had strong positions amongst the ruling bourgeoisie'; it had likewise opposed capitulation to Axis pressure, struggled against the machinations of Fifth Columnists, advocated close links with the 'peace-loving' Soviet Union, and agitated against the reactionary ruling class in favour of a 'people's government'. It had disseminated thousands of leaflets and staged demonstrations which were largely responsible for the downfall of the Government and its replacement [on 27 March] by the Simovic Government; but it had reservations concerning the latter 'because there were several explicit anglophiles in it'. During the Axis invasion, though Party activists missed some opportunities of taking over from the demoralised and reactionary officers, in those parts of the front where they were sufficiently numerous 'entire regiments took orders from them, as was the case in Montenegro, where an offensive was started against the Italians in Albania.'[6]

Was Djilas, the most prominent Montenegrin at the Consultation, responsible for this inflated version of the Party's role? The Montenegrins, as we have seen, always tended to exaggerate their heroic exploits and to go to extremes; it was a tendency which before long was to show spectacular but ultimately disastrous results. By the end of the first week in May Djilas was back in Belgrade organising the distribution of the Resolutions passed at the Consultation. A couple of days later – on 8 May – an elegantly dressed Tito arrived there from Zagreb. The Central Committee was transferring its seat to the old capital where it would be better placed to implement the tactics decided upon.

The Communist Party had escaped the havoc suffered by almost all institutions and political parties following the invasion and dismemberment of the country. No prominent leaders had been killed, and few relegated to prisoner-of-war camps. The cadres, though temporarily disorganised, were intact. The Party's illegal apparatus and experience of conspiratorial work ensured its survival. Numerically it was still weak, though in the last few years it had grown steadily. The estimate – certainly an exaggeration – given in the 'Conclusions' put its strength as 8,000 members, with 30,000 members of the Communist Youth.

Serbia was still under German military control, but an administration with limited powers was set up first under Aćimović – the Police Chief and former Minister of the Interior who had once warned Djilas to steer clear of Communist agitation – and then under General Milan Nedić. Following their arrival in Belgrade, Tito and the other leading comrades thought it prudent to lie low, though in the two weeks preceding the German attack on Russia no special steps were taken to hunt down Communists. Djilas concentrated on reactivating his agit-prop team. It included the former *Politika* correspondent Vlada Dedijer, now a full Party member, Rodoljub Čolaković, a Bosnian who had been imprisoned for helping to organise the assassination of a former Minister of the Interior and had then gone to Moscow to work for the Comintern, and Milentije Popović, an austere young Marxist intellectual. The resourceful and ebullient Tempo was in charge of the technical arrangements for producing and distributing the propaganda material. The group had the cooperation of a newsman working in the official German news agency in Belgrade where a confidential daily bulletin was prepared. Its distribution was limited to seven copies but an extra one was smuggled out each day to the agit-prop team who made it available to the Central Committee. From it they deduced that a German attack on the Soviet Union was imminent.

Djilas took the precaution of changing his lodgings frequently and finally moved in to his friend Dedijer's. They had become very close. Himself an aspiring author, Dedijer felt the impact of Djilas's strong personality and looked up to the Montenegrin, three years his senior, not only as an experienced revolutionary but also for moral guidance. Of good Hercegovinian stock himself – his late father had been a member of the Serbian secret society the Black Hand and a friend of the famous conspirator 'Apis' – Vlada had married into a still more middle-class family; but before doing so he sought his friend's advice. Being assured that Olga, the bride to be, was a doctor and a young woman of sterling character, Djilas encouraged him to go ahead; he felt sure that in time she too would make a good revolutionary. Olga showed her gratitude by interesting herself in his neglected health. Although robust by nature, Djilas had been subject from his youth to violent migraines, and towards the end of June he began to run a high temperature. Fearing pneumonia, Olga arranged for him to have hospital treatment. But the danger was too great; the Germans were already in control there as they were everywhere in Belgrade. The fever abated; it was just as well, for the tempo of life was about to become sufficiently hectic. On 22 June Hitler launched his invasion of the Soviet Union.

The Central Committee met the same afternoon. Tito drafted a proclamation which the agit-prop team then duplicated and distributed. 'A fateful hour has struck! . . . The precious blood of the heroic Soviet peoples is being shed. This is also our struggle which we are obliged to support with all our strength, even at the cost of our lives. . . . Proletarians from all parts of Yugoslavia, rally round your vanguard, the Communist Party of Yugoslavia![7] The proclamation went on to exhort them to action; not a single man or woman should go to Germany to lend the Fascist bandits their labour; no food should be surrendered to the requisitioners, no arms or ammunition produced for them. Prepare for the grim struggle, organise the masses! Stirring words; but no call yet for sabotage or armed struggle. The same day the clandestine radio station in Zagreb received the Comintern's directive.

The defence of the USSR, it declared, was also the defence of all countries under German occupation. The peoples of Yugoslavia now had 'the possibilities for developing a liberation struggle'. Its burden was much the same as the proclamation already issued by the Party's Secretary General, but with added words of caution exhorting the Yugoslav comrades to bear in mind that their concern was with the liberation of their country from the Fascists, not with Socialist revolution. And there was still no word yet of armed attacks, sabotage, guerrilla bands.

The momentous decision to begin armed resistance was not to be taken lightly, even after the invasion of the Soviet Union had begun. Five days later, the Central Committee met again and decided to set up a General Headquarters of National Liberation Partisan Detachments. The term 'Partisan' was not yet in current usage, and 'Chetnik', the traditional Yugoslav designation for patriotic irregulars, had been pre-empted by the ex-officers and their supporters whom the Communists already saw as their rivals. On 1 July a further directive from Moscow specifically ordered: 'without wasting a moment, organise Partisan detachments and start a Partisan war behind the enemy's lines.'[8]

On the morning of 4 July the Central Committee met again in the Ribnikars' villa. This session is generally regarded as signalling the start of Yugoslavia's war of national liberation. Tito, as always, presided and set the pace. Djilas, Ranković, Tempo, Lola Ribar and Swarthy Žujović were there; Dedijer and Ribnikar's wife guarded the approaches to the house. Delegates had to be assigned to the different parts of the country to promote and coordinate operations. Tito had already selected Djilas for Montenegro, and this was now confirmed. Forged papers were quickly prepared for himself and his brother Aleksa who was to go with him. The journey was likely to be dangerous. Djilas was exhilarated by the prospect of military action but had to overcome feelings of personal grief and foreboding. The Gestapo, guided by Serbian police agents, were combing the streets for known Communists, and Mitra was amongst those picked up. Since the start of the invasion of the Soviet Union, the Germans had been shooting activists out of hand. Djilas was convinced that he would not see his wife again. He took a sorrowful leave of her sister Zora and sent her his farewell messages.

The leave-taking with Tito was brisk and purposeful. Tito never allowed his preoccupation with immediate tasks to cloud the wider horizon and he talked of the Eastern Front and current reports that the Germans were carrying all before them. Djilas, with the over-confidence born of his dogmatic faith, expressed incredulity. The German claims, he said, must be sheer propaganda. It was inconceivable that the Nazis could be making such rapid headway against the heroic Red Army. Tito kept his own counsel and repeated that they must be prepared for a long struggle. Then he turned to practicalities. The Party had set up military committees but no detachments had yet been formed. The command structure remained to be worked out and the first actions to be launched. There was no overall strategic plan, no talk of any 'liberated territory' to be won and defended. No general rising in fact was envisaged; only a series of diversionary actions to distract the enemy's attention from the Eastern Front and gradually weaken him. The Montenegrins with their martial traditions and pro-Russian sentiments would clearly be quick to respond. Those who tried to hamper the struggle must be summarily dealt with.

'Shoot anyone, even a member of the provincial leadership, if he weakens or commits breaches of discipline!' Tito told Djilas. But he added with emphasis: 'Take care too not to launch a general rising! The Italians are still strong and well organised. They would break you. Just start with minor operations.'[9]

CHAPTER SIX

The Rising in Montenegro

MILOVAN and Aleksa Djilas reached Nikšić less than a week before an event which the Italians expected would consolidate their hold of the recently acquired territories. They planned to give both Montenegro and Croatia the nominal status of kingdoms, the latter under an Italian and the former under a Montenegrin prince. The only available candidate for the throne of Montenegro was Prince Michael, a grandson of ex-King Nikola; but he declined the offer. The 'Kingdom' had consequently to be administered by an Italian High Commissioner assisted by a small consultative commission composed of Montenegrin separatists – the Zelenaši or 'Greens', for the most part former ministers or court officials of the late King. Under Yugoslavia, the Belaši or 'Whites', who favoured the Serbian connection, had held power, whilst the 'Greens', forced to reduce their aims to some sort of federal status, had retained only a limited popularity. Even this now melted away once it became obvious that the expected attainment of separatist aims only served to mask an alien rule. The Italians nevertheless resolved to press on with their schemes. With the cooperation of a handful of 'Greens' they prepared to celebrate the country's fictitious independence on 12 July – the feast of St Peter according to the Orthodox Calendar, when popular assemblies used to meet in the days of the Prince-Bishops. It was a disastrous misreading of the national temper. The crowning humiliation of mock independence proved the last straw. On the following day the whole nation rose in revolt.

The social structure of Montenegro resembled that of the Scottish Highlands in the eighteenth century. Families were knit together by ties of kinship, tradition, a common name and a common *slava* – the feast-day of the patron saint – each kinship group electing its chiefs, who were chosen predominantly for their reputation for personal valour. Together they formed a clan under the authority of a *knez* or *vojvoda* and a council composed of all men capable of bearing arms. In times of national emergency the entire population of a locality would muster at traditional assembly-points, bringing with them the weapons which every family took pride in preserving for such occasions. A large quantity not only of rifles but of other arms and munitions had been salvaged from the disbandment of the Yugoslav army and there was no lack of officers, as well as trained fighters, who had avoided capture and sought shelter with their kinsmen. The problem was to give unity and cohesion to this mass of enthusiastic but disorganised volunteers who, on 13 July, began to assemble by families, villages and clans for action against the forces of occupation. This was the moment of opportunity, if only they could seize it, for which the Communists had long been waiting and of which their superior discipline and experience of clandestine activity enabled them to take more advantage than any other political party or group.

When Milovan and Aleksa arrived in Nikšić in the previous week, they had first to locate the Communist leadership, then to ascertain the extent of its authority and preparedness, and to transmit the instructions of the Central Committee. The key man, in Milovan's view, was Blažo Jovanović, the Organising Secretary, who was efficient and dedicated to the Party. The nominal head of the Provincial Committee was the Political Secretary, Božo Ljumović, who struck Djilas as a 'historic relic in the Montenegrin manner – honourable and vain, expansive, and without initiative, pretentious as a theoretician.'[1] Ljumović was one of those still infected by the dogmatic sectarianism which had characterised the Party in Montenegro and was long to remain its bane. When the Germans invaded the Soviet Union the Committee had issued its own manifesto on lines at variance with the 'popular front' position to which Tito and his Central Committee had moved. For the Montenegrin Communists, this was still an 'imperialist war' in which Britain and German capitalists were struggling for supremacy. The persistence of such dogmatic attitudes amongst the Montenegrin Communists was to bedevil the cooperation which events were before long to impose on the Partisans and their British allies.

Djilas was not sure where he would find the members of the Provincial Committee. The best course, he decided, would be to take a bus to Podgorica and to get out shortly before reaching that town and make for the home of Blažo Jovanović. They found him on a wooden ridge above the Zeta River in a peasant hut which served as look-out as well as hide-out. Messages were sent to members of the Provincial Committee summoning them to a meeting on the following day. Other leading Communists, some of them like Djilas recent arrivals from Belgrade, were also invited. Moša Pijade was not among them. In spite of his prestige within the Party and the need for the two men to cooperate closely in the coming struggle, Djilas was not anxious to have him join their deliberations. He considered Pijade not only old in years to join the ranks of the more youthful leaders whom Tito had gathered around him, but too much the product of the old Communist mentality, with its addiction to factionalism, intrigue and theorising. Pijade was not one to forget and forgive this fresh grievance.

The Provincial Committee had established itself in the territory of the Piperi, to which clan Blažo Jovanović and other leading Communists belonged. It was to furnish the Partisan movement with some of its doughtiest fighters. Though it was not his native region, Djilas speedily felt at home amongst them; he and his brother, exhausted after their journey, stretched themselves out on blankets spread under the stars and slept soundly. Nearly twenty years had passed since, as a boy, he had spent such nights out in the open guarding his father's cattle. Now he was a man in the prime of life, ready for the work to which he believed himself called.

The Provincial Committee met the following morning, 8 July, in a forest clearing an hour's walk from Blažo's hut. Djilas transmitted Tito's instructions; they were to begin armed actions at once – ambushes, surprise attacks, sabotage and other forms of guerrilla action, but no general rising. They had only to decide on targets, timing and tactics. The Party already possessed a skeleton military organisation, 'shock-brigades' of ten to thirty men attached to, but distinct from, the local party organisations. The latter however were widely scattered so, to aid liaison and control, a chain of command was set up in the form of four Regional Committees, and delegates were attached to each of them from the Provincial Committee.

Aleksa Djilas, itching for action, left the following day for the Kolašin region. His brother, being Tito's representative and a member of the Central Committee, was recognised as the virtual commander of the forthcoming operations, though he did not formally assume that title but signed his orders 'on behalf of the Supreme Command'. Plans were laid for the first actions and couriers were sent out. There were still four days to wait before the Italians and their collaborators met to proclaim the country's sham independence. Immediately afterwards, when popular indignation reached flash point, would be the right psychological moment for action. Even if they had wanted to, the Communists could not have stopped, or even delayed, the conflagration. Their role must be to bring it under control, to sustain its initial *élan* and in it to forge the cadres of a disciplined fighting force.

The Party intended to tighten its grip on that force by means of Political Commissars – something quite new, of course, in the history of Montenegrin insurrections. Djilas himself had only the vaguest idea of how such an institution should function, and despite his fervent admiration for the Soviet Union and its Red Army thought it best to avoid the use of a term smacking too strongly of mere imitation. He proposed instead the clumsy term 'liaison with the people' – a circumlocution which earned him some teasing from Tito's less inventive lieutenants. Aware of his own lack of combat experience, he also realised the need to appoint an experienced military commander. There was no lack of ex-officers impatient to demonstrate their prowess and professional skill, but none as yet in the Party's top echelons. In his heart of hearts, Djilas was not happy about Tito's resolve to combine in his own person the supreme political and military commands and he had no wish to do the same thing in Montenegro; but at least Tito had some military experience and possessed undoubted military flair. They must look beyond the Party and select a reliable sympathiser and potential Communist to command the insurrection.

The choice fell on Captain Arso Jovanović, an acquaintance and distant relative of Blažo. He was a staff officer with a reputation for patriotism and ability, not yet a member of the Party but already fully disposed to accept its dogmas and discipline. A tall, gaunt man with the tense face of a fanatic and the heart of a lion, he possessed in full measure the Montenegrin qualities of courage, obstinacy, and single-minded devotion to a movement in which he was to make a meteoric rise. His fall would be no less sudden, brought about by the corresponding defects of ambition, vanity, and infatuation with all things Russian. Arso at once agreed to everything asked of him. Though lacking the flexibility always to distinguish between the requirements and possibilities of guerrilla, as distinct from regular, warfare, he was to prove an able commander. Tito bore with his limitations and occasional errors and later made him his chief of staff.

The Military Command, since it included Arso Jovanović and other non-Communists, was kept separate from the Party leadership. But neither that Command nor the Communists themselves could keep in full control of events. They found themselves borne along on a surge of popular fury. The enemy was taken completely by surprise. The first Italian garrisons were attacked on 13 July and the rising spread rapidly throughout the country.

The scale and rapidity of the insurrection (for insurrection it clearly was, rather than a series of guerrilla actions) faced the leaders with a momentous decision. Should they – could they indeed – damp down the conflagration they had helped to kindle? Tito's orders were quite clear; harassment of the enemy, but no general rising yet. Djilas watched with anguish the way things were developing: 'The people overwhelmed their leaders, going beyond our expectations and efforts. The leadership was in a dilemma; we had Tito's instructions to begin small actions and made preparations accordingly, but the people had moved ahead of us.' He drew the logical but painful conclusion: 'We took the position – largely on my initiative – that the movement had to be scaled down to guerrilla proportions, and the people told we were not yet ready for a general rising.'[2] Delegates were sent out with this unwelcome message.

The result in most parts of the country was predictable: confusion, shame, indignation. Djilas himself was infected by the popular mood of incredulous anger and outrage. The orders he had obediently passed on simply did not correspond to the present situation. Tito had failed to appreciate the Montenegrins' vehement temperament, the force of national tradition, the intensity of their hatred for any alien invader, their single-minded and unrestrained abandon once they had risen up. Djilas knew that with his countrymen there were no half-measures; it had to be all or nothing. Now they had clearly opted for battle and they could not be stopped. Djilas would take the decision he was sure Tito would have taken: he would countermand the orders on his own responsibility. The Party must on no account be allowed to separate itself from the people. This was clearly a people's rising and the Communists must give it the leadership it required. Blažo Jovanović, the senior Political Commissar, agreed and a council of war endorsed the decision.

Djilas left for the front. Some of the fiercest fighting was around Berane, the modern Ivangrad, where the Carabinieri had barricaded themselves in the former gendarmerie post. The attackers were led by Pavle Djurišić, a regular army officer who was to become an implacable enemy of the Partisans. From Berane, Djilas moved on to Danilovgrad where a strong Italian garrison was under siege. He sent a message through an interpreter calling on them to surrender and promising that they would be well treated. Back with the Provincial Committee he received a message shortly afterwards reporting that over a thousand had answered his call and thrown down their arms. Throughout the country other isolated garrisons were following suit, and soon Cetinje, the capital, was the only enemy stronghold remaining. But an Italian counter-offensive under General Pirzio Biroli, the resolute commander of the Ninth Army, was soon under way. Strong Italian formations, amounting before long to an entire army corps, moved in from Albania. With the help of Moslem and Albanian auxiliaries, traditional enemies of the Montenegrins, the Italians undertook the systematic reconquest of the country.

The flat land round Lake Skutari, through which the Albanian-Montenegrin frontier runs, could not be easily defended. Harassed from the air and under steady pressure on the ground, the peasants who made up the bulk of the 'National Army' began to melt away. Guerrillas are no match for a regular army in pitched battles, and may need to break off contact and disperse. But these peasants, fearing for their families, homes and cattle, simply made for home and merged into the rural population again.

Kolašin had not yet fallen. Arso Jovanović, the military commander, was there together with Moša Pijade, Aleksa and other local leaders, and Djilas set out to join them. It was a long and gruelling journey and it left him exhausted and weakened by fever. Nor was the reception given him such as to cheer his spirits.

'I've been waiting for twenty-five years for this rising,' Moša Pijade reproached him, 'and now, when it comes, you send out directives that it's not needed and we should split up instead into small groups!'

Djilas attempted to explain that those had been Tito's orders, but that as soon as he realised they did not match the situation he had countermanded them.

'A revolutionary should sense that in advance!' snapped Pijade.[3]

It was no time for recrimination. Despite their animosity, the two men had to work together. Pijade saw to the disposing of the stores captured from the enemy – an important task if the struggle proved to be a long one. In temperament and cultural background the Belgrade painter had little in common with his Montenegrin comrades, though he now wore peasant dress and called himself 'Uncle Janko'. With his sardonic features and the cigarette stub continually dangling from his lower lip, he retained the air of a bohemian Marxist intellectual, in marked contrast to the trim soldierly appearance which other prominent Partisans managed to maintain. He slept, ate and worked – and he was an indefatigable worker – as the mood took him, seemingly as indifferent to Partisan conditions as he had been to those in prison.

Djilas found it strange to be back in Kolašin where, as a schoolboy, he had first defiantly declared himself a Communist. Now he and his comrades were in control, but their authority was precarious and the alliance with the more nationalist-minded insurgents was already beginning to crumble. Some of the latter were secretly in favour of passivity, or even of active collaboration with the occupying authorities, though they dared not show it yet. The peasants had already had enough, and the fighting spirit of those who still remained in the ranks was poor. Arso Jovanović left the improvised office which he had been sharing with Djilas and went off to the front in an effort to stiffen their morale. In the town itself, discontent and fear were growing, for the return of the Italians could only be a matter of time. A delegation of prominent local citizens demanded an interview. Djilas found it headed by his former teacher of catechism. Though conservative and authoritarian, the Archpriest refused to make his peace with the Italians; he sought shelter with his clan and later joined the Partisans himself. But other members of the citizens' delegation opted for collaboration. A local judge berated the Communists for having started a hopeless struggle. He raised a band of peasants on his own and forced the Communists to hand over to them a group of Italian officers whom they had taken prisoner. Aleksa Djilas urged that both prisoners and judge should be shot. His brother hesitated, then decided against it. In an order of the day issued a fortnight after the start of the rising the Partisan Command had proclaimed the establishment of 'People's Courts Martial' empowered to take action against spies, food speculators, and those guilty of 'demoralising or demobilising the ranks'.[4] These wide powers had as yet been only sparingly applied, but the shadow of civil war was already lengthening over the land.

On 5 August, three weeks after the start of the rising, units of the Venezia Division re-entered Kolašin. What remained of the 'National Army' melted away. Djilas instinctively made for Podbišće, his native village, where other leading comrades were already sheltering. With them was a young Englishwoman called Eileen. Djilas was surprised and none too pleased to find this stranger poking her freckled nose into their affairs. He suspected that she might be an agent of the British Intelligence Service whose sinister influence the Party professed to see everywhere. He gathered that she was the mistress of a party member whom she was later to leave. In the end she died fighting with the Partisans – a lone Englishwoman whose only memorial is this passing reference in his memoirs.

Djilas was none too pleased, either, with the local comrades. Podbišće, as a Communist village, had been sent a consignment of captured Italian stores for safe keeping. Serious pilfering had occurred which the comrades not only failed to prevent but were secretly involved in themselves. He called a cell meeting and berated them soundly. Then, with Aleksa and one or two others, he left the village, which was too near the highway for safety, and crossed the Tara. From the woods above the river they could look back at the house, standing lonely and forlorn on its bluff, where he had been born. There the brothers parted, Milovan heading back to the Piperi country. On rejoining the rest of the Provincial Committee there he was annoyed to find that they had held a meeting in his absence and taken a number of decisions of which he disapproved. The wording of the Resolution they had passed was not to his liking, nor was he pleased to learn that Arso Jovanović – whom he liked and esteemed personally – had been accepted into the Party by acclamation. This was an inadmissible short cut to party membership and a violation of established procedures which he held should still be observed even at times of crisis. It was also a bypassing of his own authority as a Central Committee member and Tito's delegate. To maintain discipline and unanimity was more than ever necessary now that the rising was losing momentum and the leading comrades were dispersing to save what they could of the Party organisation.

The Communists had lost control of the military situation. Feeling was turning against them even amongst those who had accepted their leadership, and they were blamed for the reprisals now being taken by the Italians and the free hand given to the Moslems to loot and burn. Where they still had the power, they hit back at their enemies by summary 'executions' on charges of betrayal or espionage. Amongst those denounced and killed as a 'renegade' was a former teacher in Djilas's elementary school, who had once been an agitator and organiser of strikes but had then withdrawn into passivity and tried to dissuade people from taking up arms against the Italians.

For the next month Djilas remained in his mountain hide-out. The days passed in a round of meetings and conferences, the receiving of reports and sending out of instructions; in the evenings they would cluster round the fire singing the old songs – epic celebrations of heroism, death and revenge, or the gentler pains and joys of love. Life, despite the summer warmth, was spartan. Their diet, varied only by an occasional bowl of milk or dish of boiled nettles, consisted of looted Italian rations of rice and sugar which ended by sickening them. In the quiet of the night Djilas relived the events of the past weeks, turning them over and over in his mind and trying to draw their lessons. He formulated his conclusions in a 'Letter from Comrade Veljko' – his *nom de guerre* – subsequently endorsed by the Provincial Committee and sent out for the guidance of the Party organisations.

Comrade Veljko's letter was at once a *post mortem* on why the rising had failed, an analysis of the errors made by the leadership with an attempt to justify the general line taken, and the deduction of important lessons for the future. The fundamental mistake was attributed to the failure to achieve a 'combination of guerrilla and frontal resistance', for 'guerrilla actions do not exclude other forms of struggle such as armed risings on a local scale.' The switch from initial discouragement to active stimulation of resistance may have led to some confusion, but it saved the Party from the danger of cutting itself off from 'the masses' and perhaps from going to pieces altogether. The masses had no wish to return to the old order; they had reached the phase of 'anti-Fascist revolution'. No mention was made of the establishment of Moscow-style Soviets, but 'Veljko's' letter ended with an invocation to Marx, Engels, Lenin, Stalin and Dimitrov, and a reminder that the Soviet Union alone was the fount of true liberation.[5]

CHAPTER SEVEN

Western Approaches, Eastern Reproaches

BY the end of the summer it seemed to the Provincial Committee safe enough to move down to Radovče, a village situated on a broad plateau overlooking the Piperi plain. There, in the mild but still invigorating air, living conditions were easier and Milovan felt his health improve. He now took on work which was much to his taste – the production of a new party organ, *Narodna Borba* or *The People's Struggle*, most of which he wrote himself. Individuals deemed dangerous to the cause were denounced in its columns, the denunciation often serving as a preliminary to their physical liquidation.[1] The Committee was beginning to regain confidence and to act more boldly, despite the reimposition of Italian rule. Its greater accessibility was soon to prove an advantage, for on 20 September an important link with the outside world was established. News was brought that a mission from the Royal Yugoslav Government in Exile had reached Montenegro. It was accompanied by a British officer who had instructions to proceed inland and make contact with the leaders of the resistance movement which was reported to be sweeping over Serbia. The mission had landed from a British submarine on a deserted stretch of the coast not far from Petrovac and had encountered a local Partisan band which sent a courier post-haste to Radovče to report its arrival.

The British had only the vaguest information about recent events in Yugoslavia. The instructions given to Captain D.T. ('Bill') Hudson, the British officer attached to the mission, were couched in correspondingly general terms: to make contact with, investigate, and report back on all groups resisting the enemy, regardless of race, creed or political persuasion. The text of the brief he carried with him has not survived, but it apparently also included an injunction 'to coordinate the forces of resistance against the enemy' – a counsel of perfection, given the fiercely independent and, in the case of the Communists at least, intransigently dogmatic mentality of the resistance leaders.[2]

The officer selected for this demanding and dangerous task was a South African mining engineer who had worked before the war in Western Serbia and acquired a good knowledge of its people and language. The daring with which he had carried out acts of sabotage on behalf of the clandestine organisation which the British War Office had hastily set up, in the months preceding the invasion, to counter German penetration bore witness to his hardy, resourceful and adventurous disposition. Djilas, whose acquaintance with the British was confined to his brief encounter with the unwelcome 'Eileen', seems to have curiously misjudged the man. Hudson struck him as 'restrained, even cold – just as we imagined Englishmen to be, and very sparing in humour – more like a civil servant than an adventurer'.[3] The hand of friendship so unexpectedly extended from the West looked to him suspiciously like a tentacle of the British Intelligence octopus. Was Hudson perhaps another 'Lawrence of Arabia', whom the Communist saw as no glamorous hero but merely as a particularly unscrupulous agent of imperialism? Djilas once remarked to Hudson, hinting darkly at his assumed role, that British Intelligence was probably the best in the world.

'No, the Soviet Union has the best Intelligence Service since it is helped by Communist Parties through the world,' the British officer replied.

'You are mistaken,' Djilas retorted, remembering perhaps his brushes with Mustafa Golubić, their man in Belgrade. 'The Communist Parties feel solidarity with the Soviet Union for ideological reasons, but they are not agents of the Soviet Intelligence Service.'

'I know,' Hudson answered. 'But the parties are reservoirs of political information such as no other state possesses.'[4]

'Comrade Veljko', like the other Yugoslav Communist leaders, was also sceptical of Hudson's assurances that his government was ready to help all who were prepared to resist the Axis powers, regardless of their political creed. Since Djilas had left Belgrade in early July his contacts with Tito and the Central Committee had been tenuous and the information reaching him about developments abroad scrappy. He knew that the Royalist Government in Exile had been taken under the wing of the British, but Moscow's attitude remained uncertain. It was not until the end of August that the Soviet Government decided to restore full diplomatic relations with the Government in Exile. This seemed, at all events, a matter of little importance to the Communists and in no way affected their resolution to make any sacrifice on behalf of the 'fatherland of Socialism'. 'The Soviet Union is at war, and we will fight to the last man,' Djilas exclaimed to his friend, the poet Zogović, during the Montenegrin uprising.[5] He never doubted that the Red Army would throw back the Germans and make possible the Communist Revolution in his own country. 'Remember that the sun will not rise in the West!' he would reproachfully remark when it was suggested that the British might prove more of a help than the Russians to the hard-pressed Partisans.[6] In point of fact, at about the time that *HMS Triumph* was preparing to land its party on the Montenegrin coast, a plan was under consideration in Istanbul for the despatch of a joint British-Soviet Mission to be flown in to Serbia from a base in Soviet Armenia. But the Royal Yugoslav Government was suspicious of the scheme, and Moscow concluded that the British and the Yugoslavs were determined to exclude its influence from the Balkans and instructed its representative in Istanbul to drop negotiations.[7] Djilas knew nothing of all this; nor was he aware that the destination intended for the abortive joint mission was not Tito's headquarters, but those of his Chetnik rival Mihailović.

The name of Colonel Draža Mihailović had first begun to appear in Intelligence reports smuggled out of Yugoslavia to Turkey during the month of August. He had been known to the British before the war as a former Military Attaché in Sofia and Prague, a staff officer with an interest in the tactics of guerrilla warfare, a reasonably competent but by no means outstanding professional soldier, and a Serb with strong royalist and nationalist convictions. The April capitulation found him holding the modest post of Deputy Chief of Staff to the Second Army in Northern Bosnia; like other patriotic officers, he refused to give himself up and made his way to the plateau of Ravna Gora, between the town of Čačak and Valjevo in Western Serbia. Though most of the men who formed the nucleus of what grew into his 'Ravna Gora Movement' were Serbian officers or NCOs, they became known collectively as 'Chetniks', the leader of the pre-war official organisation of that name having defected to the Germans. By the middle of September, the British were in contact with Mihailović through their Special Operations wireless station in Malta. But Hudson had set out on his mission without so much as having heard the name of the Chetnik leader or his claim to be leading a movement of patriotic resistance.

Djilas and his comrades received the British mission courteously but with considerable reserve. It had taken the party four or five days to reach Radovče, travelling by night and sheltering in the woods by day. They brought with them two radio transmitters, one of them a cumbersome set which had to be transported on horseback. On 26 September the mission's first message was received in Malta. It reported that they were with a band of some hundred guerrillas led by Arso Jovanović and a certain 'professor', later identified as Djilas.[8] Further messages from Hudson put the total strength of the

'Montenegrin Freedom Force' at about five thousand of whom the Communists formed the strongest and most aggressive units.[9] Hudson recommended that they should be given assistance. With the help of his hosts he even began measuring out the ground to see if planes could land there. They were encouraged to discover that with only a little levelling this should prove possible.

Djilas and the other members of the Partisan command, unaware of the tenor of his reporting, still remained wary of their British guest. With the other members of the mission – all Montenegrins – they were more expansive. There were three of them: Veljko Dragičević, the wireless operator, Zaharije Ostojić, a major on the General Staff, and Major Mirko Lalatović, an air force officer who had flown out with his squadron from Nikšić to Greece. The two Yugoslav officers had received instructions from their superiors, which were kept secret from Hudson, to the effect that they were to make contact with guerrilla bands led by fellow officers and loyal to the King, ignoring the Communists and proceeding through nationalist channels to Mihailović's headquarters in Serbia.

Though uneasily aware of what might be at the back of their minds, Djilas and his comrades made no attempt to prevent the two royalists from making contact with their brother-officers. News from Serbia suggested that the Partisans and Chetniks were making common cause as the rising spread. On the eve of the mission's arrival in Montenegro Tito and Mihailović met personally to see how they could concert their plans. In Montenegro itself, the Nationalists formed a Committee of their own with which the royalist officers at once got in touch. Differences of aim and outlook within the resistance movement had not yet hardened into irreconcilable enmity. The seeds of future trouble could however be discerned from a report which Hudson sent over his wireless transmitter on 16 October:

The Communists who are well organised are now leading an action in Montenegro. They want everybody to unite in the fight against the occupying authorities. Numerous national elements are standing on one side and waiting. Must urge on Nationalists to organize for the struggle.[10]

Reticence does not come easily to the Montenegrin temperament. Some of Djilas's comrades, particularly Arso Jovanović, aflame with the convert's fervour, were outspoken in their criticism of those who had taken the path of exile. 'The Government forced the army to surrender and then fled!' Arso exclaimed. 'They could have gone on fighting, just as we and the Communists have been doing!'[11] Lalatović and Ostojić offered only half-hearted excuses on behalf of their government and put most of the blame for the capitulation on the Croats. Ostojić spoke little and bided his time; he was to become Mihailovic's chief of operations against the Partisans in Montenegro. Lalatović seemed more open and flexible. But he too was to join Mihailović's staff and take a hard line against the Communists. Only the wireless operator Dragičević showed himself wholeheartedly sympathetic to their cause. He wanted to join them there and then and was only with difficulty persuaded to accompany Lalatović to Serbia. On reaching Serbia he did go over to the Partisans, working as Tito's wireless operator, with the rank of Major, until his death in action a year and a half later.

After some two weeks at Radovče, Hudson received a wireless message instructing him to proceed as quickly as possible to Mihailović's headquarters. He was told that the Chetnik leader was sending out his signals *en clair* and urgently needed the cyphers Hudson had brought with him. The Partisan leaders gave him and the royalist officers the help they needed for the journey and decided that Arso Jovanović, Bakić and other leading comrades should travel with them. Not everyone at Radovče, however, looked kindly on the help being given to their potential rivals. The suggestion was even made that they should be ambushed and killed.[12] Djilas took the proposal as a joke. He could be ruthless enough when circumstances required, but unlike his brother Aleksa he was not one to seek the solution of every problem in violence. He believed that the royalists and their British liaison officer had to be treated correctly but with circumspection, as one should treat unwelcome, untrustworthy but necessary allies.

Captain Hudson and the royalist officers set off for Serbia in two separate groups, for the heavy wireless equipment had to be carried on pack-horses. Soon after they had gone, the Partisan command at Radovče launched an attack on the Italians which they had been preparing in secret for some time. The place was carefully chosen in accordance with the Communists' policy of drawing down enemy reprisals on a population which tended to hold aloof, thus radicalising it. The Bratonožići had proved less militant than the Piperi, and a spot was chosen in their territory – a lonely stretch of road above a river gorge. The way was blocked with boulders and an Italian convoy of more than forty trucks loaded with troops and stores was totally destroyed. The main Partisan forces then followed a circuitous route through Bratonožići villages, taking care to leave a portion of the looted stores in them as they went.

Pirzio Biroli took drastic reprisals. Though the men who had carried out the raid had come from outside, the local population appeared to have connived and to have profited from it. A number of peasants were summarily executed, including some who had been enrolled in the Italians' own *Milizia voluntaria anti-comunista*. Many others were taken off to internment. This severity seemed to demonstrate that passivity, or even collaboration, did not pay. Anger and the desire for revenge drove many of the survivors to turn to the Communists.

Arso Jovanović was soon back from Serbia, travelling through territory everywhere under Partisan control. His stay at Tito's headquarters had been brief, but it was quite long enough to fire his imagination. The rising in Serbia was at its height. Chetnik and Partisan forces seemed still to be cooperating actively against the common enemy, and such cracks as Arso might have noticed showed no signs yet of widening into the abyss which was before long to divide them. The Central Committee and the Partisans' Supreme Staff had established themselves at Užice, in the Šumadija, the west Serbian heartland, giving the little town the air almost of the capital of some small Communist Republic. 'A real government, a real army!' Arso kept repeating jubilantly. He also brought Djilas an extraordinary piece of personal news. The rumours about his wife's execution were false; she had in fact escaped and was safely on liberated soil.

But at the beginning of November came the news that his elder brother had been killed. Aleksa had been returning from a successful raid on a bridge guarded by members of the *Milizia anti-comunista*. On passing through a village where he had once worked as a teacher he was recognised and felled by a well-aimed shot. His body was taken to Bijelo Polje and exhibited in the main square like the carcase of some beast caught in the forest. Milovan wept with grief and shame. Of all his brothers and sisters he felt closest to Aleksa and looked up to him as a fellow-fighter of heroic if over-rash courage.

The news of Aleksa's death was followed by another blow. Ivan Milutinović, a Montenegrin member of the Central Committee, arrived from Užice with a letter from Tito. This curtly informed him that he had been dismissed on account of serious 'errors' and should hand over his functions as representative of Tito and the Supreme Staff to his Montenegrin colleague. Various directives and resolutions issued by the Provincial Committee on his initiative, including the 'Letter from Comrade Veljko', were declared null and void, and Djilas was ordered to report at once to Tito's headquarters.

On 5 November, the day that Milutinović arrived, the Provincial

68

Committee met to consider Tito's letter and its analysis of their 'errors'. The letter declared that 'it was not wrong to have launched the rising, but it was wrong to have started it without grass-root political preparations.' It had been insufficiently planned and prepared and the people given no common aim beyond that of rising up against the invader. This could not be denied; but by the time Djilas had reached Montenegro, the timing was beyond his control. Only a week later the Italians were to proclaim the country's sham independence and give the signal for the people to rise in their fury, whether the Communists wanted it or not. He had tried to carry out his instructions and to delay large-scale action; it was as useless as trying to dam up an irresistible flood. So he had then taken the only possible course, countermanded his orders and urged the Party to give leadership to the anarchic spontaneous movement. If they could not stop it, then at least they must do their utmost to direct it. What other course could he have followed? The basic 'error' lay in the nature of the dilemma facing him and in the inadequate instructions he had received.

Djilas felt bitter and aggrieved. Tito appeared to be generalising from what had happened in Serbia. There the Communists had had time to build up their Partisan detachments on firm political foundations and there had been a natural development into a nation-wide rising. Montenegro had other conditions, traditions and popular mentality, and there had been a sudden, spontaneous popular explosion. However well-founded Comrade Tito's criticisms might seem in principle, was he right to put all the blame on the Provincial Committee and Djilas?

Tito also took exception to the expression 'Anti-Fascist Revolution' in place of 'National Liberation Struggle'. This was no mere terminological quibble but raised an important issue of Communist tactics. Djilas recalled that at the 'Consultation', held in Zagreb six months before, Tito had himself developed the thesis that the collapse and dismemberment of the Yugoslav state meant that the 'bourgeois-democratic stage' assumed by Leninist theory to precede every proletarian revolution might be skipped and that the Communists could make a direct bid for power. Moscow, however, ruled that the phrase 'Anti-Fascist Revolution' must be dropped and Tito complied. He wrote again to the Provincial Committee shortly after Djilas had left forbidding its use and stressing that, at this stage, they must remember that the war was being fought against the foreign invader. After all, he reminded them, did they not have 'English lords' for their allies?[13]

There were other practical matters which Tito also required to be put right. He asked for reinforcements to be sent to Serbia: 2,500 or 3,000 men, to be dispatched in batches of from one to two hundred at a time by routes which he would specify. He had made this request before, but the Montenegrin comrades had found excuses for not complying. Did Tito take this for a lack of solidarity, perhaps for something worse? Could he suspect that his Delegate to Montenegro was becoming too independent and that he might even defy his authority as the Party Secretary for Macedonia had defied it? But Djilas was absolutely loyal to Tito, and would remain so throughout the war. If he now felt a certain resentment it was because it seemed that doubts were being cast on his loyalty, or at least on his competence.

On 11 November Djilas set out for Užice. The autumn rains had set in and deepened his mood of self-reproach and depression. He and his companions had little to fear from the Italians, who seldom ventured far beyond their well-garrisoned towns, but who could now tell friend from foe? The unity which had held the Montenegrins together in the summer rising had crumbled.

CHAPTER EIGHT

The End of the Red Republic

On the day that Djilas started out for Tito's headquarters, Colonel Draža Mihailović left his on Ravna Gora for a meeting which his emissaries in Belgrade had been preparing in the greatest secrecy. At the village of Divci he was due to parley with representatives of the German High Command. He wished to discuss certain proposals put to them for discontinuing Chetnik operations against their forces in order to settle accounts with the Communist-led Partisans with whom his relations had been growing increasingly strained. In return for this – since the British, despite all their promises, had not sent sufficient help – he asked only that the Germans supply his men with arms and ammunition. The German negotiators listened courteously but declined. They welcomed the Chetnik leader's resolve to deal with his domestic rivals, but they still did not trust him to the extent of providing arms. The talks ended without result and Mihailović returned to Ravna Gora.

Several clashes between Partisans and Chetniks had already occurred, but it was not until a few days after Djilas's arrival at Tito's headquarters that the break between them became open and irreparable. Užice had been in Tito's hands for the past month and a half, together with neighbouring Požega, more recently seized from the Chetniks after they had tried to carry out a surprise attack on the Partisan capital. Beyond Požega was Čačak, also in Partisan hands, but the key town of Kraljevo, heavily invested by both Chetnik and Partisan forces, still held out. Strong German forces were pressing westwards along the valley to relieve it and fanning out to envelop the insurgent positions in the hills. The 'Red Republic' was fighting for its life.

Užice's normal population of some fourteen thousand had been swollen by an influx of troops and refugees. Tito's headquarters (marked, with a serene disregard for security, by a glaring electric sign in the shape of a red star) were in the National Bank. It was a tall, solid building fitted with up-to-date office equipment including a telephone system which still allowed Tito to communicate with Chetnik headquarters on Ravna Gora. The bank's vaults were filled with cases of silver coins and dinar notes, the latter a diminishing asset in a community where normal commercial life had come to a stop. A few sectors however still flourished. The bakeries still had stocks of flour, though most other food was short. The little tailors' shops were busy turning out items of uniforms – Djilas had a fine leather jacket made for himself – the new brand of 'Red Star' cigarette was being produced from commandeered tobacco stocks, and every two days a new number of *Borba* came off the press and was distributed free from the kiosks.

Most important of all was the state factory producing small arms and ammunition. Output was stepped up to four hundred new rifles a day, some of which, by agreement between Tito and Mihailović, were passed to the Chetniks; but the bulk, each stamped with a red star on the butt, remained with the Partisans. Ammunition and other explosives were stored in one of the two large tunnels which had been dug into the hillside to serve as vaults for the bank. The other was used as a shelter during the air raids which were now becoming alarmingly frequent.

The facades of the houses were everywhere gay with flags, red stars and the defiant slogan 'Death to Fascism – Freedom to the People!' But the mood of the population had grown sullen and apprehensive. The early enthusiasm evaporated as reports came in of the methodical reconquest of the country by the Germans and the terrible reprisals taken against the civilian population. For every German killed, one hundred hostages executed – such were the orders. Kraljevo had been cowed by mass executions, Kragujevac by a still more terrible holocaust. Reports spoke of five, even seven thousand marched out to execution there, including schoolchildren taken straight from their classrooms. The Chetniks were openly proclaiming that continued resistance could lead only to the physical extermination of the Serbian people. They had taken to handing over captured Partisans to the Germans, or to butchering them on the spot. The fiction of a common struggle against the forces of occupation could not disguise much longer the reality of an undeclared civil war.

Djilas's first thoughts were to report to Tito and to find Mitra. Tito, to his immense relief, welcomed him with unaffected warmth and without a word of reproach. The Secretary-General was not one to bear grudges or to waste time over spilt milk. What was important now was not why things went wrong in Montenegro but how to stop them going wrong in Serbia. Rapidly, he sketched in the chief events of the last weeks; the arrival of the royalist officers Lalatović and Ostojić and the assurance they brought Mihailović that he would have the support not only of the Royal Government in Exile but of the British, and perhaps, if the British could talk them into it, of the Russians as well. Almost immediately after their arrival, Mihailović's attitude had hardened and led to the first treacherous but abortive attack by the Chetniks on Tito's forces. This was in spite of a personal meeting with Mihailović, who had made only vague promises and refused Tito's proposals for a joint command and joint operations. A fresh attempt to patch things up was now in progress and Ranković was at present away in Čačak negotiating. Djilas talked to his old friend by telephone and learned the terms of the proposed agreement which Tito then authorised. It was fated, however, to remain a dead letter.

Tito told Djilas to resume his agit-prop duties and take charge of *Borba*, which Dedijer and other comrades had been producing. They had made themselves comfortable in the still undamaged Palace Hotel where he also found Mitra at work. She seemed to have altered. The experiences she had undergone since her arrest that summer had left their mark and made the restoration of their former easy relationship difficult. Mitra's appearance too had changed, and scarcely for the better, for she had dyed her hair to make it harder for the police to recognise her when she escaped from Belgrade; the result, Djilas thought, gave her the air of a hostess in some dubious night-club. Mitra had become harder, more sure of herself, and obviously pleased with the part she had begun to play in the terrible drama of resistance and civil war. She related how she had first feigned illness so as to be transferred from the internment camp, and probable execution, to a Belgrade hospital where Ranković had also been brought in, half-conscious and unrecognised; and how, in response to a message she and other comrades smuggled out, a band of armed comrades had forced their way in and rescued him. Eventually she too had escaped and made her way through a countryside in flames to join the Partisans.

In the early afternoon of 22 November, when Djilas and Mitra were at work in the Palace Hotel, a powerful explosion was heard, followed by a fainter muffled one. It came from the direction of the National Bank. They rushed out to find Tito and other members of his staff standing outside, shaken and begrimed. Smoke was pouring from the entrance to the tunnels only a few yards away. The dull thud of explosions continued to come from the interior. Someone suggested that the entrance should be blocked up so as to cut off the supply of air and prevent the fire from spreading. Tito gave the necessary orders. It was only on the following morning, when the vaults were opened and bodies found, handkerchiefs still tightly pressed over their mouths, that it was realised that some had been trapped inside.

The disaster was probably the outcome of the hasty improvisation which was the strength and weakness of the Partisan movement. Tito reported to Moscow over the Zagreb radio link that Chetnik saboteurs had smuggled in 'a time-machine' – a charge which Ranković investigated but could not confirm.

The obsession with spies and fifth columnists grew as the German advance continued. Ranković, back from his negotiations at Čačak, was tireless in rooting them out. He had exchanged his role from hunted to hunter, and with ruthless efficiency he was to continue playing it for almost a quarter of a century. Djilas had little aptitude or relish for such work, but he too was dragged in occasionally whenever his friend thought he might be of help. 'The prison was well run on the whole, and did not differ essentially, as far as I could tell,' Djilas recalls, 'from the prisons of post-war years. Torture was applied selectively, in special cases, and executions were carried out secretly at night.'[1]

The Germans and their agents were not the only enemy; to support, or even to sympathise with, the Chetniks in Partisan-held territory was as dangerous as being thought pro-Communist in areas under Chetnik influence. Each of the rival factions was intent on destroying the other. Hudson, under instructions to do his utmost to unify all resistance forces, was faced with an impossible task. Lalatović and Ostojić, with their secret directives and their assurances of British moral and material support, confirmed Mihailović in his intransigence. When, two days after Hudson's arrival on Ravna Gora, Mihailović and Tito met to parley, the latter's suggestion that Hudson should join them was turned down by the Chetnik leader who declared that this would be to interfere in a purely Yugoslav affair. Ten days later, the first British supplies were dropped to Mihailović – a small consignment, but the earnest, it was hoped, of things to come. Yet only two days afterwards Mihailović was assuring the Germans at Divci that nothing could be expected from the British and that the arms he wanted for use against the Partisans could only be supplied by them.

On 13 November Hudson signalled his headquarters that he proposed to go to Užice to urge on the Partisans the need to cooperate with the Chetniks. He attended the talks at Čačak and reported optimistically: 'Draža Mihailović has now agreed to recognise the Partisans. I told him that if both sides turned against the Germans I believed that British aid would be at his disposal and we would help to establish him as the unconditional Commander-in-Chief.'[2] The signal was followed by one from Mihailović claiming that he had 'succeeded in ending fratricidal strife provoked by the other side' and that all would now unite under his command against the Germans.[3] This was believed in London, and Hudson instructed to convey the government's congratulations. But by this time Hudson was in Užice. A young Communist doctor, whom Tito had entrusted with the formidable task of arranging the evacuation of the wounded, records in his memoirs:

A strange figure was then to be seen at our High Command . . . I came upon him once in Tito's room trying to persuade Tito of the need to cooperate with Draža Mihailović's Chetniks. The methodical persistence with which he pressed this on Tito caused sparks to fly. How could there be any cooperation after such treachery and intrigues with the invader?[4]

The Communists' doctrinaire distrust of the British and of their attempts at mediation is reflected still more sharply in the diary kept at this time by Djilas's friend Dedijer. 'An Englishman, an Intelligence Service spy called Captain Hudson, has landed by submarine in Montenegro,' it records. 'I believe that the [Chetniks'] attack on us was ordered by the English and Yugoslav Governments. The bourgeoisie has little interest in liberating our people; they have started the class war. Oh you English, how dearly those who don't know you are made to pay for it! You certainly have a finger in this pie!'[5]

On 28 November Tito made a last appeal to Mihailović for a joint stand against the advancing Germans. The 'hot line' to Ravna Gora was still working, though the enemy had broken out of Kraljevo and were rapidly pushing on down the valley as well as converging on Užice from Valjevo in the north. Mihailović repeated that to try and resist them was hopeless; what remained of the Chetnik and Partisan forces should withdraw, each to their own territory. The telephone conversation was to be the last contact between the rival leaders. The following morning Tito gave the order to evacuate Užice.

Many had already left, Mitra and the agit-prop team amongst them. Djilas and other members of the Central Committee stayed on with Tito and the headquarters guard. Tito's plan was to withdraw over the Zlatibor range into the rugged country comprising the former Turkish province, the Sandžak of Novi Pazar, where his forces could regroup and then move either west into Bosnia or south into Montenegro, or reinfiltrate back into Serbia. He was preoccupied with the problem which was to dog the Partisans throughout the war – the evacuation of the wounded – as well as with salvaging as much as he could of the ammunition, food and other supplies needed for carrying on the struggle. Koča Popović, a young Belgrade *littérateur* who had displayed a flair for military operations during the Spanish Civil War, was entrusted with organising the defence of Užice, but the Valjevo Partisan

Detachment on which he chiefly relied was already in flight and not even the planned mining of the roads was put into effect. Around noon, Tito ordered Djilas and Ranković to leave with the headquarters guard for Zlatibor, telling them that he would follow later. Like a captain standing on the bridge of his sinking ship he was almost the last to abandon the capital of his short-lived republic.

Whilst German planes strafed the retreating Partisans, a flying column of enemy infantry continued in hot pursuit. Alarmed for their chief's safety, Ranković and Djilas turned back to look for Tito. They found him eventually with Hudson and an escort. The evacuation turned into a rout as scattered bands of Partisans sought safety in the Sandžak. This was Italian-held territory into which they hoped their pursuers would refrain from penetrating. On reaching the small river which formed the boundary, the Germans turned back and devoted their efforts to hunting down stragglers and wounded. They gave no quarter; neither, from then on, would the Partisans. Amongst the wounded in the fighting round Užice was Milivoje Djilas, Milovan's idealistic younger brother. He was captured, sadistically tortured, and executed.

Following the rout of his forces and the collapse of the brief period of Communist rule, Tito seems to have underestimated the extent of the popular revulsion against the Partisans in Serbia. The bulk of Mihailović's men melted away into the countryside or merged with the troops of the Serbian Quisling General Nedić in helping the Germans hunt down suspected Communists. The peasants, willing enough generally to feed and shelter the Partisans so long as things seemed to be going their way, were now cowed or openly hostile. 'The peasant goes with whoever is the strongest!' Tito observed philosophically to Djilas.

Captain Hudson, cut off from radio contact with his British superiors, also decided that he must return to Serbia. Tito did not try to dissuade him. The Partisan leaders were indignant at the broadcasts from the BBC – and also at those from Moscow – attributing the fighting against the Germans to the Chetniks rather than to themselves, and some of them blamed Hudson for misinforming the British, but Tito knew that he was without a set or wireless operator of his own. Dragičevic had opted to stay with the Partisans, and his cumbersome set was out of action. Djilas, in fact, had given orders that it should be concealed and Hudson told that they were still trying to find it. Tito did not approve. 'There's no point in that!' he told Djilas. 'After all, the man's our ally!' So Hudson recovered his transmitter and transported it with immense difficulty back to Serbia. But he was unable to make use of it again, or to rejoin Mihailović who had made his way with a few followers into East Bosnia. The Chetnik leader refused to receive a liaison officer who had been with the Communists. Hudson was left to drag out a wretched existence, hunted and alone, a dangerous guest for the cowed peasantry of the Šumadija to harbour.

For the first two weeks of December Tito's shattered forces remained just inside the borders of the Sandžak. The Germans had temporarily abandoned the pursuit and the Italians, instead of seizing the opportunity to crush their enemy between the Axis pincers, cautiously withdrew from their nearest garrison town, Nova Varoš. It was decided that the main body of the reinforced Partisan army should veer east, along the borders of Montenegro, into Bosnia; but first, some painful stock-taking had to be done and important political decisions taken. Djilas had made Radonja, a village friendly to the Partisans, his temporary headquarters and was busying re-forming the detachment destined to infiltrate back into Serbia. Tito, Kardelj, and most of the other leaders were at the neighbouring village of Drenovo. There, on 7 December, the Central Committee – or such leading Party members as could be mustered – met to review the situation. Kardelj, always ready with a theoretical analysis, did most of the talking. The war, he declared, was changing its character. It was still a struggle against the forces of occupation but also something more – a class war in which workers and peasants were pitted against the Fascist-minded bourgeoisie. Djilas and the others agreed; this was, in fact, a development which Tito had forecast, not altogether to the satisfaction of the Comintern, at the 'Zagreb Consultation' the previous spring. To give practical expression to this thesis it was decided to form the First Proletarian Brigade, a twelve-hundred-man-strong amalgamation of Serbian and Montenegrin units prepared to fight anywhere in Yugoslavia, a shock force wholly at the service of the Party and imbued with its dogma and discipline. Its formation was to take place – significantly enough – on 21 December, Stalin's birthday. This was proudly reported to Moscow, but again the response was discouraging. 'Study of all the information you give,' the Comintern eventually replied, 'leaves the impression that the adherents of Great Britain and the Yugoslav Government have some grounds for suspecting the Partisan movement of acquiring a Communist character and aiming at the Sovietization of Yugoslavia. Why, for example, did you need to form a special Proletarian Brigade?'[6]

By the time the Comintern's reaction was made known to him Tito was in Bosnia and his army's fortunes were somewhat restored. But now, uneasily clinging to the edge of the Sandžak, the Secretary-General suffered one of his rare moments of depression. He blamed himself for the collapse of the Užice Republic, the disorderly retreat, the fate of the wounded. In the cramped living room of the Drenovo cottage, where exhausted soldiers had fallen asleep around them, he announced to his comrades that he felt compelled to resign his Party office. Kardelj, he went on, should take over; the Party must not be blamed for misfortunes for which he felt responsible. He, for his part, would go on working body and soul for the Party as he had always done; but Kardelj should assume the Secretaryship. Djilas was the first to recover his composure and express the general consternation. 'Out of the question!' he expostulated. The 'Old Man's' resignation would only make matters worse. It would be taken as an admission of defeat, of disunion within the Party, of general demoralisation. And which of them could do the job better? Kardelj and Ranković were equally insistent that there must be no change. Tito was clearly pleased with his comrades' reaction, though his offer to resign had been made in all good faith.

He quickly recovered his habitual confidence, but the Partisans' situation remained precarious. Five or six days later, an Italian raiding party nearly succeeded in surprising the High Command at Drenovo. Tito moved for greater security to Nova Varoš, evacuated by the Italians and favourably disposed to the Partisans. He called together the Central Committee for a final meeting before moving off with the main body of the army towards Bosnia.

After nearly two months of rest and reorganisation in the Sandžak the units earmarked for operations in Serbia were ready to move. Djilas, though weakened by dysentery, had been indefatigable in his efforts to ensure that the Party – since the struggle was now considered to be a 'class war' as well as a war of 'national liberation' – had thoroughly consolidated its authority over all fighting units. 'A merciless courage, a merciless unity permeated our forces,' he recalls. It was a unity forged at the cost of a ruthless elimination of those whom Djilas judged to be politically unreliable or physically or psychologically incapable of continuing the struggle. They were dismissed from the ranks, given a handful of the money the Partisans had brought with them from Užice, and told to shift for themselves. Old scores were settled and serious infractions of discipline punished with summary execution, regardless of the culprit's past services. Mile Cvetić, a Communist who had once been expelled from the Party as a Trotskyist but had fought well with the Partisans in Serbia, was shot as a fractionist. A similar fate befell a young Partisan whose bravery had been officially commended, as Djilas somewhat ruefully reported to Tito on 28 January 1942:

Navikov (Novozilov) has been executed for organising and assisting a group of deserters. It was rather awkward that he should have been praised in a recent bulletin of the High Command, but there was nothing for it, as they were hostile elements – really nothing but scum.[7]

But whilst the Partisans had been reorganising, so had their enemies. The Germans were preparing to take over Nova Varoš and the Italians were coming to terms with the Chetniks. Communists hitherto neutral or defenceless now had their own village guards. In Serbia the forces of the Nedić regime were reinforced by many who secretly sympathised with Mihailović. Heavy falls of snow and the restricted terrain made movement difficult. The Partisans' advance units quickly encountered opposition which rendered their standard tactics of infiltration and surprise ineffective. All they could do was to take a few prisoners whom they cross-examined and then, in their frustration, killed. Finding that they were hemmed in and unable to advance in strength, Djilas decided that they must pull back. The few detachments which did push on, to the Kosmaj mountains and elsewhere, were decimated.

Plans had to be changed. Instead of attempting an impossibly costly return to Serbia, Djilas decided that the Partisans must move south round the wooded slopes of Mount Zlatar, cross the Lim and veer westwards, skirting the borders of Montenegro, to link up with Tito in Bosnia. He had some 1,500 Serbians and 500 men from the Sandžak under his command, hampered by the usual train of sick and wounded. The Moslem hamlets through which they passed were hostile but too weak to oppose them. Food was short, and even the Orthodox peasantry well disposed to them begrudged the grain and cattle needed by the army. Villages known to be pro-Chetnik were simply looted. In the last week of February, Djilas brought his guerrillas, exhausted but virtually intact, into Bosnia. There, on 1 March, Tito incorporated them into his newly formed Second Proletarian Brigade.

CHAPTER NINE

Bosnian Interlude

THE next two weeks Djilas spent at Foča, where Tito's headquarters had been established for over a month. The little Bosnian town, pleasantly situated amidst smiling orchards, had escaped the ravages of war; the High Command was installed in the Hotel Gerstl, Tito in a small villa by a gully which offered cover in the event of an air-raid. But the peaceful, welcoming appearance of the place was deceptive. Lying within the frontiers of Pavelić's 'Independent State of Croatia', it had been the scene of atrocities committed first by the Ustashe, then by Chetniks who had taken terrible revenge on the predominantly Moslem population. Bosnia and Hercegovina were torn by communal strife which the German and Italian occupying forces each strove to turn to account in their respective zones. For the first few months Chetniks and Partisans, bent on self-protection and revenge, had made common cause. But here too, though lasting longer than in Serbia, the alliance had begun to break down, particularly after the arrival of emissaries sent by Mihailović. The Communist Party organisation in Bosnia had never been strong and the authority of its commissars and commanders over detachments which were Partisan in name but mostly Serbian nationalists at heart was easily undermined. Though Tito now had his Proletarian Brigades to rely on, serious defections kept occurring amongst the rank and file of many Bosnian units.

Djilas nevertheless found his chief in good heart. Tito seemed glad to see him and evidently still regarded him, despite the 'errors' in Montenegro, as one of his staunchest lieutenants. The two of them had several long talks together. The Old Man spoke frankly of his plans and problems. Now that the Partisans once again had a stable base, they were in regular radio contact with Moscow instead of having to rely on the risky and circuitous route via Zagreb. It was important to have direct access to 'Grandpa' – as Tito called the Comintern – now that there were so many reports to make, matters to arrange and misunderstandings to clear up. Amongst them was the urgent question of aid from the Allies. Anything the Russians could send him, Tito kept insisting, would be of enormous moral and material value. His men desperately needed arms, munitions, clothes and medicines. These could be dropped in to Montenegro, where there was a suitable area ready to receive them near Žabljak, at the foot of Mount Durmitor. He sent Moša Pijade there to supervise their reception. But there was no sign of the Russians or their planes. After keeping his vigil on the snow-covered plateau beneath Mount Durmitor for thirty-eight nights, Pijade was told to give up and return to headquarters.

In the meantime, Tito had received news of other and less welcome arrivals. Milutinović reported that a small military mission consisting of a British major and his wireless operator and a Yugoslav captain had landed from a submarine on the Montenegrin coast near the spot where Hudson and the royalist officers came ashore six months before. Milutinović was instructed to send them on to Foča. Tito warned Pijade not to fall on their necks in the belief that they were Russians and added that he had asked the Comintern not to send him any more such guests, 'as we had enough trouble with them in Serbia'.

But the British did not take their orders from Moscow. They seemed to be playing a devious game of their own, backing Mihailović and the Chetniks in Yugoslavia whilst remaining allies of the Soviet Union. 'Grandpa' appeared to put much of the blame on Tito for following a narrow sectarian line and stressing the revolutionary nature of the Partisan movement. 'We earnestly beg you to give serious thought to your tactics and actions,' Moscow had signalled him, 'and to make sure you have done all you really can do to achieve a true united front of all enemies of Hitler and Mussolini.'[1] Tito was irritated by such exhortations. He replied that he was doing his utmost to rally all patriotic elements against the foreign invaders, but that it was the Chetniks, and the western imperialists who stood behind them, who were frustrating his efforts and secretly conniving with the enemy.

Even experienced party workers could get things out of proportion, as can be seen from the following entry for 10 March in Dedijer's diary:

Yesterday evening the second Consultation of Party activists was held. Mitar [Bakić] spoke about the international situation and I added a few words. We both got things wrong! Leftist deviation. Djilas put things in their proper perspective. The alliance between the USSR and Britain is strong and will become still stronger.[2]

Djilas added that they must not allow themselves to have a class war imposed on them by the occupying authorities who wanted to isolate them. He said they were waging a war for national liberation and must go on waging it. Djilas's speech was lively, light-hearted and witty.

It was a delicate course to steer. 'National liberation' or 'class-war', a patriotic struggle against the foreign invader or civil war to decide who would rule Yugoslavia? It was both one and the other, though emphasis might be switched according to tactical necessity or the dictates of international pressure. The manoeuvre would require still more skill as wartime needs imposed closer relations with the Western Allies – and not with them alone. There was certainly a fear, which was to become obsessive as the end of the war approached, that the Western allies would land in force and prevent the Communists reaping the fruits of victory; but there also seems to have been some presentiment that a powerful Soviet ally might claim to have liberated Yugoslavia, and so also claim the right to call the tune and impose its protectorate.

Djilas found his short stay in Foča a rare interlude of calm and comfort. To be billeted in a hotel was in itself an unaccustomed luxury. There was even time for a little hunting, though he failed to bring down the wild ducks which would have made a welcome addition to the unpalatable bread concocted from barley and dried pears which was their staple fare. Thanks to the zeal of the Partisans' medical teams, the little town was kept clean and free of the typhus which had been thinning their ranks elsewhere.

A fortnight after Djilas's arrival, Tito broke the news that he wanted him to go back to Montenegro where things were not going well. 'All right,' said Djilas, surprised that he should have been reassigned to that area in spite of his previous 'errors' there.

Tito attributed his apparent lack of enthusiasm to the prospect of separation from Mitra and added that she might go with him. After all, Tito was seldom separated for long from his secretary and mistress Zdenka. So Djilas was accompanied by Mitra, Bakić and Svetislav Stefanović, the security officer who was Ranković's right-hand man.

Before they set out, Tito impressed upon them the seriousness of the situation they would find in Montenegro and the need to take drastic measures to halt the growing influence of the Chetniks. Djilas records the occasion as follows:

All along we were troubled by the peasants' excuse that they were going over to the Chetniks for fear of having their houses burned down and other reprisals. This issue came up at the meeting with Tito, and the following argument developed: If the peasants realize that if they go over to the invader we will also burn their houses they will change their minds. This argument seemed logical to me too, though I did not support it resolutely. Finally Tito made up his mind, though hesitantly: 'Well, all right, we can burn a house or a village here and there!' Later Tito issued orders to that effect – orders that were fairly bold, by virtue of being explicit. Armed with this bold new decree, we set out on 15 March 1942 for Montenegro.[3]

CHAPTER TEN

Montenegro Revisited

AFTER a week's march Djilas and his party arrived back at Montenegrin headquarters. It was still in the same house, in the territory of the friendly Piperi clan to which Milutinović and other leading Communists belonged. The two men got on well together, although they did not always see eye to eye. Djilas respected him for his probity and revolutionary dedication but doubted whether he possessed the political vision or firmness to curb the extremism of the more fanatical comrades and rally non-Communists to a common struggle against the occupying authorities and their agents. This had become all the more difficult since many nationalists had now come to terms with the Italians. Not only Stanišić, but Colonel Pavle Djurišić, who had fought heroically against the Italians at Berane, had since entered into formal agreements with them. To give cohesion to their individual initiatives, the leading nationalists gathered together at Cetinje on 9 March and elected one of their number, General Blažo Djukanović, to be commander of their joint forces in Montenegro. This was done with the approval of Mihailović and the tacit agreement of the Italians with whom Djukanović later (24 July 1942) concluded a formal understanding specifying the forms their collaboration should take.[1]

After a few days at Montenegrin headquarters, Djilas sent to Tito his appraisal of the situation. He described it as very bad but by no means beyond the possibility of putting right. Many mistakes had been made. 'Our comrades have failed to understand that the masses do not want a fratricidal war, but a war against the forces of occupation,' he declared.

In the meantime, the new British mission had reached Tito's headquarters from Montenegro. It was headed by Major Terence Atherton, who had worked as a journalist in Belgrade before the war and knew the country and its language well. Atherton appeared well disposed towards the Partisans and impressed by everything he saw at headquarters. But Tito, from the outset, was suspicious of his guests' movements and intentions. On 8 April, when the mission had been at his headquarters for a couple of weeks, he drafted a confidential letter addressed to the Communist leaders in Croatia warning them to be on their guard against any similar visitors.

For your information, but not for general publication [he wrote], we have to acquaint you with some very interesting matters which we have established beyond the possibility of doubt. We have now certain proof that the British, through their agents in Yugoslavia, are working not to remove, but rather to intensify, the differences between ourselves and other groups such as the Chetniks. England is supporting different Chetnik bands just as the Germans are doing and egging them on to attack us. We have proof that British policy aims at sabotaging and compromising the struggle for national liberation so that when the situation is favourable and Italy leaves Hitler and comes within their grasp, the British will land troops in Dalmatia and elsewhere and appear as 'liberators' to save the country from chaos. To this end about ten so-called 'military missions' have already arrived and are doing their dirty work in different parts of Yugoslavia. One such mission has arrived at our headquarters, another has landed in Dalmatia and others are in different parts of the country, exactly where we do not know.

What they are aiming at can clearly be seen from what has been happening in Montenegro. Around Kolašin and elsewhere there suddenly appeared strong and well-armed Chetnik bands, led in the main by pro-British leaders and assisted by the Italian occupation forces who are cunningly turning the situation to their advantage. These Chetniks bands fell upon our Partisan troops at Kolašin, captured the town and shed the blood of many of our best fighters. As you know, the only fighting force up to now in Montenegro has been the Partisans. Yet here arc Chetnik bands suddenly springing up throughout Montenegro under the leadership of Fifth Columnists and pro-Britishers. This cannot be explained away simply by Italian guile. It is quite clear that the pro-British elements who have hitherto fought on our side have not suddenly turned against us overnight on orders given by the Italians. A hint must have been dropped in London. . . . I must emphasise again that all this is not for general publication, but for the confidential information of leading persons in the army and Party. In public, the alliance between the Soviet Union, Britain and the United States must continue to be stressed, and the latter two Powers are to be depicted as our allies. But their agents and pawns inside our country must be opposed, just as we oppose the henchmen of the invaders and the enemies of the people who are out to crush our struggle for national liberation.[2]

A week after Tito had sent this warning, Atherton disappeared from Foča without a word of explanation, taking his wireless operator and the Yugoslav captain with him. With him too vanished another individual with whom he had latterly become friendly – General Ljubo Novaković, the only officer of that senior rank in the royalist army to have escaped capture and internment. The general was an enigmatic character. He had turned up at Foča after being for a time with Mihailović, whom Tito suspected he wished to supplant in the good graces of the British. Neither Atherton nor his wireless operator were seen alive again. Mihailović sources put it around that they had been murdered by the Partisans, but an investigation by Ranković indicated that Atherton had probably encountered and been killed by a Bosnian, more of a bandit than a Chetnik, who was later found to be wearing his boots and had probably stolen the large quantity of gold sovereigns in his possession. Novaković subsequently perished at the hands of Montenegrin Partisans.[3]

The affair deepened Tito's suspicions of the British and their machinations. The day after Atherton's disappearance from his headquarters he wrote to Djilas:

Our British guests have sprung a great surprise on us. Last night all three of them vanished without trace together with that old fox General Novaković and a couple of civilians. I think they are making for the Sandžak or Montenegro . . . Do everything you can on your side to catch them if they appear in your territory.[4]

The indignation and suspicion engendered in Tito's mind by the Atherton affair was natural enough, but the assumption that the growth of Chetnik influence in Montenegro was due to the intrigues of 'pro-Britishers' and to 'a hint dropped in London' was unfounded. The savage extremism of the Montenegrin Communists themselves was in large measure to blame. 'It became increasingly clear to me', Djilas writes, 'that our unpopular, hasty executions, along with hunger and war weariness, were helping to strengthen the Chetniks.'[5] And he asks, 'How is one else to explain that on territory cleared of Chetniks by the Partisans, such panic has been aroused that the Partisans do not encounter a single soul?'[6]

How many fell victim to the Partisans' terror in Montenegro and the Sandžak at this time? Djilas puts the number at several hundred.[7] 'In Hercegovina,' he adds, 'it was still more terrible and ugly. Communist sons confirmed their devotion by killing their own fathers, and there was dancing and singing around the bodies.'[8] One such case is described by an eye-witness in Dedijer's diary. Marijan Stilinović, an old Communist and member of the agit-prop team, had been at Piva in Montenegro, visiting a youth organisation. The cell secretary gave a report which mentioned that they had executed a rich peasant. 'An informer or a collaborator, I suppose?' asked Stilinović. 'Not at all!' replied the Secretary. 'He even donated regularly to our funds. But we had to execute him. You see, he was a kulak! And one day he would have been our enemy!' Stilinović began to remonstrate, but the

Secretary cut him short, pointing to a boy sitting with him. 'That is his son – he also voted for his father's execution – you ask him.' The boy nodded.[9]

If, in such cases, political fanaticism proved stronger than family ties, it could also be sharpened by clan loyalty and the Montenegrin tradition of the blood feud. The Communists who held power at Savnik, for instance, executed thirty men on a charge of 'conspiracy', most of whom knew of it only through the clan 'grape-vine' and were in no way directly implicated. This mass execution was taken with the blessing of Moša Pijade, then tense and frustrated by his fruitless vigil at neighbouring Žabljak. Pijade, with the intransigence of a dogmatist embittered by long years spent in prison, was inclined to favour extremist solutions, especially at the expense of the Montenegrins whose mentality and ways were alien to him. 'I disagree with the decision to release rather than shoot the Vasojevići Chetniks,' he complained. 'So many in our district have been shot or mutilated by the Chetniks that there is the utmost bitterness against them, above all against the Vosojevići clan.'[10]

Terrible and tragic could be the consequences when loyalty to clan and kin clashed with loyalty to creed and Party. The memory of one such experience remained with Djilas throughout his life. A certain student and party member called Tadija Tadić was commanding a Partisan battalion whilst his uncle, a former police agent, was with the Chetniks. The uncle took refuge in a wood and became the object of a *potjera* – a man-hunt. His nephew managed to send a warning to him, and when the pursuers closed in they were met by machine-gun fire which killed two of their number before the fugitive was taken. The nephew was arrested, but the young man's kinsmen, all party members too, took his side and rose up in arms. They were overpowered, arrested, and the leading members of the family sentenced to death for rebellion.[11]

Djilas approved the sentences passed on the Tadić rebels, as he approved or ordered other death sentences whenever the stern necessities of revolutionary war seemed to demand it. But reprisals taken so readily by the Partisans against their enemies or 'traitors' seemed to him both inhumane and counter-productive. On 8 April, largely on his advice, Tito sent instructions that such executions, except for those of prominent ringleaders, were to cease. 'On no account,' he added, 'permit a wave of general burning and destruction which can only make the present situation worse. Only in exceptional cases and for the purpose of a reprisal may you carry out the burning of the house and property of some very notorious fifth columnist or collaborator.'[12] Djilas himself never shrank from harsh measures when he judged them to be required by 'revolutionary necessity.'

I must emphasize that I have never been soft towards the enemy [he wrote at the end of April]. But against the enemy – the *real* enemy. I have perhaps pronounced more death sentences than anyone else, as it fell to my wartime lot to do. Yet my conscience is clear. But kill our own brothers – that we should never do.[13]

But it was now too late for the Partisans to restore their declining fortunes in Montenegro by simply halting attempts to impose their authority through the firing squad and scorched earth tactics. Djilas devoted his efforts to reorganising the army, while Milutinović attended to the Party, almost the entire leadership of which was replaced early in April. There was war-weariness and demoralisation amongst the rank and file fighters, though they had some excellent commanders, outstanding amongst them the Spanish veteran Peko Dapčević and the peasant hero Sava Kovačević. The latter had become a legendary figure. Tales were told of how he would take on Italian tanks single-handed or, bearing a charmed life, storm impregnable bunkers at the head of his men. He was violent and rash like a thoughtless boy; and ruthless too, with the fierce innocence of one untroubled by any scruples of good or evil. Djilas found that the staff at his headquarters ate well. The Italian commander at Nikšić had agreed to supply the seventy to eighty Italian prisoners held by the Partisans with rations, of which Sava's men took half for themselves. This continued until the Partisan Brigade was forced to move; then the prisoners, half starved and too weak to keep up, were quietly killed off.

Towards the end of April Dapčević planned a major operation – the recapture of Kolašin. It failed, even with the assistance of a battalion of the First Proletarian Brigade sent by Tito. It was now mid-May, and on almost all fronts the Partisans found themselves on the defensive. Tito evacuated Foča and withdrew his forces towards the border between Hercegovina and Montenegro.

Djilas, alone and on horseback, set out to meet him. He followed a track westwards under the peaks of Mount Durmitor. There, on the highland pastures, Moša Pijade had been trying out his pet schemes, establishing collective farms stocked with the cattle confiscated from Chetnik peasants. Mitra had been sent to help him and had been busy organising shepherd brigades, appointing instructors, drawing up inventories and regulations, prescribing production norms which the unenthusiastic peasants never approached. Neither of them knew much about farming, but the important thing was to demonstrate the benefits of collectivisation and gain experience for the revolutionary changes which they intended to introduce on a national scale after the war. The experiment collapsed and the herds vanished as soon as the Partisans began to withdraw.

The majesty of the landscape in its spring glory could not dispel the gloom which oppressed Djilas on that solitary ride. The Chetnik-Italian condominium – the Italians garrisoning the towns, the Chetniks dominating the countryside – was steadily establishing itself throughout Montenegro. What had become of the patriotic rising against the invader, the prelude to the revolution which was to sweep the grateful peasantry and workers to power? Despite all his efforts to rally and reorganise the Partisan forces, he had seen the rising degenerate into senseless and bitter fratricidal strife. 'For hours both armies climbed up rocky ravines to escape annihilation,' he wrote of the fighting round Kolašin, 'or to destroy a little group of their countrymen, often neighbours, on some jutting peak six thousand feet high, in a starving, bleeding, captive land.'[14]

Tito's forces were heading for Žabljak, and from there on to Crno Jezero, the 'Black Lake', the beauty of whose pine-clad shores and limpid water rich in trout drew many visitors in happier times. The Commander-in-Chief was quick to notice Djilas's discouragement but gave no signs of sharing it. His anxieties were however reflected in the urgency of his radio appeals to Moscow.

'Since May 20,' he reported, 'I have been on the Montenegrin sector of the front. The situation here is critical. Incessant fighting has left the Partisans exhausted. Apart from that, there is no ammunition.'[15] He said that to escape annihilation they must get the greater part of their forces out of Montenegro and that assistance was vital. 'In the name of the High Command', he implored, 'please pass on our request for help to the High Command of the Red Army.'

Crucial decisions had to be taken. Serbia remained closed to them, most of East Bosnia was in enemy hands, the Italians and Chetniks were over-running Montenegro. Some small Partisan detachments had already been reinfiltrated into Montenegro and the Sandžak, as they had been into Serbia, to harass the Chetnik rear. Should these be reinforced, or would that merely be sending good men to their death? And in which direction should the main body of the army move? Djilas volunteered to stay behind in Montenegro; he felt humiliated by the setbacks there and found it hard to take in good part the teasing from his

Serbian comrades – Mitra amongst them – about the failure of the vaunted Montenegrin heroism to hold the enemy at bay. But Tito would not let him go; he wanted to keep him by his side, for too many of the leading comrades were at present away on special assignments. Despite the younger man's long absence, a special relationship – almost that of father and son – still bound the two of them together. Though he was careful not to go too far, Djilas dared to take certain liberties which the others would not allow themselves.

There was, however, a serious and wounding blow to Djilas's self-esteem at a meeting of the Central Committee called by Tito to carry out a post-mortem into the Party's failure in Montenegro. 'Comrades Milutinović and Djilas are much to blame, and for this I believe they deserve a reprimand,' he pronounced. The real offence was simply that in Montenegro they had failed.

CHAPTER ELEVEN

The Long March

BY the middle of June Tito had moved his forces from Montenegro to the valley of the Sutjeska, between the wild mountain ranges of Maglić and Zelengora. Here the decision was taken that the bulk of the army – four Brigades – would continue their advance into Western Bosnia whilst the local Hercegovina Partisan detachments and the Fifth Montenegrin Brigade under Sava Kovačević remained in that area. The barren country could not support a larger force. The Partisans were being forced to give ground, but in a war with no fixed fronts, a withdrawal can be less a retreat than an advance, for wherever the Partisans went they fed the flames of revolt. And there were encouraging reports that in many parts of Pavelić's 'Independent State' of Croatia desperate men were resorting to arms and Partisan detachments already operating.

On 22 June Tito signed the order for the start of the Long March to Western Bosnia. The Partisans were to move north-westwards in a direction broadly parallel to that of the Adriatic coast and some forty to fifty miles inland. The thickly wooded mountains would afford them the cover they needed, and their course would lie roughly along the extended watershed which also formed the boundary between the Italian and German zones of occupation. Their first major target would be to cut the railway which linked Sarajevo to the coast and served as the Italians' most vital supply line. They then intended to push on to link up with the Partisan detachments operating in Dalmatia and with those in the Lika and Western Bosnia.

The Long March would take them further away from the Serbian lands, the possession of which they knew to be the key to victory and the mastery of post-war Yugoslavia. But they were realists enough to recognise that neither the international alignment of forces nor the mood of the population favoured any early prospect of re-establishing Communist influence there. The route to ultimate power would be a circuitous one.

Tito's forces now consisted of five Brigades, together with the inevitable train of wounded and non-combatants. The region through which the army was to pass had been fought over by Chetniks and

Ustashe but had not yet had contact with the Partisans except for occasional isolated local bands. Tito attached the greatest importance to not alienating this generally neutral population. He issued strict orders against pilfering or unauthorised 'requisitioning', and the death penalty was prescribed, and generally carried out, against offenders. ('Don't our comrades know that, for the peasant, a cow is almost a member of the family!' he once exclaimed when a woman came to complain that someone had carried hers off.) The Partisans came well supplied with silver, gold and *kunas* – Croatian currency – and could generally afford to purchase what food they needed; but in this wild mountain region, already devastated by marauding bands, there seldom remained enough even for the civilian population. As exceptions to the general rule against looting, 'confiscations' were allowed at the expense of pro-Chetnik or pro-Ustasha collaborators – terms applied broadly enough to cover the few wealthier folk encountered – local landowners, merchants, priests – and occasionally whole villages.

Mitra was assigned to the First Proletarian Brigade for work in the 'Political Section' which had recently been formed, on approved Soviet lines, 'to build up the Party in the Army'. She had developed into a zealous and disciplined Party functionary and found the task of ideological indoctrination congenial. The appointment would mean that she and Milovan would see little of one another on the Long March, but such was commonly the lot of husband and wife in wartime. Sometimes it was a separation for good. Only ten days before, Djilas had had to break the news to Ranković that his wife Andja had been killed in a clash with Chetniks. Tito alone remained close to his common-law wife throughout the war, for Zdenka was also his secretary. Her touchiness and displays of temperament, particularly at moments of crisis, made her universally disliked. She behaved as if the enemy's main objective was to destroy her personally, Djilas sarcastically observed. The others were delighted when, after one of her tantrums, Tito turned to the commander of his bodyguard and asked, in mock despair, what he was to do with her, and the old warrior replied in all seriousness: 'If I were in your place, Comrade Tito, I should have her shot!'[1]

Heavy rain fell as the army made its way through the mountains. Mist hung around the trees and slowed up progress. They had no tents, and it was hard to get the camp fires to burn. Some Partisans suffered from nausea caused by the height. Djilas wrapped himself in an overcoat taken from an Ustasha gendarme they had surprised and shot. On approaching the Sarajevo-Mostar railway the two army groups, which had been keeping together, separated for the attack. The northern group to which Djilas was attached was too close to Sarajevo for safety and did little damage to the line before being dispersed by an armoured train. The southern group, whose target was the tunnel and marshalling yard at Bradina, took the enemy unawares. The tunnel was blocked and a turn-table and several locomotives were destroyed. More wagon-loads of food were captured than could be carried away. The Partisans withdrew after burning down the station and the supplies they were obliged to leave behind. It was an added satisfaction to know that the looted town was the birth-place of the Croatian Quisling Ante Pavelić.

In the course of the attack men from the northern group had spent the night of 16 July in a Serbian village called Hurije. A few days later Djilas learned that the Ustashe had sallied out from Sarajevo and slaughtered every man, woman and child in the place. The Partisans were still in the woods near by, and he decided to investigate the report; there might be intelligence to be gleaned, wounded or orphans to be cared for. What he saw in Hurije haunted his memory for a long time. Even Tito, no sentimentalist himself, was visibly moved by the account which Djilas gave him and later wrote down for insertion in his friend Dedijer's Diary.

The morning was clean and fresh after a night's rain when Djilas and his companions reached Hurije. Under a peartree by the road side, as if resting after harvesting, lay two peasants; they had been shot through the back of the head. Djilas walked on towards the village. Round a bend in the road he came upon a heap of a dozen corpses, mostly those of women and children, some of them mutilated. The cross-roads at the entrance to the village was marked by a larger pile of armless trunks and severed limbs. Two of the dead were mothers, each clasping her unweaned child. They entered the silent cottages. In each room bodies lay sprawled on the floor in all the varied, macabre postures of death. Most of the victims were women and children; the men had been cut down as they worked in the field. In house after house it was the same picture. The dead remained unburied, for there were no survivors. No wounded, no orphans. From the fields outside came the lowing of untended cattle. Djilas caught sight of two peasant women in the distance. They had come from a neighbouring village to visit their families; but there were no families left to visit.

Hurije had not been a Partisan village. The Partisans had only spent one night there, and the peasants had not tried to oppose them. It was a Serbian village; that was excuse enough for the fury of the Ustashe cut-throats.

The Long March was resumed and Hercegovina left behind. The course was still to the north-west, the route over mountains along the borders of the Italian and German zones of occupation, with sudden descents to fan out and attack the small towns garrisoned by the armed forces of the Croatian puppet state.

At the beginning of August Livno was reached and attacked. Its population was preponderantly Moslem, but unlike that in many other places had shown little enthusiasm for the Ustashe and awaited the coming of the Partisans with apprehension rather than open hostility. It was held by a garrison of Domobrans together with a small contingent of Ustashe who had fortified themselves in a large villa after massacring its occupants. A handful of Germans had also installed themselves there – not soldiers but mining engineers engaged in the extraction of coal and bauxite. On the far side of the town stood a beautiful Gothic monastery. It was owned by the Franciscans who, in those Bosnian borderlands disputed between Catholic, Orthodox and Moslem, had developed a spirit of militancy highly untypical of their Order. They tended to sympathise with, and sometimes actively to support, the fanatical nationalism of the nominally Catholic Ustashe. Rumour had it that the Ustashe had been allowed to install a machine gun in the belfry. The Partisans took an ironic pleasure in commandeering the building, though they refrained from destroying it as they had done only recently on capturing a more overtly hostile monastery at Šćit.

Djilas went to the monastery, which had been quickly turned into a prison and interrogation centre; and then to the town to requisition a printing press for the use of his agit-prop. He was joined by Dedijer, and also by Mitra whom he had not seen since the start of the Long March. As they were leaving the monastery they passed a batch of Ustashe prisoners being brought in under guard. One of them suddenly broke loose and made a dash for cover, whilst the others struggled to undo the ropes round their wrists. Djilas drew his revolver and struck the nearest prisoner on the head, shouting they would all be shot unless they kept quiet. He then seized a rifle from one of the guards and took aim at the fugitive. At his second shot the man fell dead. 'I felt no regret,' he recalls. 'I had only done my duty like any soldier.'[2]

The seven hundred Domobrans in the town quickly laid down their arms after a token resistance, but the Ustashe held out stoutly in their fortified villa from which their mortars inflicted severe casualties on the Montenegrins of the First Proletarian Brigade investing it. But at last they too, and the few Germans with them, surrendered. On the following day they would meet their fate. That night Djilas could not sleep. Despite everything he had seen at Hurije, the thought of a just revenge somehow failed to satisfy him. Even the captured cut-throats, degraded by bestial blood-lust, were men. They too might claim to have 'ideals', however distorted, which in their eyes justified killing and being killed. 'For the first time,' he recalls, 'I thought of the Ustashe as my own people.' The next morning he went to Ranković who was heading the three-man court martial set up to deal with the prisoners. Cross-examination was short and justice summary. Those judged guilty – the majority – were separated to the right into Room A, to await execution; the others to the left, into Room B, for further interrogation. Djilas tried to make his friend understand his doubts and misgivings. Was there not a danger that these Croatian nationalists were being treated not as individual cases but as objects – the mere label 'Fascist' attached to them serving as sufficient death warrant? Were all those young men war criminals, beyond any hope of redemption? Could not some of them be rehabilitated and won over? There was even a girl amongst the prisoners – a leader of the Ustasha youth. She stood up for herself defiantly, declaring that she could not bring herself to repudiate her beliefs. She was sentenced with the others, her death being the more poignant by the signs of human weakness she showed at the end. It was rare for the Ustashe to surrender in a group; most generally preferred to commit suicide, as fifty of them were to do the following month at Jajce, blowing themselves up with dynamite rather than fall into the hands of their enemies.

From the monastery the captives were led away in batches of twenty and shot in a nearby gully. The Montenegrins, who had suffered the most casualties at their hands, did their work in a business-like way, not gloating or torturing their victims first but regarding the job, as Dedijer noted with satisfaction in his diary, simply as a 'technical matter'. Nor did Djilas, who was present at some of the cross-examinations but not at the executions, feel any particular compunction, despite the heart-searching of the previous night. Things seemed simpler in the light of day. 'What Ranković was doing, I too would have done, perhaps more expeditiously.'

It was assumed that the Germans who had been with the Ustashe would also share their fate. But the Germans were civilians, not combatants. Why, someone suggested, should they not be exchanged rather than shot, as captured Italians had sometimes been exchanged to the Partisans' advantage in the Montenegrin rising the year before? The Germans had in their power, and would otherwise probably execute, a number of Yugoslav prisoners whom the Partisan leaders were particularly anxious, for political or personal reasons, to save: Party leaders like Hebrang, who had been in charge of their underground organisation in Zagreb, and the wives of Party functionaries like Dedijer and (before his liaison with Zdenka) Tito himself. An eloquent advocate of such exchanges was a friend of Tito's who had worked until recently in Zagreb and had excellent contacts with the Germans there: Vlatko Velebit, a Party member and a man of good will, social charm and diplomatic finesse. Another was Marijan Stilinović, the agit-prop friend of Dedijer and Djilas who had worked as a theatrical producer in Berlin and Vienna and would also make an excellent go-between. He promised Dedijer that, if negotiations were authorised, he would do everything to get his wife Olga released. She was a doctor, and the Partisans badly needed more doctors. On the German side, the chief advocate of an exchange was a middle-aged engineer called Dr Hans Ott. In conversation with his captors he managed to convince them that he was personally sympathetic to their cause and had influential connections with the German command. Ott was in fact working for German Intelligence and may have had secret instructions to establish contact with the Partisans.[3]

Despite the dangers and difficulties, there was a good deal of clandestine coming and going between enemy-occupied and Partisan-held territory. Tito had sent the ebullient Tempo first to Sarajevo and then to Macedonia, Kardelj to Slovenia. Emissaries had even been despatched to Albania. Lola Ribar had extracted his father, a veteran politician well-disposed to Tito, from Belgrade. Dr Ribar brought discouraging news which convinced Tito that something had to be done, despite the risks involved, to reactivate the influence of the Party there. Djilas was chosen for this hazardous assignment; he began at once to disguise his appearance by growing a moustache.

The time was ripe, Tito believed, for important military and political initiatives. During the Long March and the liberation, albeit temporary, of large new areas of territory, the Partisans had increased in numbers, sophistication and fighting experience. They had marched two hundred miles and absorbed or linked up with detachments hitherto operating separately. It was time to give these forces an expanded and more formal structure. On 12 November Tito reported to Moscow:

So far, we have formed eight divisions of three brigades each on the territory of Bosnia, Croatia and Dalmatia. In other parts of Yugoslavia we have begun the formation of brigades from stronger Partisan detachments. The divisions are well armed, inclusive of artillery. They are no longer called Partisan units but shock divisions of the National Liberation Army of Yugoslavia. . . . We shall now set up something like a government.[4]

For the first time since the fall of Užice, the Partisans controlled an extensive stretch of territory and could install themselves in a town of some size – Bihać, on the borders of Bosnia and Croatia, captured earlier that month. The Party's agit-prop, hitherto improvised whenever circumstances permitted, was now given a more regular status under the High Command and stepped up its activities, including the regular publication of the party organ *Borba*, at first issued under the editorship of Moša Pijade. Tito considered this to be of such importance that he decided to entrust it to Djilas instead of sending him on the perilous mission to Belgrade. Until his fall from power a dozen years later, Djilas remained the head of the Party's propaganda apparatus and one of the leading ideologists of the Partisan movement.

At the end of November delegates began to assemble in Bihać for the inauguration of the Anti-Fascist Council (AVNOJ) and its executive body, the National Liberation Committee. 'Grandpa', alarmed for the effect this might have on its relations with the Western Allies and the Royal Yugoslav Government in Exile, cautioned Tito not to declare the new body a rival government or to announce the abolition of the monarchy. Tito agreed, adding that 'it would nevertheless have to look after all the state business and occupy itself with the war,' and would be obliged to coordinate the work of local national liberation committees 'since there are no other public authorities in Yugoslavia'.[5] Tito needed to allay the suspicions always entertained by Moscow that the Yugoslav comrades were going too far and too fast in their revolutionary zeal. The Anti-Fascist Council and its National Committee must therefore be given a broadly representative and patriotic character and its Communist sponsors kept in the background. Dr Ivan Ribar, who ironically enough had presided over the Constituent Assembly which had banned the Yugoslav Communist Party in 1921, was chosen as a suitable figure-head. Other well-known personalities, such as the septuagenarian Croat poet Vladimir Nazor, were also given prominence. The fifty-four delegates were not elected – this was hardly possible in war-time conditions – but nominated in a list drawn up by Ranković and vetted by the Central Committee. It included neither his own name nor that of Djilas, who continued to busy himself with agit-prop matters and did not attend the inaugural ceremonies.

The October celebrations staged in Užice had been a crude Balkan replica of the Red Square parades in Moscow. Then Tito took the salute amidst a profusion of red star and hammer-and-sickle emblems, Communist slogans and clenched fist salutes. But the mass of the Serbian people, though ready enough to respond to the call to rise against the foreign invaders, had no wish to carry through a Communist Revolution. Many still looked to their exiled king and sympathised with the Chetniks. The rising, with its attendant clashes between rival resistance organisations, had been a purely Serbian affair. But now resistance had spread to almost all other parts of the country. The Croats were joining in increasing numbers and already had some excellent fighting units, especially in Dalmatia. Their territory would become of major strategic importance should the Western Allies attempt a landing. Most Croats had hitherto supported the pre-war Croat Peasant Party which had pacifist leanings. Its leaders, mainly middle-class, remained inactive, neither supporting the Ustashe nor prepared to resist them openly. Tito aimed to discredit and isolate them and to draw the rank and file into his movement. His emissaries had been at work to this end in Zagreb and in Dalmatia. He decided to dispatch Djilas to the latter to carry the negotiations a stage further.

Towards the end of December Tito briefed Djilas on his new mission. The problem of the peasantry was one of great importance to the Partisan movement. Marxist thinking had always assumed the primacy of the industrial workers in any revolutionary movement; the peasants were regarded merely as junior partners in a worker-peasant alliance, if not as actual reactionaries. But experience compelled a reappraisal of this view. In Yugoslavia the industrial working class was small and weak, and relatively few members of it were active in the Party. The bulk of the Partisan army was made up of peasants, even the proudly named Proletarian Brigades. Insofar as the Croatian peasants still thought themselves loyal to the movement founded by the charismatic Stjepan Radić and now led by his ineffectual successor Maček, a place might be accorded them within the framework of the Partisan Movement. The Communists were prepared to allow them a degree of nominal autonomy whilst of course ensuring that real power remained in their own hands. The British still seemed to think highly of Maček, and a 'popular front' relationship with his party under the umbrella of the recently formed Anti-Fascist Council might help to secure the Allied recognition, and consequently the military supplies, that Tito badly needed. But were the British to be trusted? They were still supporting and assisting Mihailović, and Tito suspected that they might try to play a similar game with the Croat Peasant Party in order to undermine the influence of the Communists. In the confidential letter he had sent the Croat Communist leaders the previous April, putting them on their guard against the intrigues of the British, he had warned that 'in Croatia, their military missions will probably try to make contact with members of the Croat Peasant Party.'[6]

Djilas was due to meet the Peasant Party delegates from Dalmatia at Imotsko, a valley in the bleak uplands south-east of Livno. The road from Bihać was ice-bound. He and his companions were constantly losing their way, and each other, in the blizzards. He was accompanied as far as Drinići, the village where the agit-prop team was installed, by Mitar Bakić and Dr Olga Dedijer. The latter had been discovered alive and well and, as promised by their friend Stilinović, had been included in the prisoner exchange recently negotiated with the Germans. They arrived at Drinići on Christmas Eve – 6 January, by the Orthodox calendar – and decided to spend a couple of days resting. It was to prove the last carefree break before the still greater testing time ahead. Mitra was there too, and all were in high spirits. Djilas suggested a Christmas hunt. They came on the tracks of a fox, but seeing no sign of the animal, loosed off their guns at a distant beech-tree. Djilas, the only one to hit the target, was acclaimed the best shot. The hunt ended in laughter and a romp through the snow-drifts, followed by a long evening round the fire exchanging stories and memories of other Christmas Eves spent at home. The snowflakes piled up softly against the windows and war seemed far away.[7]

The march was resumed and Djilas at length reached the outskirts of Imotsko. He could see no sign of the Peasant Party delegates. Either they had been intercepted on the way or had had second thoughts about cooperating with the Communists. After waiting for them a whole day he decided that there was nothing for it but to turn back. Later, after the capitulation of Italy, he was to make another and equally fruitless attempt to reach agreement for joint operations with the Croat Peasant Party. By then the Partisans would have grown stronger and their terms stiffer, but now it was to be a matter of sheer survival. The enemy were mustering their forces to attack and overrun this defiant island of freedom in the heart of Hitler's *Festung-Europa* and to make an end of the Partisans and their supporters. Before Djilas left Bihać there had been ominous signs that operations against them were about to be resumed. Not even Tito, with his shrewd intuition, could foresee just how grave the danger and the ordeal would prove to be.

CHAPTER TWELVE

Operation White

THE campaign code-named Operation White, generally referred to by the Partisans as the Fourth Enemy Offensive, opened in January 1943. In the early hours of the thirtieth, Djilas was aroused by Dedijer who had just arrived with instructions that the agit-prop team was to dismantle the printing press and evacuate Drinići at once. The attack had begun ten days before; the Germans, supported by some of Pavelić's troops, were advancing on Bihać from the north and east, the Italians, with their Chetnik auxiliaries, from the west and south. The operation as a whole was directed by General von Löhr, the German Commander-in-Chief for South-East Europe.

The enemy offensive anticipated the plan which Tito himself had been preparing for an orderly withdrawal to the south-east in the spring, roughly retracing the route of the Long March. His intention was to break through again into Montenegro, and thence into southern Serbia. This still seemed to him the best course of action, though now it would have to be accomplished against fearful odds and under pressure from a determined enemy vastly superior in numbers and resources. The Partisans had some artillery and even a few tanks of their own, but no aircraft. Their vulnerability was increased by a train of three to four thousand wounded, together with ten times that number of civilian refugees who were anxious to withdraw with them. It was the exodus of an entire population anxious to escape from reprisals and the reimposition of an odious tyranny. Most were with difficulty persuaded to disperse or return home.

The Partisans had been well liked at Drinići, but the welcome given them elsewhere was not always so warm. Priluke, a village ten miles from Livno where the agit-prop headquarters were next set up, favoured the Ustashe, and the women and children who were its only inhabitants met them with silent hostility. Djilas had little doubt that before long their whereabouts would be reported to the enemy.

Straffing and bombing played havoc with the columns of refugees and wounded moving along roads where snow was now turning to slush. The snow clouds which would have afforded some respite from air attacks had given place to a cruelly clear sky. The wounded proceeded in orderly formations, those still able to walk forming one group, those who could ride another, the stretcher-cases a third. Dedijer and other agit-prop personnel were reassigned to help them. The fighting units protecting the flanks of the retreating army did what they could to ward off, or at least to slow down, the enemy's tightening embrace. But the real test would come when they approached the Neretva River.

The gorge of the Neretva cuts its way through the Dinaric Alps which block off central Bosnia from the sea. Above Mostar, with its mosques and its famous sixteenth-century bridge, the river flows deep and swift under cliffs which in places reach a height of three thousand feet. At Jablanica, the Partisans found it some seventy yards wide and spanned by an iron railway bridge. From there the Neretva makes a mighty loop eastwards, and on the left bank of that curve, below the massive bulk of Mount Prenj, the Chetniks had taken up strong positions in bunkers and redoubts among the scrubby foothills. They were twenty thousand strong, and the Germans, suspecting that they would prove unreliable allies in the event of an Allied landing, had agreed to their participation in the battle against the Partisans on condition that the Italians would disarm them afterwards.

In the night of 17 February Djilas and his remaining agit-prop comrades left Priluke for Prozor, a nearby town commanding one of the approaches to the gorge which had fallen to the Partisans the same day. Except for a few drivers needed to transport the wounded and the captured munitions, its Italian garrison, having rejected earlier demands to capitulate, were slaughtered and their bodies thrown into the river. 'I shared with our officers a malicious joy,' he recalls, 'at the thought of Italian officers on the bridges and embankments of Mostar stricken with horror at the sight of the Neretva choked with the corpses of their soldiers.'[1]

Five days later Jablanica fell to the Partisans. Tito expected that they would quickly take the town of Konjić, where there was a bridge over the Neretva, and so would be able to move the wounded into eastern Bosnia where the broken hill country offered them better security. But the beleaguered Italians, fearful of suffering the fate of their countrymen in Prozor, held out desperately until relieved by the German 718 Division, rushed out from Sarajevo. In the meantime, an over-confident Tito had ordered the demolition of the railway-bridge at Jablanica.

On the last day of February, Djilas joined Tito, Ranković, Swarthy Žujović and other leaders in a council of war. The enemy continued to hold Konjić and the destruction of the Jablanica bridge was now realised to have been dangerously premature since it blocked the easiest escape-route to the south. Tito, quickly recovering from a moment of frustration and indecision, resolved to make a virtue of necessity. 'Well then, perhaps we can turn that demolition into a stratagem of war!'[2] he declared, and explained that if their forces were pulled back from the river and shifted their full weight against the Germans advancing on Prozor, the enemy would be misled into imagining that the break-through was intended in that sector. But instead, the Partisans would rapidly regroup round Jablanica, and improvise a bridge on the ruins of the old one. Their shock-troops would then surprise the Chetniks on the far side of the river and clear a way for the passage of the wounded. The success of this bold plan hinged largely on the Partisans' ability to hold, and temporarily throw back, the German forces round Konjić and Prozor.

A makeshift bridge of planks was quickly thrown over the tumbled girders of the railway bridge, and in the night of 6-7 March the Partisan shock-troops crept over it to destroy the Chetnik advance-posts on the far side. The following day, in the face of sustained bombing and machine-gunning, there began the slow and hazardous passage of the wounded, patiently waiting their turn in the shelter of a disused tunnel by the bridge. This feat of endurance and heroism continued for a week. By the middle of March, the High Command, the wounded, and the bulk of the army were across the Neretva and the Chetniks in headlong flight.

In the fighting round Prozor a number of Germans were taken prisoner including a certain Major Stoeker. Tito decided to see whether an agreement could be reached, as it had been in Livno the previous November, for an exchange of prisoners. This time wider issues could be raised – the recognition of the Partisans as a 'belligerent force', which would entitle their prisoners and wounded to be treated according to international conventions, the possibility of a truce, and even of joint resistance to any landing by the British. Official German archives published after the war confirm that these talks took place, but since the relevant papers have not been published or the matter openly discussed by Yugoslav historians it is difficult to know exactly what was agreed. Djilas's account remains our main source of information, but even this is not specific on all points. It tells us that on 9 March, whilst the crossing at Jablanica was in full swing, a reply was received from the German command agreeing in principle to negotiations for an exchange of prisoners. Tito thereupon conferred with Ranković and Djilas as to the composition and terms of reference of their delegation. They agreed that it should consist of Velebit, as an experienced negotiator and lawyer, Djilas, for the Central Committee, and Koča Popović, as a leading military commander.

'What will the Russians say?' Djilas asked.

'Well, they also think first of their own people and their own army!' Tito replied with some irritation.[3] He had already referred the matter to Moscow and had not been pleased with the reply. Is it possible, 'Grandpa' had countered, that you who have until now been an example to all enslaved Europe and shown such heroism, will give up the struggle against the worst enemy of mankind?[4] Tito had mentioned only the possibility of negotiating an exchange of prisoners, but the Russians had not failed to perceive the implications of a truce. Irked by their failure to respond to his many urgent appeals for help and now by their lack of appreciation of the critical situation in which the Partisans found themselves, he had replied with some asperity: 'If you cannot understand what a hard time we are having, and if you cannot help us, then at least do not hinder us!'[5]

The significance of these exchanges was not lost on Djilas. He recalls: 'That was the first time that a Politburo member – and it was Tito himself – expressed so vehemently any difference with the Soviets.'

The Partisan negotiators liked to think that in addition to striking a mutually beneficial bargain with the Germans they were also tricking them. They intended to conceal their true objective – a return to Serbia – and to make out that they were primarily interested in pushing on into the Sandžak in order to settle accounts once and for all with their domestic rivals the Chetniks. They knew that the latter were not fully trusted by the Germans who would not be sorry to see their destruction. In any case, the encouragement of fratricidal strife was a favourite German tactic. Tito seems to have given no specific instructions that they should conclude a truce, but since the Partisans were growing stronger and the Germans weaker, it could only be to the Yugoslav advantage to play for time. 'There was not a word about the cessation of fighting between the Germans and ourselves,' Djilas recalls, 'but that too was understood.'[6]

In the evening of 10 March, after giving a final briefing to his negotiators, Tito left with his bodyguard for the Jablanica crossing. The same day the Germans entered Prozor. Dedijer noted in his diary: 'In the night Djido, Vlatko [Velebit] and Koča [Popović] set off under a white flag for a parley with the Germans with a view to exchanging

Major Stoeker, who was captured at Vakuf. He is an old Nazi. We shall get a number of our comrades back in return for him. The lives of our own people will be saved and the Nazi will anyway fall into our hands again sooner or later. . . !'[7]

The three Partisans took the high road to Prozor, hoping that it would be the Germans, and not the Ustashe, whom they would encounter first. A sentry on guard outside an old fort saw them coming and reported their approach. They handed over their arms and identity papers to a German escort then they were blindfolded and driven out of the valley to Upper Vakuf where they were brought before the German General commanding the 717th Division. He received them with cold courtesy, motioning them to some chairs and listening without comment to their proposals. They were then put in the charge of two officers from the Abwehr, the German Military Intelligence, whilst the General made his report and waited for further instructions. The Abwehr officers were curious but correct; it was their first contact with Partisan leaders. Popović told them his real name and introduced himself as commander of the First Division. Velebit, to protect his family in Zagreb, gave his as Petrović. Djilas called himself Miloš Marković. One of the officers observed to the other that he was obviously not a divisional quartermaster as he claimed, but probably a political commissar.

They were kept waiting for three days at Upper Vakuf until instructions were received that they should be sent on to the Commander-in-Chief's headquarters at Sarajevo. By the time they left they had become almost friendly with the Abwehr officers. The latter did not try to question them about their mission, and the conversation turned on the way the war was going, each side claiming that it was developing in their favour and was bound to end in their victory. The two Germans had fought against the Russians and expressed rather differing views of the Red Army's fighting spirit, the Major claiming that they had surrendered in droves when the invasion began, the Captain that he had seen them ready to die to the last man in the defence of Moscow. Both spoke with contempt of the Chetniks and with irony of their Italian allies; they described the Ustashe as cut-throats who fought ferociously but without real military skill. Djilas agreed, noting with surprise that these 'Fascist' officers never once mentioned their Fuehrer's name.

In the corridors of the German command Djilas came across a deserter from the Partisan ranks. He was sure the man recognised him; but whether the deserter reported him or not, the Germans never discovered his true identity, and 'Dr Marković' and 'Petrović' were sent on their way to Sarajevo. Popović, chafing at the delay, was allowed to return to his command.

On the talks conducted with senior Abwehr officers in Sarajevo Djilas has this to say:

The conversation was informative and restrained on both sides. They mostly asked questions, and we tried to say as little as possible. We stayed within the limits of set positions. The Germans made no commitment other than that they would exchange prisoners. The atmosphere was not menacing or even unpleasant. The Germans then demanded that, prior to any negotiations, sabotage on the Zagreb-Belgrade railroad be stopped immediately. However, we did not commit ourselves to this, but tied everything to the recognition of our rights as a belligerent.[8]

The Germans gave the impression that this was only the start of negotiations which might drag on for some time whilst issues were referred to higher authority – perhaps to the Fuehrer himself. Djilas decided that he ought to go back, to report to Tito and to arrange for the captured major to be sent back and the other German prisoners to be assembled, as a token of the Partisans' good faith. This was agreed, and leaving Velebit to maintain contact in Sarajevo, he set off for Konjić by truck, with a German NCO as an escort. He planned to cross the Partisans' lines at a point previously agreed with Ranković a couple of miles south of that town. The Germans held the highroad and their opponents the heights, from which desultory bouts of firing came. From time to time waves of Stukas swept down to plaster the range with bombs. When the firing and the bombing died down, Djilas and his NCO advanced gingerly up the hill, cautiously walking towards the rocks and scrub where he assumed the Partisans had taken up fresh positions, and calling out at the top of his voice: 'Don't shoot, comrades! I'm a Partisan returning from a parley!'

The only reply was a shower of bullets which forced him to take cover. He shouted again: 'Don't shoot! I'm a Partisan!'

The bullets continued to play. There was nothing for it but to wait until nightfall. Djilas was facing troops who evidently knew nothing of the orders to expect the return of a Partisan delegate. After nightfall he tried again, shouting out that he was a Partisan with an important message. This time he was allowed to proceed until halted by the command of a sentry. He was then recognised by an officer and taken to brigade headquarters where he found the commander of the Fifth Brigade, Sava Kovačević, who arranged for the German NCO to be given safe-conduct. Major Stoeker was also found and held in readiness, whilst Djilas went on to Tito's headquarters in the woods.

Tito was overjoyed at his safe return and listened intently while Djilas reported on his mission. He immediately approved the hand-over of Major Stoeker and, once they had been brought together, that of the other prisoners. He was confident that the Germans would keep their side of the bargain. They already had a list of the captured Yugoslavs whose return was particularly requested. It included the name of Herta Hass, a Slovene girl with whom Tito had been living in Zagreb before the war; every effort, he kept repeating, should be made to find her and secure her release. Though her place had now been taken by Zdenka, Herta was, after all, the mother of his son Alexander.

With regard to the wider question of a truce and the Germans' precondition that Partisan attacks on the Zagreb-Belgrade railway should cease, Tito seemed dubious. 'Ah, I knew it! That's where it hurts them!' he exclaimed. 'But we can't agree to that until they stop attacking us.'[9]

No harm could come from continuing the talks and exploring the possibility further, so much Tito agreed, but nothing more specific was decided.

As soon as the German prisoners had been brought in, the whole party set out under a white flag for Konjić. They reached it without incident, and from there the Germans took the party on to Sarajevo, where they were joined by Velebit and Ott, the engineer who had taken the initiative over the prisoners captured at Livno. After a night's rest they continued to Zagreb. Arrangements for the new exchange proceeded smoothly, though the Ustashe sometimes made difficulties.

When the question of the proposed truce was raised, the German negotiators repeated their condition that all sabotage of the Belgrade-Zagreb line must first stop. Whether Tito had already issued orders to this effect is not clear from Djilas's account; he says only that 'some progress was made towards a truce.'[10] In Slavonia, the territory through which the vital railway ran, the local Partisans were at first reluctant to cease their attacks. They suspected that orders to do so were faked, and Velebit, who was sent to persuade them, an agent provocateur. Croat Partisan headquarters had to intervene firmly to enforce compliance. The two senior German officials in Zagreb, Glaise von Horstenau, the Plenipotentiary General, and Siegfried Kasche, the Nazi Party's envoy, at odds with each other in much else, both set high hopes on these developments. 'I see the possibility of saving our manpower and blood and thus of succeeding more quickly,' Kasche hopefully predicted in a report of 26 March stressing the Partisans' apparently growing willingness to agree to a cease-fire. But their chiefs thought otherwise. As Ribbentrop explained in an instruction dated 21 April, 'It is not our purpose through clever tactics to play off Chetniks and Partisans against each other, but to annihilate them both.'[11] Or, in the more brutal words attributed to Hitler: 'One does not negotiate with rebels; rebels must be shot!'[12]

Rumours that their Partisan rivals were negotiating with the Germans quickly reached the Chetniks, though the scope of the parleys and the identity of 'Dr Miloš Marković' remained unknown to them. Some ten days after Tito's delegates had met the German General the Cairo headquarters of the Special Operations Executive (SOE) controlling the military missions still with the Chetniks received a coded message from Colonel Bailey, Hudson's successor with Mihailović, that some talks were in progress. London appears not to have become aware of this until a month later, possibly through deciphering delays, but its intercepts of German military radio traffic probably confirmed that changes were taking place in the Partisans' order of battle and that they seemed to have suspended their operations in Slavonia. British policy towards Yugoslavia had reached a turning point. By the spring of 1943 preparations were in train for the first Allied missions to be sent in to the Partisans; a start would soon be made in switching support from Mihailović to Tito. But what was behind Tito's secret contacts with the Germans? Were the Partisans tarred with the same collaborationist brush as their Chetnik rivals? Were the Germans cynically inciting both sides to exterminate one another, and could German connivance explain the rout the Partisans had inflicted on the Chetniks after their recent crossing of the Neretva?

Had the British suspected that the Partisans' talks with the Germans went further than the question of prisoner exchange, or even of a truce, and envisaged the possibility of joint action against a future British landing, might they not have had second thoughts about switching support to such dubious allies? Djilas does not conceal that the possibility of such action *was* discussed with the Germans:

We didn't shrink from declarations that we would fight the British if they landed. Such declarations didn't commit us, since the British hadn't yet landed, and we really believed that we would have to fight them if – as could still be concluded from their propaganda and official pronouncements – they subverted our power, that is, if they supported the Chetnik establishment.[13]

This standpoint had its logic in Partisan thinking. Dedijer, recording a conversation with Djilas some time before about the prospect of a

British landing, had put their case very frankly towards an operation of this sort. He said that, if its purpose were to weaken the occupation forces they would support it. But if the British landed in order to put down the Partisan uprising at a time when the Germans and their supporters had been driven from Yugoslav territory by the Partisans, then such an intervention would be a violation of the principles of the Atlantic Charter and an attack on the independence of the National Liberation Movement. 'In that case', he said, 'we should oppose it.'[14]

Such was the Party line. But now, it seems, a disturbing new factor had entered into the calculation. The Germans were being assured that resistance to a hypothetical British landing would be to their mutual advantage.

For the time being, the Germans' offensive had certainly slackened, allowing the Partisans to drive home their victory over the Chetniks, and they had got their prisoners back. Though their contacts with the Germans were never, even after the war, officially admitted, 'neither I nor the other Central Committee members,' Djilas declares, 'had any pangs of conscience that by negotiating with the Germans we might have betrayed the Soviets, internationalism, or our ultimate aims. Military necessity compelled us. The history of Bolshevism – even without the Brest Litovsk Treaty and the Hitler-Stalin Pact – offered us an abundance of precedents.'[15]

CHAPTER THIRTEEN

Operation Black

OPERATION White had failed. The Partisans had broken out of the ring and in doing so inflicted a mortal blow on their rivals. 'Our most important task is now to annihilate the Chetniks of Draža Mihailović and smash their administrative apparatus which constitutes the greatest obstacle to the spread of our national-liberation struggle,' Tito instructed the Party's Provincial Committee for Bosnia and Hercegovina, adding that they should avoid clashes with the Germans and raids on the railway running along the Drina valley in order to concentrate on mopping up the Chetniks.[1]

The Partisans had won a breathing-space – a short respite between 'Operation White' and the still more dangerous 'Operation Black'. Djilas was glad to make the most of it. He had so far come through unscathed; the rigours and exertions of Partisan life seemed actually to have benefited his health. He threw himself into the task of organising a training course for the cadres whose job it would be to consolidate politically the areas of Montenegro, the Sandžak and South Serbia which had to be purged of all Chetnik influence. The basic text used was Stalin's short *Foundation of Leninism*: this seemed to sum up with admirable clarity and unimpeachable authority the Marxist view of the world and its blueprint for the new society they were resolved to construct.

There was also another task which Tito wanted Djilas to take on – the organisation of a security and counter-intelligence service to police the new territories. Ranković had so far been in charge of activities of this nature; with his patient, methodical and ideologically conventional mind, he seemed the Party leader best fitted for such work, the ideal 'apparatus-man' essential everywhere for the smooth functioning of Communist power. It is not clear why Tito should have preferred Djilas, his agit-prop chief and political trouble-shooter instead of the experienced Ranković. Did he see the danger of concentrating too much authority in the hands of a man who had shown such skill in developing the personnel side of the Party and extending its influence over the armed forces? The new body was to bear the grandiloquent name of *Commission for the Suppression of Fifth Column and Terrorism* and to be unashamedly modelled on the pattern of the Soviets' dreaded CHEKA. Later the name was changed to the more euphonious and euphemistic OZNA – *Odelenje zaštite naroda*, or Department for the Protection of the People.

Djilas had only made a start on selecting its staff and building up its framework when the resumption of intense enemy activity made it necessary to put the whole scheme into cold storage. It was to be a year before Tito had the time and the new territorial base needed to take up the idea again. By then he had entrusted Djilas with other duties, and it was Ranković, after all, who was to become the founder and remain the boss of OZNA. Djilas tells us that had Tito still wished him to assume the responsibility he would not have demurred. 'Though I am glad that this duty by-passed me, I don't doubt to this day that I would have carried it out conscientiously and perseveringly, even though not with Ranković's calm equanimity.'[2]

Tito had two aims which were not easily compatible – to establish and consolidate Communist power and to win and keep the good will of the people, without which a Partisan army cannot long sustain itself. In the early stages, the two things might not seem difficult to combine. In territory recently freed from alien officials and Chetnik bullies, any new authority might at first seem preferable. As Djilas observed, 'the Partisans brought with them a government whose concern for all did not yet reveal a desire to control everyone.'[3] To many it really did seem a liberation; OZNA had not yet cast its shadow over the land. The possible loss of popular good will seemed less likely to result from an overbearing centralised authority than from the excesses of individual Communist leaders. An entry in Dedijer's diary for 21 April records one such case:

Uncle Janko [Moša Pijade] down in the dumps. The Old Man gave him a sharp dressing down over the case of the Montenegrin – a member of the Proletarian Brigade – executed at Kalinovik. Great importance is now attached to correct behaviour towards the population – avoidance of looting and other acts of violence.

He referred to the case of a Montenegrin who had assaulted a girl in her mother's house. When Uncle Janko heard about this he had disarmed the man and shot him with his own sub-machine gun there and then in front of the Orthodox church.

Ranković deplored the fact that Moše had behaved like this in the first liberated place they had returned to since 1942. Executing people without trial was exactly what the Chetniks always accused the

Partisans of. Uncle Janko, though sorry for what he had done, wanted justice and had felt the culprit must be punished.[4]

In a later account of the affair, Dedijer adds somewhat casually that the Partisan shot down by Pijade without a chance to utter a word in his defence was later found to have been quite innocent. The mother, who had Chetnik sympathies and did not wish to see her daughter courted by a Partisan, had falsely accused him of trying to rape the girl.[5]

At the beginning of May 'Grandpa' radioed that the Comintern was proposing to cease its activities. This apparently drastic step was intended as a gesture to reassure the Western Allies. Moscow was asking for the views of the national Communist Parties which theoretically comprised the 'sections' of the Comintern. The start of a new enemy offensive delayed Tito's reply, and it was June before he was able to inform Moscow that he had consulted his Central Committee which fully endorsed such a wise decision. 'Thanks to the assistance of the Comintern,' he assured Moscow, 'the Communist Party of Yugoslavia has grown into a powerful mass party which in these fateful days is conducting the struggle for national liberation and has won the good will of the people. The Party will always remain faithful to the principles of the International.'[6] In practice, 'Grandpa's' demise (decreed, in any case before the parties 'consulted' gave their answer) made no difference whatsoever to the relationship with Moscow. Tito continued, until the arrival of the Soviet Military Mission, to send it his reports and to receive its directives just as before.

May also saw the start of a new relationship. On the night of 27-8 May a British Military Mission was dropped by parachute into the same reception area near Žabljak where Pijade had once kept his long vigil for the Russians. It was headed by two young captains – Bill Stuart, who had lived in Yugoslavia and spoke the language, and Bill Deakin, who Djilas gathered, somewhat vaguely, was 'a secretary of sorts to Churchill'. Deakin was, in fact, an Oxford history don who had helped with research for Winston Churchill's life of his famous ancestor, the Duke of Marlborough. At all events, the first impressions made on Djilas by the two British officers were not particularly favourable. They struck him, like Hudson before them, as 'silent and expressionless – exactly as we had pictured them'.[7] Deakin's impressions of Djilas were more appreciative:

My first clear impression of him [he writes] was in the last hours of the battle in one of the Bosnian villages north of the encircling ring, which had been just breached by Tito's forces. Milovan Djilas was endowed with the outstanding physical courage of the Montenegrin clans. In the immediate moment of our tired escape from destruction, Djilas departed with a handful of companions southwards to the desolation of the battlefield. . . . Saturnine and darkly handsome, he seemed to embody the legends of his divided land. This was the single impression first borne upon us. Shortly afterwards Djilas reappeared at Tito's headquarters deeper in Bosnia. He was holding a bayonet, wrenched from a member of a German patrol which had been liquidated by his band. . . . By character intransigent, arrogant in the superficial certainties of Marxism as simplified in a student world . . . his nature was both complex and simple; rigid political beliefs of urban intellectuals had been imposed by a deliberate effort of will on the realism and honesty of a clansman. The tragedy of Djilas was to emerge long after the events at hand: the irreconcilable conflict between a rigid and pitiless doctrinaire and the reflective imaginative artist of a mountain community of epic traditions.[8]

Only a few hours after the arrival of the British Mission, the High Command moved off on the start of the most gruelling month-long ordeal of the war. The Partisans were encamped on the shores of the Black Lake, under the peaks of Mount Durmitor, from where they had set out on their Long March a year before. The bulk of their forces – nearly twenty thousand together with their inseparable burden of some four thousand sick and wounded – were concentrated over an area of wild mountain ranges, forest and rock-strewn upland pastures slashed by the precipitous gorges of the rivers – the Kormarnica, the Piva, the Tara, the Sutjeska – which converged to form the headwaters of the Drina. By tradition an impenetrable refuge for irregulars defying Turkish rule, it could also become a merciless death-trap if closed by a determined enemy sufficiently superior in numbers and armament. And the Germans, together with their Italian, Bulgarian and Croat allies (except for scattered bands, the Chetniks whom they distrusted had been disarmed) outnumbered the Partisans by nearly six to one. By blocking every potential loophole in this circle of steel, and by employing sustained air attacks, specially trained and equipped mountain troops, even bloodhounds to sniff out the defenceless wounded, and by using against them their own guerrilla tactics of ambush, infiltration and the like, they were confident that they could destroy the Partisans to the last man.

The Germans expected that Tito would try to break out to the south-east, into the Sandžak; they deduced as much from their talks with Velebit and Djilas in Zagreb. Tito hoped to mislead them by ordering his spearhead, the First and Second Divisions, to move instead against Foča and break through over the Drina to the north-west. But the enemy was too strongly entrenched and the Partisans had to shift their thrust further to the west – across the Piva, then over the Maglić range and across the Sutjeska valley, to the Green Mountain (Zelengora).

The first stage of this route was a nine-hour night march, through mist and rain and slippery mud, across the flank of Mount Durmitor. It was hard going for man and beast. Pijade was so exhausted that he kept falling off his horse. Zdenka was in a state of near hysteria, until Djilas lost his temper and shouted that unless she stopped whining he would seize her by the hair and throw her over the cliff. To the roar of enemy artillery was added the occasional thud and clatter of rocks dislodged by some mule, horse or comrade falling to his death. The Piva canyon was more than three thousand feet deep and reached by a slippery track appropriately known as zlostup – 'bad step'. Flares marked the whereabouts of the flimsy suspension bridge which was the only remaining means of crossing the turbulent torrent below. Getting the stretcher cases down was a particularly slow and hazardous job. Some of the stretchers were carried by Italian prisoners, and to the British officers these helots seemed 'stunned with misery and touching in their mute anxiety to serve'.[9]

On 3 June, Djilas was sent back to be with the wounded lagging behind on the far side of the gorge and the Third and Seventh Divisions who were protecting them. He would be in effective command, though Milutinović, like himself a member of both the Central Committee and the High Command, was already there so that decisions would have to be taken jointly. Sava Kovačević was given operational command.

Djilas decided to try to cross the Tara into the Sandžak, but the Germans had already mined the bridges over the lower course of the river, and the only spot where a crossing might still be effected was the shallows where a small tributary, the Sušica, flowed into the river. There it might still be possible to improvise a pontoon from logs or inflated sheep-skins.

Djilas sent a party there to begin work at once, but on 8 June he had to radio to Tito: 'Situation very grave. Enemy occupied both banks of Tara. If our penetration fails, we shall fight to the last man.'[10]

Not all the combat troops were fighting fit. The four thousand men of the Seventh Division had been ravaged by typhus and reduced to fifteen hundred. In consultation with Milutinović, he decided to send them back across the Piva to rejoin Tito's main forces, taking with them those of the sick and wounded still capable of walking (about six hundred in all) and also a number of prominent civilians such as the poet Nazor and Dr Ribar, President of the Anti-Fascist Council. After crossing the

Piva, they were to scale the mountain range and descend to the next valley, that of the Sutjeska, where the shock troops of the First Proletarian Brigade had secured a bridge-head.

There remained the question of what to do with the Third Division and the remaining wounded – the seriously disabled and ill, the hopeless cases. At a council of war Djilas decided to propose to Tito that the Third should follow hard on the heels of the Seventh and that the sick and wounded should be left behind, hidden in the woods and caves of their upland retreat, whose area was already beginning to contract as the enemy advanced. There they must stay, with the courageous nurses who volunteered to look after them, in the hope that the Partisans would be able to reinfiltrate the area and bring them succour. It was a counsel of desperation – to abandon those no longer battle-worthy in order to preserve the remaining combat troops. The responsibility for so grave a decision was one which Tito, as Commander-in-Chief, and the High Command, had to take. Djilas waited impatiently for a reply to his urgent message, but Tito too was beset by pressing problems. To speed up his troops' withdrawal and increase their mobility he had ordered them to bury their heavy equipment. They had no defence against attacks from the air except for the darkness of night and the flimsy cover of the trees. In one attack Captain Stuart of the British Mission was killed and Tito himself wounded in the shoulder.

During the two days he waited for a reply, Djilas could do little but see that hiding places were prepared for the wounded they were to leave behind. 'Don't worry about us, Comrade Djido. You just break through,' one of them said. 'Only, I beg you, let us keep our weapons.'[11] Djilas knew that many would prefer to take their own lives rather than fall into enemy hands. 'The last stand of pockets of the disabled disconcerted the enemy patrols, causing them unexpected casualties,' records Deakin. 'But one by one, using police dogs and local scouts, almost every hidden group was discovered and done to death.'[12]

When at last Tito's awaited authorisation arrived the Third Division moved off down into the Piva gorge. The suspension bridge by which the others had passed was now held by the enemy. Further downstream a new one was improvised, but it was too flimsy to bear the weight of the horses, which had to be driven into the torrent and hauled across by ropes. The frail bridge itself was not hit, but many who set out to cross it never lived to start the long ascent out of the gorge. Others completed the climb and fought their way across the Vučevo plateau in the wake of the rest of the army. But the wedge driven by the Germans between the rearguard and their comrades ahead was to cost both sides dear. It is at this point that Djilas laconically relates a particularly grim episode:

The Supreme Staff's order was carried out to execute the Italian prisoners. . . .
These prisoners had been decimated by disease, hunger, desertion and
bombing. I don't know how many of them there were altogether – maybe two
or three hundred, maybe more, but no more than ten were attached to the
Third Division. Though there was a stifled opposition inside of me to that
order, I accepted its necessity, all the more so since I could not change it. . . .
There were Partisans who wept as they executed the Italian prisoners, with
whom they had grown close in suffering and travail, even fondly giving them
Yugoslav nicknames.[13]

Now that there were fewer sick and wounded to tend – though still
perhaps as many as six hundred – it was thought as well to reassign some
of the 'political workers' who had been doing duty as medical orderlies.
Those from Montenegro set out on the perilous task of infiltrating back
through the enemy lines in order to begin rebuilding the shattered Party
network. Amongst the political workers turned medical orderlies was
Mitra, but since she was not a Montenegrin Djilas felt justified in
keeping her by his side. They would at least be together in the perils
ahead. Only a few days before, Vlada Dedijer's wife Olga had had her
shoulder blown off by a bomb. On the stony soil of Mount Romanija her
husband scooped out a shallow grave and buried her with his own
hands.

The Vučevo plateau was crossed. The Third Division was now within
a couple of days' march of the Seventh who had already crossed the
Sutjeska. They could tell that their comrades had passed that way, for
there had been no time to bury the dead. The Sutjeska itself was shallow
and offered no great obstacle. Those who had horses splashed through
without dismounting; others held on to a cable and waded. They began
to climb the slope on the far bank, and it was then that they realised that
the enemy had inserted a steel wedge between them and the main
Partisan forces beyond and were merely holding their fire. At daybreak
on 13 June, the men of the Seventh were thrown back by bursts of
machine-gun fire from a line of bunkers. Sava Kovačević, with his usual
reckless disregard of personal safety, tried to rush the bunkers and fell
at the head of his troops. His body was hastily covered to prevent the
sight of it from spreading panic amongst the men who idolised him.

Standing there beside the fallen Montenegrin warrior as suddenly the
guns grew silent, Djilas felt a strange mood of detachment, almost of
exaltation, sweep over him. The curtain dividing life from death had
suddenly been drawn aside. He had never accounted himself a

114

particularly brave man, though others had; he had often felt afraid, and provided duty or honour did not hold him back, had often sought to avoid danger. But at this instant he seemed to have passed beyond all fear. Death had become altogether just, natural and even desirable. 'It was,' he afterwards declared, 'the most extraordinary, the most exalted moment of my life.'[14]

The way ahead was blocked. The Partisans, suddenly checked, decimated and bereft of their commander, threatened to become a rabble. A report was received that other German units were advancing up the valley from the plain. A hasty consultation with the officers near him and the decision was taken to veer left, up the valley towards the cliffs and forests of the Green Mountain. The best hope of safety was to scatter into small groups, but to keep contact by means of couriers and patrols.

The Germans were all around them, concealed in bunkers or liable to steal upon them in ambushes and patrols, but by nightfall the Political Commissar of the Fifth Montenegrin Brigade, a courageous and resourceful man who was to survive the war to become Rector of Belgrade University, found a way through and brought out two battalions, together with some 350 wounded. In the relative safety of a thick wood the exhausted men threw themselves down and fell asleep.

At this point in his narrative Djilas records a singular experience. It is true that, under the stress of intense nervous and physical exhaustion strange cases of mass hallucination are on record. We hear of men making off through the trees towards what they believed to be the lights of a great city. Once a whole column formed up, mess-tins in hand, in front of a large snow-drift, convinced that they were waiting their turn in front of a field-kitchen. But Djilas's experience of that night seems to be of a different order and is best given in his own words:

After I fell fast asleep, something seemed to awaken me. Suddenly, in my mind, Christ appeared: the one from the frescoes and ikons, with a silky beard and a look of pity. I knew that this image was synthesized from the stories and impressions of my childhood, but his presence was pleasing to me, as if I found myself in some safe and glowing warmth. I tried consciously to dispel that image, but in vain: it only melted into a still sadder gentleness, firm in its contours. I opened my eyes. Around me, the trees and my slumbering comrades. And silence, endless and lasting, as if there had never been any firing or screaming. I closed my eyes, and there was Christ again – tangible, close enough to touch. I began to speak to him: 'If you came into the world and suffered for goodness and truth, you must see that our cause is just and noble. We are, in fact, carrying on what you began. And you have not forgotten us, nor can you abandon us. You live and endure in us.' As I was saying this, I knew that I was not ceasing to be a Communist, and kept telling myself that this was in fact brought on by nervous tension and exhaustion.

I don't remember how long this lasted, or when and how it stopped. But I am quite sure that I was awake, and that the image appeared only when I closed my eyes. It never even crossed my mind that this was a miracle or that miracles occur, though the apparition inspired calm and courage. Even today I am of two minds about setting this down. Yet it seems to me that without it my own personality and the circumstances would remain unclarified. Thus I include it in this work, though my atheism and the dogmatic purity of the revolution may suffer for it.[15]

Morning light revealed that though the wood had afforded them a safe night's shelter, the Partisans were not yet through the enemy lines. The Germans had taken up positions in depth and were still all around. The hungry men could see groups of them preparing breakfast round camp-fires. They themselves had no food, though a forest stream supplied good drinking water. Djilas reckoned that the Partisans within his vicinity numbered about 150. After a brief reconnaissance and council of war, they decided to make their way down through the wood, recross the Sutjeska at a point which a shock force of about thirty of them could go ahead to secure, and eventually to regroup in the forest of Peručica beyond. That day, 15 June, they rested under the sheltering trees and at nightfall they moved off.

When they reached the river Djilas led the way into the water. The patter of machine-gun bullets mingled with the splash of bodies. On the far bank they pulled themselves up through the bushes and rested in a thicket.

When they reached the Peručica forest they came upon a band of Partisans in a clearing roasting a horse, and joined hungrily in the feast. Someone dried a piece of its hide in the sun and fashioned Djilas a pair of makeshift shoes. For three days they rested in the depths of the forest, living on horse-flesh and the plants and berries which a boyhood spent amongst the mountains had taught Djilas to recognise as edible. At the hamlet on the slopes of Mount Maglić selected as their rendezvous they found more than a hundred exhausted and emaciated comrades waiting for them. Milutinović, an indefatigable organiser, was already reforming them into fresh units and had laid on a supply of milk from the local peasants.

Djilas decided that his first task must be to find Tito and the High Command. Radio contact with them had long been lost and he had no idea what had become of them. He did not even know for certain that the bulk of the army had got through. With one or two companions he set out a few days later to retrace the hard and perilous route along the Sutjeska valley. The Germans had already buried their dead in neat cemeteries, but had left the corpses of those they had killed rotting in the sun and rain. A sour stench of putrefaction infected the mountain air, and where the gorge narrowed, became unbearable.

The villages through which they passed marvelled that the Partisans had escaped annihilation; some marvelled with joy, others – where there were Ustashe or Chetnik sympathisers – with sour regret. Some had remained unscathed; in others nothing had been left to plunder and nobody to kill. In one village, the pro-Chetnik inhabitants were cowed and wavering. They talked and bartered with the Partisans, and one of them exclaimed: 'We're Chetniks now, but if you Partisans take over tomorrow, then by God we'll be Partisans!'

On 3 July, Djilas discovered Tito and his staff in a cave overlooking the little town of Kladanj in East Bosnia – the sort of location Tito liked to choose as a safe headquarters. Ranković was with him, so worn and emaciated that he struck Djilas as being in the last stages of consumption. Tito also had lost a good deal of weight; his fingers had become so thin that the ring he liked to wear had slipped off and been lost. He looked careworn and lined, but he had brought his army through, even if every second man in it had been lost. Its numbers had shrunk from twenty to ten thousand, but were already picking up again as fresh recruits came in. Help was beginning to arrive by air from the British, even if so far it was more token than substantial. Morale was high. The Partisans were coming to believe that they and their leader were truly invincible.

But they still had to keep on the move. The Germans had let their prey escape from the trap, but they continued the chase through the hills of eastern Bosnia. Djilas was still in fairly good physical shape, but soon after rejoining Tito he fell ill with a high fever. Weakness made the night marches particularly trying, but gradually he recovered. The news from the wider world was cheering; the Red Army continued its advance, the British and Americans landed in Sicily, and on 25 July came the report that Mussolini had fallen. Before long the Western Allies would force their way up the Adriatic, with unpredictable military and political consequences. Tito decided to send Peko Dapčević back with his Second Division to strengthen the Partisans' position in Montenegro. Djilas, with the battered Seventh, was to proceed to its home base in western Bosnia, whence he would go on to a new assignment. On the night of 10-11 August he set out for Croatia.

CHAPTER FOURTEEN

Croat Problems

THE Partisan leaders were aware that Croatia was assuming growing importance in their twofold struggle – the patriotic struggle against the forces of occupation and the Quislings and the struggle for post-war power against their domestic rivals. Serbia, Montenegro, Hercegovina and Bosnia had so far been the scenes of their bloodiest battles; the grand finale too would probably be fought out when they returned in force to Serbia. But more and more Croats were now taking up arms under the Red Star. Croats inhabited the coastal areas where the Western Allies were most likely to land, and Croats still made up the largest of Yugoslavia's old political parties, whose rank and file must be induced to transfer their allegiance if the Communists were to count on a truly popular base. But all had not been well with the Croat Communist Party itself, nominally independent of the Yugoslav Party with whose Central Committee it had sometimes had its differences. Tito also felt that the army, though it had excellent qualities, had not been sufficiently active in Croatia and needed changes at the top. These were amongst the problems which Djilas and his fellow Central Committee member 'Swarthy' Žujović were instructed to look into.

The journey from East Bosnia began with a twenty-eight-hour forced march with less than an hour's break for food. Such haste seemed necessary as important enemy-controlled lines of communication had to be crossed as they traversed territory otherwise largely under Partisan control. Their party included old Nazor, now so exhausted that he had to be carried much of the way by a stretcher-party composed of peasant girls – the men were away with their units. Vlada Dedijer, suffering severe pain from a head wound, also travelled with them. In the neighbourhood of Glamoč they parted from the Seventh Division and crossed into Croatia proper. There they were met by the chief Political Commissar, Vladimir Bakarić, son of a judge before whom young Josip Broz had once appeared on a charge of Communist subversion. Bakarić, whose quiet manner and rather flabby appearance concealed a quick intellect and an astute political sense, was to become Tito's right-hand man in Croatia after the war. The Secretary of the Croat Communist Party was Andrija Hebrang whom Djilas knew from his prison days.

The two men had then sometimes found themselves at odds, Djilas representing the leftists and Hebrang inclining to the right. Hebrang had been a friend of Tito's and head of the Party's underground organisation in Zagreb. After his arrest by the Ustashe Tito attached great importance to his inclusion in the prisoner exchange negotiated with the Germans. Since his arrival at Croat headquarters he had become the acknowledged Party boss for the whole of Croatia and exercised locally an authority comparable to that of Tito himself. He had also begun to show Croat nationalist sympathies which aroused the misgivings of the Central Committee.

A brush with Hebrang could not be altogether avoided, though both he and Djilas took care to prevent it becoming a serious rift. Hebrang had established his personal headquarters in a wood outside Otočac where he had ensconced himself with his printing-press, his own staff and bodyguard, and his pretty young wife Olga. His aloof and lavish style of living jarred on the puritanical strain in Djilas's temperament and seemed to him all the more offensive since Hebrang prided himself on his proletarian origins. Worse still, it offended many comrades in the Croat Communist Party who resented the blatant favouritism shown to Olga and her friends when it came to desirable pickings from 'confiscated' goods. Djilas felt constrained to raise this delicate matter with Hebrang, who had difficulty in suppressing his resentment at his Montenegrin comrade's interference. They found themselves at odds too on other and more weighty issues.

First and foremost, there was the 'Croat question' on which some Communists seemed to feel as strongly, and to share the same prejudices, as the 'bourgeois' politicians. The Party stood officially for the theoretical equality of the Croats and other 'oppressed nationalities' with the Serbs who had hitherto dominated Yugoslavia. The Croat comrades had been allowed to set up not only their own nominally autonomous Communist Party but also their own Regional Anti-Fascist Council of National Liberation (ZAVNOH), with Nazor as its President. Both that body and its President tended to overstep their authority and to show a much greater degree of real independence than Tito wished to allow them. Without reference to him or his Central Committee, and just as if it were a sovereign body, ZAVNOH had proclaimed the annexation of Istria and the Dalmatian islands, hitherto Italian, and their inclusion in the Croat Federal Republic which was to form one of the components of the new Socialist Yugoslavia. Such matters Tito considered to be the prerogative of himself and his government. As for Nazor, who had recovered from the fatigues of his journey and was beginning to order others about like a *real* president, Djilas had to have a firm but tactful talk to explain that his office was purely symbolic. The old poet yielded with a good grace.

Djilas gained the impression that some Croat comrades were infected with a nationalism which left the Serbs, who had suffered so much from Ustasha persecution and given so much to the Partisan cause, resentful and uneasy. Captured Communists were generally executed out of hand by the Ustashe, as Ustashe prisoners were executed by the Partisans, but Hebrang had been spared, though his importance was known to them; Pavelić himself was rumoured to have come to the hospital to take a look at him as he lay wounded after his capture. When under interrogation Hebrang was said to have defiantly declared: 'You are Fascist; I am a Communist. But I am no less a Croat patriot than you are. The difference between us is that you want a Fascist Croatia whilst I am fighting for a Communist Croat state!'[1]

Djilas studied the productions of the Croatian agit-prop and found them highly unsatisfactory. Too much emphasis on Croatia, too little on Yugoslavia! Hebrang argued that this was necessary in order to win over the Peasant Party rank and file who thought of themselves first and foremost as Croats. Djilas remained unconvinced; that was not the line taken by Tito and the Central Committee. They realised indeed that the Communists could never gain a popular power basis in Croatia until they had won control over the Peasant Party and smashed its pre-war near-monopoly of influence over the peasantry, but to attempt to do so by pandering to Croat nationalist sentiment was playing with fire.

The Ustashe, the fanatics of extreme Croat nationalism, had also failed to win the peasantry's genuine support. They had managed only to enlist the cooperation of a handful of opportunists whilst the peasant masses remained largely indifferent or even hostile. But this hostility was for the most part passive. Maček, the Peasant Party leader, spurned repeated German and Ustasha offers of collaboration; but he would not urge his followers to active opposition either. He was now living quietly on his farm outside Zagreb, under virtual house arrest, after spending some time in an internment camp. August Košutić, his right-hand man and the son-in-law of the late Stjepan Radić, was also kept under close supervision. Tito's representatives had put out feelers to the Peasant Party leaders but nothing came of their secret negotiations. Communist tactics were now to drive a wedge between the Peasant Party's nominal leaders and the rank and file whom they hoped to spur into militant action and cooperation with the Partisans. Kardelj recommended that the Ustashe should be provoked into burning down Croat villages, as they did Serbian, as a means of radicalising the peasantry. These tactics were tried out but achieved little result beyond arousing hatred for the Communist provocateurs.[2] Only in a few regions, such as Dalmatia and its mountainous hinterland, where there was fierce hatred and scorn for the Italian occupation authorities, were the peasants at last becoming more militant.

Such was the situation in the late summer of 1943 when Partisan headquarters in Croatia received an approach from a group of Peasant Party leaders in the strategically important area of Slavonia, the fertile plain lying between the Sava and Drava rivers, through which the vital Belgrade-Zagreb artery ran. The Slavonian Peasant Party leaders offered their active cooperation on certain conditions: they wished to have their own units, called after the Radić brothers who had founded their Party, and their own representatives instead of Communist Political Commissars attached to them; and they should not be required to go into action against the Domobran, the Croat regular army, in whose ranks many of their own members were forced to serve. These proposals were considered by Hebrang, Djilas and Kardelj who decided that, though some of their conditions seemed unacceptable, they afforded a basis for negotiation. It was decided that Djilas and one or two other comrades should set out for Slavonia for a parley. They left Otočac at the end of August.

The Peasant Party representatives failed to show up at the rendezvous. Once again, as at Imotsko, it seemed that they had been intercepted or had changed their minds. The decision to start open resistance against the Germans was a grave one. For another year the leaders of the Croatian Peasant Party were to continue vacillating; and when at last their spokesman Košutić appeared at Partisan headquarters to negotiate, the Communists held all the cards. They needed the Peasant Party's cooperation no longer, only its complete subordination.

Djilas's political mission proved abortive, but he had at least been able to establish contact with the Slavonian Partisan units. They had recently been regrouped – somewhat to the annoyance of military headquarters in Croatia which had not been consulted – to form a Second Croatian Division. Its core was still composed mainly of Serbs, but more and more Croats were coming forward, and Djilas was impressed by their quality and fighting spirit. A British military mission had recently been sent to them, but Djilas found that relations with it were anything but cordial. The local Partisan command complained that the British were sending in supplies of food, of which they had more than enough, instead of badly needed dynamite. There was even talk of impounding the mission's signals equipment which the Partisans coveted for their own use. Djilas remembered just such an incident after the withdrawal from Užice when Tito had ordered the prompt restitution of Captain Hudson's 'lost' set. He now took the same line himself. 'Don't do that sort of thing in future!' he told the Slavonian comrades. 'Remember the British are our allies. But just make sure they're not trying to recruit our own people!'[3]

Relations with the Western Allies had now assumed new importance. Since the sending in of a British military mission at the start of 'Operation Black', Britain had been steadily moving towards *de facto* recognition of Tito and the Partisans. On 17 September a senior officer, Brigadier Fitzroy Maclean, who was also an MP and the personal representative of the British Prime Minister and the Allied Commander-in-Chief in the Mediterranean area, dropped in by parachute at the head of an expanded mission. Its function was primarily military, but the political implications were also clear, for the Brigadier quickly formed the impression that the end of the war would find Tito and his movement as the decisive factor in Yugoslavia. This made it all the more urgent to end the British support hitherto given to Mihailović and the Chetniks, and to regard the Partisans as allies and probably the future government of Yugoslavia. The immediate need, however, was to provide them with the maximum support in the war effort against the Germans. This had become all the more urgent following the announcement, on 8 September, of Italy's surrender to the Allies. The Partisans raced to seize as much as they could of Italy's store of arms, munitions and other vitally needed war supplies before the Germans could fill the military vacuum. Italy's capitulation thus brought an immense accession of material and moral strength to the Partisans, and a sudden, if temporary expansion of the territory under their control. Djilas decided to take advantage of it to visit Slovenia, where Kardelj had invited him and Swarthy Žujović to attend a rally organised by the 'Freedom Front'. It would be an opportunity to see an aspect of the Partisan movement that was entirely new to him.

CHAPTER FIFTEEN

Preparing for Power

IN Slovenia, the Partisan movement had developed along lines of its own. After the disintegration of the Yugoslav state, Slovenia had been partitioned between Germany and Italy, the latter receiving the lion's share including the capital, Ljubljana. Resistance, against fearful odds, had begun almost at once. The 'Freedom Front' started as a genuine coalition of patriotic groups and parties brought together by a common resolve to save what they could of the physical existence of the Slovene people and their national identity. The two largest pre-war parties, the Liberals and the Clericals, stood aloof, the latter even collaborating with the Italians; but smaller groups, particularly the Christian Socialists and the strongly Yugoslav-orientated Sokol organisations, made common cause with the Communists. The latter then steadily whittled away all real independence on the part of those groups, though their members were welcomed into the Front as individuals provided they recognised the 'leading role' of the Communist Party. Certain prominent non-Communists, such as the respected literary critic Dr Josip Vidmar, were still accorded an honourable place as figureheads, but any attempt to exert influence outside the narrow limits allowed them by the Party was sternly repressed. Ugly rumours were current that the capture and subsequent execution by the Italians of Dr Aleš Stanovnik, the leader of the Christian Socialists, had resulted from a Communist tip-off. By the time of Djilas's visit, in September 1943, the Freedom Front, though an authentic resistance organisation enjoying considerable popular support, had been brought under exclusive Communist control.

The Slovenes were the least 'Balkan' of the Yugoslavs. During his time in prison Djilas had come to know some of them well and to appreciate the contribution such steady, industrious, well-educated folk could make to the revolutionary movement. Kardelj was in many respects typical of his people. Though inclined to be pedantic and prolix, he had a subtle mind and an interest in theoretical questions for which the more conventional Ranković and the pragmatic Tito showed little concern. Djilas got on well with Kardelj and liked discussing points of ideology with him. But the quiet demeanour of the Slovene schoolmaster concealed the dogmatist's untroubled ruthlessness. Kardelj fully approved the work of the Communist assassination squads and the burning down of villages to radicalise the peasantry, and dismissed the wholesale execution of seven hundred members of the collaborationist White Guard, after the Partisans' capture of their stronghold at Turjak, by calmly remarking to Djilas: 'That ought to demoralise them!'[1]

Whilst in prison Djilas had also come to know Boris Kidrič, Kardelj's boyhood friend and now second to him in importance in the Slovene Party. A pale young man with a large head and protruding blue eyes, Kidrič took great pains to belie his bourgeois origins – his father was a well-known university professor – by affecting the coarsest of language and proclaiming a creed of implacable class war. Most Slovenes are notably hard-working, but Kidrič drove himself and those around him in a relentless flurry of activity as if resolved that death should not catch up with him until he had fulfilled the work to which he believed himself called – the transformation of Yugoslavia into as faithful a copy as possible of the Soviet Union. He was to die of leukemia at the age of thirty-four.

Djilas admired his Slovene comrade's energy and devotion but did not altogether trust his judgement. Three years before, Kidrič had alarmed Tito by reporting that most of his comrades in the Slovene Party were disguised Trotskyists. Djilas was sent to investigate and reached the conclusion that the charge was unfounded; he even wondered whether the accuser might not himself be a Trotskyist provocateur. His suspicions on that score were dispelled by Tito, but the incident continued to rankle with Kidrič and led to a certain coolness between the two men. Kidrič's zeal for the Party was buttressed by a dog-like devotion to his wife Marijeta, a relentless militant who controlled the party's counter-intelligence arm VOS, the main function of which was the liquidation of collaborationists and dissidents. Its victims, struck down in Ljubljana in broad daylight, included a former provincial governor and the leader of the Catholic youth.

Djilas and his companions reached Slovenia on 27 September, four days before the Freedom Front rally was due to start. It was to take place at Kočevje, to the south of Ljubljana, under Mount Rog where the Partisans had established their forest headquarters. The Slovenes were excellent organisers and had laid in a store of food, blankets and other necessities in well-built and cunningly concealed hide-outs. All the same, it was cold and damp in the woods, and they were glad to move to the comfort of Soteska Castle, the late residence of Prince Karl

Auersperg who had invited the Italians in and ringed the place with bunkers. When his protectors fled, the Prince abandoned the castle with all its furnishings and art treasures intact. Djilas had never set foot in such a magnificent dwelling. He ensconced himself in the Princess's boudoir, Kardelj in the Prince's study. In the evening they gathered in the great hall beneath the portraits of Maria Teresa and the Auersperg ancestors, savouring this foretaste of the luxury and grandeur to be theirs once they were masters of the land. The castle itself did not survive their brief occupation. Kidrič and Kardelj gave orders that it should be burned to the ground with all its contents 'in case it might prove of use to the Germans'.

The assembly, held during three consecutive nights in the town cinema, was of a type that was to become familiar in the new Yugoslavia. The walls were festooned with bunting and the white-blue-red Slovene flag, a five-pointed star superimposed on its centre. Portraits of Stalin, Churchill, Roosevelt and Tito hung over the platform, together with Partisan slogans and a quotation from a Slovene poet: 'The people shall write their own destiny!' In such an atmosphere, in a hall packed with cheering delegates from all parts of Slovenia, the Communist Party might really seem what it claimed to be, 'the vanguard of the popular masses'. On the platform were ranged the functionaries of the Freedom Front, the military commanders, peasant representatives and a lone priest included to show that the Partisans were not against religion. In a place of honour beside them sat a recently arrived British liaison officer. Major William Jones was a First-World-War veteran from Canada and already a warm admirer of the Partisans. They struck him as 'the most friendly, frank, unpretentious, matter-of-fact, simple-in-taste, modest folk imaginable', and their leader Comrade Kardelj as 'an honest, sincere gentleman of noble purpose and high ideals'.[2]

Djilas addressed the assembly on behalf of the Central Committee. Though politely applauded, he felt far from satisfied with his performance. The Slovenes welcomed the presence of their Slav brothers, but their mentality was so different. Dedijer, who also attended the rally, noted disapprovingly in his Diary:

Vidmar made a speech, but it could have been better. Too much still of the old Slovene bourgeois mentality about it. He did not so much as mention the other peoples of Yugoslavia; no mention either of the army. Kardelj was quite annoyed.[3]

The rally had been held in a mood of patriotic euphoria. The Italians who had briefly occupied Slovenia had been expelled and their supporters discomfited. But their place was now being taken by a still more formidable enemy. The Germans were seizing control of key points along the coast and throughout the country. Djilas and his comrades had to cut short their visit and hurry away before the Germans barred the way back.

Tito had moved his headquarters to Jajce, a picturesque town at the confluence of the Vrbas and Pliva rivers which had once been the seat of the Turkish Governor of Bosnia. The High Command was installed below the ruined fortress, next to a little mediaeval church, half underground, which did duty as an air-raid shelter. The British military mission had found quarters a short distance away across the river. Its head, Brigadier Maclean, had gone to report to the Allied Commander-in-Chief and to Mr Churchill. His assessment that the Partisans undoubtedly constituted a force of military importance to the Allies and would probably rule Yugoslavia after the war was to accelerate the British Government's change of policy in their favour.

Djilas had not himself had much to do with the British. He still shared the Communists' distrust of the 'Intelligence Service', seeing its finger in every pie and suspecting it of being behind the poisonous rumours current in London, and even reaching Moscow, to the effect that the Yugoslav Communists were really Trotskyists.[4] Now Vukmanović-Tempo in Macedonia was reporting a proposal, emanating from the British officers attached to the Greek Partisans, for the establishment of a joint Balkan headquarters. This Djilas took to be a ruse calculated to rob the Yugoslav Partisans' High Command of its independence by subordinating it to a body which the British hoped to dominate. He drafted a letter on behalf of the Central Committee rejecting the proposal and putting Tempo on his guard.[5]

Jajce was preparing to celebrate the great October Revolution. Djilas spoke in the name of the Central Committee. His speech was a profession of the Partisans' faith in the Soviet Union. 'History knows no event which has made so great an impact on the destinies of mankind as the Great October Revolution!' he declared. It had given birth to a new type of state in which man's exploitation by man, one nation's oppression of another, were unknown; it represented the coming of a new civilisation, a beacon of light to every other nation struggling for freedom. He justified the Partisans' decision to launch their rising as soon as Hitler invaded the Soviet Union and gave an optimistic survey of the course of the war. He praised the new sense of brotherhood between Serbs, Croats and other peoples of Yugoslavia who were fighting shoulder to shoulder in their common struggle, and he attacked the government of King Peter and his runaway politicians who supported Draža Mihailović's Chetniks with the connivance of certain 'reactionary circles' in Britain and America. But now the governments of those countries were beginning to see the light and to send the Partisans material help, 'though not as much as we deserve'. He called on them to step up their assistance and also to open a Second Front – not in the Balkans, as some might wish, but in Western Europe, thereby taking the pressure off the Soviet Union and enabling the Red Army to accelerate its glorious advance.[6]

Tito and Kardelj approved the draft of Djilas's speech and made a few minor amendments. He was just putting the finishing touches to it when news of a fresh Russian victory came through. Kiev had fallen to the Red Army – 'Holy Kiev', a name which even to the atheistic Communists held a certain magic. Djilas gave vent to his elation in the way characteristic of his countrymen. Rushing out onto the walls of the old fortress he began discharging his revolver into the air. Soon there came answering shouts of 'Kiev!' 'Kiev!' and bursts of firing from rifles, pistols, machine-guns, in which even the gun-crews joined in. Tito shared in the general rejoicing but remarked ruefully: 'All the same, an awful lot of ammunition has been used up!'[7]

At the end of November the Anti-Fascist Council (AVNOJ), founded the previous year at Bihać, was due to hold its second session. The time seemed ripe for a new step forward; the institutionalisation of the Partisans' political power as a preliminary to formal recognition by the Allies. The Foreign Ministers of the Soviet Union, Britain and the United States were meeting in Moscow to prepare for the conference between Stalin, Churchill and Roosevelt at Teheran the following month. Tito sent a cable to 'Grandpa' (still his link with Moscow, despite the nominal demise of the Comintern earlier in the year) requesting that its contents be brought to the Foreign Ministers' attention. *We recognise neither King Peter nor his government*, it ran, *and will not allow them to return to govern the country after the war. The only legal government will henceforth be the Anti-Fascist Council and its executive, the Committee for National Liberation.*

The communication was not placed on the agenda and seems to have gone unnoticed. Yugoslavia was indeed mentioned, but in an unofficial conversation between Eden and Molotov. To the former's surprise, the Soviet Foreign Minister said that his government was thinking of sending in a mission – to Mihailović! Did the Russians believe that Tito, their own nominee, was misinforming them? Did they suspect that the

127

Chetnik Leader was in fact the major force to be reckoned with and that the British and Americans would manipulate him in their interest unless they too had their representatives with him? Whatever may have been in their minds, the strange proposal was not pursued at Teheran and Tito remained in happy ignorance of it.

The Partisan movement had been Tito's creation, and in the new political order which was beginning to emerge it was clear that he would play the leading role. No one in the Party dreamed of challenging his authority; not even Swarthy Žujović who was sometimes envious of his power and privileges. Ranković, Kardelj, Lola Ribar and the others deferred to the 'Old Man' unconditionally. So did Djilas. 'I do not know anyone in the Yugoslav Communist Party,' he had once in all sincerity assured the High Command, 'who loves and esteems Comrade Tito more than I do, or is more ready to face death on his behalf than I am!'[8] As for the rank and file of the army, and for the masses for whom the name of Tito was only now becoming familiar, they needed a hero, a father figure, who could embody and express both their patriotic defiance of the foreign invader and their yearning for a better life and a juster world. In Tito they found and acclaimed such a leader. At Bihać, the year before, he had been accorded the style of President of the National Liberation Executive Committee, the embryo of a future government. But Presidents lack glamour, and something more was now needed, some gesture which would strike the popular imagination. The Slovene delegation proposed that Tito be proclaimed a Marshal – a distinction without precedent in Yugoslavia. Tito flushed and showed some embarrassment when he first learned of the proposal. 'But isn't that going too far?' he exclaimed. 'And the Russians – what will they think?'

Kardelj and the others quickly reassured him. The Russians had Marshals; why should not the Yugoslavs have theirs?[9]

The resolution conferring on Tito the rank of Marshal, carried unanimously of course like all the Council's resolutions, unleashed wild popular applause. Off-stage, it proved a rare occasion for euphoria. There was much kissing and hugging in exuberant Slav style. Djilas joined in as enthusiastically as anyone. 'I too was absorbed by the delirium,' he writes, 'conscious that my own future was being decided then and there, that by my surrender to this frenzy I was willingly accepting Tito as my ruler, my master, despite my ideas and desire for a world without masters, despite my own integrity and my own vanity.'[10] A personality cult was in the making which struck none of the Yugoslav comrades as in any way incompatible with their Marxist creed. After all, did not the Russians have their Stalin?

One event occurred to mar the euphoria of the Jajce Assembly. On the eve of the opening session it was learned that Lola Ribar had been killed. The circumstances were dramatic and distressing. Tito had been anxious to send a military mission to the Allied Commander's headquarters in Italy, with young Ribar, who spoke good English and enjoyed Tito's fullest confidence, as its head. It was proposed that the mission, with its escorting British officers, would fly out in a Dornier aircraft which had recently come over to the Partisans from the Croat Air Force. When on the point of taking off from an improvised air-strip near Glamoč, it was spotted and destroyed on the ground by German planes. Ribar and two British officers were amongst those killed. The Partisan leader's body was brought back for ceremonial burial at the close of the Jajce Assembly. Amongst those who delivered the funeral orations was his father, the President of the Anti-Fascist Council, who had already lost his younger son, also a Partisan and a painter of promise, one month before. From the days of their revolutionary work together at Belgrade University, Djilas had felt particularly close to the dead youth leader, though they had not shared the same wartime duties. At the funeral he could not keep back his tears.

Three days before the opening of the Jajce Assembly, Tito radioed 'Grandpa' that the National Committee would be declared the provisional government of Yugoslavia. But he said nothing about another resolution which the Assembly would also pass: the resolution forbidding King Peter's return after the war. Tito confided to his intimates – Ranković, Djilas and Kardelj – that he did not intend to give the Russians this advance information for fear that they might veto his plans. When, after the event, the Russians learned that they had been kept in the dark on this point they became extremely angry. Manuilsky, Stalin's man on the Comintern, sent for the Yugoslav representative and told him that 'the Boss' was furious and regarded what they had done as a 'stab in the back for the Soviet Union and the Teheran decisions'. Radio Free Yugoslavia was not permitted to mention the resolution about King Peter for fear of annoying the British and American governments who would be bound to suspect that Stalin had secretly put Tito up to forcing their hand. But the reactions of the Western Allies to the Jajce resolutions, even when their full scope became known, were not particularly hostile, as they had no wish to make this another bone of contention with their Russian allies. Seeing

129

their mild response, Moscow relented; Free Yugoslavia was belatedly permitted to broadcast the full texts, which even received favourable comment in the Soviet press. Tito's ploy had every appearance of paying off; but the Yugoslav comrades' show of independence had not passed unnoticed in Moscow.

For the time being, the Russians not only chose to overlook Tito's lack of candour but took a step for which he had long been pressing, the despatch of a Soviet military mission to his headquarters. They made their intentions known a fortnight after the Jajce meeting, though it was not until the end of the following February that the mission reached Tito's headquarters, now moved once again, as the result of renewed German pressure, to the Bosnian town of Drvar. The mission was headed by a lieutenant-general, with Major-General Gorshkov, an expert in Partisan warfare, as his second-in-command. It included at least two Serbian-speaking KGB agents, one of whom Djilas had known slightly as a newspaper correspondent in Belgrade. Some Yugoslav emigrés, Moscow employees of the same organisation, also accompanied the mission.

It was Djilas's first contact with the Red Army he had so often glorified in his speeches and articles. If the Russians seemed at first something of a disappointment in the formality of their relations with what they appeared to regard as a still rather makeshift Partisan force, their coldness thawed once the mission began to get its bearings. Then, Djilas noted, whilst 'maintaining an official exterior, it became thick with us and penetrated into our affairs and our commands and organisations. . . . Everything was accessible to the Soviet Mission and all of us were predisposed towards it in spirit. And all of us would have remained devoted to it but for its own Great Power standards of loyalty' – standards which the Yugoslav Communists at first readily justified as a necessary protection against the duplicity of the Western Allies.[11]

But in one respect at least the Russians were still manifestly lagging behind the West – the supply of much needed arms and munitions. Deliveries by air from British bases in Italy, though still far from adequate, were steadily increasing; the Red Army was sending nothing. There were British missions with Partisan units in many parts of the country and the Yugoslav mission which the late Lola Ribar was to have headed was now in contact with the British and American army chiefs. Its leader, Vlatko Velebit, had even been received by Mr Churchill. This one-sided state of affairs Tito regarded as highly unsatisfactory; for reasons both of prestige and practical support he needed to send a mission to Moscow. The Russians would welcome it and Stalin himself was prepared to receive Tito's envoy.

At the beginning of March Tito told Djilas that he had been picked for the job. A senior officer would go with him to look after the technical side of the war-supplies; but he, as a member of the Politburo and the High Command, would be the mission's political head. The prospect threw Djilas into ecstasy; he felt overwhelmed by the honour and the responsibility. He would now see for himself the Fatherland of Socialism, the land of his dreams, speak with its great leader face to face. And he would go as the representative of the Party which had won recognition for its heroic achievements, a Party which would lead Yugoslavia along the same Socialist path and take its place next to the Soviet pioneers who had blazed the trail of world revolution.

CHAPTER SIXTEEN

To the Kremlin

DURING the last three years Soviet-Yugoslav relations had undergone many vicissitudes. The Treaty of Friendship signed on the eve of Hitler's invasion of Yugoslavia remained a dead letter, but after the Soviet Union was herself invaded the Russians reactivated their contacts with King Peter's government, now in exile in London. However, despite attempts to improve relations by such gestures as raising their respective missions from Legation to Embassy status – a step that greatly irritated Tito – things had been deteriorating as a result of the Partisan-Chetnik conflict. Although not wholly convinced by Tito's allegations that Mihailović, with the collusion of the Government in Exile, was secretly collaborating with the Germans and their allies, the Russians were finally, in the spring of 1944, moving closer to giving formal recognition and support to the Partisans. The most important objective of his mission, Tito told Djilas, was to accelerate this process.

Tito briefed him carefully before he left. General Velimir Terzić, a Montenegrin regular officer who had been chief of staff at the High Command during the grim days of Operations White and Black, was to head the military side of the mission. They were to ask the Russians for a loan of $200,000 to finance Tito's mission to the Western Allies and also obtain, through Soviet or other channels, a pledge of United Nations help in relief and reconstruction work. They should entrust to the Russians' safe keeping the precious Yugoslav Communist Party archives; a trusted comrade was detailed to guard them day and night, for it was suspected that the ubiquitous British Intelligence Service might try to lay their hands on them during the journey.

There was the question to be looked into of the Yugoslav Brigade which the Russians were already forming, despite objections raised by the Government in Exile, from captured members of the Croat Legion sent by Pavelić to fight with the Germans on the eastern front. Finally, Djilas was confidentially instructed to find out from Dimitrov, the former Secretary-General of the Comintern, or better still from Stalin himself, whether there were any grounds for dissatisfaction in Moscow with the Yugoslav Communist Party. 'This order of Tito's,' it seemed to Djilas, 'was purely formal – to call attention to our disciplined relations with Moscow, for he was utterly convinced that the Communist Party of Yugoslavia had brilliantly passed the test, and uniquely so.'[1] Minor misunderstandings and irritations there had certainly been, but what were they compared with the achievement of creating a whole new Communist-controlled army and laying the foundations of what the Yugoslavs believed would be, after the Soviet Union, the world's second 'Socialist' state?

There were many things to arrange before the mission was ready to start. Gifts worthy to be presented to the great Stalin had to be found. A rifle made in the Partisan workshops at Užice – there were few of these now left – was deemed suitable, together with a selection of embroidered bags and stockings and pairs of peasant sandals collected by the Association of Anti-Fascist Women. There were also passports, hurriedly printed and bearing Tito's signature, to be prepared. Uniforms were put together from the gear of captured Italian officers; Djilas's bore a general's insignia. The Party archives were loaded into sacks, to which Djilas added the war-diary entrusted to him by Dedijer who had been sent out for medical treatment in an Allied military hospital. Then the mission boarded a British plane which was to fly them via Bari and Cairo to Teheran, where their Soviet hosts would take charge of them.

They arrived at Moscow on 12 April. The welcome at the airport was cordial but subdued. His hosts would no doubt have been more exuberant, Djilas told himself, had they not needed to avoid arousing the resentment of their touchy Western Allies by too great a show of enthusiasm for the representatives of a new Communist power which was yet to receive official recognition. His emotion and excitement reached such a pitch that he could hardly refrain from kneeling to kiss the soil of the great country which was at once the cradle of the Slav race and the heartland of the new socialist world order. His arrival seemed both a longed-for homecoming and the start of an exciting new phase in his own life as a man and a Communist.

In so vast and mighty a country, he constantly reminded himself as the days passed with no sign from the Kremlin, the pace of things must necessarily be slow. Did not Stalin bear on his shoulders not only the burden of ruling his own people and conducting the war but the cares of all humanity struggling towards the light? As he himself had written not long before:

Stalin is the most complete man. Yesterday he was concerned about the quality of wheat, kindergartens, workers' dwellings, heavy industry, world politics and dialectics. He knows all and sees everything; nothing human is alien to him . . . There are no riddles in the world that Stalin cannot solve.[2]

No wonder then that his guests had to wait a while before Stalin could attend to their concerns. All the same, Djilas found it difficult to be patient, even with so many wonderful things to see in the Soviet capital, when he knew that the comrades who had sent him were in such dire need and looking so fervently for relief.

The mission was comfortably billeted in the Red Army Centre, a hotel reserved for Soviet and visiting officers. The Yugoslavs were given a chauffeur-driven car and a liaison officer who solicitously provided them with tickets for the ballet, concerts and the theatre. They were shown the sights, wined and dined. The Pan-Slav Committee, in its ornate mock-baroque palace, took them under its wing and regaled them with toasts, receptions and cordial speeches about Slav brotherhood. A month passed, and still no word came from the Kremlin. The nearest they approached – and it was clear that a great gulf separated even those high-ranking Communists from the seat of all power – was to the ex-Secretaries of the defunct Comintern, Manuilsky and Dimitrov, now leading lights in the International Department of the Central Committee which was the chief channel of Soviet control over foreign Communist Parties. Manuilsky at first struck Djilas as a lively, intelligent and cultured man of the world; later, he came to look on him as superficial and sycophantic, and ultimately as nothing but 'a lost, senile little old man'. But Dimitrov, though aging and sick, seemed to him still mentally alert and genuinely well disposed towards the Yugoslavs. Dimitrov was proud that he had befriended 'Walter', as Tito had been known in Comintern circles during the purges which carried away so many of his compatriots, and that he had helped to launch him on his career: 'When the question arose of appointing a Secretary of the Yugoslav Party, there was some wavering; but I was for Walter! He was a worker, and he seemed solid and serious to me. I am glad that I was not mistaken!'

Dimitrov went on to explain the technical difficulties which had prevented Moscow from sending help to the Partisans, and he also touched on the delicate question of their parleys with the Germans: 'We were afraid for you then,' he said, 'but luckily everything turned out all right!'[3]

Through Dimitrov Djilas met other leading Bulgarian Communists. There was Chervenkov, married to Dimitrov's sister, with whom the Yugoslavs were later to wage bitter polemics; and Kolarov, now over seventy, who opened his mouth only to ask: 'And the language spoken in Macedonia; is it nearer, in your opinion, to Serbian or Bulgarian?'

'I don't know whether the Macedonian language is closer to Bulgarian or to Serbian,' Djilas retorted. 'But I do know that the Macedonians are not Bulgarian nor is Macedonia Bulgarian!'

Dimitrov, who was partly of Macedonian descent himself and wished to avoid taking sides, flushed with embarrassment and changed the subject.

The Bulgars were looked on with favour in Moscow. In so far as they trusted anyone, the Russians trusted them. The masters of the Kremlin, like their predecessors the Tsars, considered themselves the protectors or 'liberators' of that small Slav nation – a claim which many Bulgarians tended to accept. Though the half-German Coburg dynasty ruling them brought Bulgaria in on the side of the Central Powers in the First World War, and on that of the Axis in the Second, it was no secret that its people still looked on the Russians as their friends and could never be relied upon to bear arms against them. Dimitrov was one of the rare non-Russians for whom Stalin had any regard, and his authority over the Bulgarian Communist Party was absolute. Bulgarians supplied a high proportion of the foreign agents used by the NKVD. One of them, a certain Šterija Atanasov, had turned up at Jajce, shortly before the second session of the Anti-Fascist Council, on his way from Moscow to a secret mission in Bulgaria and had stayed for a time with the Partisans' High Command. Although Djilas saw as yet nothing incompatible between a Communist's loyalty to his own party and people and service on behalf of the Russians, the role played by men like Atanasov left him with a certain uneasiness and contempt not altogether to be explained by that individual's mediocre capacities. He seemed to Djilas 'a combination of romantic Bulgarian and NKVD man – the more zealously he served the NKVD the more fervently he imagined he was carrying out some exalted assignment.'[4] Even in his present mood of unquestioning enthusiasm for all things Soviet this did not seem to him quite right.

Djilas was soon to have his own faintly uncomfortable experience with the NKVD. One day his Russian liaison officer introduced him to a nondescript stranger who hinted that he had come on behalf of Soviet Intelligence. With this man for a guide, Djilas was taken to the flat of an attractive young woman who began to ply him with questions about his comrades in the Yugoslav Communist Party. It felt to Djilas 'uncomfortably like a police interrogation, and yet I knew that it was my duty as a Communist to give them the information they wanted. Had some member of the Central Committee of the Soviet Party called me, I would not have hesitated. But what did these people want with data about the Communist Party and leading Communists when their job was to wage a struggle against the enemies of the Soviet Union and possible provocateurs within the Communist parties?'[5] Nevertheless, he answered the questions put to him, 'taking care to say nothing precise or negative, nor to give any hint of inner friction'. The little man sat quietly taking note of what was said. Then sensing perhaps that her guest was ill at ease and providing little of value, his hostess brought in a tray of refreshments and the session ended in polite trivialities.

The weeks of waiting were sometimes varied by trips outside Moscow. Once they were taken to visit the former Croat Legion, now in the process of being turned into the Yugoslav Brigade – men with dead, expressionless faces drilled by relentless Soviet instructors under the harshest army discipline. The commander whom Pavelić had appointed was still with them, accepting as mechanically as his men the fate which was converting them from anti-Communist volunteers into obedient if unenthusiastic auxiliaries of the Red Army. It was the first time Djilas had seen 're-education' at work. The Partisans had tried it with little success on German prisoners during their occupation of Užice, and he felt dubious about both its practicality and its morality. These turn-coats would fight, if fight they must, but without the conviction and comradeship which alone redeemed the hardships and horrors of war. It was a total breaking and submission of the mind which was required of them rather than true 're-education'; and what value could the robots it produced have as soldiers or human beings?

They found a very different spirit amongst the Red Army officers and men at the front. First they were flown to a little town in the Ukraine, where Djilas could not help noticing the reserved and sombre attitude of the local population towards the war and the fortunes of the Red Army. Then on by car to a village in Bessarabia where Marshal Koniev had his headquarters. Here the Yugoslavs were warmly received and invited to a banquet where huge quantities of food and drink were served by girls who struck Djilas as too provocatively pretty to be mere rustic waitresses. The Marshal himself, like the officers on duty at the front, was controlled and abstemious, but the gusto with which the other officers fell upon the good things and quaffed the endless toasts repelled Djilas. The Yugoslav Partisans, especially Tito himself, enjoyed such rare luxuries as came their way; but the prevailing spirit amongst them, bred by idealism and ideology as much as by necessity, was one of asceticism. This Russian sensuality, bursting at times through the correct exterior of 'Soviet man' into violent brutality, was something which would not cease to trouble Djilas. Poor Terzić suffered still more: 'Drink up, General! Drink to the success of the Second Ukrainian Front!' Terzić downed his vodka with soldierly discipline and as good a grace as he could muster. Djilas, never much given to alcohol, pleaded the migraines from which he continued to suffer and kept his drinking to the minimum.

The party was accompanied by a Russian writer who was also a correspondent for *Pravda*. On his return to Moscow, Djilas was invited to contribute an article to that paper on the Partisans' struggle in Yugoslavia and another for *Novoe Vremia* on Tito. He accepted without foreseeing the difficulties. The *Pravda* article was sub-edited to exclude everything about the political aspects of their movement. The war had to be presented as a purely military, patriotic affair; any suggestion that a revolutionary situation existed and that social changes were occurring was struck out. His author's pride was hurt too by the deletion of all lively figures of speech, every touch of individual colour. The article became impersonal and drab; Djilas scarcely recognised it as his own. But finding it hopeless to argue with the bureaucrats who occupied the editorial chairs he reluctantly let the corrections pass. His piece on Tito fared even worse. Any praise of the Yugoslav Marshal's personality or exceptional qualities was pruned away or reduced to cliché. The editor was apologetic but firm. 'It's awkward because of Comrade Stalin!' he finally explained. 'That's the way it is here!'[6]

The summons from the Kremlin, when at last it came, was sudden. One evening Djilas was invited by Lozovsky, Molotov's Deputy, to speak on Yugoslavia to a small but select gathering. He had just finished his address when someone whispered in his ear that his presence was urgently required elsewhere. With a hurried excuse to the meeting, he made his way quickly to the car which was waiting to drive Terzić and himself to the Kremlin. On the way a thought occurred to him which increased his agitation. 'The gifts! The gifts for Stalin!' There was no time to fetch them. But the NKVD officers who had conveyed the Kremlin's message and were now accompanying them, had already thought of that, as they thought of everything. Dusk was falling as they arrived. Another officer took charge of them at the gates and escorted them through the courtyards, past Ivan the Great's massive bell-tower and a row of ancient cannon to a low building traversed by long, silent corridors. 'It's more like a museum or a university than the nerve-centre of the Soviet Union!' Djilas thought to himself.

The Progress of a Revolutionary

They were taken to an ante-room leading to Stalin's office. The door opened, revealing in the background the outline of a large globe and the stocky figure of Molotov standing by it, with Stalin in the middle of the room to greet them. Djilas stepped forward and introduced himself. Terzić did the same, reeling off his official titles with a military click of the heels. Their host held out his hand and said simply: 'Stalin!' There was something unreal, almost comical, about the manner of their meeting.

The Yugoslavs shook hands with Molotov and sat down at a table. On the walls were the inevitable photographs of Lenin and portraits of the great Russian war-chiefs of the past, Suvorov and Kutuzov. Stalin wore a Marshal's uniform and the gold star of the Order of Hero of the Soviet Union. In the description of the great man which he afterwards published to satisfy the curiosity of *Borba* readers (and which greatly pleased Stalin himself) Djilas wrote that:

he was not at all as you would expect from the pictures of him. His moustache, and particularly his hair, are greyish-white, his face pale. His cheeks are more rosy and rough. His build is slightly below average; he has fine, small hands with rather long fingers, long legs, narrow shoulders and a large head.

He added that Stalin's face seemed pleasant, because it showed a gentle strength, thoughtful, lively and smiling. He appeared to have caring brownish-yellow eyes and an expression, though stern, of beautiful, simple serenity. These were features missing from his photographs.[7]

Also missing were other features which Djilas noted and later described in less flattering terms. Stalin seemed to him to be really:

of very small stature and ungainly build. His torso was short and narrow, while his legs and arms are too long. His left arm and shoulder seemed rather stiff. He had quite a large paunch, and his hair was sparse, though his scalp was not completely bald. His face was white, with ruddy cheeks – a characteristic of those who sit long hours in offices and known as the 'Kremlin complexion'. . . . His teeth were black and irregular, turned inward. Not even his moustache was thick or firm. Still, his head was not a bad one; it had something of the common people, the peasants, the father of a great family about it – with those yellow eyes and a mixture of sternness and mischief.[8]

Their conversation began with the small talk usual on such occasions. The Yugoslavs were asked their impressions of the Soviet Union. They were thrilled, they answered – full of enthusiasm over everything!

'We are not so enthusiastic,' Stalin rejoined, 'though we're doing everything we can to make things better.'

The talk then turned to the Yugoslav Government. Stanoje Simić, its Ambassador in Moscow, had declared himself for Tito, but the Soviet Government still maintained diplomatic relations with the Royal Government in Exile. The politicians, mostly Serbs, who succeeded each other in its empty cabinet posts, had at first, with the British Government's support, tried to induce Moscow not only to declare itself for Mihailović but to compel Tito to submit to him. They had rebuffed Soviet offers to conclude a treaty with them and vetoed Molotov's suggestion of sending a military mission to the Chetnik leader whom they appointed their Minister for Defence. Gradually – much too gradually for Tito's liking – the Russians had come to accept the charges not only of Chetnik inactivity but of collusion with the enemy. The Royalist Government, conscious of its growing weakness, belatedly offered to conclude a treaty, but now it was Moscow's turn to refuse. British pressure was brought to bear on King Peter to appoint a new Prime Minister, Dr Šubašić, the former Governor of Croatia, to attempt the difficult task of coming to terms with Tito. Britain's aim was to bring about some form of united government compatible with their obligations to King Peter and the realities of the situation created by the rise of the Partisan movement.

Stalin too supported this policy. He did not promise to grant early recognition to Tito's National Committee, but Djilas gained the impression that he was willing to treat it as the effective provisional government. The subject was not directly broached but left for discussion at a subsequent meeting. But Stalin did turn to Molotov with the mischievous remark: 'Couldn't we somehow trick the English into recognising Tito, who is doing all the fighting in Yugoslavia?'

'No, that is out of the question,' Molotov replied. 'They are quite aware of what is happening in Yugoslavia!' Djilas noted his ironic and self-satisfied smile, but could not foresee what an unyielding opponent of Tito and the Partisans he would prove to be. What now struck Djilas was the intimacy, the identity of views and purpose, which characterised the relationship between the two Soviet leaders. Stalin's darting intuition and ruthlessness and Molotov's solidity and caution seemed admirably to complement each other. 'They were always talking to each other,' Djilas observed in his *Borba* article, 'Stalin constantly asking Molotov about something, and Molotov adding something more to Stalin's comments. For a moment one got the impression that there was one person talking aloud to himself. Molotov's broad, fair Russian face would smile heartily at Stalin's jokes which, it seems, were always new and fresh to him.'[9]

For Stalin had a sense of humour, Djilas was surprised to discover – a crude, rough humour apt to turn nasty and crush its victim, or at least to score a telling political point against him. His jokes and sarcasms were calculated to discredit an opponent or a potential rival, to sow suspicion and to make bad blood. The talk turned to young King Peter, who had unwisely chosen this moment to get married; Tito's agit-prop was to hold him up to contempt by popularising the ditty

The King got wed
Whilst his people bled!

When Djilas observed that the bride was a Greek princess, Stalin jovially interjected: 'How would it be, Vjacheslav Mikhailovich, if you or I were to marry some foreign princess? Perhaps some good might come of it!' Molotov gave one of his noiseless laughs. They turned to discuss other things.

Djilas enquired if the Partisans could have a loan of $200,000. 'A trifle!' Stalin exclaimed, and promised that they should get it at once. Djilas gratefully declared that they would repay this debt after the war, together with the full cost of all the arms and other war supplies they hoped to obtain.

'You insult me!' Stalin appeared genuinely angry. 'There you are shedding your blood, and you expect me to make you pay for your arms! I'm not a merchant; we're not merchants in Russia! You're fighting for the same cause as we are. We're in duty bound to share with you whatever we have.'

Djilas noticed that Stalin constantly used the term 'Russia' – not even 'Soviet Russia' – rather than 'the Soviet Union'. As the leader in the Great Patriotic War, it seemed as if his Communism had been submerged in the exalted nationalism which inspired his people in the heroic defence of their Russian fatherland.

They went on to discuss how military aid could best be sent to the Partisans. It was agreed to ask the Western Allies to set aside an air base in Italy from which Soviet supplies could be flown in.

'Let us try,' said Stalin, as if intent on disparaging in advance any assistance which the Allies might offer. 'We'll see how far they are really prepared to go to help Tito!' Then he added: 'But planes are not enough. An army cannot be supplied by air, and you're already an army. Ships are needed. But we have no ships. Our Black Sea fleet has been put out of action.'

'We have ships in the Far East,' put in the general who had been escorting the two Yugoslavs. 'We might transfer them to the Black Sea.'

Stalin turned on him savagely: 'Whatever are you thinking about! Are you in your right mind? There's a war on in the Far East. Somebody will make sure of sinking those ships. We have to *buy* ships. But where from? There's a shortage of ships at present. From Turkey? The Turks have got many, and they won't sell us any of those they have. From Egypt? Yes, we could buy some from Egypt. Egypt will sell. The Egyptians will sell anything, so they'll certainly sell us ships.'

The general silently made a note of Stalin's decisions. But no ships were in fact bought and no supplies sent in to the Partisans by sea. The rapid advance of the Red Army rendered such plans out of date. But Djilas gained the impression that Stalin was in earnest about wanting to help.

They had been talking for more than an hour. When they rose to go Djilas presented the gifts. They seemed to him, in the vastness and power of the Kremlin, a pathetically humble offering.

Stalin picked up the rifle, toyed with it, and then said: 'Ours are lighter!'

He glanced casually at the other things. '*Lapti –*' he said, 'leather sandals!' Those worn by the Russian peasants were not so very different. There was no trace of contempt in his voice, and Djilas even detected a certain sadness as if the great man was touched by nostalgia for the region where he had his own humble origins, or by compassion for the poverty of the far-away Slav people who had sent those gifts.

Djilas left the Kremlin and emerged into the spring twilight suffused with the mysterious shimmering of the northern lights. He was more than ever convinced of the greatness, the humanity, the uniqueness of Stalin.[10]

CHAPTER SEVENTEEN

An Evening with Stalin

DJILAS was to have a second and longer meeting with Stalin before returning to Yugoslavia. By then, dramatic changes were taking place in his own country and were imminent on the world stage. The British and Americans were preparing to land in France. In Yugoslavia the Germans, though weakening, were still strong and determined enough to make a bid to decapitate the Partisan movement. On the morning of 25 May, when Drvar was getting ready to celebrate Tito's birthday, the enemy came within an ace of success. In a well-planned concerted attack, their land forces converged on Partisan headquarters whilst parachutists and glider-borne troops swooped on the cave where Tito, Kardelj, and other leaders had thought themselves virtually impregnable. They escaped, letting themselves down by a rope from the rear of the cave, whilst the escort battalion put up a heroic defence and outlying units fought delaying actions. Many lives were lost on both sides, and savage reprisals taken against the population of Tito's captured headquarters. After a series of forced night marches and days spent concealed in the woods, the Marshal was evacuated by aircraft flown in by Soviet pilots from a base in Italy under British operational control. New and more secure headquarters were established on the island of Vis.

Djilas knew no further details and was anxious about Mitra who had been billeted in a cottage not far from the mouth of the cave. It was only later that he heard she was safe and could look back on her narrow escape with wry humour. Other details he learned after his return: the warnings given by Arso Jovanović, who had succeeded Terzić as Chief of Staff, and how they had been brushed aside; Swarthy's jealous impatience at Tito's passivity whilst his bodyguard fell fighting off the attackers; Zdenka's hysterical clinging and screaming 'They'll kill us, they'll kill us!' Even the Soviet military mission, according to cynical old Pijade, showed unseemly panic during the hurried retreat from Drvar.[1]

It was ten days after the Germans' attack on Drvar and on the eve of the Normandy landings that Djilas received his second summons from Stalin. At 9 o'clock on the night of 5 June a car called to fetch him to the

Kremlin where he found Molotov waiting for him. Without more ado, the Soviet Foreign Minister announced that they were going to have dinner with Stalin. During the twenty-mile drive to Stalin's *dacha*, Molotov questioned his companions about the German attack and the conversation was continued *à trois* in Stalin's study.

'What will happen to the Partisans on the run in Bosnia?' Stalin asked. 'They'll all starve to death!'

Djilas tried to reassure him. 'In our country one can always find something to eat!' he declared. 'We have been in worse straits before and no one starved.'

Stalin was not convinced. 'Soldiers have often starved to death,' he repeated. 'Hunger is the terrible enemy of every army.'

The conversation reverted to the question of aid. Soviet inability to send in aid had long been a grievance with the Partisans, as Stalin well knew. At one point he angrily put the blame on his pilots. 'They're afraid to fly during the daytime!' he exclaimed. 'Cowards – that's what they are! By God, they're cowards!'

Molotov interjected that the front was still too far away for fighter planes to escort transports. Their range was too limited; and without fighter escort the transports would simply be shot down before reaching their targets. It was not a question of cowardice, Molotov explained; they had to fly by night, and even then they could carry only small loads on account of all the fuel needed to get back. But the Allies had already agreed to Soviet requests for an air-base to be placed at their disposal in Italy. It was in fact planes from that base which had just evacuated Tito and his staff to Italy after the Drvar attack.

The question of the Western Allies and the Partisans' relations with them was one to which Stalin constantly returned. Djilas realised that his wish to put the Yugoslavs on their guard – or rather, to strengthen their existing prejudices – was probably the chief reason for this second meeting. The British must not be 'frightened' at this stage, Stalin kept repeating; nothing must be said or done to scare them into believing that a revolution was already in progress in Yugoslavia or that the Communists were bent on taking all power into their hands.

'Why, for instance, do you want to wear red stars in your caps?' Stalin asked irritably. 'Stars aren't important. It's the substance, the reality, that matters. You've no need of stars!'

Djilas tried to explain that the red star had by now won general acceptance as the Partisan emblem. It was too popular amongst the troops to be done away with now. But Stalin gave no sign of being convinced. He simply switched the talk onto Churchill and the iniquities of the British Intelligence Service: 'Perhaps you imagine that just because we are their allies, we have forgotten who the British are, and who Churchill is! They like nothing better than tricking their allies. During the first world war they were always tricking the Russians and the French. And Churchill? He's the kind of man who'll pick your pocket if you don't watch out. Yes, pick your pocket for a kopek! Pick your pocket, by God, for a kopek! And Roosevelt? Roosevelt's different. He dips in his hand only for bigger coins. But Churchill – ! Churchill will do it for a kopek!'

Stalin turned his guns on the Intelligence Service. 'They were the ones who killed General Sikorski in a plane, and then neatly shot the plane down!' he declared. 'No proof, of course; no witnesses.' He kept repeating that they might try something of the sort to get rid of Tito.

Stalin also had advice to give about the Royal Yugoslav Government and the line to take with its new Prime Minister Dr Šubašić, a man of good will but naive and irresolute.

'Don't refuse to talk with Šubašić. On no account must you do that. Don't attack him straight away! Let's see what he wants. Just talk to him. You can't win recognition over night. You must find a half-way house. You should talk with Šubašić and see whether you can't reach some sort of compromise.'

As they walked towards the supper-room, Stalin paused in front of a map of the world in which the Soviet Union was coloured red, and pointed to it saying: 'They' – he was still thinking of the British and the Americans – 'they will never accept the idea that so large an area should be red! Never! No, never!'

A number of other guests were already waiting for Stalin in the large dining-room in front of tables loaded with food and drink. They were mostly high officials and officers of the High Command whom Djilas did not know. Such gatherings generally lasted six or more hours. Between the leisurely eating and drinking there was much exchange of rambling conversation, news and rough jests. Djilas related several jokes at the expense of his countrymen, and Stalin laughed uproariously at the story of the Turk and the Montenegrin discussing what they were fighting for. 'For plunder,' said the Montenegrin bluntly. 'For honour!' boasted the Turk, to which the other replied: 'Everyone fights for what he has not got!'

'That's good, by God,' Stalin exclaimed. 'Yes – everyone fights for what he hasn't got!' He kept turning to Djilas and asking him what different things were called in Serbian and, noting the frequent similarities, commented with satisfaction: 'By God, there's no doubt about it; we're the same people!'

Then, turning to their neighbours the Albanians, he asked what was happening in their small country and whether they were of Slav origin too, as some of their place-names might suggest. Djilas explained that they were descended from the ancient people who inhabited the Balkan peninsula before the coming of the Slavs.

'Ah – I had hoped that there was at least something a little Slavic about them!' Stalin exclaimed mischievously. As with so many of Stalin's remarks, Djilas was later to discover that his allusions to the Albanians were not so casual as might appear. The questions Stalin put about Yugoslavia itself, he noted, were not about the extent of the war damage or the sufferings of the people, but the strength and alignment of the various forces pitted against each other. It was clearly power, in all its manifestations and permutations, that chiefly interested him.

Stalin spoke of the Comintern and the reasons which had prompted its dissolution. That body, he said, had served its historic purpose and had become merely a source of suspicion and discord with the West, though they never mentioned the subject. He claimed that the situation within the Comintern itself was also becoming more and more 'abnormal'. 'Here were Vjacheslav Mikhailovic [Molotov] and myself racking our brains, whilst the Comintern was pulling in a different direction of its own! So the discord only grew worse.' Was he alluding to the occasional misunderstandings and irritations revealed by the exchanges between Tito and 'Grandpa'? Was he trying to shift all blame for them away from the Russians? With Dimitrov, Stalin went on, it was easy to work, but with some of the others it was harder. More important still, there now seemed something unnecessary and unnatural about the persistence of a Communist forum at a time when each Communist party should be trying to find its proper national language and adapt its struggle to the conditions prevailing in its own country.

In the course of the evening two dispatches were brought in. Stalin handed them to Djilas to read for himself. One reported a conversation that Šubašić had been having with the State Department in which the Yugoslav Prime Minister was reported to have stated that the Yugoslavs could never be prevailed upon to pursue a policy directed against the Soviet Union on account of their traditional pro-Russian sentiments.

'That's Šubašić trying to put the wind up the Americans! But why, I wonder – why?' remarked Stalin. Then, noting the expression of astonishment on Djilas's face he explained: 'They steal our dispatches and we steal theirs!'

The second dispatch was from Churchill announcing that the landings in France would begin the next day. Stalin pretended to show surprise and disbelief. He was playing his old game of holding the British and Americans up to ridicule.

'Yes, there'll be a landing – if there's no fog. So far they've always found excuses for putting it off. Tomorrow, I suspect, they'll find something else. Maybe they'll come across some Germans! Maybe there'll be no landing – just promises as usual.'

Molotov observed in his ponderous way: 'No, this time it will be the real thing!'

Stalin played the game with gusto, sowing suspicion in the mind of his Yugoslav guest, harping on their common distrust of the West, particularly of the British, casting doubt on his ally's military capacity and political sincerity. By so doing he hoped to bind the Yugoslavs, whose very successes in the war were breeding a spirit of confidence and independence which might one day become dangerous, ever more closely to the Soviet Union, their one and only genuine ally and friend. The links which the Yugoslav Communists – like himself – had been forced to establish with the West were a regrettable wartime necessity. They should never be allowed to become more than that, and at the first opportunity they should be relaxed if not broken off altogether. Stalin's tactics were to become clear to Djilas only in hindsight, particularly following Tito's break with Moscow three years after the war. Now, intoxicated by the confidence apparently reposed in him by the great Soviet leader, surrounded by the full panoply of Soviet power, he felt nothing but boundless admiration and gratitude. Stalin's scheming appeared to him as statesmanlike foresight, the tortuous and suspicious working of his mind only commendable revolutionary vigilance.

When Djilas at last took his leave his host presented him with a magnificent sword as a gift for Tito, and Djilas seized the opportunity to ask whether Stalin had anything to say about the work of the Yugoslav Communist Party.

'No, I have not,' Stalin answered. 'You yourselves know best what to do!'[2]

CHAPTER EIGHTEEN

Island Fortress

BY the middle of June, Djilas was back again at Partisan headquarters. Before leaving Moscow he sent Tito a cable through the Soviet Military Mission. It stated that he had had a long conversation the previous day with Stalin in the presence of Molotov, Beria and Mikoyan. 'I urge you to take the greatest care. Be on your guard when you return to the mainland and be sure to keep your time of departure strictly secret. Bear in mind that accidents happen to planes when they are in flight. Beware I beg you of foreign friends.' He recommended Tito not to refuse a meeting with the Šubašić government if it was suggested.[1]

The seeds of suspicion against the Western Allies which Stalin had been careful to sow in his visitor's receptive mind were visibly burgeoning by the time he was halfway home. Djilas broke his journey in Teheran where the Russians laid on a reception for him and plied him with the strong drink from which he normally abstained. Rumours of the tirade delivered in his cups against Churchill and Roosevelt, and euphoric prophecies of the post-war triumph of world Communism, were picked up by the alert ears of the Office of Strategic Services and passed to Washington. They confirmed the reputation Djilas was already acquiring as the most fanatically pro-Soviet of the Yugoslav Partisan leaders.[2]

By the middle of June he was back again at Tito's headquarters. Much had happened in the two months he had been away. The last British liaison officers had been withdrawn from the Chetniks – a sure sign that full recognition for Tito could not be long delayed. In Serbia, Mihailović's commanders were deserting him and Koča Popović had been sent to coordinate and command the revival of Partisan activity there, pending the northwards advance from Montenegro and East Bosnia of a strong force of nine divisions under Peko Dapčević. In Croatia, a plot involving Pavelić's Ministers of Foreign Affairs and War, and even the collusion of the German General Glaise von Horstenau, showed how shaky was the puppet regime. Šubašić was in Italy preparing to put proposals to Tito for the formation of a united government. And all the time the Red Army was continuing its relentless advance into south-eastern Europe and towards the frontiers

147

of Yugoslavia. Djilas felt an exhilarating sense of being on the threshold of great and exciting events.

A jeep was waiting for him when he landed in the little port now teeming with British launches, torpedo-boats, landing-craft and Partisan shipping of every description. Vis had now become virtually a Yugoslav-British condominium. A British Commando Brigade shared the general defence of the island with Tito's troops, whilst RAF officers commanded the landing strip cut through the vineyards in the centre of the island from which a squadron of rocket-carrying Hurricanes operated against enemy shipping and targets on the mainland. British units manned the coastal defences and the anti-aircraft batteries protecting Tito's headquarters in the hills. British instructors were running a 'Balkan School of Artillery' where Partisan soldiers learned to handle 75 mm guns. All this reliance on Western assistance, whilst it made for greater security and fighting efficiency, Djilas found disturbing in view of Stalin's stern warnings against the perfidy of the British allies.

The jeep sped through the Dalmatian twilight up the steep sides of Mount Hum and past the sentries guarding the approaches to the cave where, once again, Tito had chosen to make his headquarters. All the leaders were there, full of curiosity to learn the news from Moscow. Djilas was the first Yugoslav Communist to be personally received by Stalin. How had the great man received him, what did he think about their Partisan movement, the achievements and prospects for their Party? What words of commendation or guidance did he have? They could hardly wait to hear or Djilas to tell. He began, rather stiffly, for he was conscious of the solemnity of the occasion, by formally reporting his arrival to Tito as Commander-in-Chief and Secretary to the Party. Tito listened for a moment in silence, then came forward with a smile and embraced him, saying: 'Come on, Djido, tell us what's new in the Soviet Union!'[3]

There was so much to tell, and so many eager listeners hanging on his words! He talked on late into the night; to Mitra, hardly able to contain her own longing to see the wonders of the Socialist fatherland for herself; to Dedijer, back from hospital treatment in Cairo and Italy; to Zogović, alert to gather material for fresh panegyrics. On the matter of supplies, Djilas could only say that Stalin had made the most generous promises; Terzić was staying behind to work out the practical details with Soviet officials. With regard to recognition, everything seemed promising. He related to Tito the advice given to meet the royal government half-way and reach some compromise – for the time being.

Three or four days later, Dr Šubašić arrived on Vis to begin negotiations. He was greeted with military honours but deep suspicion and scepticism on the part of his hosts. They were conscious of the inherent weakness of his position; no basis of popular support, no territory to control, no army to command. He could not even count on full support from his political colleagues or his confused and vacillating young king. The only card in his hand was the promise of diplomatic recognition on the part of the Allies and the favour he enjoyed from the British. This, however, was a liability rather than an asset in Partisan eyes, confirming their suspicions that the Yugoslav Prime Minister was a mere tool of the imperialists, appointed at their behest. Mr Ralph Stevenson, the smooth and smiling British Ambassador, kept a little too ostentatiously close to him, accompanying him almost to the mouth of Tito's cave headquarters and then leaving him there, as if saying: 'Now, just do as you've been told!' In the negotiations which followed Šubašić was alone – uncomfortably alone, surrounded by Tito and his uniformed generals and disciplined political workers. Djilas was amongst them and noted that he seemed aware of his isolation. Nevertheless, the Prime Minister opened in a confident tone. The time had come, he declared, when all must sink their differences and work together for victory over the enemy, for which they could count on the blessing and backing of all the Allies. He produced and read out his draft agreement: a coalition government under the King as Commander-in-Chief of their joint forces, and Tito as his Minister of War. It was implied that the National Liberation Committee and the Anti-Fascist Council would quietly cease to exist.

His listeners were dumbfounded by the unrealistic nature of the proposed deal. What armed forces apart from the Partisans, someone asked, could the Prime Minister call upon? Well, Šubašić replied vaguely, there was the Domobran, the Croat regular army, which had recently sent an emissary to Italy. Was he then really intending to take command of the Quisling forces, Šubašić was asked? The absurdity of the situation struck even the unfortunate Prime Minister who joined in the general laughter. Then Tito announced that he too had a draft agreement which he asked Kardelj to read out. It proposed collaboration with the royal government, but not a coalition, though some individuals favourable to the National Committee, but not representing it, might be included in Šubašić's cabinet. The National Committee itself would continue to function as the only effective authority inside the country. The question of the monarchy should be settled after the war.

There was no serious discussion of Tito's proposals. Šubašić read through the draft again, suggested a few minor stylistic amendments, and said simply: 'I accept this draft as a basis!' A formal agreement on the lines proposed by Tito was signed on 16 June. It seemed a complete victory for the Partisans. The Royal Government undertook to regard the provision of aid to the Partisans as its main task, endorsed the decisions taken by the 1943 session of the Anti-Fascist Council at Jajce, and recognised the institutions there set up. Both sides agreed to work for the formation of a united Yugoslav Government representing the fusion of the Royal Government and Tito's National Committee. The advice which Djilas had brought back from Stalin for a temporary compromise with Šubašić had been followed to the letter and promised excellent results. Moscow had every cause for satisfaction.

The British less so. They too welcomed the prospect of an ultimately united Government as foreseen in the agreement, but Šubašić seemed to have given way too quickly and too completely. The British Government, and in particular its Prime Minister with his romantic view of kingship, were conscious of their obligations towards the luckless young king living under their protection. The bland declaration that the question of his return to Yugoslavia would be settled after the war did nothing to improve his chances. Djilas put the Communists' case with complete frankness: 'that he was a monarch was enough for us to depose him.'[4] Nor did it weigh with them that Šubašić was a man of genuinely good will, one of the few politicians in exile always to have believed in and worked for unity between Serbs and Croats, and now committed with equal sincerity to the search for common ground between non-Communists and Communists. The latter were concerned only with the seizure and consolidation of their power. Besides, they nursed a special grievance against the former Governor of Croatia for having failed to release the imprisoned Communists before the Ustashe took over and murdered them. Djilas on one occasion taxed him with this to his face and contemptuously rejected the explanation that orders had been given for the Communists' release but were sabotaged by Fifth Columnists in the Governor's administration.

In August Tito went to Italy for talks with the Allied Commander-in-Chief, Churchill and Šubašić. A compromise agreement was reached, to which King Peter reluctantly consented, for a united government under a three-man Regency pending a settlement of the monarchy issue. Tito returned to Vis well pleased with his visit and impressed by Churchill's personality and good will towards the Partisans. 'The English are clever!' Swarthy Žujović commented caustically. 'An escort of warships and naval manoeuvres laid on in honour of the Old Man and I see it's had its effect!'

But though he may have felt flattered by the attentions shown him by the Western Allies, Tito had no intention of tying himself too closely to them. He was well aware of where his chief support and his political loyalties lay. In the second half of September, the British were disconcerted to discover that the Marshal was no longer on Vis. He had taken off secretly one night from the island airfield, accompanied by General Korneyev and one or two companions, and headed for an unknown destination. He eluded the RAF security guards and no one in the High Command would say where he had gone. Only Ranković, who arranged his departure with some assistance from Djilas, and a very few others were in the secret. Tito was on his way to Marshal Tolbukhin's headquarters in Rumania and from there he would go on to Moscow. Djilas had impressed on him what Stalin had said about General Sikorski's death at the hands of the perfidious British, and Tito, despite his reassuring experiences as their guest – which of course might have been devised to put him off his guard – had no wish to court a like fate. To complete the confusion of his allies, Djilas permitted himself a little exercise in disinformation. He circulated a report that Tito had landed in Western Serbia.

At the end of September Tass issued a communiqué declaring that, with the authorisation of Marshal Tito's Liberation Committee, the Red Army had entered Yugoslavia in pursuit of the retreating enemy. Three weeks later the Germans were driven from Belgrade. Djilas was impatient to return to Serbia. He had been forced to spend most of the torrid summer months on Vis recovering from a severe attack of dysentery. Drained of energy, he had spent his time on the beaches and attempting to resume his agit-prop activities. He wrote two long articles – one giving his impressions of Stalin, the other singing the praises of the Red Army. When he was well enough to travel, Tito wished him to undertake two missions of some delicacy before joining him in Serbia. One was to go with Kardelj to Croatia, where Hebrang's nationalist deviations continued to cause concern, and the other to discuss with the Italian comrades the question of Trieste and its adjacent territory which Tito intended to claim for Yugoslavia after the war.[5]

In Rome they talked with Togliatti whom Kardelj had known as a Comintern official in Moscow. Togliatti suggested a Yugoslav-Italian condominium in Trieste, but the issue was one which aroused strong nationalist emotions on both sides and was to remain an apple of discord for many years. In Croatia too, nationalism was still a disturbing factor. 'Things will never go well there so long as Andrija [Hebrang] is Secretary of the Croat Communist Party,' Kardelj wrote to Tito. 'His whole mentality and character are such that they tend to weaken everything which links Croatia to Yugoslavia. He is an autocrat more feared than loved.'[6] Tito took his emissaries' advice and recalled Hebrang to Belgrade where he was compensated with high office in the new Government. It was a solution that was to create fresh problems which none of them could foresee.

CHAPTER NINETEEN

Friendship and Friction

ON 22 October, two days after Russian and Yugoslav forces had battled their way into Belgrade, Kardelj and Djilas flew from Croat headquarters to Serbia. They landed at an airfield near Valjevo, half way between Užice and Belgrade, and went on to the capital in a jeep which Djilas hurriedly taught himself to drive. The days of foot-slogging though the moutains were over and the heady prospect of power was opening before him.

Belgrade had been taken at a heavy cost in human lives. Some thirteen thousand Germans had been killed in the battle and eight thousand captured. The Chetniks and Quisling formations had disappeared, most of them in the wake of the Germans. The Partisans and the Red Army also suffered severely, their respective contributions to victory becoming later the subject of bitter controversy. The official Russian accounts state that 'the Soviet command courteously complied with the wishes expressed by Partisan leaders, and by Tito personally, that Yugoslav troops should be the first to enter the capital.'[1] But stories were current that General Zhdanov, the Soviet operational commander, had met Partisan requests for cooperation with the brutal words: 'I am advancing according to my own plan, and you may use yours and advance if you can. The enemy is weak and I shall simply walk over him. . . . Come tomorrow and have tea with me in Belgrade!'[2]

The general was given to walking over others, friend and foe alike, as Djilas was soon to discover. After installing his agit-prop unit in the Majestic, one of the few hotels to have escaped damage, he made his way to Partisan headquarters and was conferring with the Yugoslav commanders when Zhdanov entered the room and gruffly accosted him: 'Why don't you salute?'

Djilas was wearing the recently introduced insignia of a lieutenant-general and retorted in Russian: 'And you should be able to recognise the ranks of allied officers!'[3] The conqueror of Belgrade turned on his heel and stormed out.

This brush reflected a growing unease. Almost from the moment of Djilas's setting foot in Serbia, people had been coming to him with complaints of outrages committed by Red Army men against the Yugoslav citizens whom they should have treated as friends and allies.

There had been looting and raping – to say nothing of the grabbing of watches and revolvers even from Partisan officers – which the Russian commanders had made little or no effort to control. Later, when these abuses reached such proportions that attempts were made to collect statistics, the Yugoslav tally amounted to 121 cases of rape, 111 rapes with murder, and 1,204 robberies with violence.[4] How could the glorious Red Army which Djilas had so eloquently extolled for its lofty morale as well as for its incomparable heroism permit such things? The question kept gnawing at his mind amidst the excitement and preoccupations of those first days in liberated Belgrade.

The agit-prop team lost no time in getting to work. Its first task was to start up the presses again. The pro-Nazi *Novo Vreme* (New Times) reappeared as the Communist Party organ *Borba*; Djilas was to use it as his chief mouthpiece for the next nine years. *Politika*, the capital's most prestigious daily with a long tradition of objectivity and independence, re-echoed the party line in more muted tones. Djilas later claimed with pride that he had prevailed on Tito not to sanction the establishment of formal censorship, but Serbia's post-liberation publications nevertheless were all careful to speak with much the same obedient voice. His trusted agit-prop colleagues were with him again – Dedijer, Zogović, Mitra and others – assigned to new and more weighty duties. After a couple of weeks at the Majestic he moved into the *Borba* building and took over the apartment which had been occupied by the former owner. Later, he and Mitra, like many other ex-Partisans competing for comfortable quarters, moved into a commandeered villa in the elegant suburb of Dedinje. It was by no means one of the most luxurious, and he shared it with Zogović and his wife who occupied the ground floor.

By the end of the year they had moved again into more spacious accommodation where they were joined by the surviving members of the Djilas family. The war had taken a merciless toll; his elder brother Aleksa had been killed by Montenegrin Chetniks, his younger brother Milivoje by the Gestapo, his father by Albanian Fascists, and one sister, pregnant at the time, had also been slaughtered by Chetniks together with her husband. Other families had suffered similar losses. The revenge now taken by the triumphant Partisans was correspondingly savage. OZNA, though still imperfectly organised, was already at work hunting down and executing known enemies, not a few of the innocent perishing with them. Djilas does not conceal or minimise the blood-letting. 'Even before our entry into Belgrade,' he writes, 'we had established the criteria according to which the adherents of Nedić and [the Serbian Fascist leader] Ljotić would be killed on the spot.'[5] Known Chetnik supporters generally received equally short shrift.

Domestic tensions added to the bitter-sweet aftertaste of victory. The gradual return to normal life saw the end of many wartime relationships. Zdenka had contracted tuberculosis which medical treatment in the Soviet Union failed to cure; a resting place was found for her body in the grounds of Tito's private villa. Ranković remarried, unobtrusively and almost secretly, as with everything he did. Dedijer found himself a new wife from Slovenia. Milovan and Mitra resumed married life together but could not recover their former intimacy. Their relationship was punctuated by periods of emotional estrangement and stormy scenes. Mitra was bent on pursuing a political career of her own and resented any suggestion of political or personal ascendancy on the part of her husband.

Tito did not reach Belgrade from his operational headquarters near the Rumanian border until nearly a week after its liberation. His mood was one of angry dissatisfaction – in unconscious imitation, Djilas suspected, of the Soviet commanders – that so little seemed to have been done. Fifth Columnists, he delcared, were still at large; a start had not even been made on relieving the urgent needs of the population and getting life back to normal; and pressure was not being kept up against the retreating Germans. The war, indeed, was far from over. Six months' hard fighting still lay ahead; the hardest, for the Yugoslavs, of the war. Forces forged in guerrilla combat confronted a regular army which, even though withdrawing, could only be finally destroyed by the resources and techniques of regular warfare. Tito's troops were carried forward for a time with the momentum of the Red Army's advance, but headway was desperately slow and costly.

The Soviet command was anxious to switch the weight of the attack to the Hungarian flank, leaving the Yugoslavs to keep up pressure in Slavonia. The last Russian operational units were withdrawn from Yugoslav territory by the middle of November, when a communiqué was issued expressing gratitude for the unselfish help and friendly attitude shown to the Red Army by the Yugoslav people. Soviet military intervention had indeed been of tremendous, perhaps decisive, importance; but it had also given grounds for sentiments other than gratitude. The outrages perpetrated had become so frequent and scandalous – one *Partizanka* orderly had been raped by a Soviet officer when she was actually in the process of delivering an important message during the battle for Belgrade – that the matter had to be brought to Tito's attention immediately on his arrival. In conference with Djilas,

155

Ranković and Kardelj he decided that the matter must be taken up with General Korneyev, the head of the Soviet Military Mission. During the eight months and more which the General had spent with the Partisans they had come to know each other well. Plump and affable-looking, this ex-Tsarist officer might have been taken for an elderly bank manager rather than a general. He liked his drink – 'The poor man is not stupid, but he's a drunkard, an incurable drunkard!' Stalin once said to him[6] – and in his cups he was apt to grow genial to the point of sentimentality. But when he believed his personal dignity or the honour of the Red Army to be in question he could become as harshly arrogant as any of his brother-officers. Tito rightly anticipated that this was likely to be the case in the coming interview. To lend it greater solemnity he decided to speak with Korneyev in the presence of his closest Central Committee colleagues and of his two senior generals, Koča Popović and Peko Dapčević, the latter two in full uniform and wearing the Order of Kutuzov lately conferred on them.

The meeting took place in Tito's villa. Tito came straight to the point but spoke in restrained and courteous tones. As he listened, the General grew more and more angry and scarcely heard him out. 'In the name of the Soviet Government I protest at such insinuations against the Red Army!'

Tito tried to convince him that these were no isolated cases, as the General kept declaring, exaggerated by counter-revolutionaries to make bad blood between the Yugoslavs and the glorious Red Army. They had become sufficiently frequent and widely known, he explained, to be having an unfavourable effect on an otherwise well-disposed public opinion.

'The problem is that our enemies are exploiting them,' Djilas put in. 'They keep comparing the assaults by Red Army soldiers with the conduct of the English officers who do not indulge in such attacks.'

This was too much for Korneyev. Flushed with anger he turned on Djilas and shouted: 'I protest most strongly against this insult to the Red Army in comparing it with the armies of capitalist countries!' The interview ended in an atmosphere of tension.[7]

Despite Soviet indignation, the meeting did seem to have the desired effect, and the Yugoslav leaders noted that the Soviet commanders appeared to be dealing more severely with cases of gross misconduct by their troops. But it was never admitted that the Yugoslav complaints had any justification. On the contrary, they were treated as an unfriendly act, and Yugoslav protests – in particular, the remarks made by Djilas – were themselves made the subject of repeated protest.

Korneyev lost no time in reporting the affair to Moscow, no doubt adding a gloss which showed his own reaction in a most favourable light, and before long Tito received the following notification of Stalin's displeasure:

You must know that the Soviet Government, in spite of colossal sacrifices and losses, is doing everything in its power and beyond its power to help you. However, I am surprised at the fact that a few incidents and offences committed by individual officers and soldiers of the Red Army in Yugoslavia are generalized and extended to the whole Red Army.

Stalin added that the Yugoslavs should not be offensive to the Soviet Army which was shedding its blood to get rid of the German occupiers in Yugoslavia. He said that there were black sheep in every family, but the whole family should not be condemned for the actions of one black sheep. He went on that if the soldiers of the Red Army found out that Djilas considered the British officers to be morally superior to Soviet officers, the latter would 'cry out in pain at such undeserved insults'.[8]

The stormy interview with Korneyev was not the only affair, though it was the most important, to trouble the course of what appeared to the outside world as a honeymoon period in Yugoslav-Soviet relations following the liberation of Belgrade. An unpleasant incident occurred at Marshal Tolbukhin's headquarters, and once again it was a Montenegrin – the ebullient and outspoken Vukmanović-Tempo – who acted as a catalyst. The Yugoslav leaders had never been reconciled to Bulgaria's sudden *volte-face* and too ready acceptance by the Russians as an apparently favourite ally. Memories of the harsh rule imposed during their occupation of Yugoslav Macedonia were still too fresh to make them welcome comrades-in-arms. Tito therefore decided to request that, in deference to his people's feelings, their troops should be transferred from Yugoslav soil to the Hungarian sector of the front. Arso Jovanović, his Chief of Staff, and Vukmanović-Tempo, now in charge of political work in the army, were sent to Tolbukhin's headquarters to convey his request. They received a dusty answer from the Marshal: 'I have made my dispositions and have no intention of changing them. The Bulgarian units will remain where they are!'

Arso Jovanović backed down at once, but Tempo refused to take no for an answer. By temperament he was even more impetuous and plain-spoken than Djilas. He declared that they were speaking under instructions from the Commander-in-Chief of the Yugoslav forces and asked that Tito's request be referred to the Soviet Government. Tolbukhin hardly troubled to conceal his anger. He was not used to being contradicted, and certainly not by foreigners and mere Partisans whom he looked on simply as auxiliaries to the Red Army. He dismissed them after brusquely declaring that he had no intention of referring such stupidities to his government. Nevertheless, Tito's request was transmitted to Moscow and orders were given for the transfer of Bulgarian troops to another sector of the front.[9]

Yugoslavia's distrust of Bulgaria was to persist for a considerable time to come. An eventual union between the two countries had long been on the cards which Stalin chose to play close to his chest. In conversation at the end of November with Šubašić and Kardelj, who were visiting Moscow in an attempt to settle the final details of the proposed united Yugoslav Government, he urged them to go ahead with plans for the federation. Kardelj prepared a draft and took it with him to Sofia for discussion, but he returned to Belgrade at the end of the year discouraged and frustrated; he had found the Bulgarians slippery and always ready to raise fresh difficulties. The following month Pijade headed a delegation to Moscow for further talks with the Russians and Bulgarians. All agreed in principle that federation was desirable, but differences remained about the form it should take. The Russians appeared to favour first the Bulgarian, then the Yugoslav, proposals, but only halfheartedly, as if suspecting that a South Slav state enlarged on those lines might become undesirably strong and independent. So plans for a federation hung fire and Tito and Dimitrov had to be content with a Treaty of Yugoslav-Bulgarian Friendship, signed a year later.

The Yugoslav Communists were also much concerned with developments in Greece, where British intervention foiled a bid for power by the Greek comrades. Might not the British attempt to play the same game in their country? They had not yet formally recognised Tito as the legitimate ruler of Yugoslavia and the projected United Yugoslav Government was still unformed. The Partisans' domestic rivals, though driven from Serbia, were not yet completely crushed. There were also elements in Croatia who hoped to do an eleventh-hour deal with the western allies, switching their allegiance to them and so ensuring the continuance of a separate anti-Communist Croat state. Mihailović remained at large and not all his followers had given up hope. After the fall of Belgrade, the Germans' main line of withdrawal from the Balkans had been cut but they still hoped to continue making an orderly retreat through Montenegro and Bosnia. At the end of October Tito authorised the British to land field artillery at Dubrovnik to harry their retreat; but towards the end of November the Partisans' policy changed. The British were ordered back to the coast, unblocking the Germans' escape route. This sudden change of attitude reflected Communist fears that the British would intervene in Yugoslavia as they had begun to do in Greece.

The British, for their part, distrusted Yugoslav intentions, particularly with regard to Greece. A fortnight after returning to liberated Belgrade, Djilas addressed a rally at which he complained that the Slav inhabitants of Aegean Macedonia were suffering persecution at the hands of the Greek authorities. Tempo also spoke, bluntly demanding the incorporation of both Aegean and Bulgarian Macedonia within the borders of Yugoslavia's new 'Macedonian Republic'. The British Embassy (still accredited to the Yugoslav Government in Exile) grew alarmed, seeing such demands as interference in the domestic affairs of another state and a threat to Greece's territorial integrity. The British Military Mission was instructed to lodge a protest with Marshal Tito whilst the Ambassador in Moscow addressed a note to the Commissariat for Foreign Affairs conveying his government's concern and expressing the hope that 'the Soviet Government will likewise feel able to express to Marshal Tito its disapproval of irresponsible remarks of this kind which only damage relations between Allies.'[10] London evidently regarded the Yugoslav Communists, particularly such firebrands as Djilas and Tempo, as answerable to Moscow and subject to control by the Kremlin.

Djilas, in fact, had been left shaken and dejected by the incident with Korneyev. It was not that his colleagues seemed to hold the affair seriously against him or that his functions had been curtailed as a result of it; he was chosen soon afterwards to pronounce the customary eulogy at the October Revolution celebration. He had spoken to the Soviet General in good faith, both in the interests of his own people and in those of the Russians themselves, in a genuine concern to prevent further damage being done to their good repute. But they had deliberately exaggerated and distorted his words and seemed determined to hold them against him. They refused to admit the awkward facts, insulting the allies they had injured and behaving with all the callous arrogance of a great power towards a weaker one. For the first time he was made painfully aware – though he still could not bring himself to admit it fully – of the contrast between his ideal picture and the reality of the Soviet system and Soviet Man. The Russians were even spreading the rumour that Djilas was a Trotskyist. Ranković traced the rumour to its source and scotched it, but his hands were tied by his dependence on Soviet help in building up his own secret service. Colonel Timofeyev, in charge of Russian intelligence, was always most cordial. All the same, the Soviet intelligence chief continued busily recruiting his agents, particularly from amongst Yugoslavia's numerous White Russians, many of whom had previously worked for the Germans, and even within the organisations of the Yugoslav Communist Party. Tito was indignant when he learned of it; nevertheless, the work went surreptitiously on.

Early in 1945 a Yugoslav government delegation visited Moscow. It was headed by Hebrang, now Minister for Industry and Chairman of the Economic Council and the Planning Commission. It included Mitra, who had long been eager to see the Fatherland of Socialism for herself. She had much to tell her husband on her return, some of it disquieting. The delegation had been sumptuously entertained but also subjected to a series of taunts and recriminations. Stalin wounded them by comparing the Yugoslav Army unfavourably with the Bulgarian and blaming it for letting the guns given by the Russians fall into the hands of the Germans on the Srem front. The Yugoslavs reacted volubly to these taunts, General Arso with tears of shame and frustration in his unavailing effort to convince Stalin that he was doing them an injustice. Only Hebrang remained surprisingly silent until remarking that, as good Communists, they ought to take what Comrade Stalin said to heart and admit that their government was to blame for many failures and mistakes.

Finally Stalin raked up Djilas's alleged outburst against the glorious Red Army: 'And to think that such an army was insulted by Djilas! By Djilas, of all people – Djilas, the last person of whom I would have expected such a thing – a man whom I had received so warmly!' Stalin appeared to be actually in tears. 'An army which did not spare its blood for you!' he went on. 'Does Djilas, himself a writer, not know what human suffering, what the human heart is? Could he not understand it if a soldier who has crossed thousands of kilometres through blood and death has fun with a woman or takes some trifle?'

The actor then crowned his performance by throwing his arms round Mitra and kissing her, exclaiming that he could not refrain from showing his love for the Serbs in that way even at the risk of being charged with rape![11]

Djilas listened to Mitra's excited account with astonishment and dismay. What could it all mean? What was behind these extraordinary antics, this harping on his alleged insults to the Red Army? Nothing that Stalin did was without its reason, though it might have to be sought in the recesses of a pathologically tortuous mind. Later reflection convinced Djilas that this was Stalin's way of trying to win over a man whom he regarded as a key figure in Tito's intimate entourage, a man whom he might perhaps some day need to replace Tito himself. First, that man had to be reduced by feelings of acute guilt and shame, a craving for the Soviet leader's forgiveness. The penitent must come to desire above all else to prove by his slavish submission that he was worthy of being restored to Stalin's paternal favour. There were others too whom Stalin appeared to be trying to woo by similar tactics – Arso Jovanović, for instance, whom Hebrang rebuked for daring to defend himself and his army from the Soviet charges. Hebrang himself was clearly already unconditionally committed to Stalin. He had even been heard confiding to the Russians that Tito seemed more interested in the alterations being made for his benefit to Prince Paul's White Palace than in the military operations on the Srem front.[12] And Mitra? Like the rest of the delegation, she had been overwhelmed by what they had experienced. 'How could you keep from weeping,' she told him, 'when you see even Stalin himself in tears?'[13]

CHAPTER TWENTY

Return to Moscow

ON 7 March 1945 it was announced that the long-awaited United Government had at last been formed. Under a nominal three-man Regency, Tito ranked as Prime Minister, Dr Šubašić as Foreign Minister, and Djilas as Minister without Portfolio, later as Minister for Montenegro. The first act of the new government was to send a high-ranking delegation to Moscow to sign a Treaty of Friendship, Mutual Aid and Post-War Collaboration with the USSR. Tito, who headed it himself, wished to take Djilas with him in the hope of liquidating the Korneyev incident once and for all and clearing up any remaining misunderstandings.

Djilas set out on his second visit to Moscow burdened with a sense of failure and isolation. It was not so much apprehension at the prospect of the unpleasantness, or at least the embarrassment, awaiting him in the Soviet capital. He had never been one to shirk a good fight, if a fight seemed inevitable and in a just cause, and he still believed passionately in the cause which he served as revolutionary and Partisan. Only the smallest wisp of doubt as yet clouded his mind, quickly dispersed by the confident assertions of his Marxist creed. His low spirits were nevertheless in marked contrast to the excitement and elation he had felt on his first encounter with the Soviet Union.

Molotov was amongst those at the airport to meet them. He shook hands with Djilas without a glimmer of recognition. Tito was escorted to a separate villa, the others to the Hotel Metropole where that same evening the visiting comrades were each offered – so they discovered on comparing notes the following morning – the opportunity of enjoying a dubious form of Soviet hospitality. The telephone in his bedroom rang and a seductive female voice suggested an assignation.

'Let me alone!' Djilas slammed down the receiver angrily. Surely such tactics by the ubiquitous NKVD were inappropriate in the case of trusted Communists, whatever might be necessary for gaining a hold over bourgeois visitors!

The days in Moscow were spent sight-seeing, the evening in a round of official receptions. The terms of the treaty had been agreed in advance, and there was little work to be done apart from checking the translation of the text. The signing ceremony took place in the Kremlin on 11 April – little more than four years after the conclusion of the stillborn Treaty of Friendship and Non-Aggression entered into with the bourgeois Yugoslav Government. It was followed by supper at the Kremlin and the showing of a film about the happy life led on a collective farm. Stalin shook hands with Djilas without saying a word. At a subsequent banquet a few days later he was in jovial mood but still said nothing about his guest's alleged misdemeanour. Some evenings afterwards there followed a supper at his *dacha* where the subject was finally broached. Filling a small glass with vodka, Stalin offered it to Djilas who, not liking hard liquor, was drinking beer. Thinking it was intended as a toast to his host which could not be refused, Djilas raised the glass to his lips.

'No, no!' Stalin said with a smile, 'not to me – to the Red Army! What, you won't drink to the Red Army?'

Djilas drained his glass and Stalin came to the point. What was all that trouble with General Korneyev about? he asked. Djilas explained that his remarks had been misinterpreted. He had never intended – far from it – to disparage the Red Army but only to call attention to certain cases of misconduct on the part of some of its members that were having an unfortunate effect on Soviet-Yugoslav relations. Stalin hardly let him finish before launching into a discussion of Dostoevsky and that writer's unparalleled insight into the human soul. Could not Djilas, himself a writer, learn from him what a complex thing was that soul and could he not make allowance for man's weaknesses? The ordeals through which the Red Army men had passed made intolerable demands on them and it was no cause for wonder or complaint if they did not always behave like angels.

'The Red Army is not perfect,' he concluded. 'The important thing is that it fights Germans – and is fighting them well. The rest doesn't matter!'

There was nothing more to be said. Stalin seemed to regard the incident as closed, but he went on teasing Djilas and pretending to compare him – not without a touch of malice, for who at the end of such a war would like to be compared to the enemy? – to the beer-swilling Germans. 'He drinks beer like the Germans!' Stalin repeated with relish. 'Yes, by God, he's a German, a German!'

Tito was not spared either. Stalin began talking sneeringly of the Yugoslav army, as he had talked to Tito's Chief-of-Staff. The subject he knew to be a sensitive one, as the untrained conscripts called up to the Srem front had been suffering heavy losses and some defeats. 'Your men are still Partisans, unfit for serious, front-line fighting!' he said.

'Last winter one German regiment broke up a whole division of yours!'

Again he compared the Yugoslavs unfavourably with the Bulgarians, fully aware of the traditional rivalry between them and the still smouldering resentment over Macedonia. He wanted to give Tito a salutary reminder that the Bulgarians, as grateful protégés of the Russians, had a special claim on his favour. And they made good fighters too, he kept repeating – much better than the Yugoslavs. Bulgaria had a well drilled and disciplined army.

Tito, who had borne Stalin's sallies with a patient smile, could endure this goading no longer. He shouted out that the Yugoslav army would quickly overcome its weaknesses. It had, in fact, already seized the initiative and a day or two after the signing of the Treaty of Friendship began to break through the German lines.

The talk shifted to firmer ground. Djilas had regained confidence and joined in the conversation which was mainly between Stalin, Molotov and Tito. The other Soviet leaders present said little. Djilas observed them closely; Bulganin, rather stout, but handsome with his neat goatee beard and general's uniform; Antonov, also a general, but younger and more handsome still; Malenkov, small, plump and slightly pock-marked, whose reserved manner masked an adroit intelligence which had gained him Stalin's trust in handling the Party's internal affairs; Beria, with his pale, nondescript appearance and his shifty, protruding eyes glinting behind pince-nez. Djilas was suddenly struck by his likeness to a notorious police official who had hunted down and tortured Communists in pre-war Belgrade.

Amongst his cronies Stalin allowed himself to express opinions he would not dream of airing openly. Sometimes they sounded distinctly unorthodox. After noting the exchange of recriminations early that month between British Conservative and Labour ministers and guessing that these presaged the end of the war-time coalition and a general election which might bring Labour to power, Stalin observed: 'Today, Socialism is possible even under the British monarchy. Revolution is no longer necessary everywhere! Recently we had a British Labour Party delegation here and we spoke particularly about this. Yes, Socialism is possible even under an English King!'

Tito chose his words carefully, remarking somewhat enigmatically that in Yugoslavia something new was certainly taking shape; Socialism was not everywhere being achieved only by the ways which had been followed in the past. Though sometimes smarting under Stalin's needling, Tito treated him with the respect due to a senior. There seemed to be little or no divergence of views between the two leaders.

Djilas was more ready to generalise, though as yet he had few ideas of his own to propound and still thought in terms of the existing orthodoxy. The government they had just established in Yugoslavia, he asserted, was already of the standard Soviet type. All key posts in it were held by Communists – he did not need to mince his words, since the non-Communist Šubašić had not been invited to the evening's festivities – and there was no effective opposition.

'No,' Stalin interjected. 'Your government is not yet Soviet! You have something in between De Gaulle's France and the Soviet Union.' Djilas could not agree. He felt aggrieved that their regime was not yet recognised as being in essence, if not in form, fully Communist.

Stalin propounded a new thesis about the nature of the war and the consequences to be expected to stem from it for the peace. The Yugoslavs did not challenge it, though it was later to account in good part for the distrust with which the Soviet Union came to regard them. 'The war is not as in the past,' Stalin declared. 'Whoever occupies a territory now also imposes his own system on it. Everyone imposes his own system as far as his army has power to do so. It cannot be otherwise.'

The Red Army had fought only briefly on Yugoslav soil. Though they were later to claim the credit for having driven the Germans out, they could not maintain that they had been long in occupation of Yugoslav territory. Thus, according to Stalin's dictum, it followed that the social system imposed on it must be that of the Yugoslavs themselves. They might choose to call it 'Socialist', but it was not necessarily what Moscow understood by Socialism. Stalin could feel sure only about a Socialist Government which had been set up and, if necessary, maintained in power by the Red Army. Hence his preference for the Bulgarians. Their Communist-led Partisans had in reality done little or nothing to drive out the Germans and overthrow the Fascist Government. That was directly due to the Red Army, and the Bulgarian Communists had been able to form a government only as the result of the Soviet presence and Soviet power. For this they had to pay a price. They were masters of their country, but only by grace and favour of their Russian protectors. Dimitrov was by far the most powerful and best known of the Bulgarian Communists, and he even seemed to enjoy the friendship and a certain regard on the part of Stalin. Yet Stalin still kept him more or less idle in Moscow whilst his comrades laid hands on the levers of power in Bulgaria. 'It's not yet time for Dimitrov to go to Bulgaria: he's well off where he is!' Stalin remarked with a roguish smile at the dinner party with the Yugoslavs.

Djilas pondered these words when they spent an evening with Dimitrov before leaving Moscow. What was Stalin up to? Was he really reluctant to risk upsetting the western allies, as he alleged, by letting such a notorious Communist as Dimitrov return to his country, even though by the spring of 1945 Soviet, and so indigenous Communist, influence was already dominant there? Could it be rather that Stalin simply wanted to keep all the reins in his own hands rather than pass them to the most adroit and experienced of the Bulgarian leaders? Was that the measure of the trust which existed at the summit of the international Communist movement between representatives of nominally independent national parties?

The evening at Dimitrov's was pleasantly relaxed. Tito and his host reminisced about their time in the Comintern. The future union between their two countries was also touched on, but only in general terms. That would have to await a favourable international juncture, and above all, the nod from Stalin. Dimitrov struck Djilas as tired and dejected. Bulgaria's hour had struck but he was kept in virtual exile and would be allowed to go home, after everything had been settled, only as an honoured figurehead.

At the conclusion of their Moscow visit it was arranged that the Yugoslav delegation should return by train via Kiev and be shown something of the Ukraine. Stalin telephoned to N.S. Khrushchev, at that time secretary of the Ukrainian Communist Party and Prime Minister of its nominally independent Government. 'Lay on a good reception and look after them well!' Stalin told him. 'Make Tito feel that our country harbours a deep sense of friendship towards Yugoslavia.'

Khrushchev did his best, though a visit to a collective farm, in an area which was still suffering from the ravages of war, was perhaps no great treat. He took a liking to Tito, whom he found lively and sympathetic. He also liked Djilas. 'When I first met him, he impressed me with his quick and subtle wit,' Khrushchev later recalled. 'He struck me as a good man. I won't deny that I now have quite a different opinion of him, but that's beside the point.' Khrushchev later reported to Stalin that the Yugoslavs had had a good time and enjoyed themselves. Stalin was pleased. 'At that time,' Khrushchev concludes, 'Stalin wanted us to have, and was sure we would have, the best, the most fraternal relations with Yugoslavia.'[1]

Djilas too formed a favourable impression of Khrushchev. The latter seemed to him 'unlike other Soviet leaders, unrestrained and very talkative,' fond of interlarding his conversation with proverbs, common sayings and Marxist tags, with an inexhaustible, lively and somewhat crude sense of fun. He was less bureaucratic – 'the only one who delved into details, into the daily life of the Communist rank and file and the ordinary people'. Yet for all his obvious ability, it struck Djilas as odd to find a Russian at the head of the Ukrainian Party and Government. He noticed too the marked russification of all sectors of public life – Russian newspapers in the kiosks and Russian spoken in the theatre – in a country theoretically independent enough to have representatives of its own in the United Nations. Despite the ebullience of Khrushchev and the beauty of Kiev, the dominant impression made on him by the Ukraine was one of 'loss of personality, weariness and hopelessness'. Was this all the Soviet 'federal' system had to offer a national republic credited with a vigorous cultural life and a considerable degree of autonomy – a federal system which the Yugoslav Communists were to adopt as the model for their own multi-national state?

If such disturbing thoughts passed through his mind as the delegation continued on its way home, Djilas did not permit them to mar the general satisfaction left on him by their visit. Things had, on the whole, gone very well. The misunderstanding over his own remarks about the Red Army had, he hoped, been put right. He could bask again with the others in Stalin's favour, assured of Soviet friendship and goodwill at the outset of the great task before them – the implementation of the Revolution and the transformation of their country into a Socialist state. 'The new Yugoslavia', he assured his *Borba* readers, 'pursues, and will consistently pursue, the most friendly policy towards the Soviet Union.' He said that the Partisans would never forget how the Red Army under Stalin's leadership both came to the assistance of the Yugoslavs at the most difficult moment in their history and fought shoulder to shoulder with them for the liberation of the Yugoslav homeland. 'There is no force on earth which could break the fraternal alliance, born of the war, of the peoples of Yugoslavia with the peoples of the Soviet Union.'[2]

CHAPTER TWENTY-ONE

The Power and the Glory

THE 'fraternal alliance' with the Soviet Union would also, the Yugoslav Communists hoped, help them to achieve their immediate post-war gains *vis-à-vis* the Western Allies. The most coveted prize was Trieste. On 3 May 1945 New Zealand units of General Alexander's Fifteenth Army Group found themselves facing Yugoslav troops who had already begun to take over the city's administration. It was the end of the Partisans' precarious wartime alliance with the British. The West was determined to deny the USSR and her allies this strategic foothold on the Adriatic. Reinforcements were brought up and the Yugoslavs forced out. A compromise was reached by which 'Zone A' – the city itself and a strip of land to the west – remained under allied occupation, and 'Zone B' – the rest of Istria and Venezia Giulia – under that of the Yugoslavs. Tito's forces were also compelled to fall back over the Austro-Yugoslav frontier and evacuate Klagenfurt and Villach which they had seized to make good their claim to Austrian territory inhabited by the local Slovene minority.

In both these ventures Tito failed to receive the backing from the Soviet Union which he expected. Moscow feared a clash with the western allies and an affront to Italian nationalist sentiment which would ruin the electoral chances of the Italian Communist Party. In a speech at Ljubljana he complained that the country's interests were being subordinated to great power barter and bargaining. His outburst was aimed against the West but it was also taken in Moscow as an implied criticism of the Soviet Union. Their Ambassador in Belgrade was instructed to lodge a sharp protest. Kardelj, according to Ambassador Sadchikov's account, made an obsequious admission that 'he regarded our opinion of Tito's speech as correct' and 'agreed that the Soviet Union could no longer tolerate similar statements'. The published version of Sadchikov's despatch goes on to give an extraordinary account of their interview. It describes how Kardelj said that he would like the Soviet Union to think of the Yugoslav leaders not as representatives of an independent country but as representing one of the future Soviet Republics; that the Yugoslav Communist Party should be considered as part of the Soviet Communist Party and that relations between Yugoslavia and the Soviet Union should be based on the idea that Yugoslavia would at some time in the future become part of the USSR. Kardelj added that he would like the Russians to criticise the Yugoslavs frankly and openly and give them advice about internal and external policy which Yugoslavia would rightly follow.

Sadchikov said that he had replied to Kardelj that the Yugoslavs must face facts as they were, that is Yugoslavia must be treated as an independent state and its Communist Party as an independent party. 'You can and must', he said, 'present and solve your problem independently, while we should never refuse advice should you ask for it.'[1]

Did the Yugoslav Communist leaders then really think of themselves as 'part of the Communist Party of the Soviet Union' and their country as potentially a 'constituent part of the USSR'? The authenticity of Sadchikov's account has been denied by the Yugoslavs and it is certainly possible that it may have been doctored to make it more damaging and to drive a wedge between Kardelj and Tito. But Moscow itself does seem at the time to have been seriously considering the possibility of simply annexing the recently 'liberated' countries of Eastern Europe. 'From Stalin's stated position at the time and vague allusions by Soviet diplomats,' Djilas writes, 'it seemed that the Soviet leaders were also toying with the thought of reorganising the Soviet Union by joining to it the "People's Democracies" – the Ukraine with Hungary and Rumania, and Byelorussia with Poland and Czechoslovakia, whilst the Balkan states were to be joined with Russia.'[2]

Probably the Yugoslav Communists were not greatly concerned at this stage with long-term plans for their country. Their immediate task was the speedy and total establishment of their power, the neutralisation of all opposition, and the reconstruction of the devastated country according to their 'Socialist' blue-print. Djilas, as the only member of Tito's cabinet from Montenegro, took special responsibility for that region. Blažo Jovanović, the Secretary of the Provincial Committee who had worked closely with him in the 1941 rising, was now its 'Prime Minister'. Djilas found him installed in the Cetinje villa which had once housed the British Legation to the tiny kingdom. The ravaged land had not yet bound up its wounds. Roads, railway-tracks and bridges lay wrecked, whole villages, and many of the towns, in ruins. The bulk of the Montenegrin Chetnik forces had withdrawn through Bosnia in the hope of reaching Austria; many were slaughtered on the way by Ustashe, others by Partisans. Some four to five hundred desperate men, Djilas reckoned, were still at large in the hills and forests of Montenegro and were being tracked down by soldiers and OZNA squads. Mihailović, with a handful of followers, was lured back into Serbia by faked signals purporting to show that he could still count on popular support there. Djilas helped Ranković concoct the counterfeit messages which, in March 1946, resulted in his capture. The Chetnik leader was then executed after a show trial in Belgrade.

Pavelić and some other leading Ustashe escaped to Austria and Italy, gave the Allied authorities the slip, and eventually found asylum in South America. The bulk of the Croat forces, together with a number of Slovene and other Quislings who attempted to surrender to the Allies, were turned back and slaughtered by their Partisan pursuers. Kill or be killed had been the rule since the outset of the civil war, and the Communists did not now stay their hand.

Tales of horror reached Montenegro, along with groups of crushed Chetniks [Djilas records]. No one liked to speak of this particular experience – not even those who made a show of their revolutionary spirit – as if it were only a horrible dream. No one spoke of it either in the Central Committee or privately amongst ourselves . . . until late in 1945 when, at a meeting of the Central Committee, Tito cried out in disgust: 'Enough of all these death sentences and all this killing! The death sentence no longer has any effect! No one fears death any more!'[3]

In Montenegro the blood-letting was accomplished with particular relish. Djilas, so representative in many respects of his countrymen, had never himself shared this particular trait; but neither did he denounce or do much to curb it; such violence seemed to him both inherent in the national spirit and justified by revolutionary necessity. He relates that one day in the summer of 1946, when he was in Slovenia with an official of the Polish Ministry of Foreign Affairs, his companion described how Stalin had rebuked the Polish Communist leaders for being soft with their enemies and had commended Tito for dealing with them very differently. 'Tito is a tower of strength,' Stalin had exclaimed. 'He wiped them all out!' Djilas related this to his comrades in the Central Committee. 'We felt,' he admits, 'a cruel but not unpleasant pride.'[4]

The liquidation of collaborators, rebels and class enemies was the business of Ranković and OZNA; Djilas was more concerned with rallying support for the new regime. When the Partisans entered Belgrade, he declares, they could not find a single member of the original local party organisation alive. Though many had taken the

The Power and the Glory

place of the fallen comrades, and recruits were now coming in fast, the cadres were still too weak for the manifold tasks of administration and government facing them. The Party's solution to such problems had always been the formation of a front organisation – the National Liberation Front (later renamed the People's Front), or the Freedom Front in Slovenia, the Fatherland Front in Bulgaria – comprising an outer shell of non-Communist well-wishers, fellow-travellers, sympathisers and aspirants and an inner core of Party members; a 'mass organisation' controlled by a 'directing nucleus'. The 'United Government' recently recognised by the Allies was an expression of this trend which had been theoretically in process since the Communists began to prepare for armed opposition to the invaders and their domestic rivals. Now it needed to be formalised and given a suitable post-war face, thus supplementing and legitimising the numerically weak Communist Party. The People's Front was accordingly conceived as a transitional expedient pending the Communists' ability to take total control of the political, economic and social life of the nation, after which the need for it would disappear.

Djilas played an active part in the formation of this People's Front. On behalf of the Central Committee he started talks with representatives of the few political groups which could be considered uncompromised by wartime collaboration or by close association with the pre-war regimes. They boiled down in Serbia to the numerically insignificant Republican Party and the Agrarians led by Dragoljub Jovanović, the Professor of left-wing but non-Communist views whose lectures he had once attended (without much enthusiasm) at Belgrade University. In 1941, in accordance with Comintern instructions to build up a broadly-based resistance front, Tito had negotiated with Jovanović, who had indicated his support in principle but had never joined the Partisans in the field. He was now approached again and agreed to accept the post of Secretary General of the People's Front. He did so in the belief that he could preserve his small party's independence and eventually break with the Communists when the post-war euphoria had evaporated and left them without popular support. He underestimated their ruthlessness and guile. Two years later, when he was deemed to have played his part, he was ousted, brought to trial on a trumped up charge of working for 'British Intelligence' and sentenced to nine years' imprisonment. The Communists might accept left-wing politicians as temporary allies, but unless they were prepared to follow the Party's lead unconditionally, they would be cynically discarded. Such allies were, in fact, regarded as particularly dangerous enemies.

171

Djilas describes the peasant party leader somewhat contemptuously as 'incorruptible and fearless, but without verve or any great ideas, Utopian, an amalgam of visions and pettiness. We leaders, particularly in Serbia, secretly nursed a pre-war hatred of him and lamented our error in not having liquidated him during "that mess" at the time of Belgrade's liberation.'[5]

The democratic politicians with whom the Communists had been obliged to cooperate in the 'United Government' received even shorter shrift. Five months after the end of the war Šubašić had ceased to be Foreign Minister and was under house arrest. With the 'bourgeois' politicians there also disappeared the vestiges of an independent press. By November the scene was set for elections to the National Assembly which were officially declared to have resulted in a ninety-six per cent victory for the People's Front, the sole contenders. In January 1946 a new Constitution, based on that of the Soviet Union, declared Yugoslavia to be a Federal People's Republic.

Whatever the constitutional form – and it was to undergo many changes in the coming years – the substance of political power, now strengthened by all the resources of an authoritarian state, remained much as it was in Partisan days. Tito, Marshal and Commander-in-Chief, Prime Minister or President, Secretary-General of the Party, wielded absolute authority. Immediately under him came the triumvirate Kardelj-Ranković-Djilas. The latter, through his control of agit-prop and his articles in the party mouthpiece *Borba*, exerted enormous influence. Foreign observers regarded him as one of the more extreme members of the government and a leading exponent of Soviet policies. A British assessment of that time classes Tito as a relative 'moderate', open to reason and anxious to preserve some ties with the West, increasingly bypassed by more militant subordinates who might end by manipulating him altogether.[6] 'The reason for this,' according to this appraisal, 'is that, in our opinion, Tito puts Yugoslavia first and these subordinates put Communism first. Amongst them we would include Kardelj, General Arso Jovanović, Ranković and Djilas – the latter, though only Minister for Montenegro, is a very powerful figure behind the scenes – Pijade and Hebrang. All are Communists of long standing.'

Tito, in fact, was no more 'moderate' than his 'extremist' subordinates; only his unerring timing and sense of what was politically practicable tended to conceal the drastic nature of his policies. He was jealous of his prestige and the retention of supreme power, though allowing his intimates a share in its exercise and enjoyment. Djilas was

172

no exception in this respect. Later he was to write of power as something which 'once it has been savoured, poisons everyone with its lotus-like sweetness, divine or diabolic, or most probably a little of both.'[7] Unlike other leading comrades, he cared little for its trappings, seldom donning a general's uniform or even a tie or a dark suit, and preferring to keep to his Partisan top-boots and the mackintosh and cap which denoted plebian origins; but it could be noted that his jacket was cut by the best tailor in Belgrade and made from the finest English stuff. He developed too a taste for powerful cars and discovered the thrill of driving at high speed, regardless of traffic regulations, through the streets of the capital. Mitra too, whilst eschewing the bourgeois fashions which other party workers were beginning to find attractive, was still young enough to keep her zest for life. Two years after the end of the war, though still determined not to let such domestic ties interfere with her independent political career, she presented her husband with a baby daughter. Milovan was pleased with the arrival of little Vukica, but still enough of a Montenegrin to attach only minor importance to a merely female addition to his family.

The new regime had been so occupied with crushing its enemies that there were few signs as yet of the Yugoslav Revolution, like others before it, beginning to devour its own children. Some comrades who had distinguished themselves in war but shown themselves less capable of discharging peace-time responsibilities had indeed lost their jobs. General Arso ceased to be Chief of Staff and was transferred to Moscow where he was soon to make trouble. Swarthy Žujović, tackling formidable problems as Minister of Finance and then of Transport but still envious of Tito's primacy, frequented the Soviet Embassy. Hebrang, responsible for Planning and Industry, adopted the Soviet view that his country had no need of an ambitious five-year plan of its own but should come to depend more, both economically and politically, on the Soviet Union. Ambitious and frustrated comrades such as these could not only count on receiving a sympathetic hearing from the Russians but could serve them too as a potential Trojan horse within a party deemed to be growing too independent.

In the spring of 1946 Tito went to Prague and Warsaw where Treaties of Friendship were signed with Yugoslavia. Djilas was a member of the strong delegation accompanying him. Hebrang took advantage of their absence to challenge the Secretary-General's authority over the Central Committee, to which he addressed a letter complaining of the personal animosity shown him by Comrade Tito. Following a stormy debate a Commission of Enquiry was set up which rejected Hebrang's charges and stripped him of his offices as Minister for Industry and President of the Economic Council. Both he and Swarthy Žujović, who had supported him, were expelled from the Politburo. From Warsaw Tito went on to Moscow and Djilas to France to attend a congress of the French Communist Party. In Paris he met Molotov who received the news of Hebrang's demotion in his usual impassive fashion.

The Americans had launched the Marshall Plan for Europe's economic recovery, but Europe was already hardening into two camps. Moscow vetoed the Plan and began to consider ways of strengthening her influence over the Soviet bloc. Tito discussed with Stalin and Dimitrov the possibility of setting up some machinery to take the place of the defunct Comintern. Djilas and Molotov touched on the same subject when they met in Paris and agreed that the journal *La Nouvelle Démocratie* published by the French Communists did not answer this need as they claimed. 'That isn't what is needed or what ought to be done,' Molotov remarked.[8] A year and a half later a new organisation, the Communist Information Bureau or Cominform, was launched at a meeting in Poland.

Andrei Zhdanov, the Soviet hard-liner, opened proceedings by denouncing the western imperialists for splitting the world into two blocks and preparing to unleash a new war against the progressive forces led by the peace-loving Soviet Union. Kardelj and Djilas, with his encouragement, then trounced the Italian and French Communist Parties for lack of militancy and mistaken tactics. Re-echoing Zhdanov's attack in *Borba*, Djilas declared that the 'imperialists in Washington and some other capitals' and 'the sharks of Wall Street' were a major threat to humanity. 'While their so-called aid corrupts a nation's ruling circles,' he wrote, 'they are in reality milking that country's wealth and thwarting its development'; whereas 'Moscow radiates freedom and justice for all mankind, pursues a policy of aid to liberation movements and to peoples struggling for independence, peace and democracy.'[9]

The Cominform included no representatives from Greece or Albania. A month before its inaugural meeting, a Greek Communist delegation had met secretly with Yugoslav, Bulgarian and Albanian representatives in Slovenia to discuss a resumption of the insurrection which had failed to carry them to power the previous year. The Yugoslav comrades now agreed to take the lead in providing food, transport facilities, and the use of camps, ostensibly for refugees; they subsequently provided arms, ammunition, artillery, and a military mission under their most experienced general Peko Dapčević. To what extent the campaign was undertaken on direct instructions from Moscow or whether it was left primarily to the initiative of the Balkan Communists, to Tito in particular, remains unclear. Stalin must certainly have given it at least his initial approval, but he may have left the detailed implementation to the Yugoslavs, who would also have to foot the bill and take the blame should the venture fail.

The Albanian case was different. There the Communist Party and its Partisans had developed under direct Yugoslav tutelage and the links which bound them to Belgrade had become so numerous and so close that the absorption of the weaker partner was assumed to be only a matter of time. The Yugoslavs exercised the same sort of patronage over their Albanian comrades as the Russians considered themselves entitled to exercise over the Yugoslavs. They had encouraged the Albanians to form their Anti-Fascist Council and their Committee of National Liberation, and now a completely Communist government. 'Without the struggle of the peoples of Yugoslavia, resistance by the small Albanian nation would have been unthinkable,' the Albanian Communist leader Enver Hoxha admitted to Yugoslav journalists. 'Without that, the small Albanian nation would have been defeated whatever sacrifices it was prepared to make.'[10] The two states were linked together in a Soviet-style Treaty of Friendship and their economies cemented by a Commercial Treaty and bolstered by a number of joint stock companies – a method of economic integration which the Russians were attempting to apply to their own advantage in Yugoslavia. Albania, with its Party, its army, its government and its economy was fast becoming a Yugoslav protectorate. Not all the Albanian Communists could bring themselves to accept this humiliating dependence. Resentment came to a head when the Central Committee member responsible for economic affairs was driven to suicide. Others turned for protection to the large diplomatic mission the Russians had established in Tirana.

At the end of 1947 Stalin sent a message to Tito declaring that the Albanian situation had got so out of hand that he should send someone to Moscow to sort out their policy differences. He suggested that Djilas should go. Why Djilas – who had not been directly involved in Albanian affairs? Stalin may have reckoned that Djilas had now been sufficiently chastened by the displeasure shown over his criticisms of the Red Army and could be more easily influenced than other Yugoslav leaders, perhaps even induced to turn against Tito if need be. At all events, Djilas was asked for and Tito agreed that he should go. 'I was flattered that Stalin had invited me specifically,' Djilas recalls, 'but I also had vague, unspoken suspicions that this was not by chance and that Stalin's intentions towards Tito and the Yugoslav Central Committee were not entirely honourable.'[11]

It was decided that Koča Popović, now Chief of Staff, and Vukmanović-Tempo, in charge of political work in the army, and a number of other officials should go with him. They set off in good spirits and with high expectations, confident that the small cloud on the horizon could be quickly dispersed. It seemed a cloud no bigger than a man's hand; or was it rather, Djilas uneasily asked himself, a cloud in the shape of a fist – Stalin's fist?

CHAPTER TWENTY-TWO

The Bear's Hug

WITHIN a few hours of his arrival in Moscow, Djilas received a message through the Yugoslav Ambassador that, if he was not too tired after the long train journey, Stalin would like to see him that same evening. Visitors to the Soviet capital generally had a very different experience. They were often kept waiting for days, even weeks, before the desired interview could be arranged, even with less exalted officials. Djilas had himself been made to kick his heels in this way on his previous visits, and he felt flattered but flustered by this unusual treatment. Was it a mark of esteem and cordiality or merely a sign that Stalin was irritably impatient? His excitement was tinged with apprehension.

At around 9 o'clock that evening Djilas was ushered into Stalin's office in the Kremlin, where he also found Molotov and Andrej Zhdanov. Stalin lost no time, after the usual greetings, in getting down to business.

'So, Central Committee members in Albania are killing themselves on your account! That's very awkward, very awkward!'

Djilas began to explain that Naku Spiru, the Albanian who had committed suicide, was against linking his country with Yugoslavia and so had found himself isolated from his comrades in the Central Committee. Stalin broke in with the unexpected remark: 'We have no special interest in Albania. We agree to your swallowing Albania!' He illustrated the words with a coarse gesture, putting his fingers to his mouth as if about to swallow them.

Djilas tried to conceal his astonishment by treating the performance as a joke. 'It's not a matter of swallowing, but of unification!' he attempted to explain.

'But that *is* swallowing!' Molotov put in, most affably.

'Yes, yes – swallowing!' Stalin repeated. 'We agree with you. You ought to swallow Albania. The sooner the better.'

Stalin too appeared to be more than cordial.

'And what about Hoxha? What's he like, in your opinion?' Stalin asked.

Djilas avoided a direct reply and let Stalin answer his own question.

'He's a petty bourgeois, inclined to nationalism? That's what we think too. Doesn't the strongest man there seem to be Xoxe?'

Djilas agreed. Koči Xoxe, a veteran Communist, was Minister of the Interior and in control of the police; he was also reputed to be stoutly pro-Yugoslav – a repute which within a short time was to lead to his disgrace, trial and execution.

They talked no more about Albania, and Stalin again surprised Djilas by a still more astonishing remark: 'There are no differences between us! You personally write Tito a despatch about this in the name of the Soviet Government and let me have it by tomorrow!' Djilas could hardly believe his ears. Stalin repeated that he wished him to draft a despatch to the Yugoslav Government in the name of the Soviet Government.

The conversation turned to trivialities. Stalin asked about Tito's health, the location of the new Cominform headquarters, and the like. Djilas managed to put in a word for his military colleagues who, he said, wished to discuss urgent questions relating to supplies for the army. Soviet officials, they found, were sometimes apt to be unhelpful and to make excuses that they could not give away 'military secrets'.

'We have no military secrets from you!' cried Stalin. 'You are a friendly Socialist country. We have no military secrets from you!'

He went to his desk and spoke to Marshal Bulganin on the telephone: 'The Yugoslavs are here – the Yugoslav delegation. They should be heard immediately!'

The meeting in the Kremlin had lasted half an hour and was now over. Stalin took the three of them off to dinner in his *dacha*. The veneration and awe which Djilas had always felt for his host were now tinged with something like affection. Was not the great Stalin in reality just 'a little old grandfather who, all his life, and still now, looked after the success and happiness of the whole Communist race?'

Stalin's *dacha* had not changed, nor the way in which their host and his guests spent their evenings. Djilas noticed that the large wall-map still hung in the entrance-hall, with its blue pencil mark encircling Stalingrad. As they glanced at it, their attention was caught by a cluster of villages round Leningrad which still had their German names dating from the time of Catherine the Great. 'German names! It's absurd that those places should still have them. See that they're changed!'

Zhdanov pulled out a pocket book and noted down Stalin's orders. Leningrad was his fief. He had been its Party Secretary and organised the desperate defence of the city against Hitler's armies in the war. Latterly, his victories had been more ingloriously achieved at the expense of the country's most talented writers, musicians, artists and scientists. Though a docile amanuensis in his master's presence,

Zhdanov had become the dreaded agit-prop dictator of Soviet literary life, exercising a real terror in all cultural matters as well as dominating the fraternal parties grouped together in the Cominform. The rest of the Politburo regarded him as an intellectual of great authority.

Djilas noticed that Molotov, the *alter ego* whose close psychological and political accord with Stalin he had written about so warmly, no longer seemed to enjoy his chief's confidence. The tension between the two men was in fact almost palpable, though Molotov had not yet had to suffer the indignity of seeing his wife arrested and exiled for alleged involvement in another of Stalin's imagined conspiracies – the proposal to turn the Crimea into a Jewish Soviet Republic which the Americans would be sure to use as a Trojan horse.[1] What Djilas chiefly noted about Molotov was his coarseness. 'We call this unloading before loading!' the Soviet Foreign Minister remarked as he started undoing his fly-buttons whilst they walked downstairs together to the men's lavatory.

Beria was again among the guests. Djilas was struck anew by his uncanny resemblance to the anti-Communist Belgrade policeman he had observed on first meeting him. Beria was a heavy drinker. Fixing Djilas with his glazed, greenish eyes, he raised a small glass of vodka mixed with pepper and invited him to drink. It had a marked effect on the sex glands, Beria assured him with a snigger. Djilas had no liking for strong liquor or coarse witticisms and complied without pleasure. Even in their cups, Stalin's guests did not dare reveal their mutual hatreds, fears and mortal intrigues. Only Stalin himself sometimes indulged in outbursts of terrifying passion. 'Without warning, he would turn on you with real viciousness,' Khrushchev recalls. 'A reasonable interrogator could not behave with a hardened criminal the way Stalin behaved with friends whom he'd invited to eat at his table.'[2]

Djilas personally had no grounds for complaint that evening. Stalin picked no quarrel with him, refrained even from broaching the delicate subject which had prompted his presence in Moscow – the deepening though as yet unacknowledged differences with Tito and the Yugoslav Central Committee. Djilas deliberately left a few openings in the evening's conversation, but no one took them. It was as if Stalin, with his uncanny intuition, sensed his guest's unspoken resolve to resist. If forced to take sides between the Soviet and the Yugoslav comrades, Djilas would go with his own people, both out of national solidarity and also because he sincerely believed in the rightness of the policies he himself had helped to frame. The Yugoslav Communists were beginning to build Socialism in their own country and in their own way, just as the Russians had built it in their way in their country. He and his comrades would of course continue to look to the Fatherland of Socialism as they had always done; but life imposed its own pattern and looking was not the same as slavish imitation. Djilas still had a deep admiration for the Soviet Union, although he had begun to find in it things which were far from perfect, or at least not suitable for emulation. And though certain of Stalin's intimates did and said things which jarred on him, as did Stalin himself at times, his sentiments towards the great leader had not in essence changed. He even felt sorry for him; sorry that no human greatness could confer immunity from nature's inexorable law that men grow old and die.

And Stalin was manifestly in decline. Djilas could not fail to note that he no longer exhibited the same confident alertness, the intellectual vigour and physical toughness which had struck him before. The war had made gigantic demands on the Soviet leader from which he would never recover. He drank less, as though afraid his health might be further impaired, though he ate more voraciously than ever. His wit, cruel, coarse and quick, had degenerated into mere love of buffoonery. He laughed at empty jokes or missed the point of some anecdotes altogether. He was more given to reminiscences than before. Only the pathological suspicion of everyone around him, and the malicious delight in testing and if possible humiliating them, were stronger than ever. Djilas by then was familiar with this trait and remained on his guard as the inconsequential talk flitted from one subject to another. Stalin suddenly asked whether there were many Jews in the Yugoslav Party. Only one of any consequence, Djilas told him; Moša Pijade, a veteran Communist and the translator of Marx's *Kapital*.

'There are no Jews in our Central Committee!' Stalin exclaimed; then, laughing triumphantly, as if he had discovered a secret: 'You are an anti-Semite; you also, Djilas, you too are an anti-Semite!'

Djilas laughed quietly and said nothing. He did not feel *touché*, as he had never been an anti-Semite, though he suspected his questioner was one. He tried to steer the conversation away and onto subjects which interested him. He asked Stalin his opinion of Dostoevski, a writer who had always fascinated him. He was given quite a straightforward answer: 'A great writer and a great reactionary! We are not publishing him because he is a bad influence on young people. But a great writer!'

They spoke about Gorki and some Russia's contemporary writers. Zhdanov laid down the law, then ingratiated himself with Stalin by quoting a remark the latter had made about a poet who had published a large edition of his own works: 'Two copies would have been enough; one for him and one for her!'

Stalin seemed pleased at being reminded of this sally. He liked to be regarded as a critic and theoretician. A couple of years later he was to astonish his entourage by publishing in *Pravda* an article dealing with some abstruse theory of linguistics of which he happened to disapprove. His last major contribution in the field of learning had been published before the first world war, *The National Question in the Light of Marxism* which Sima Marković, the former Secretary of the Yugoslav Communist Party, had unwisely tried to invoke in the polemics with Stalin which led to his downfall. Djilas was curious to learn how Stalin would define the difference between a 'nation' and a 'people'.

'They are one and the same thing!' Molotov put in.

'Nonsense!' retorted Stalin. 'They are different. A nation is the product of capitalism, with certain characteristics. By "people" we mean the workers of a given nation – workers having the same language, culture and customs.'

The conversation did not long remain on this level but drifted off again into trivialities. Before proposing the final toast to Lenin, Stalin turned to Djilas and asked him why he had not accepted an invitation passed to him through Tito to go to the Crimea for medical treatment. 'Tell Djilas that I'll cure his headaches for him!' he had said to Tito.

'I waited for an invitation through the Soviet Embassy,' Djilas explained. 'I felt awkward about forcing myself on you and causing you trouble.'

'Nonsense – no trouble at all!' Stalin replied. 'You just didn't want to come!'

Before the party broke up, Stalin put on the record of a dance from his native Georgia. He performed a few steps and then gave up.

'Age has caught up with me and I'm already on old man!' he said.

His guests vied with one another in reassuring him: 'No, no; not at all. You look fine. You're bearing up marvellously. Yes, indeed – for your age. . . . '

Stalin had, in fact, over five more years to live.

What did it all mean, Djilas asked himself as he turned over the evening's events in his mind? Nothing had been said or done to offend him; on the contrary, Stalin had gone to considerable lengths to be affable and had stopped short of any overt attempt to win him over or extract from him even an implied criticism of his comrades. He had started by disclaiming any Soviet interest in Albania and inviting the Yugoslavs to 'swallow' that small country. The idea repelled Djilas, and involuntarily he thought of those three small Baltic states which the Soviet Union had unceremoniously 'swallowed', even though he had himself found justification for it at the time. What if they had not wanted to be 'liberated' from the capitalist exploitation they were said to suffer? Perhaps the Albanian people, although already living under Communism, had no wish to enjoy the blessings of unification with an alien state. Though the Albanians, being Moslems, were his country's traditional enemies and had murdered his father, Djilas felt a good deal of sympathy for them as a nation. They and the Montenegrins were two mountain races which had much in common; a similar clan system and a fierce attachment to their independence. He remembered how his own people had been divided on the issue of unification with the Serbs – their own flesh and blood. For the Albanians, union with the Serbs and the other Slav peoples might seem even less natural. Why then should Stalin be pressing it upon Belgrade? He was left with an uncomfortable suspicion that it was all a 'provocation' – a ruse to allow the Yugoslavs enough rope to hang themselves, branded as chauvinistic aggressors in the eyes of the rest of the world.

This might explain Stalin's extraordinary request that he, a member of the Yugoslav Government, should draft a despatch purporting to come from the Soviet Government authorising the 'swallowing' of their intended victim. This could then be repudiated by Moscow and the 'despatch' shown to have been faked by Djilas. Determined not to fall into any such trap, he composed his draft in the briefest and most innocuous terms possible:

Djilas arrived in Moscow yesterday and, at a meeting held with him on the same day, there was expressed complete agreement between the Soviet Government and Yugoslavia concerning the question of Albania.

That should be safe enough; no mention of 'swallowing'! The draft was duly submitted but never sent; nor was any attempt made to use it as ammunition against Yugoslavia in the ensuing dispute.

There were still no signs so far that anything was wrong, only Djilas's vague foreboding. He and his military colleagues were not kept waiting long. At five o'clock the next afternoon they were summoned to a meeting chaired by Bulganin and attended by Marshal Vasilevsky, the Chief of the General Staff. A detailed note was made of all their requests. 'A mere trifle – you shall have everything!' Bulganian declared, and set up a committee of experts with instructions to look into things and report the following Monday.

Monday came, but there was no word of any meeting; nor on the days following. It began to look as if things were starting to go wrong – very wrong. At the end of the week they were told that 'complications' had arisen and that they must wait. They spent the time sightseeing, going to theatres, joining the reverent queue waiting to gaze on Lenin's embalmed body. They had endless discussions together. Djilas moved into a double room in the Hotel Moskva which he shared for company with Koča Popović, but not before a 'technician' had been called in to attend to the electrical installations – no doubt to install a listening device. The Yugoslav comrades chose their words carefully and generally talked to a background of radio music. Lesakov, the liaison officer assigned to them, struck them as a cross between a Party official and an intelligence agent. He seemed well informed about the affairs and leading personalities of their Central Committee and once paid them the compliment of remarking: 'In no Party in Eastern Europe is there such a closely watched foursome as yours!' No ordinary Soviet citizen dared make contact with them although they were comrades from another Communist country. They felt isolated, frustrated and uneasy.

Still no word came from the Kremlin about the nature of the 'complications' which were holding things up. Djilas wondered whether progress might be possible on some other front. By now they had been joined by an economic expert from Belgrade. They went together to call on Mikoyan, the Soviet Minister of Foreign Trade. He received them coldly, rejecting without discussion a suggestion that they might renegotiate the onerous terms of an agreement regarding the sale of Soviet films and their request for the return of railway wagons removed from Yugoslavia.

'My job is trade – not giving away gifts,' he replied curtly, showing signs of interest only when there was talk of Yugoslavia's copper which Moscow was eager to buy. Djilas quickly realised that the minister was indifferent to their country's economic needs.

Moscow's attractions were soon exhausted. The Soviet capital, on closer inspection, struck the Yugoslav visitors as for the most part little more than a vast, sprawling village. These 'men from the woods' did not take kindly to sightseeing. Tempo, as blunt in his criticisms as he was enthusiastic in his naive expectations, could be particularly awkward. Asked by his escort (an NKVD officer) what he thought of the Red Army Museum he answered that he found it frankly disappointing and went on to write down his criticisms in detail in the Visitors' Book.

The Yugoslavs, still kept waiting, asked if they might see Leningrad, and a visit was arranged. The whole atmosphere of the place, still struggling back to normal life after its terrible wartime ordeal, seemed to them altogether more human, and its people more friendly, decent and better educated. They felt they had more in common with its people and party officials than with the bureaucrats of Moscow; little could they foresee how savagely and unjustly those followers of Zhdanov would be purged after his death. Zhdanov, who had authorised their visit, received Djilas with little of his previous warmth. He asked Djilas for his opinion of an interview with Dimitrov which *Pravda* had just published. Djilas replied guardedly that the references Dimitrov was reported to have made on the desirability of a customs union between Bulgaria and Rumania seemed to him premature and insufficiently related to other questions involved. Zhdanov gave little indication of his own reactions, but it was clear that they were not very favourable either to Dimitrov's statement or to Djilas's comments.

The *Pravda* interview gave a clue to the 'complications' which had arisen between Moscow and Belgrade. Dimitrov had made his statement whilst on an official visit to Bucharest. The previous summer he had visited Tito at Bled and resumed discussions aimed at an eventual federation between Yugoslavia and Bulgaria. This was followed, in November, by the signing of a Treaty of Friendship and Mutual Assistance, the text of which had been vetted in Moscow, envisaging close economic and political cooperation between the two countries. As Tito had explained before an enthusiastic crowd in Sofia: 'We shall establish cooperation so wide-ranging and so close that the question of federation will be a mere formality!' Now Dimitrov had begun to talk as well about a customs union between Bulgaria and Rumania, and a wider federation or confederation embracing all the countries of Eastern and South-Eastern Europe.

This talk of federations and confederations seemed to the suspicious men in the Kremlin to be going too far and too fast. It is true that Dimitrov, in the course of his press conference, had taken the precaution of declaring that such questions were not at present on the agenda, but would be settled 'without consulting the Imperialists' when the time was deemed ripe. But this was by no means enough. To Stalin it seemed that the ex-Secretary-General of the Comintern was taking too much upon himself, trying to usurp the functions of the Soviet government which alone had the right to pronounce on such weighty matters, thereby promoting indiscipline amongst the ranks of the client Communist Parties of Eastern Europe and complicating Moscow's relations with the western powers. *Pravda* was made to publish a declaration disavowing the views expressed by Dimitrov and declaring that the countries concerned 'had no need of such a doubtfully constructed federation or confederation, any more than of a customs union.' Dimitrov had to eat his words and hurry to Moscow with other leading Bulgarian Communists.

A Yugoslav delegation was also summoned. Stalin expected it to be headed by Tito, but the latter prudently pleaded ill health and sent Kardelj and Bakarić in his place. They arrived on 8 February and were lodged in a village outside Moscow where Djilas related how, after a promising start, everything had come to a halt. Kardelj said that matters had come to a head in Belgrade when the Russians had objected in violent terms to Yugoslav plans to send two divisions into Albania to protect it from possible aggression on the part of Greek 'monarcho-Fascists'.

On the evening of 10 February Kardelj, Djilas and Bakarić were summoned to the Kremlin where they were joined by a Bulgarian delegation consisting of Dimitrov, Kolarov, another Comintern veteran, and Kostov, a critic of Tito but nevertheless subsequently executed on charges of 'Titoism'. Beside Stalin, Molotov, Malenkov and Zhdanov, the Soviet side included Zorin, Ambassador to Prague at the time of the recent Communist coup, and Suslov, a hard-liner and implacable enemy of Tito. Molotov opened the attack, which was directed primarily against the Bulgarians, though the Yugoslavs also knew themselves to be in the dock and perhaps looked upon as the principal accused. Serious differences had arisen, Molotov declared, between Bulgaria and Yugoslavia on the one hand and the Soviet Union on the other. This was quite 'impermissible both from the Party and the State point of view'. Stalin, doodling irritably on his scribbling block, scowled his agreement.

Molotov went on to specify the recent differences: the Bulgarian-Yugoslav Treaty, concluded, he declared, against the wishes of the Soviet Government, which believed that Bulgaria should first sign a peace treaty; the exchanges with Belgrade over Albania; Dimitrov's statement on a customs union with Rumania and an East European federation. Stalin broke in to say that Comrade Dimitrov permitted himself to get carried away at press conferences and cited a recent example of how awkward this could make things for the Soviet Union. As for Dimitrov's subsequent attempt to explain his blunder away, that had done nothing at all to improve matters, Stalin added. Dimitrov tried to excuse himself by pointing out that he had only referred to federation in general terms.

'But you agreed on a customs union, on the coordination of economic plans!' Stalin interrupted. That was tantamount to creating a unified state, Molotov added. Dimitrov continued lamely defending himself.

Yes, he admitted, he had got carried away at the press conference. But Bulgaria was in such a mess economically that closer cooperation with other countries was absolutely necessary. Stalin would not let him finish.

'You wanted to cut a figure – to say something original! But that is all wrong. Federation with Rumania is quite out of the question. What historical links are there between your two countries, or between Bulgaria and Hungary or Poland?'

Dimitrov tried to take refuge in generalities.

'But there are no essential differences between the foreign policies of Bulgaria and those of the Soviet Union!' he said weakly.

'There are enormous differences!' Stalin contradicted. 'Why deny it? Lenin's practice was always to recognise errors and repair them as quickly as possible.'

'True, we did make a mistake. But we are trying to learn from our mistakes and so do better in our foreign policy.' Dimitrov was anxious to be conciliatory, but Stalin was not to be appeased.

'Learning from your mistakes?' he sneered. 'You've been in politics all these years, a veteran political worker, and yet you are still learning from your mistakes! It's not a question of mistakes. The trouble is that the line you are taking is quite different from ours.'

Kolarov summoned up courage to come to the help of his comrade who was becoming flushed and flustered under Stalin's battering. He reminded them that the draft agreement with Rumania had in fact been previously submitted to Moscow and approved. Molotov rather shamefacedly agreed. Stalin became angrier than ever. 'So we've been making fools of ourselves too!' he shouted.

Dimitrov tried to make the most of this loophole but Stalin was not going to let him off. 'You've been behaving like a raw youth from the Komsomol!' he asserted. 'You want to make a sensation, just as if you were still the Secretary of the Comintern! You and the Yugoslavs never tell us what you're up to. We have to find out for ourselves. You simply confront us with a *fait accompli*.'

Kostov pleaded economic necessity: 'It's hard, being a small, under-developed country. . . . ' Stalin cut him short and told him to take his problems to the Ministry concerned.

The Bulgarians had had enough; it was now the turn of the Yugoslavs. Stalin turned to Kardelj and told him to state the Yugoslav case. It was impossible to know what Stalin was thinking, what line he would take. At one point he interrupted Kardelj to say: 'What about waiting a while with the federation with Bulgaria? Perhaps in the meantime the USSR could join the Yugoslav federation!'

Was this one of Stalin's sarcastic jokes or was it meant to be taken more seriously? Did Stalin wish to humiliate Kardelj by reminding him of his remarks to the Soviet Ambassador in Belgrade about Yugoslavia becoming part of the Soviet Union? It was no secret that the grouping of the East European states into federations linked with the Soviet Union was one of the possibilities then under consideration in Moscow.[3] But Stalin quickly changed tack and took a different line.

Like Dimitrov, Kardelj was flushed with embarrassment and could not get his words out easily. He began by making the point that the Bled agreement with Tito and Dimitrov had also first been vetted by Moscow. It had been approved, except for the question of its duration which they had amended, at Moscow's request, from perpetuity to twenty years. Molotov, uncomfortable too under Stalin's disapproving glare, could not deny it. Apart from the point he had mentioned, which had been put right as Moscow wished, Kardelj concluded that he knew of no foreign policy difference.

Stalin refused to admit it. 'Nonsense! There are differences – serious differences! What about Albania? What have you to say on that? You did not consult us about sending your army into Albania!'

Kardelj said that they had obtained the Albanian Government's consent, but that did not satisfy Stalin either. 'This will lead to international trouble!' he went on. 'Albania is an independent state. The fact remains that you didn't consult us about sending in two divisions.'

Kardelj said that the matter of sending in Yugoslav troops was not, in any case, finally settled. He repeated that he could not think of any issue of international politics on which his government had failed to consult the Soviet Government.

Stalin remained adamant. 'No, you don't consult us at all! It's not simply just a mistake on your part. It's your policy; yes, your policy!'

Seeing it hopeless to convince him, Kardelj fell silent. Molotov reverted to the Bulgarian-Yugoslav Treaty and asked Dimitrov for an explanation of one of its clauses. Dimitrov said something about it signifying solidarity with the United Nations in 'resisting hot-beds of aggression'.

'No – that means preventive war!' Stalin thundered, and began berating him again. Molotov renewed the attack on the proposed Bulgarian-Rumanian customs union. Kardelj cautiously cited the case of the Benelux countries where a customs-union had proved beneficial. Stalin pooh-poohed the example; it was just an unimportant arrangement between Belgium and tiny Luxembourg, he said. Djilas had it on the tip of his tongue to point out that the customs union included the Netherlands – hence the *ne* in Benelux – but managed to restrain himself.

Stalin then returned to the subject of the Bulgarian-Yugoslav federation and surprised them by declaring that it was quite different from the Bulgarian-Rumanian case and that it ought to be carried into effect at once.

'Let it be done immediately! First Bulgaria and Yugoslavia should unite – and Albania should join them later!'

He turned to the problem of Greece, asking Kardelj what prospects he considered the insurrection to have. Provided there was no foreign intervention and no serious political or military blunders were made, Kardelj said he thought its prospects very good.

Stalin disagreed. Did he really think that Britain and the United States – the most powerful state in the world – would let Greece be lost to them? Of course not. There was no chance of success at all of the insurrection succeeding and it was folly to go on encouraging it. 'The rising in Greece must be stopped; and stopped as quickly as possible!'

The discussion tailed off in other directions – to China, to Somalia, to economic matters – and then came back again to the proposed Bulgarian-Yugoslav federation. The two delegations were to get together and discuss the details further amongst themselves, he told them. Stalin then brought the meeting, which had lasted some two hours, to a close with the customary invocation to Lenin: 'We who were disciples of Lenin sometimes had our differences – and even quarrels – with him. But later on we would talk things over amongst ourselves, reach our conclusions – and go forward again!'

That evening at the Kremlin was a shattering experience for the Yugoslav comrades. The treatment meted out to them left them with such a sense of bewildered indignation and frustration that when Djilas began to commiserate with Kardelj as they were being driven back to their villa, Kardelj motioned him to be quiet. He had not recovered his customary composure when, twenty-four hours later, he received a midnight summons to report again to the Kremlin where he was handed two sheets of paper by Molotov who curtly told him to sign. It was the text of a proposed Treaty of Consultation devised so as to tie the unreliable Yugoslavs still more tightly to Stalin's apron-strings. Such was Kardelj's agitation that he put his name in the wrong place. The documents had to be retyped and the signing repeated the following day; but the treaty itself was to remain a dead letter.

The same day the Yugoslavs gathered for lunch at Dimitrov's to work out details of the proposed federation. They had not much heart for their task; they did it mechanically and without their former conviction simply because it was required of them. Why, after giving them such a drubbing, had Stalin told them to go ahead? The more Djilas and Kardelj thought about it, the more convinced they became that it was nothing but a trick. Stalin was out to destroy the unity of the Yugoslav Party, its independence, its loyalty to Tito. He knew the Bulgarians to be more subservient and dependent on the Soviet Government. He could count on them to do whatever they were told, and he intended to make use of them, by amalgamating the two parties and states, to extend his full control over Tito's domain. Djilas and his comrades agreed that they must not fall into the snare and that pressure for immediate federation with the Bulgarians must be resisted. This was what they would recommend to Tito. The delegation left Moscow as soon as Kardelj had signed the undertaking required of him. Djilas could not wait to get back. Even the perils and hardships of their Partisan days seemed preferable to this humiliating stay in the Soviet capital. 'The sooner we can get back to our hills and forests the better!' he exclaimed to Kardelj.

Yet even now he still looked on the Soviet Union's great and terrible leader with much of his former veneration. It was with a pang of disappointment that he left the Kremlin after their long session without an invitation to dinner at Stalin's *dacha*. 'I felt a sadness and emptiness because of this,' he confesses. 'So great was my human, sentimental fondness for him still.'

Back in Belgrade, where Djilas presented his report to the Central Committee, he could still end by declaring – and still believe what he said – 'But there is no need to doubt for a moment the great love Stalin bears our entire Party, the Central Committee, and particularly Comrade Tito.'[4]

CHAPTER TWENTY-THREE

The Bear's Claws

As soon as the delegation got back from Moscow Tito called a meeting of the Central Committee. They gathered on the morning of 1 March 1948 at his residence at 15 Rumanska, the commodious villa on Dedinje where the Marshal preferred to live when not occupied with official duties in the White Palace. He began by painting a sombre picture of the difficulties and misunderstandings which seemed to be multiplying daily. Moscow was not providing the aid and trade on which the plans for Yugoslavia's economic recovery were based. The Soviet-Yugoslav joint stock companies, of which only two had so far been formed, were in any case most unfairly weighted in favour of the Soviet side. The Russians refused to agree that the Yugoslavs needed any heavy industry or a strong army and were withholding the arms and supplies needed for the nation's defence. Kidrič, who had taken over Hebrang's responsibilities for heavy industry, cited further details of the economic pressures being applied against the country.

Abroad, the trouble over Albania was growing more serious. On the proposed federation with Bulgaria Tito said that, as matters now stood, this could only place them at a disadvantage and should be resisted.

'We should then have a single Party with the Bulgarians. But our strength lies in unity of will and action. They differ from us ideologically and would act as a Trojan horse.' And he added: 'Bulgaria would at present merely be a dead weight. She is a poor country, and besides, she still has heavy war reparations to pay to Greece.'

Ranković supported Tito's remarks, adding that in Bulgaria the Russians had a finger in every pie and the Minister of the Interior was completely under their thumb.

Kardelj, Tempo and Djilas then described their experiences in Moscow. They all agreed that the Russians had struck them as interested only in the aggrandisement of the Soviet Union rather than in true cooperation between countries advancing towards Socialism.

'I do not believe they will stop at economic pressure on our country,' Djilas declared. 'In my opinion, the basic question is whether Socialism is to develop freely or by the expansion of the Soviet Union!'[1]

His comforting conclusion that, all the same, he still believed that Comrade Stalin and the Russians genuinely cherished real affection for their Yugoslav comrades had a hollow ring.

One thing was certain; the situation had become critical – so critical that Tito disconcerted the company by offering to resign as President of the Government.[2] He wanted to test whether the others were firmly behind him and was clearly relieved when his proposal was turned down with loud protestations of support. There was general agreement that the projected union with Bulgaria would spell the end of Yugoslavia's political independence and must therefore be rejected. Feeling on this was all but unanimous; only one member of the Central Committee had reservations. Swarthy Žujović sat there saying little but taking careful note of everything. Some days later Djilas happened to drive past the Soviet Embassy and noticed Swarthy's car parked in front of it. Challenged as to what business had brought him there, Swarthy became embarrassed and produced some lame story about settling difficulties which had arisen over the import of a new car for the Ambassador.

'So a Minister of the Yugoslav Government goes kowtowing to the Soviet Ambassador to get him a car!' Djilas exclaimed sarcastically. No one believed Swarthy's explanation; they also suspected that Hebrang, although no longer in office, was busy intriguing with the Russians and feeding them with reports highly critical of the Party leadership.

The tone of the exchanges between Belgrade and Moscow continued to grow sharper. Eighteen days after the Central Committee meeting Tito wrote to complain about the offensive way Soviet officials were behaving towards their Yugoslav colleagues in Tirana and the refusal of the Soviet Minister for Foreign Trade to conclude a commercial agreement for the current year. On the same day General Barskov, who had succeeded Korneyev as head of the Soviet Military Mission, called on the Yugoslav Chief of Staff to inform him that all military advisers and instructors had been ordered back to the USSR since they found themselves 'surrounded by hostility' in Yugoslavia. The day after that – 19 March – the Soviet *chargé d'affaires* broke the news to Tito that he had received similar instructions with regard to all civilian advisers. Tito at once drafted a letter to Molotov declaring that he was 'amazed and deeply hurt' at the injustice of these measures and stating that, on the contrary, the Soviet representatives had always been treated in the most friendly and cooperative fashion. He believed that such allegations must be based on serious misunderstandings and he asked to be told frankly what grounds the Russians had for their complaints and dissatisfaction.

A week later the Russians sent their reply. It was handed to Tito, who was in Zagreb at the time, by Ambassador Lavrentijev who was accompanied by his Counsellor. The letter consisted of eight closely typed pages and bore the signatures of Stalin and Molotov. Tito at once sensed trouble from the opening sentence: 'We consider your answer untruthful and therefore completely unsatisfactory.' He felt shattered by its harsh, uncompromising tone but managed to reply coldly without betraying his emotion: 'We shall give the letter our attention!'

He kept his visitors standing and within five minutes the interview was over.[3]

When they had gone he read the letter over several times with great care. It bore the date 27 March 1948 – the seventh anniversary of the famous coup which had provoked Hitler's wrath and the destruction of the old bourgeois state; the implied reminder of Yugoslavia's vulnerability was ominous. The letter reiterated the charges that the Soviet advisers had been meeting with hostility and recalled the derogatory remarks ascribed to Djilas about the conduct of Red Army officers. Not only were Soviet officials denied information to which they a right but they were subjected to surveillance, just as if they were in a hostile bourgeois country. Though lip-service was paid to friendship with the USSR, Soviet achievements were constantly belittled by 'such questionable Marxists as Djilas, Vukmanović, Kidrič, Ranković and others'. In this connection, Stalin and Molotov observed menacingly, 'we think the political career of Trotsky quite instructive'. They went on to criticise the Yugoslav Party for maintaining its conspiratorial character. Its Central Committee was run on non-democratic lines; most members had been coopted rather than elected, and there was virtually no criticism or self-criticism practised within it. Instead of the Party controlling the secret police, the police controlled the party. Rather than the Party being the 'controlling the force in the country' it had merged its identity with that of the Popular Front and could not be regarded as truly Marxist-Leninist. Nor did it show the proper spirit of class struggle, for 'capitalist elements' were still dominant in the villages. Finally, the writers of the letter expressed indignant surprise that an 'English spy' in the person of Vlatko Velebit, Tito's skilled negotiator who had been stubbornly defending Yugoslav interests in the recent discussions over the joint-stock companies, should hold the key post of Assistant Foreign Minister.

Tito sent urgently for Kardelj, Djilas, Ranković and Kidrič. Whilst waiting for them to arrive he began drafting his reply. The unthinkable had happened; the Soviet Union, which had nurtured him politically and in whose image he believed that he was rebuilding his own country, had disowned and denounced him! This was the terrible news he now had to break to his closest comrades, though he was confident of their loyalty. The outside world had not yet begun to suspect the existence of such hidden tensions. Trieste continued to sour relations with the West. His government was also in dispute with Washington over the return of Yugoslav gold which the Americans claimed should be offset against the value of expropriated American property.

On the Yugoslav side, however, revolutionary euphoria seemed as great as ever. Djilas waxed particularly enthusiastic to the Ambassador of Czechoslovakia over the recent Communist takeover in that country. Politicians and commentators in the developed countries, he declared, liked to claim that Socialism had nothing to offer them; they said it was only suited to primitive societies like Tsarist Russia. Czechoslovakia had a highly developed industry, a long tradition of democratic freedom, and good contacts with the West. Now the latter would see that Socialism could flourish too in advanced countries. This had great historical significance and would hearten the working classes of Italy and France in their struggle too.[4]

When they learned the contents of Stalin's letter, Tito's comrades were as thunderstruck as he himself had been. Ranković, Djilas and Kidrič, branded as 'dubious Marxists' (Kardelj had not been named, perhaps in the hope of splitting the ranks of the leadership) at once offered to resign from the Central Committee as a gesture to pacify the Russians. Tito would not hear of it. What would he do without them? They were all much moved. The only differences arose over the tactics to adopt for resisting. Ranković, and at first Tito himself, favoured taking a stand simply on the basis of state-to-state relations, whilst Kardelj, Djilas and Kidrič thought the field should be widened to embrace theoretical points as well. At all events, the step most urgently needed was to rally the broadest possible support from the Party. A plenary session of the Central Committee was fixed for 12 April. It would be the first genuine plenum to be held since the Committee was set up in Zagreb in the autumn of 1940. Since then, 'Central Committee' meetings had in fact been no more than meetings of its Politburo – Tito and the Kardelj-Ranković-Djilas triumvirate – to which other leading Communists might also be invited. The place chosen for the plenum was the library of the old Royal Palace, a residence kept for official guests and considered less likely to be 'bugged' or vulnerable to a raid or sabotage. Tito believed that the Russians would now stop at nothing and he was taking no chances.

Tito opened the debate by reading the letter from Moscow. It was primarily a question of relations between one state and another, he told them; the nation's independence was involved. All the rest was secondary. Then he called on each of those present to give his opinion. Seventeen spoke briefly in full support.[5] Moša Pijade raised a laugh by remarking in his most caustic manner: 'The first thing that surprised me about the Moscow letter, Comrades, was its really almost illiterate style!'

When the turn came for Swarthy Žujović to speak he startled everyone by declaring that he thoroughly disagreed: 'I appeal to your revolutionary conscience, Comrades! I am against sending a letter on these lines to the Soviet Central Committee. Make no mistake about it – great issues are at stake. I'm opposed to taking this stand against the USSR and the Soviet Central Committee. Our place is beside them and against the Imperialists! We did our bit in the war and now we've come to power and into contact with the Soviet Union. Each and every word from Stalin deserves to be carefully weighed. What will our own people think if we start taking issue with Stalin? If we do that, we should be making a terrible mistake!'

Then he turned to the various charges levelled against the Yugoslav Party. He was interrupted by angry cries, whilst Tito, much agitated, rose from his seat and paced up and down muttering: 'But this is treason! – treason against the people, the state, and the Party!'

'Can you really think me a Trotskyist, Swarthy?' Djilas asked him.

'No, I don't, but – '

'And are we really guilty of taking the capitalist path, of merging the Party in the People's Front?' Tito went on. 'Are there really people spying for England in our government?'

It was at this point that Ranković brought up Swarthy's visit to the Soviet Embassy and Djilas contemptuously described his explanation of the affair as mere kowtowing.

The Plenum went into recess. When it reassembled, its first act was to set up a three-man commission to investigate the cases of Swarthy Žujović and Andrija Hebrang, both under suspicion for informing, or rather for misinforming, the Soviet Embassy of confidential matters relating to the Yugoslav Party. 'That would be treason!' Tito warned. 'No one has the right to love his own country less than the Soviet Union!' The Plenum then went on to approve the reply which was sent to Moscow after some slight amendments had been made to Tito's original draft. Many years later, Tito was to accuse Djilas of having tampered with the text. Since the final version bore Tito's and Kardelj's signatures it is difficult to see how the letter could have been sent out without their full endorsement.

The Yugoslav reply began by deploring the harsh tone of the Soviet letter and expressing indignant surprise that it seemed to have been based on the fabrications of malicious informants. All the criticisms were rejected. The request to reduce the number of Moscow's military advisers was in no sense due to anti-Sovietism but simply a measure of economy. The remarks attributed to Djilas about the Red Army officers were grossly distorted, the comparison with Trotsky unmerited and insulting. The Yugoslav Communist Party had never belittled the achievements of the Soviet Union and its Party; on the contrary, it had zealously inculcated love and admiration for them. But though looking for inspiration to the Russian Revolution, the Yugoslav Party was 'developing Socialism in somewhat different forms.' It was not controlled by the secret police nor had it lost its identity in the People's Front. Far from lending encouragement to capitalist elements, it was mercilessly rooting them out. As to Velebit, his case was being looked into, but there were no grounds so far for suspicion. Passing over to the offensive, the letter went on to accuse Soviet Intelligence of spying on Yugoslavia's state and party leaders and trying to suborn its citizens. It concluded with an appeal for the restoration of good relations and the despatch of delegates from the Soviet Party who could see the situation for themselves.

Tito wound up the Plenum with a further denunciation of Žujović and a reaffirmation of Yugoslavia's right to preserve her independence. He defended the Party and its policies and appealed for unity: 'Our Revolution has clean hands, Comrades, and it does not devour its children!'

All the same, the Commission of Investigation quickly found against Hebrang and Žujović who were expelled from the Party and arrested. Žujović later recanted, but Hebrang was declared to have committed suicide in prison. Time was to show that the Yugoslav Revolution, like others, *did* devour its children, though it may have lingered rather longer than others over the meal. Tito had nothing of the sadism, the pathological suspiciousness and vindictiveness of Stalin; but he was no less determined than the Soviet dictator to hold and retain absolute power; and power constantly feeds on those who might otherwise destroy it. 'The Revolution which does not eat its children is not a true Revolution,' Djilas was to discover, 'just as the children who, because of their revolutionary illusions, allow the Revolution to devour them are not real genuine revolutionaries.'[6]

The clash with Moscow was quickly to test the value of those political friendships to which so many eloquent tributes had been paid during

The Progress of a Revolutionary

Tito's recent round of visits to the East European capitals. Gomulka, the Polish leader, had been particularly fulsome in his praises on his return visit to Yugoslavia. Dimitrov was an even older and more trusted friend. A week after the Central Committee meeting at the Old Palace he passed through Belgrade on his way to Prague. Djilas was at the station to meet him. The Bulgarian leader took advantage of a quiet moment together to clasp him warmly by the hand and whisper: 'Stand firm!'[7] But such solidarity could not stand long against Moscow's pressure. When passing through Belgrade again on his way back to Bulgaria, Dimitrov took care not to show himself at the station, and this time there was no Djilas there to greet him. As for Gomulka, before long he would find himself dismissed and under arrest. Khrushchev, speaking from his intimate experience of the methods favoured by Stalin and the Stalinists, explains that 'Gomulka's opponents used those [pro-Tito] speeches against him, saying he had sympathised with Titoist positions. This was enough for Stalin; he considered anyone who had close contacts with Tito to be little better than Tito himself.'[8]

Stalin lost no time in whipping up support for his campaign against the Yugoslavs by circulating copies of his letter of 27 March to other members of the Cominform. Soon the Central Committees of those parties began to react in the manner required of them. On 16 April Yudin, the Cominform representative in Belgrade, handed Tito a note from Zhdanov enclosing a letter from the Hungarian Party couched in even more offensive terms than Stalin's. Similar missives were shortly sent by the Czech, Polish, Rumanian and Bulgarian comrades. The Yugoslavs must be left in no doubt as to their isolation. We know from Khrushchev's famous 'secret speech' to the Twentieth Congress of the Soviet Party how confident Stalin was that he could soon bring Tito to heel. Once, Khrushchev elsewhere recalls, he heard the Soviet leader boast: 'I have only to shake my little finger – and there will be no more Tito!' 'We have paid dearly for the shaking of that little finger,' Khrushchev went on to say. 'No matter how much or how little Stalin shook not only his little finger but everything else he could shake, Tito did not fall. Why? The reason was that Tito had behind him a state and a people who had gone through a severe school of fighting for liberation and independence, a people which gave support to its leaders. . . . This does not mean that the Yugoslav leaders did not make mistakes or did not have shortcomings. But these mistakes and shortcomings were magnified in a monstrous manner by Stalin which resulted in a break of relations with a friendly country.'[9]

Stalin's reaction to the Yugoslav's attempts to exculpate themselves was an even harsher and fuller denunciation dated 4 May 1948, rehearsing all the former grievances and adding a number of new ones; not only Velebit, but the Yugoslav Ambassador in London and three members of his staff were accused of being English spies; the Soviet Ambassador to Belgrade was treated like the representative of a bourgeois state whilst the American Ambassador acted 'as if he owned the place'; even after Tito's offensive speech in Ljubljana, of which Moscow had already complained, the Yugoslavs expected the USSR to back their claims to Trieste to the point of war; their boasted social reforms were 'almost negligible' and no serious attempt was being made to collectivise the peasants; the Party was not truly Communist and its leaders were guilty of 'boundless arrogance' and Trotskyist errors; they exaggerated their military achievements, whereas their movement had been all but destroyed after the German attack on Drvar and was only saved when 'the Soviet Army came to their aid, crushed the German invader and liberated Belgrade.' The letter ended by declaring that since the Yugoslav Party arrogantly persisted in its errors, no delegates would be sent to it from the Soviet Party.

When, on 9 May, the Central Committee met again to consider this fresh onslaught, Djilas found to his dismay that his own alleged offences figured prominently amongst Stalin's charges. His unfortunate references to the Soviet officers accused of misconduct were again dragged up and the explanation given by 'this pitiful Marxist' brushed aside, because 'Comrade Djilas did not recall the main difference between the Socialist Soviet Army, which liberated the peoples of Europe, and the bourgeois English army, whose function is to oppress and not to liberate the peoples of the world.' Stalin's letter concluded by pointing out that Djilas's anti-Soviet attitude had not been challenged by other members of the Yugoslav Politburo although it had been the basis for what the Soviet leaders considered to be a slanderous campaign conducted by the Yugoslav Communist leaders against representatives of the Red Army in Yugoslavia, and all this had been the reason for the withdrawal of Soviet military advisers. Stalin pointed out that the whole matter had ended with Djilas, as member of a Yugoslav delegation, visiting Moscow, where he apologised to Stalin and asked that his 'unpleasant error' should be forgotten. Stalin concluded that the Soviet version was very different from that given in the letter of Tito and Kardelj and added that unfortunately Djilas's error 'was no accident'.

The Central Committee decided to send an answer that was short and firm, yet not intransigent. It expressed regret that the explanations given had been brushed aside and declined a proposal put to it by Moscow to meet with other Cominform delegates to discuss matters which were already clearly prejudged. The letter concluded however by expressing readiness to 'show by our deeds that the accusations against us are unjust' and stating that 'we are resolutely building socialism and remain loyal to the Soviet Union, loyal to the doctrine of Marx, Engels, Lenin and Stalin.' The Central Committee also endorsed the findings of the Commission of Investigation into the cases of Hebrang and Žujović, whose arrests quickly followed. This provoked a fresh outburst from Moscow threatening to brand them as 'criminal murderers' should any harm come to the two men and demanding that Soviet representatives be present at their interrogation – a demand which was at once indignantly refused. A renewed call to submit the dispute to the judgement of the Cominform was similarly rejected. An emissary arriving from Moscow with a final summons to this effect was recognised as an NKVD officer who had taken a leading part in the arrest and liquidation of Gorkić, Tito's predecessor as Secretary-General of the Party, and other leading Yugoslav Communists in Moscow in 1937.

The Yugoslavs were told that, whether they attended or not, the Cominform meeting scheduled to take place at Bucharest would be held at the end of June. It was then that the dispute was made public. In a violently worded communiqué the Cominform pronounced anathema on the Yugoslav leaders and appealed to 'healthy elements' in the Party to replace them. The Central Committee riposted with a vigorous rejection of the Soviet-inspired accusations and a reaffirmation of confidence in the Party leadership. It was drafted by Djilas, working all through the night, with some amendments formulated chiefly by Kardelj and approved by a plenum held the following day. A full-scale Party Congress, at which the rank and file would be called upon to express themselves on the dispute, was called for the end of July.[10]

The sensational announcement that the leaders of the Yugoslav Communist Party had 'placed themselves outside the ranks of the Information Bureau' was made on 28 June, St Vitus's Day, a date charged for the Yugoslavs with deep symbolic significance. On that day in 1389 the Orthodox Serbian Empire had gone down at Kosovo before the Moslem armies and given way to four centuries of Turkish rule. On the same day in 1914, the murder of the Austrian Archduke at Sarajevo by Bosnian terrorists sparked off World War I. On 28 June 1919 the Treaty of Versailles ending that war was signed, and exactly two years later, the constitution giving the South Slavs their new state. Now, on

St Vitus's Day 1948, Tito and his fellow rebels saw themselves expelled from the Communist family in which they believed themselves entitled to an honoured and prominent place. The world looked on amazed. Some said it was all a trick to take in the West. Other predicted Tito's immediate fall and his country's capitulation to Soviet pressure. For Tito and his close-knit band of 'dubious Marxists' the excommunication was a traumatic experience. It shattered their assumption that the interests of their nation, their Party and themselves were necessarily identical with those of the world revolutionary movement headed by Moscow, and that their future would be based on material and doctrinal solidarity with the 'Socialist camp'. The bottom had been knocked out of their Marxist world.

CHAPTER TWENTY-FOUR

Destination Unknown

THERE was less than a month in which to prepare the Party Congress which would test the loyalty of the rank and file. No such gathering had been held for twenty years; the last was the Fourth Congress held at Dresden, when the Party was small and weak and its pre-Tito leadership in ineffectual exile. The purpose of the present Congress was to celebrate the Party's wartime and post-war achievements, to reaffirm loyalty to its leaders, and to reject the Cominform's calumnies.[1]

Criticism of Stalin and the Soviet Union was to be avoided. The Congress hall (the same in which Draža Mihailović had lately been tried and condemned to death) was bedecked with the obligatory portraits of Marx, Lenin and Stalin as well as Tito's own; the speeches were interlarded with quotations from Stalin's works and punctuated with shouts of 'Tito-Stalin! Tito-Stalin!' Only twenty minutes of Tito's marathon review of events since 1928 were taken up with the 'monstrous accusations against our Party and its leaders', and his repudiation of them, though proudly firm, was moderate and counciliatory. He ended by declaring that 'we shall do everything in our power to restore relations between our Party and the Communist Party of the Soviet Union . . . and show by deeds, through its steadfastness and unity, through its utter loyalty to the teachings of Marx, Lenin and Stalin, that it has not swerved from their teachings.'

Was this pure expediency? Did Tito still hope against hope for a reconciliation which, with his intimate knowledge of Moscow's ways, he knew in his heart he could never expect? Was it a defiant gesture to show that those under attack were better Marxists than the attackers? Later, Tito was to confide to Vlada Dedijer, the Partisan diarist now turned court biographer: 'I had to give Stalin time to behave in such a way that people in Yugoslavia would say "Down with Stalin!" of their own without my having to suggest it to them!'[2]

Other speakers at the Congress were equally circumspect. Kardelj kept his harsh words for the American warmongers and the Marshall Plan and reaffirmed the aim of Yugoslav policy as 'close cooperation with, and all-round support for, the peace-loving, democratic, anti-imperialist policy of the Soviet Union and the People's Democracies.' Ranković stressed that the Yugoslav Party had always 'successfully utilised the immense, comprehensive experiences of the Communist Party of the Soviet Union'.

Djilas took a similar line in acknowledging that 'the ideological struggle in the Soviet Union during the period of transition to Communism will have far-reaching significance for all countries, but particularly for us on our way to the development of Socialism,' though he did appeal for more attention to be given to 'elaborating *our* reality and the results of *our* Revolution and the paths of development *here* on the basis of Marxism Leninism!' He sang the praises of Socialist Realism and lashed out against 'the excesses of various Cubists, Surrealists, Existentialists, "artists" and "writers" such as Picasso and Sartre,' and warned that unjustified Cominform criticism should not mislead the Yugoslav comrades into 'under-rating the progress and achievements of contemporary philosophical-theoretical thought in the Soviet Union'. In short, he assured the Congress, 'there is no divergence whatsoever between the principles of our Party and the general Marxist-Leninist principles expounded in the letters of the Central Committee of the Communist Party of the Soviet Union and in the so-called resolution of the Information Bureau.'

The Fifth Congress ended with a resounding vote of confidence in Tito and the leadership. Few of the two thousand and more delegates, representing half a million Party members, had not served under Tito in the war. They were proud and moved to be reminded of the perils and hardships they had passed through together and the victory to which he had led them. They were relieved too to be told that the misunderstandings which had led to Moscow's puzzling displeasure would assuredly be removed and good relations restored. All the same, some alarm and bewilderment remained and were apt to reappear when the euphoria of the rally had worn off and the delegates returned home. A typical case was that of Ilija Bulatović, Secretary of the Party's Regional Committee for Bijelo Polje, an honest, semi-educated peasant whom Djilas had known before and during the war. After the publication of the Cominform denunciation at the end of June, Bulatović sent a letter appealing to the Central Committee to remain true to the Socialist Fatherland. When he came to Belgrade as a delegate to the Congress Djilas talked with him and thought he had convinced him that the Party was following the correct line. But back amongst his comrades the old doubts returned. Bulatović and a dozen others took to the woods in a typical Montenegrin gesture of protest. They were hunted down and killed out of hand.[3]

There were many like Bulatović whom, sooner or later during the ensuing months, the Party failed to carry with them. Some acted out of conviction, others from opportunism or as a result of Soviet enticement. Žujović and Hebrang, whom Moscow had apparently favoured as the political leaders to replace Tito, were safely behind bars. But a few, like the Yugoslav Ambassador to Rumania and some of those on courses in Moscow, opted to remain where they were. Others fled, or attempted to flee, from Yugoslavia to join them. On the night of 12-13 August General Arso Jovanović was shot by frontier guards, it was announced, as he was illegally trying to cross the frontier into Rumania. Tito's former Chief of Staff, aggrieved at his demotion and inveigled, it is said, by the daughter of a Red Army general with whom he had become infatuated whilst in Moscow, was apparently groomed to play a principal part in the anti-Tito movement. Imbued with the same Russophil fanaticism were a number of other prominent Montenegrins. General Petričević, deputy head of the Army's political department, and Colonel Vlado Dapčević, brother of the famous general, were both arrested whilst trying to escape with Arso. Another prominent figure was Pero Popivoda, a pre-war Communist well known to Djilas. Thanks to his rank of air force general, he was able to steal a plane and fly to join the Cominformists.

Such defections worried Djilas and complicated his task, as head of agit-prop, of defending the Party's stand without openly criticising the Soviet Union and its formidable chief whose initiative in instigating the Cominform's anti-Tito campaign it was becoming increasingly difficult to disguise. 'We certainly recognise the leading role of the USSR in the struggle for Socialism in the world,' he wrote in *Borba*, but added that those 'who think they can strengthen the leading role of the USSR by belittling the struggle of Yugoslavia or other nations are mistaken.'[4] The struggle, he continued with unabated revolutionary optimism, 'is one to create a new man, a man whose consciousness and emotions will be different from those of capitalist man. The new man will be unselfish, sincere, brave and modest, holding the people's welfare and the people's property above all else. He struggles courageously for truth. He fights relentlessly against lies, denunciations and cheating. He is sincere and open, trained to recognise the enemy.' This new man, Djilas concluded hopefully, was already emerging out of the blood and sweat of the struggle for national liberation and the struggle to construct Socialism. The creation of the new man, in short, was the crowning achievement of the Party.

Truth to tell, there were precious few signs as yet, after three years of revolutionary birth-pangs, of any such paragons emerging, least of all in the ranks of the Yugoslav Communist Party. Nor did its sister Party in the Soviet Union, though so much older, seem any more successful in producing them. Almost every day brought to light fresh examples of trickery, venomous spite and arrogant egoism on the part of the Soviet Communist Party towards its Yugoslav comrades. Those Yugoslavs who happened to find themselves studying in Soviet institutions were hindered by every means possible from returning home. Soviet Intelligence was active in recruiting from amongst them and from Yugoslav citizens at home. Every form of economic pressure was applied against the government – the withholding of credits and capital resources, restrictions on trade, interruption of rail and postal communications, exclusion from Moscow's new Council for Mutual Economic Assistance (COMECON). The Yugoslav-Soviet Treaty of Friendship was denounced, Tito's Ambassador expelled from Moscow. Yugoslavia's neighbours, the 'Peoples' Democracies', were purged of all those suspected of Titoist sympathies and spurred on to acts of hostility.

Menacing manoeuvres were held and frontier incidents provoked as threats of invasion intensified. 'I am absolutely sure,' Khrushchev was later to declare, 'that if the Soviet Union had a common border with Yugoslavia, Stalin would have intervened militarily. As it was, though, he would have had to go through Bulgaria, and Stalin knew that he was not strong enough to get away with that. He was afraid the American imperialists would actively support the Yugoslavs – not out of sympathy with the Yugoslav form of Socialism but in order to split and demoralise the Socialist camp.'[5] Tito too was quick to take this possibility into account. Once, in the summer of 1948, when they were on a visit to Split together, he remarked to Djilas: 'The Americans are not fools! They won't let the Russians reach the Adriatic!'[6] Did the preservation of Yugoslavia's independence then ultimately depend on help from the 'American imperialists'? Could the 'new man' be saved only through the help of 'capitalist man'? It was a startlingly new and ideologically shocking thought, but somehow Djilas found it strangely reassuring.

But those who predicted that Tito's break with Stalin would drive him at once into the arms of the West were quickly disillusioned. Belgrade took the line that this was a dispute between comrades, a quarrel within the Communist family which in no sense affected its common stand against the 'imperialists', even where at least diplomatic support from the latter would clearly strengthen the Yugoslavs' hand. This was demonstrated within a month of the Cominform's anathema when delegates from the Soviet Union, the East European countries,

Britain and the United States met to adopt a new Convention governing their joint use of the Danube. Though insultingly ostracised by their fellow Communists the Yugoslav representatives voted in solidarity with the 'Socialist camp' for an arrangement which assured the Soviet Union full control of the international waterway, though it would clearly have been to their advantage to have Britain and America represented on the governing body as a counterweight to Moscow.

Had not Tito replied to Stalin's charges by declaring that 'we will show by our deeds that the accusations against us are unjust, and that we are resolutely building Socialism and remain loyal to the Soviet Union, loyal to the doctrine of Marx, Engels, Lenin and Stalin'?[7] This implied not a liberalisation but a radicalisation of existing policies; the strengthening of the already formidable power of the Communist Party, the intensification of its stranglehold over the Popular Front; the nationalisation of all small trades, crafts and services; the direction of class enemies and 'social idlers' into mines and factories. Above all, it meant the sharpening of the struggle in the countryside by forcing peasants into collectives, with the inevitable results of fierce resistance, falling agricultural production and food shortages. 'We will show by our deeds. . . . '

Attempts to placate Stalin by such measures, which only intensified social unrest and economic distress within the country, were doomed to failure. The core of the dispute was not over the rate of collectivisation, the merging of the Party into the People's Front or its lack of democracy, or any of the alleged shortcomings of the Yugoslav Communist Party. It was a question, as it had been in the civil war waged within the war, of power and authority – of 'who whom', of 'them' or 'us'. And 'they' were no longer the domestic enemy, those who collaborated with the invaders or set up rival resistance movements. 'They' were now the avowed standard-bearers of world revolution, the masters of the Kremlin and of the 'fraternal parties', and all those who could be persuaded or inveigled into supporting them inside Yugoslavia. Ranković now had his hands full tracking down and arresting not only the 'bourgeois reactionaries' and 'counter-revolutionaries' but militants suspected of siding with Stalin rather than Tito. The prisons were full to overflowing. In the autumn of 1948 Tito decided, without consulting his Politburo or anybody else, that it was necessary to set up a special internment camp for the 're-education' of such dissidents. A bleak island in the northern Adriatic, Goli Otok or Naked Island, was selected for this purpose. Djilas heard the news when he was on a visit to Montenegro where there were Cominform sympathisers even on the Provincial Committee. They were arrested, bundled into the holds of prison-ships and despatched without ceremony to a camp not yet ready to receive them. The Stalinists were to be crushed by Stalinist methods.

How long could this go on, Djilas began to ask himself, without a breath of criticism of Stalin himself? How long could agit-prop sustain the fiction that the great man was simply being kept 'misinformed' and was not personally involved in the anti-Tito campaign? At the beginning of October – nearly four months after the Cominform had unleashed the storm – *Borba* admitted the first glimmer of the unwelcome truth. Stalin was, of course, the greatest living authority in the 'international workers movement'; but 'authority is not everything; truth is above authority'. In the present dispute between the Central Committees of the Soviet and Yugoslav Parties, Stalin was quite simply wrong.[8] This mild but firm admission was the first milestone along a path which, after five years of wandering through tangled thickets of ideological and personal heart-searching, was to lead Djilas to a destination which he was still far from imagining.

By the end of 1948 the effects of a poor harvest and a virtual economic blockade imposed by the 'Socialist camp' were making themselves felt. Yet 1949 started in a mood of still unshaken Stalinist confidence. In January the Central Committee met and decided, despite reservations expressed by Bakarić and Kardelj, to step up collectivisation and other radical measures. The Five Year Plan was to go ahead in all its ambitious scope and coercive rigour. The 'leading role' of the Party was to be emphasised more than ever. In his report to the plenum on agit-prop Djilas stressed however that the conflict with Moscow could no longer be seen as due to 'misunderstandings' which could be explained away or put right; it had much deeper roots and must 'inevitably sharpen'. 'It is incorrect,' he declared, 'to concentrate only on denials, to defend ourselves merely from lies and attacks. We must assume a more active stance, devote more serious effort to analysing the essence of the problem.' Yugoslavia was doing more, he argued, than standing up for her national independence; 'we are defending proletarian Marxist-Leninist internationalism from those who distort it.'

The harsh, radical measures approved by the January plenum resulted in a further erosion of popular support at a time when Tito, the Party and the government most needed it. There followed a year of flux and floundering. Though Stalinism continued to flow at full tide at home and Tito still proclaimed that Yugoslavia's place was in the front line against the 'imperialists', some concessions had nevertheless to be made to the latter if the country was to avoid complete international isolation. By the summer of 1949 Yugoslavia had withdrawn support from the Communist-led Greek rebels. By the autumn she was beginning to receive the American loans and assistance which were to keep her afloat economically. The 'Peoples Democracies' sharpened their attacks and staged show trials to discredit and liquidate their own alleged 'Titoists', and Cominform hostility reached a fresh pitch of virulence in a new Soviet-inspired denunciation entitled 'The Yugoslav Communist Party in the grip of murderers and spies'. In the United Nations the Soviet bloc tried, but without success, to complete Yugoslavia's humiliation and isolation by blocking her election to the Security Council.

Ostracised by the 'Socialist camp' with which it still professed solidarity, the Yugoslav government was forced willy-nilly to change its line. At the end of the summer Djilas attempted to provide a theoretical justification for its new stand in an essay entitled *Lenin on relations between Socialist states*. His defence required considerable ingenuity, since in Lenin's time no Socialist state existed other than the Soviet Union. He succeeded nevertheless in unearthing from the master's works sufficient material to prove, to his own satisfaction at least, that Moscow had seriously deviated in this respect from Lenin's teachings. One quotation was to figure with particular prominence in the polemics which subsequently developed round the thesis of 'separate paths to Socialism' and the emergence of 'National Communism': 'All peoples will arrive at Socialism – that is inevitable. But they will not arrive there by exactly the same road. Each will introduce a modicum of specific characteristics into this or that form of democracy, this or that rhythm of the Socialist transformation of various aspects of social life.'[9] This truth, Djilas went on, was being ignored by the Soviet leaders who 'under the mask of Soviet patriotism, are propagating the most vulgar nationalism'. They had evolved the thesis of a given nation developing superior qualities – a theory which 'in a somewhat different form has long been spread by all kinds of racialists and nationalists'.[10]

This was going further than anything that had yet been said to impugn Moscow's assumption of a 'leading role'; further perhaps than might be prudent for good Communists eager to 'show by their deeds' that they remained loyal to their creed. Djilas hastened to reaffirm in all other respects his Party's Leninist, even Stalinist, orthodoxy. Lenin was still 'the creator of the greatest revolution in the history of mankind, the founder of the first workers' state'. Djilas attacked the 'Trotskyites, Bukharinites and others who accused Stalin of having betrayed the

Revolution'. All the same, there was no denying the historical fact that the phase when a single Socialist State existed, encircled by Imperialist states in constant rivalry among each other, has ended. A new phase has begun – the phase of coexistence between a series of Socialist states which can no longer be encircled by the Imperialist states. . . . By failing to comprehend the essential nature of the new conditions and by revising Leninism, the leaders of the USSR have reached extravagant conclusions in theory and in practice. They have divided the world into two sectors – a capitalist sector led by the American Imperialists, and a Socialist sector led by the USSR – while in fact there is a capitalist world where individual nations strive to liberate themselves from American domination, and the world of completely equal Socialist states, completely equal workers' parties and democratic movements. . . . In Socialism there are no leading nations or states.[11]

The dispute was being widened and carried onto dangerous ground – more dangerous and fraught with far-reaching implications than Djilas perhaps foresaw at the time or at least dared to admit even to himself. His Marxist creed assumed that it is the material base – the economic structure of a given state – which determines the intellectual superstructure and the lines of its foreign policy. If the latter is seen to be clearly at fault, implying the hegemony of one Socialist state over others, it must reflect certain distortions and contradictions within that state. It followed that the Soviet Union could not be regarded as a model in everything apart from its international stance, since the latter was the logical projection of its internal reality. And if the Soviet system, which the Yugoslavs had taken as their model, was no longer found to be exemplary, what of the system they were themselves trying to build?

These were dangerous, heretical thoughts. But by the end of the year, after returning from New York where he and his comrades had been venomously attacked by the Soviet and satellite delegates attempting to deny them their rightful place in the Security Council, Djilas had begun to think them. The enormities of the show trials being staged in Prague, Budapest and Sofia drove the same lesson home. If Moscow, and those who followed her line, were capable of such patent falsifications in order to discredit Tito and any who sympathised with him, could it any longer be doubted that the earlier Moscow trials of Zinoviev, Radek, Bukharin and the like must have been similarly rigged? Vyshinski, then the State Prosecutor, was now Soviet Foreign Minister and the architect of the Soviet Union's anti-Yugoslav policies.

Even Tito, in one of his speeches, hinted that the Moscow trials had been a shameful travesty of justice; and Moša Pijade, with his caustic wit, did not fail to point the parallels in *Borba*. It was time, he declared, to take a closer, more critical look and see where Soviet society had gone wrong, to probe more deeply into first causes. Such boldness alarmed others in the Party leadership. Even Djilas continued to hope that criticism of the Soviet Union could be limited to her attitude towards other Socialist states and remarked to his friend Tempo that though what Pijade was saying about the Moscow trials might be true, 'one should keep quiet about some things for the present.'[12] But by the end of 1949, portraits of Stalin were disappearing from their accustomed place at Yugoslav official functions in 'spontaneous' popular demonstrations. Delimitation was becoming more and more difficult, and the dispute was acquiring a menacing momentum of its own.

Was there still a chance that the Soviet leaders would see the error of their ways and put an end to the dispute? 'The Yugoslav peoples and their state organs desire that all questions considered contentious by the Soviet government and the governments of the East European countries should be solved by an understanding, and in such a form that neither the prestige of those countries nor the sovereignty and equal rights of our country suffer in any way,' Djilas declared in the summer of 1950 in what appears to be his last public offer of an olive branch. 'They have said so all along and it has been their constant and earnest desire.' Did he still believe in the likelihood of any such offer being accepted by the men in the Kremlin? Or was he simply concerned to show the Party faithful that it was not the fault of the Yugoslav leaders if the Cominform countries refused to bury the hatchet? He was addressing a 'peace conference' called a few weeks after the outbreak of the Korean War, when the Yugoslav government was anxious to avoid appearing to take sides. Their international isolation was still acute, and to break out of it without falling into the arms of the West they had been courting the attention of independent leftists of every description – men like Konni Zilliacus, recently expelled from the British Labour Party, the East German maverick Communist Wolfgang Leonhard, even small Trotskyist groups in France, Germany and elsewhere. An Indian journalist called Banerjee, representing the Fourth International, secured an interview with Tito and had talks with Kardelj, Pijade and Djilas; the latter struck him at the time as the most dogmatic and Stalin-minded of the Yugoslav leaders.[13] But such men, whom it had apparently been hoped might form the nucleus of some 'third force' with which the Yugoslavs could identify without drawing nearer to either East or West, clearly represented no parties or movements of consequence, and the Trotskyists at least declared themselves on the side of the Soviet Union over the Korean War.

Djilas had been assiduously rereading Marx and Lenin in his search for some explanation of how the 'Socialist Fatherland' could have come to adopt such a wrong attitude to other Communist parties and states; why, in short, Socialism under Stalin was bad, but under Tito – as he still firmly believed – it was good. In an address to the students of Belgrade University on 18 March 1950 he gave what he believed to be the answer. The Soviet Union was still a Socialist state since it had abolished capitalist exploitation and socialised the means of production. But she had succumbed to a disease which Marx had foreseen – 'bureaucratic degeneration', the hypertrophy of an administrative apparatus which had come to rely on arbitrary rather than democratic rule. This was reflected in an incorrect and arbitrary attitude towards other states and other parties.[14]

Before long Djilas was writing in *Borba* that the disease had become so serious that the system could no longer be regarded as Socialist but rather as a form of state capitalism. This had spawned all sorts of abuses and distortions including treatment of national minorities so callous that it was comparable to Hitler's extermination of the Jews.[15] The Peoples Democracies were being transformed in turn into state capitalist despotisms with the status of colonies (e.g. Rumania) or semi-colonies (e.g. Poland). Far from withering away, as Marx foretold, the state established by the proletarian Revolution had grown more powerful, more oppressively totalitarian, its economic monopoly more absolute and its society more polarised; 'on the one side, workers and wage-earners, on the highly salaried, unscrupulous, shifty, malicious and brutal bureaucrats of State Capitalism' – an early vision, in fact, of what Djilas would later describe in merciless detail as the 'New Class'. The much vaunted Soviet society appeared to him in reality as 'a grey, monotonous mental world diversified by mad, inhuman, drunken doses of officially patented "happiness" and a pressure of the iron heel so fierce and total (informers spying on the smallest social cell, on the relationship between man and wife, parents and children, on the artist, his inspiration and his work) that human history has never known the like.'[16]

If this was the horrifying picture of life in the first state established and still ruled by Communists, what reason was there for the Yugoslav comrades to imagine that they were likely to do any better? This question too had obsessed Djilas in his rereading of Marx and resulted in the discovery of what he believed to be a safe antidote to the contagion of 'bureaucratic degeneration'; the principle of 'self-management' by the workers which was to become, so its practitioners later claimed, the hallmark of Yugoslavia's distinctive path to Socialism. The results were to assume such far-reaching importance that the account of its modest genesis is best given in Djilas's own words:

One day – it must have been in the spring of 1950 – it occurred to me that we Yugoslav Communists were now in a position to start creating Marx's free association of producers. The factories would be left in their hands, with the sole proviso that they should pay a tax for military and other state needs 'still remaining essential'. With all this, I felt a twinge of reservation: is not this a way for us Communists, I asked myself, to shift the responsibility for failures and difficulties in the economy on to the shoulders of the working class, or to compel the working class to take a share of such responsibilities from us? I soon explained my idea to Kardelj and Kidrič while we sat in a car parked in front of the villa where I lived. They felt no such reservations, and I was able all too easily to convince them of the indisputable harmony between my ideas and Marx's teaching. Without leaving the car, we thrashed it out for little more than half an hour. Kardelj thought it was a good idea, but one that should not be put into effect for another five or six years, and Kidrič agreed with him. A couple of days later however Kidrič telephoned me to say that we were ready to go ahead at once with the first steps. In his impulsive way he began to elaborate and expound on the whole conception. A little later, a meeting was held in Kardelj's cabinet office with the trade-union leaders, and they proposed the abolition of the workers' councils, which up to that time had functioned only as consultant bodies for the management. Kardelj suggested that my proposals for management should be associated with the workers' councils, first of all in a way that would give them more rights and greater responsibilities. Debates on issues of principle and on the statutory aspects soon began, preparations that went on for some four or five months.

Tito, busy with other duties and absent from Belgrade, took no part in this and knew nothing of the proposal to introduce a workers' council bill in the parliament until he was informed by Kardelj and me in the government lobby room during a session of the National Assembly. His first reaction was: our workers are not ready for that yet! But Kardelj and I, convinced that this was an important step, pressed him hard, and he began to unbend as he paid more attention to our explanations. The most important part of our case was that this would be the beginning of democracy, something that socialism had not yet achieved; further, it could be plainly seen by the world and the international workers' movement as a radical departure from Stalinism. Tito paced up and down, as though completely wrapped in his own thoughts. Suddenly he stopped and exclaimed: 'Factories belonging to the workers – something that has never yet been achieved!' With these words, the theories worked out by Kardelj and myself seemed to shed their complications and seemed, too, to find better prospects of being workable. A few months later, Tito explained the Workers' Self-Management Bill to the National Assembly.[17]

By sponsoring the principle of workers' self-management, which a compliant parliament passed into law without further discussion at the end of June 1950, Tito gave a new dimension to his quarrel with Moscow – an ideological dimension. He did so in the belief that it would strengthen his hand. Not much interested personally in theoretical questions, he had at first insisted that 'the issue was that of the relationship of one state to another'. Whilst still firmly championing the Yugoslav state's right to defned its own interests and follow its own policies, the argument was now reinforced by the thesis that his state was just as truly 'Socialist' as its critic, indeed more so since it was returning to a principle enshrined in Marxist-Leninist writ but never effectively practised in the Soviet Union. 'Factories to the workers' or 'workers' self-management' was a slogan which would give the Yugoslav comrades the comfronting assurance that they were evolving someʰhing different, something distinctive, whilst remaining exemplary Communisʳ·. The new course proclaimed by Tito was as yet more a declaration of .ntent than an immediately realisable policy; its limitations, and the contradiction inherent in any attempt to combine grass-roots democracy with rigidly centralised planning and monopoly control by a single Party, were not yet apparent. Nor was the economic climate, aggravated by another disastrous harvest and the persistence of forced collectivisation and coercion, favourable to such a tender plant. The system itself thus remained essentially Stalinist despite its theoretical new look. But at least the Yugoslav Revolution had been given an attractive new banner.

Power remained concentrated as firmly as ever in the hands of Tito, whose autocratic, ostentatious and regal life style jarred on more puritanical comrades like Ranković and Djilas. They themselves indeed had contributed not a little, perhaps without realising where it was to lead, to fostering Tito's personality cult; Djilas, through his eulogistic writings, Ranković, through his ready acceptance of Russian suggestions for transforming the free-and-easy relationship between Tito and his commanders into the hierarchical rigidity of the Soviet command structure. Soon after the arrival of the Soviet Military Mission in February 1944 Ranković, on their advice, sent out instructions to all corps commanders that they should in future address Tito in the respectful second person plural form of address *Vi* instead of the customarily comradely *Ti*.

From such small beginnings the Marshal's personality cult had been assiduously built up. Djilas had noticed too, when a delegate to the United Nations in New York at the end of 1949, that it projected an unfavourable image of Yugoslavia and its leader just when that country needed to get on better terms with the West. He brought back with him a copy of *Life* containing an article which portrayed Tito as a parvenu South American dictator. Tito looked at it in some embarrassment and for a time was more circumspect with foreign correspondents and press photographers; but he made little change in his preferred life-style. The quarrel with Moscow and the need to rally maximum Party support had forced him to consult more fully with its leading members on important issues. Even so, the Central Committee held only two plenums in the course of 1949, whilst power remained in the hands of the Politburo of which Ranković and Djilas were joint secretaries, the former responsible, his friend jocularly remarked, for twisting people's arms whilst he had the job of twisting their minds.

As head of agit-prop Djilas continued to wield enormous power, charting the course (with Kardelj, Bakarić and later Kidrič) for the theoretical innovations and experimentation which were to mark the Yugoslav path to Socialism. But there was a central paradox in this power. Here was the arbiter of the nation's literary and artistic life laying down the law like a sort of Yugoslav Zhdanov, yet speaking out ever more loudly in favour of intellectual independence and freedom of expression – a cultural dictator who, as he put it, 'yearned for the power of law, not the law of power'.

Djilas was not of course alone amongst intellectuals in wanting such things, but none had more say than he had in deciding the extent and the timing of any step towards greater freedom of thought and expression. He used his powers arbitrarily, slapping down those who judged matters differently, as he himself would in turn be ultimately slapped down by Tito.

A revealing case was the controversy which raged during 1950 over the special privileges enjoyed by high officials of the Party, government and army, an issue on which Djilas himself came to feel strongly and to express himself forcefully. Branko Ćopić, a popular writer who had crossed swords before with Party leaders whilst with the Partisans, published a satirical article, on the delicate subject in the literary journal *Kniževne Novine*. The editor had at first been reluctant, or too frightened, to publish it but Ćopić appealed to the Central Committee who gave their approval. A week later, *Književne Novina* published an article denouncing the satirist. Ćopić riposted wittily in another journal, to the delight of most readers. *Borba* than joined the fray, trouncing the humorist in two violent articles, whilst Tito himself delivered the *coup de grace* in a speech denouncing Ćopić's 'heretical stories' and branding him as an unwitting ally of the Cominform. Djilas was commonly believed to have inspired the *Borba* campaign against Ćopić. But later, with the support of Kidrič, he secured the closure of the controversial shops where the privileged few could buy imported quality goods at token prices. Tito, realising the strength of public feeling over such unwarranted privileges, raised no objections.[18]

The shock of the break with Moscow and the continuing tension under which he lived during the rest of Stalin's lifetime took their toll of Tito's naturally robust physique. In May 1948 he suffered the first of a series of increasingly painful gall-bladder attacks and was operated on nearly three years later. The operation proved successful and his recovery rapid. One of the woman who had devotedly nursed him was a Serbian girl from Croatia, Jovanka Budisavljević, a former *Partizanka* and a member of the Marshal's household. In April 1952 it was announced that she and Tito had married. Two months later Djilas, whose increasingly strained relationship with Mitra had finally come to an end, also took a new bride. Štefanija (Štefica) Barić hailed from Tito's native region, the Croatian Zagorje, and worked in the Central Committee organisation. She was a long-standing Party member and had been active for the Partisans from the early days of the rising. Politics, as always in the life of a revolutionary, had helped to shape personal life. 'But I am not at all sure,' Djilas wrote in retrospect, 'that Tito would have married Jovanka, or that I would have taken Štefica as my second wife, if we had not become less bound by Leninist dogma and our private lives freer and more independent of the Party.'[19]

CHAPTER TWENTY-FIVE

Windows on the West

UNTIL the war, none of the Yugoslav Communist leaders had much contact with the West. The intellectual world was confined to their own country, its Balkan neighbours, the Soviet Union, Austria and Germany; a few knew Italy, France or Belgium and a number had served their military apprenticeship in Republican Spain. Some of the old Party members, including Tito himself, had lived under the Austro-Hungarian empire. Not one of them knew much of Britain or North America, despite the presence in the latter of a large Yugoslav immigrant community. Of Tito's immediate entourage, only the well-educated Lola Ribar, killed as he was setting out to head the first Partisan mission to the British, had some familiarity with the latter's language and ways. His successor Velebit, later to become one of Tito's most effective envoys, knew no English at the outbreak of the war. Vlada Dedijer had received part of his education in England and passed for something of an authority, though he never belonged to the top Party leadership and his attitude towards the British was ambivalent. Tito himself picked up some English in the course of the war and made his first acquaintance with the British through their Military Mission representatives Deakin and Maclean, and later through Alexander and Churchill, whose personalities, if not their policies, impressed him. This lack of familiarity or sympathy with the western world proved a handicap when the Yugoslav Communists had willy-nilly to turn to it in order to survive.

Djilas shared this general ignorance of the West and the prejudices against it inculcated by Marxist-Leninist orthodoxy. Britain and the United States were for him the classic lands of capitalist exploitation of the workers. He saw their malign influence exercised abroad primarily through the British Secret Service, whose finger seemed to be in every Balkan pie and whose agents were only waiting for opportunities to penetrate the Party and the Partisan Movement – dubious characters like 'Eileen', Hudson and Atherton. Had not Tito's predecessor Gorkić been known to have spent some time in Britain and was he not finally unmasked as a British spy? In the military missions sent to the Partisans during the war, there had been members of the British Communist Party, such as James Klugman who later became a leading light in its Central Committee, and the intelligence officer Kenneth Syers, but their duplicity was revealed when they came out for Stalin after the break with Tito.[1] The nature of Djilas's responsibilities during the war, being principally those of agit-prop, had not brought him into close contact with the British or Americans. Their language, literature and political thought remained *terra incognita*. It was only after 1948 that he began to perceive the need, and then the fascination, of exploring those new worlds.

The West's attitude towards the Belgrade heretics (like that towards the Partisans during the war) was compounded of bewilderment, admiration, suspicion and irritation. Nor did the heretics' own conduct and past history inspire confidence or make for clarity. The wartime cooperation between them and the West, born of necessity and bedevilled by mutual distrust, had quickly become a thing of the past, though Tito personally never permitted his comradely associations to lapse completely. After the war, the clash of interests became manifest. Yugoslavia's support for the Greek rebels, her territorial claims against Austria and over Trieste, her half-disclosed designs for the absorption of Albania and for union with Bulgaria, her fervent support for Moscow's most aggressive Cold War policies – all these things stamped Yugoslavia as the most committed and intransigent of Moscow's satellites. The ruthless imposition of Communism and the distorted picture of the West projected by the propaganda machine, the show trials of Mihailović (slanted so as to implicate the Allies), of Archbishop Stepinac and of prominent persons known to have links with the West alienated even well-disposed opinion. Disputes over the gold deposited in New York by the Royalist Government and American claims for compensation for expropriated assets, and above all the shooting down in 1946 of United States planes with the loss of American lives, embittered feelings still more. Nor did frenzied efforts to 'show by their deeds' that the Yugoslavs were still staunch pro-Soviet Communists, and consequently hostile to the West, make rapprochement any easier. Not until more than a year after the start of the Cominform dispute did the United States government formally declare its support for Tito and accept the reality of his break with Moscow.

The first modest American bank-loan was made in the autumn of 1948 and a formal aid programme was inaugurated a year later. Other western governments – Britain, France, West Germany – followed suit, but it was primarily the United States which came to Yugoslavia's rescue. How could this *volte face* of 'aid without strings' be explained away? Djilas had been categorical in decrying and rejecting the Marshall Plan. Even in the spring of 1950 he could still declare: 'Our Socialist regime is so contrary to the western capitalist world that its

215

very nature does not permit us to agree to anything, nor to expect anything, other than the trade relations which are common to Capitalism.'[2] The subsequent change of attitude towards aid he attempted to justify in a series of articles on 'Contemporary Problems'. Capitalist development, he argued, had reached the stage when it became in the United States' own interest to give 'aid' – the word was still in quotation marks. Nevertheless, it was aid and not concealed exploitation and could therefore be accepted without a Communist government incurring unacceptable obligations or doing violence to its principles. From this it was only a short step to demanding aid as a right and resenting any suspension of aid as 'imperialism'.[3]

By this time Djilas had also begun to establish personal relations with some of the more ideologically congenial circles in the West. Immediately after the rift with the Cominform, when the Yugoslav Communists were trying to break out of their isolation without departing too far from their anti-capitalist principles, they had been content to form links with independent, but totally unrepresentative, left-wing politicians. Now it was recognised that more influential friends were needed. The Yugoslav Communists began to turn to Britain's Labour Party, as Europe's most important Social Democrat movement and a likely sympathiser with their new stance, and they invited a delegation to visit their country. In September 1950 Tito, Moša Pijade, Djilas and other leading figures received members of its Executive Committee and declared themselves gratified to find that they had much in common.

The British visitors were guests not of the Yugoslav Communist Party but of the People's Front which, Moša Pijade blandly assured them, was the means by which 'the Masses' could exercise control over the Party. Djilas spoke more frankly. There were at present, he admitted, 'too many democratic forms without substance', and 'a new form of supreme authority' needed to be developed. The control supposedly exercised by the Presidium of the National Assembly over the government was purely nominal. The government was in reality controlled, in the Soviet manner, by the Party. The problem of democracy in a Socialist, one-party state, he continued, was not whether its citizens should be allowed to advocate a return to capitalism but how to let those who supported Socialism express their viewpoints. The Russians had not succeeded in doing this; that was why their form of Socialism was defective. The Yugoslavs were making some headway and intended to press on in this direction, though things were as yet far from perfect.[4]

216

Djilas surprised his visitors by the frankness with which he spoke of the recently held elections to the National Assembly. He admitted that the officially declared results, almost unanimously favourable to the government, did not reflect the true state of feeling within the country. The pro-regime majority 'exercised a certain psychological and political pressure on the others'. Some two per cent of the Party's members had been expelled for supporting the Cominform, but there were still some within it who sided secretly with the Stalinists, either because they had been recruited by Soviet Intelligence or because of undiminished loyalty to the Soviet Union or out of fear that Yugoslavia would be forced before long to give in. The Party would not act against such people unless they attempted to form a subversive faction. He was confident, in any case, that the Cominform would never command enough ideological or political backing amongst the people at large to launch a popular rising. The only real danger was a deterioration in the economic situation grave enough to cause the people to lose their will to work and their faith in their leaders.[5]

Such views showed how far Tito's agit-prop chief had travelled from the crude dogmatism of his earlier pronouncements. The Yugoslav leaders, as the British Ambassador reported, were being forced by economic necessity to turn more to the West and they no doubt presented developments in their country in a light which would gain them sympathy. But the delegates' visit had been an undoubted success, and the invitation extended to their hosts for a return visit to Britain in the summer was accepted with alacrity. As President of the International Commission which the Central Committee had set up the previous year, Djilas decided to lead the delegation himself. Dedijer, who had been appointed Secretary to the Commission and who knew England already would go with him.

But Tito had Djilas in mind for another and more delicate mission to England before then. The threat of Soviet invasion, to be launched probably by surrogate Warsaw forces, loomed more menacingly than ever. Yugoslavia urgently needed arms and equipment which only the West could supply. Informal approaches were already being made to the French and the Americans, and Djilas was now instructed to put the Yugoslav request officially to the British Government. An invitation to deliver a lecture at the Royal Institute for International Affairs and to meet Labour Party leaders would serve as a suitable pretext for his visit to London. Its real purpose must be kept strictly secret in order to avoid provoking Moscow and its supporters in Yugoslavia. Djilas was to stress that there was no question of the Yugoslavs joining NATO. He was

217

to make clear that they simply shared a common interest in resisting Soviet aggression and that Western assistance must be given unobtrusively. The Yugoslavs would also welcome a declaration by His Majesty's Government affirming Britain's interest in the maintenance of their country's independence.

At the end of January 1951 Djilas came to London and put his request to the Prime Minister. Mr Attlee and his colleagues were sympathetic but cautious. They appreciated Yugoslavia's predicament and applauded her stand, but they explained that HMG had many commitments to its allies but only limited resources. A list of Yugoslavia's most pressing needs was promised by the Yugoslavs and presented a few days later by their Ambassador. Mr Attlee repeated his assurance that their request would be given urgent and sympathetic consideration, and Djilas and Dedijer returned to Belgrade well pleased with their reception.[6]

Before they left, Djilas was taken by Brilej, the Yugoslav Ambassador, to call on Mr Churchill. Dedijer, who went with them, has described their surprise at finding the door of the house in Hyde Park Gate opened to them by Mrs Churchill herself, who then took them up to the bedroom where the great man customarily spent his mornings working:

It was a spacious room with a large bed and several tables piled with books and manuscripts. A green candle was burning on the bedside table, which Churchill used to light his cigar. When I looked at him in his voluminous white night-shirt, edged in red, and took in the whole atmosphere I recalled a picture from early childhood: that is how I had imagined the wolf in 'Little Red Riding Hood' dressed in the grandmother's clothing and waiting for his victim. All that was lacking was the nightcap. I was just about to whisper this to Djilas and Brilej when Djilas, who knew me and could image what I was about to say, kicked me under the table. The talk began with formalities. Churchill offered us something to drink – port I think. He poured it himself, his hand steady. . . . Churchill began to recollect his meeting with Tito. Djilas interjected: 'In 1945, you said that Tito had tricked you. We Yugoslav partisans considered that a great compliment!' Churchill liked that kind of talk. He winked and said with a laugh: 'I don't remember having used those words, but I was so angry at all of you that I could have said something worse.' Laughing again, he continued: 'It was a mistake to say that and it shall never happen again!'

At the end of their conversation Djilas steered the conversation round to Churchill's relations with Stalin. Dedijer records Churchill as saying:

'I don't think there will be war. Stalin has grabbed enough and would not want to risk anything now; besides, he is afraid of the atomic bomb. I do not believe he will attack Yugoslavia – he is not so foolish as to stir that hornet's nest. He would more likely turn west, where the way is open.'

Churchill stressed that he did not want war with the Russians, but that if he were in power he would force Stalin into an agreement by not laying down his arms. He added that already he had once come to an agreement with him about Greece, Rumania and Bulgaria.

Djilas broke in: 'And Yugoslavia?'

Churchill calmly replied: 'Fifty-fifty. Naturally in terms of influence, not territory.'[7]

Ambassador Brilej reported their visit in the following telegram to Belgrade:

Djilas, Dedijer and myself paid a visit to Churchill, as he expressed through his secretary the wish to see Djilas. The conversation was confidential, informal and friendly.

1. Churchill mentioned Anglo-Yugoslav relations during the war and their deterioration immediately after the war.

2. He mentioned also the agreement with Stalin on the Balkans, among other matters, and the 50/50 agreement on Yugoslavia, pointing out that it was not on a territorial basis but the division of influence.

3. Speaking about the world situation, Churchill expressed the opinion that it is possible to achieve an agreement with Stalin but only on condition that the West is strong enough. He considers that the Soviet Union is not yet ready for a war.

Minister Djilas will inform you in detail about the contents of the conversation after his return.[8]

1951 was a memorable year for Djilas not only on account of his visits to London and further contacts with British politicians but for the beginning of a close and fruitful friendship. Milovan Djilas and Aneurin Bevan, then Minister for Health in the Labour Government, felt drawn to one another by an instinctive and natural affinity. It was not only a question of the common political ground, which each had reached by his own path, but a matter of temperament and approach. 'They were both poets, romantics, unrestrainable individualists, strong unpredictable mountain types,' noted Jennie Lee, who came to share no less cordially in her husband's friendship with the Djilas family.[9] Each found stimulation in the other's company, the lively interchange of ideas, the thrust and counter-thrust of arguments constantly renewed and carried forward in the search to probe more deeply into the political and social reality of their respective countries and the universal principles behind them.

In April Bevan resigned from the Attlee cabinet, and three months later he accepted an invitation to visit Yugoslavia. Djilas acted as his host in Belgrade and then took him and Jennie Lee to visit Tito on Brioni, the North Adriatic island where the marshal liked to hold court, to work and relax with the men who had been his closest comrades and were the chief officers of the Party and State. Djilas himself, though still intimate with the 'Old Man' and more active than ever in helping to shape Yugoslavia's rapidly evolving new institutions and ideology, was not a very frequent visitor at Brioni. Some aspects of Tito's life-style were becoming less and less to his taste; the luxury and self-indulgence, the exaggerated though discreetly camouflaged security, the arbitrary nature of a power structure still dominated by the will of one man beneath the surface of the camaraderie forged in war and revolutionary struggle. Tito, who was extraordinarily sensitive to the subtlest changes of atmosphere, was not unaware of this tacit disapproval. Once, when he had commissioned a new villa which was being built largely by the labour of political prisoners, he teased Djilas by sending Tempo with a message for him: 'Tell Djido what my villa is like, and tell him that all that is great in history was built by slaves!'[10]

The 'simple life' on Brioni was based on an infrastructure of boundless and unquestioned privilege enjoyed by its owner and his circle, and was thus, for all its attractions, repugnant to one with deeply held egalitarian beliefs. But to the foreign guest of this legendary Partisan hero, this Yugoslav David to the Soviet Goliath, as they sat with his comrades in a rough stone shelter open in one side to the azure Adriatic round a trestle table laden with choice Dalmatian wines and exquisite if simple food, the scene might well seem idyllic. For the Socialists from Britain it had the authentic flavour of some Partisan headquarters where there was now leisure and freedom to discuss the problems which interested them. The atmosphere seemed one of carefree, trusting give-and-take. Where else amongst Communists, or even among Social Democrats, could one find such spontaneity and open-mindedness, such a stimulating and uninhibited exchange of ideas? The Bevans threw themselves into the discussion with their accustomed verve, savouring to the full the lively exchanges in the most beautiful of Mediterranean settings. They came away, Bevan's biographer tells us, 'with indelible memories of the special qualities of Yugoslav bravery, of their absolute resolve to resist Soviet encroachment, of the greatness of Tito, and with another possession more peculiar to Jennie and himself – an immediately established affinity with Milovan Djilas.'[11]

220

The friendship was nourished by a spirited and wide-ranging correspondence. 'It is understandable that – in different countries under different conditions – identical or similar viewpoints are being born,' Djilas wrote to them not long after their return to England. 'I think that the personal relationship established between both of you and ourselves is only the beginning of something much more lasting and deeper, the beginning of that unbreakable link between people who through different methods and even from different ideological positions truly fight for the freedom of men and peoples.'[12]

It would only be later, when his ideas had crystallised still further, that Djilas became aware of the natural demarcation line between his thinking and Bevan's – a demarcation determined by the differences in the social reality within which each had to operate.

In Britain, according to Bevan, what was happening was that private enterprise was gradually being nationalized in sectors where this makes for greater efficiency, all without weakening the British parliamentary system; while in Yugoslavia the problem is to achieve political freedoms and the liberation of huge nationalized industries and private concerns from the managerial grip of a self-perpetuating party bureaucracy.[13]

Yet however great these differences, the friendship which developed between the two men and the cross-fertilisation of their ideas was no less of a reality.

Moscow's feud with Belgrade raged as fiercely as ever. Shortly before the Bevans' visit, Molotov delivered one of his most violent distribes against Yugoslavia and its leaders, branding them as 'spies and provocateurs who betrayed their people and sold out to the Anglo-American Imperialists, re-established the capitalist system and deprived the people of its revolutionary victory.'[14] Tito gave measure for measure, declaring that such outbursts were nothing but attempts to cover up the Soviet leaders' own crimes.

They have been murdering in Albania, Bulgaria, Hungary, Romania, Poland and Czechoslovakia, not to mention Russia itself. They had exterminated whole communities – the Crimean Tartars, the Chechens of the Caucasus, the Germans of the 'Volga Republic'. Tens of thousands of Estonians, Latvians and Lithuanians had been uprooted to perish in the forest of Siberia. And it was these practitioners of genocide, who were now accusing and threatening Yugoslavia![15]

In the autumn, the Yugoslav Government decided to take the dispute to the United Nations. Despite Russian attempts to dismiss the charges as a tissue of lies, the General Assembly, by an overwhelming majority, took sympathetic note of the Yugoslav complaints and urged both parties to settle their differences. Kardelj, as Foreign Minister, presented the Yugoslav case in the General Assembly, Djilas in the Special Political Committee which considered it in detail. Dedijer, in his account of the affair, claims much of the credit for making Djilas rewrite the first unsuitably polemical draft of his speech, thereby unleashing a violent quarrel between them. Kardelj, according to this account, had to intervene and talked Djilas into completely revising his text. 'Djilas took this good-humoredly,' Dedijer writes. 'He slept on it, and the next day I begged his pardon for being so clumsy. He never mentioned it again, nor did he ever try to 'get even' with me.'[16] Milovan Djilas, so perceptive in his writings on the Montenegrin character and its obsession with revenge, was singularly free from this trait himself. Impulsive and intemperate he could often be, but he was never moved to bear grudges or to settle old scores. He was to pay dearly for failing to realise that many of his comrades in high places were.

CHAPTER TWENTY-SIX

Reshaping the Party

THE next year and a half – 1952 and much of 1953 – saw Djilas at the height of his political career; it was also, following his remarriage in June 1952, a time of new happiness in his personal life. His place in the triad closest to Tito seemed as assured as ever. The Party's powerful agit-prop machine, and particularly its official mouthpiece *Borba*, now edited by Dedijer, remained at his unfettered disposal. The ferment of new ideas, fertilised by his rereading of the Marxist classics and by his contacts with stimulating minds outside his own Party and country, was not only intoxicating in itself but afforded him the satisfaction of seeing theory accepted and shared by others and embodied in new legislative forms and institutional experiments. The conflict with Stalin had served as a stimulus, reviving the camaraderie of Partisan days whilst infusing into it the excitement of ideological innovation, broadening personal experience and new friendships. It was a time which combined the enticements of power, the satisfactions of emotional fulfilment and the fascination of intellectual exploration.

Official responsibilities had not lessened the natural informality of Djilas's character. Because he was himself the least bureaucratic of Party pundits, he could the more readily discern and denounce the symptoms of 'bureaucratic degeneration' in the Soviet Union, and then nearer home. A dogmatist who had outgrown the familiar dogmas, he took an iconoclastic pleasure in demolishing the structure he himself had helped build up. His *gout de déplaire* might sometimes shock; but his comrades had grown used to tolerating him in the role of *enfant terrible*. For beneath the charm, they recognised rare qualities of which the Party and country stood in great need. As a Swiss newspaper correspondent who saw much of him at this time observed:

In him the others did not resent what they rejected in any outsider – the fact that he towered over them all in intelligence and mental agility. He was one of them, and they were proud of him. And then, there was the relaxedness, the unselfconsciousness, the personal charm of the man. It was easy to forgive him the foibles and contradictions of character which he exhibited so unconcernedly. He was forgiven capricious and erratic conduct, too; for gentle and lovable 'Djido' would suddenly turn domineering and arrogant, intolerant of any contradiction, and would fail to keep to arrangements, neglect his promises, and coolly shrug his shoulders when he was reminded of them. Even the inconsistency in his style of life was readily pardoned; the enemy of formality, who draped his gangling body in wrinkled suits and went about without a tie, with a proletarian cap on his head, lived at the same time in a palatial villa with a park watched over by a member of Tito's Guard, and was so crazy about beautiful cars that he always had to drive the newest Chrysler or the latest Mercedes-Cabriolet.

And finally he was forgiven his cynicism, his game of *épater le communiste*, the disagreeable home-truths and the dreadful heresies with which he loved to shock his comrades. After one of his heretical outbursts, it was enough to look into his clown's face, at the radiant, irresistible, kindly-mocking and somehow timid smile of the Montenegrin charmer – and to forgive him everything. Because the pure fanatical fervour was so clearly recognisable behind his cynicism, because he was so utterly convinced of the cause and believed so imperturbably in its final victory, Djilas could dare to think and say all the evil nagging thoughts weaker men had to suppress.[1]

1952 was notable for the Party's Sixth Congress, held in Zagreb in early November, which set the seal of approval on the new trends and pointed the way ahead.[2] Its dominant figure, as always on such occasions, was Tito, whose opening speech was largely a forthright denunciation of Stalin's foreign policy and the distortions disfiguring the pattern of Socialism under his rule, coupled with a defence of his own party and its policies as the most authentic expressions of Marxism-Leninism. A far cry indeed from the Fifth Congress of four years before, with its earnest protestations of loyalty to the father figure in the Kremlin and of filial resolve to 'show by their deeds' that his criticisms were undeserved! What their deeds had in fact shown, so they now claimed, was the Yugoslav comrades' right and ability to shape their own destiny and blaze their distinctive trail towards the Socialist goal.

Milovan Djilas drafted the Congress Resolution, delivered an impassioned speech in its defence, and afterwards expounded its significance to western correspondents, relaxed and confident as he puffed away contentedly at his briar pipe when all the applause had died down. He did more than anyone to make the Congress a notable milestone in the Party's history, the high-water mark of the trend towards liberalization. But in retrospect, even these advances, since they stopped short of introducing a multi-party system, seemed to him fated to end in the triumph of a dogmatic and entrenched bureaucracy, the New Class he was so vehemently to denounce, and a reversion to at least an attenuated form of Stalinism. Tito, on the other hand, later claimed that he himself had 'never liked' the Sixth Congress and had

224

always had misgivings and reservations about its decisions.[3] None of this could however be suspected at the time. The leadership, except for one Serbian member of the Politburo who resigned because he disagreed with the Party's western trend, and a demented Partisan hero, the former commander of the famous Second Proletarian Brigade, who seized the opportunity to denounce a high-ranking colleague for enticing away his wife, seemed united in their approval of the new course.

Self-management – the 'epoch-making act' of two years ago vesting control of the factories in their workers' councils – was given Tito's imprimatur as the distinguishing feature of Yugoslavia's path to Socialism. The wildly over-ambitious Five Year Plan was quietly abandoned; its chief architect Kidrič, in his last public speech before dying of leukemia, adumbrated a new and more realistic economic system where market forces would have free play subject only to the essential minimum of overall planning. Kardelj expatiated on a law making the People's Committees at district and municipal levels 'the basic organs of state authority' – a scheme formally embodied in a new Constitutional Law passed two months later.

It is true that Tito still spoke of collectivisation as representing 'the most important element of Socialism in the villages', without which the ultimate victory would not be complete, but the disastrous effects that the drive to impose collectivisation was having an agricultural production and in eroding the support of the peasants had prompted Kardelj, Bakarić and Djilas to urge that it should be jettisoned. Four months after the end of the Congress legislation to that effect was passed.

These were all important steps towards dismantling what were generally taken to be the props essential to any Communist régime. What of the cornerstone itself – the Party's monopoly of authority over the policies and administration of the state and of every branch of public life? It was difficult to know, as bewildered activists were to discover, exactly how to regard the changes announced at the Congress. They learned that the apparatus to which they belonged was no longer to be called the Communist Party but the 'League of Communists', and its Politburo the 'Executive Committee'. Djilas fought hard for this innovation and persuaded Tito and all the other leading comrades except Ranković, the apparatus-man *par excellence*, by reminding them that Marx himself had coined the phrase 'Communist League'. The new name was supposed to reflect new functions; the Party was still to retain its 'leading role' but would henceforth exert influence by persuasion and guidance rather than by simple command, allowing more initiative to be taken by the People's Committees and the Workers' Councils. The People's Front, which was renamed the Socialist Alliance and which convened a congress of its own three months later, was also expected to promote democratisation by being given more scope.

A number of other new regulations and organisational changes designed to further the same process were introduced. The outcome, the leadership explained, should not be any down-grading of the Party's importance but rather the contrary, since it would now have fresh and more exacting responsibilities. It was expected to wield less direct power but to achieve better results, becoming more democratic in itself and encouraging a freer interplay of democratic processes in others. But the principle of 'democratic centralism', which in fact meant a rigid obedience to decisions handed down from above, would be upheld.

The attempt to achieve and harmonise such differing effects proved an impossible task. The rapid post-war expansion of the Party had gathered in many members of inferior calibre who were ready enough to exercise authority by command but quite unsuited to the more subtle role of persuaders and educators. They either continued to wield power in the old way or else lapsed into passivity.

The Party had been disorientated by the rift with Moscow to a more serious extent than was officially admitted. Ranković, in his report to the Sixth Congress, gave the number of members 'penalized' since 1948 as 11,128, with 2,572 sentenced by the Courts for pro-Cominform activity.[4] Neither Djilas nor any of the Party leaders believed that the necessity for the Goli Otok camp could have been avoided. Without it, Djilas writes, there would have followed 'not only the removal of our present leadership and bloody purges within the Party, but also the subjugation of Yugoslavia to the Soviet Union.'[5] Whilst in New York attending the United Nations session at the end of 1949 he had noticed that 'the official West viewed the persecution of the Cominformists with understanding but not without malice,' and on his return he suggested to Tito that some thought should be given to dissolving the camp and dealing with suspects through court procedures. 'But we need the camps now desperately!' Kardelj objected, and Ranković supported him. Tito, though clearly unhappy over the situation, dismissed Djilas's suggestion.[6]

But need the treatment meted out to the prisoners have been so inhuman? The avowed purpose was their 're-education', and it was claimed by Tito and others that this was being achieved with the cooperation of those inmates who saw the errors of their ways and organized themselves into 'self-management units'. But against those who remained obdurate torture was freely employed.

On landing, they were herded through a double row of guards who punched and kicked them. There were lynchings, too. Those who would not recant were subjected to humiliating abuse which could only result from the dogmatic fury and the ingenuity of those who had reformed. Prisoners had their heads plunged into pails of human excrement. They were forced to wear placards that read 'Traitor'. They were required to confess publicly even their non-political sins. All of this was deliberately planned.[7]

It later seemed to Djilas that he could not escape a share of the blame for these excesses. 'Although I was not myself involved directly in the organization or administration of the camp,' he writes, 'my ideological activity played its part. The sharpness and depth of my criticism of Stalin and the Soviet system contributed to the sufferings of the inmates.'[8]

How much of the true state of affairs did Djilas and the others suspect at the time? Even Ranković, it seems, was kept in the dark to a certain extent. In the summer before the Congress he visited the island where a great reception was laid on for him by the prisoners who had been 're-educated'. He returned, Djilas says, 'moved and delighted', and convinced of the success of his campaign. But Djilas and some others were beginning to have doubts. Rumours, and the retraction of statements made by some of the ex-convicts who had previously praised the treatment given them, suggested a more disturbing picture. Some ten months after the Sixth Congress, when Djilas was relaxing at Niška Banja spa, his friend Dobrica Ćosić, the Serbian writer, confided that he had visited Goli Otok out of curiosity and been horrified by what he had found; he described the 'corrective methods' being applied there as 'possibly the most diabolical in history'. Djilas arranged for Ćosić to tell Ranković and Kardelj in person of his impressions. The worst abuses were then corrected, but the camp itself was not closed. According to Djilas, around fifteen thousand Party members and sympathisers passed through it, some of them interned on mere suspicion.[9]

There could be no leniency towards the Cominformists, nor any healing of the rift with Moscow, so long as Stalin remained alive. On 3 March 1953, Dedijer telephoned Djilas to say that the Soviet dictator was dead. He was rewarded with the gift of a gold wrist-watch inscribed: 'To Vlado, for the good news – Djido.'[10] What would Stalin's death mean for Yugoslavia? The possibility of reconciliation, certainly;

perhaps also a change of course, or at least of emphasis, in both foreign and domestic policy. That was still the subject of lively discussion and speculation a fortnight later when Djilas invited his friends to celebrate a joyful family event – the birth of his son Aleksa. Ranković, Tempo and Dedijer came with their wives. Tito had left on a state visit to Britain, an event which marked the point of Yugoslavia's nearest rapprochement to the West. Now, with the expected relaxation of pressure from the East, it might be safe for the pendulum to swing back a little in that direction. Tito had never wished to set a course which would take his country out of Moscow's orbit only to see it drawn into that of the West. He was searching for a position of equilibrium which would become known as the policy of non-alignment.

Djilas had recently returned from a visit to the Far East. Asia, and later Africa, seemed the most promising fields where new friends and allies could be cultivated. Yugoslavia offered military aid to Burma, opened an embassy in India, and gave advice and encouragement to the newly formed Asian Socialist Alliance – a forum likely to lend a willing ear to talk of independent roads to Socialism. Djilas was confident that, despite the differences of background, Yugoslavia's experience was deeply relevant to countries at a similar stage of development.

He was also eagerly responsive to the sights and voices of this unfamiliar eastern world. The writer in him, as well as the politician, hungrily absorbed a host of new impressions to which he was later to give literary expression.[11] Beyond the immediate political objectives of his visit he sensed the impact of a new cultural universe whose values spoke more eloquently to the human condition than those offered either by the capitalist West or the pseudo-Socialist Soviet Union. His talks with the philosopher Rada Krishnon, Vice President of the Indian Republic, persuaded him that the sage's idealism was 'incomparably more "progressive" than the vulgar and subjective idealistic materialism of the Cominform.'[12] He was impressed by the humanity and wisdom of Gandhi's creed of non-violence, so different from that which had brought him and his comrades to power, and also of the effectiveness of civil disobedience as 'not only a possible form of class struggle' but the tactics most in tune with Indian traditions and present possibilities for forcing the British rulers to leave India. Alien as it might be to the European mind, Europeans could not ignore it without being impoverished, as the Soviet mind had been impoverished by ignoring the wisdom of Tolstoy. Djilas, like other perceptive travellers, returned from his encounter with Asia conscious that he would 'always carry something of the radiance of its beauty, as if he had found his true self, as if he had cleansed himself and returned to the well-springs of human values.'[13]

Djilas was never, however, one of those who believed that the panacea for human ills was to be found in eastern mysticism. To expect that salvation would come to the west from that quarter seemed to him an illusion. Even after his Communist faith had dimmed, he looked for no substitute in any religion, either of the east or of the west. No religious creed appealed to him as an alternative to a political creed. The most it could do – and perhaps that was after all enough – was to open a window onto another world of timeless reality, a world whose very existence was denied by the materialist philosophy which, despite occasional glimmerings of something beyond, he still professed. Some months after his Indian tour he was sitting with Tito in the latter's special Blue Train bearing the body of Boris Kidrič back from Slovenia for burial. The man who had done most to devise, and then to dismantle, the Five Year Plan was the first of their intimate circle to die, and the talk turned on death and the transience of human life. Nothing existed, Djilas declared, beyond matter itself, indestructible though endlessly changing. 'Don't dwell on that now!' Tito broke in; adding reproachfully, but with a smile: 'And anyway, who knows what it's all about – who really knows?'[14]

Tito was not given to philosophical or religious speculation. His concern was with the here-and-now, with the affairs of men and government, the practical problems of state and Party. The latter had recently been causing him increasing anxiety and he decided that it was necessary to summon the Central Committee to a plenary session to consider the situation. A letter circulated to all Party organisations drew attention to the 'negative tendencies' which had been manifesting themselves – 'all kinds of uncertainty and anti-Marxist theories . . . petty bourgeois anarchist ideas,' and the like. The concept of 'the withering away of the Party' stressed at the Sixth Congress had been made an excuse for inactivity instead of being taken as the goal of a distant future once all class-enemies had been liquidated and all internal contradictions overcome; only then would a strong, unified leadership be no longer necessary.[15]

The Plenum was due to be held in June on Brioni. Djilas, who had just returned from London where he had represented Yugoslavia at Queen Elizabeth's coronation, was displeased at the choice of this venue instead of Belgrade or Zagreb, since it implied that the Party was subordinate to the authority and convenience of its Secretary-General. He made no secret of his disapproval, but, as he later recalled:

Kardelj replied that this was of no importance, and the others kept a downcast silence. There was an uneasiness in the atmosphere and the arrangements: there we were, former guerrilla fighters and defenders of the oppressed, in the lap of luxury, but also in a sort of fortress, with a superfluous escort of guards everywhere. And during the actual session Tito whispered to me significantly, using my familiar nickname: 'You will have to speak, Djido, so people won't think we're in disagreement!' I was staggered by his manner, and particularly by his oblique insistence that we must be in agreement. I did make a speech, although there was nothing on the agenda that obliged me to speak or touched on my interests. It was the muddled, contradictory speech of a man doing his best to please someone else without being false to himself. Overnight I considered my position, and on the following day, on the road through Lika on our way to fish for trout, I told Kardelj that I would not be able to support the course we were now adopting. He, very wisely, avoided the issue, remarking merely that I was exaggerating what was a transitional stage in 'our socialist development', not an essential feature of it.[16]

The change of course decreed for the Party seemed likely to coincide with moves towards a closer relationship with the Soviet Union. In June Tito announced that Moscow had shown a desire for an exchange of ambassadors – since the break diplomatic contacts had been only at *chargé d'affaires* level – and he believed it was right to accept this olive branch although it 'does not necessarily mean a normalisation or improvement of the relations between our two countries'. That would depend, he continued, on whether Moscow was prepared to 'modify her Stalinist foreign policy' and respect the rights and independence of other nations. As to Yugoslavia, she was quite ready to bury the hatchet and be friends again. He was only sorry, he somewhat complacently concluded, 'that they have not followed our path of self-management on their own soil'.[17]

The Soviet Union could scarcely be expected to copy the institutions of those she had been denouncing as heretics. It was more likely, Djilas feared, that attempts would be made to force the Yugoslavs back to the old Stalinist patterns. He was resolved to do his utmost to prevent it.

CHAPTER TWENTY-SEVEN

Collision Course

UNLIKE other leading comrades, Djilas was not burdened with administrative responsibilities. From the end of the year he would exercise the duties of President of the National Assembly, but otherwise he had no institutions or departments of state to supervise. He remained free for special political or representational duties, free to head delegations, free above all to write. For the past two years, since the Central Committee had, on his initiative, decreed freedom of theoretical discussion, the Party leadership had formally renounced the claim to monolithic ideological control and the huge agit-prop apparatus had been partly dismantled. Theoretical discussion, the exchange and ventilation of constructive ideas, was supposed to be unfettered. Actually, the Central Committee's decree remained a dead letter. The Party was not really prepared to let itself wither away at its intellectual roots, and whatever its leading idealogues like Kardelj, Djilas and Pijade said or wrote continued to be regarded as having the sacrosanct character of official pronouncements. Up to the middle of 1953 they spoke, with only minor differences of emphasis, with much the same voice. But after the June Plenum on Brioni, one voice began to be raised in increasingly personal and distinctive tones.

Because Djilas had for so long been the supreme agit-prop chief, and because he held forth at such length, and in such confident if often confused tones, whatever he said was still taken to be authoritative Party thinking. His political-philosophic articles were long, rambling disquisitions couched generally in an involved and cloudy style. It was difficult for his readers, and apparently often for the author himself, to know exactly what he was driving at. He seemed to be thinking aloud – thinking thoughts that were generally stimulating, often obscure, and sometimes, to Orthodox Marxists, smacking dangerously of heresy.

In the autumn, *Nova Misao*, a favourite mouthpiece for such ruminations, published a long essay cryptically entitled *The Beginning of the End and of the Beginning*. This apparently meant the ending of the old Stalinist regime and the start of new trends in the Soviet Union heralding the transition from 'bureaucratic state capitalism to Socialism' on Titoist lines. But his strictures on bureaucratic despotism and its intellectual sponsors in the Soviet Union could equally be applied to Yugoslavia. The broadside was clearly aimed against the totalitarianism of Djilas's own Party with its 'intrigues, mutual scheming and trap-laying, pursuit of posts, careerism, favouritism, the advancement of one's own followers, relatives, "old fighters" – all of it under the mask of high morality and ideology'. To carry out a revolution, he argued, professional politicians and tight party discipline were necessary; but in a post-revolutionary period, these were no longer essential and could become brakes on social development. Power inevitably corrupts; revolutionary leaders, like any others, are loth to relax their grip on it. They may claim that it would be wrong for them to think of doing so as long as there is a danger that others – counter-revolutionaries and class enemies – would then seize it and undo their good work. This poses a dilemma: the revolution ossified in the power of a corrupt bureaucracy but with no acceptable alternative in view. Djilas was to return again and again to this theme.

The forum chosen for further instalments of Djilas's continuing ideological soliloquy was *Borba*, the Party organ. The articles at first attracted no particular attention; they seemed to differ little from the prolix commentaries and exhortations readers of those columns had come to expect. But soon the more perceptive noted that they were assuming an increasingly astringent flavour; or, as one critic later put it, that they were being 'sprinkled with more and more venom'. Every two or three days a fresh broadside would be discharged, to the readers' growing delight or consternation.

The first group of half a dozen such articles appeared between mid-October and 22 November – the date fixed for elections to the National Assembly. Polling on that day was conducted with a slight but perceptible relaxation of official pressure. For the first time, voters could make use of ballot papers and separate, closed pooling booths and were given a choice of at least two candidates, not all of them nominated by the Socialist Alliance. The result still, of course, remained a foregone conclusion – over 95 per cent of the votes cast for the official candidates. A measure of the popularity then enjoyed by his articles was that Djilas was declared to have won no less than 98.8 per cent of the votes cast in his constituency – a higher proportion even than that claimed for Tito![1]

The eyes of the world, Djilas warned his readers, were now on Yugoslavia; 'the Yugoslav battle is part of the world battle.' Now was the chance to show that 'our revolution may end in the splendour of a new democracy' provided the working population succeeded in 'preserving their ownership of the means of production and in proving their ability to administer it more efficiently than the capitalists or the "bureaucrats'". The new form of Socialism they were establishing was under attack from two quarters; from remnants of the old bourgeois ruling class, which still enjoyed some, though declining, support from the West, and from 'bureaucracy' – the power structure into which revolutionary fervour tended to ossify. This latter trend, which looked East for support, was now the greater danger to 'Socialist Democracy'. 'The [Yugoslav] Revolution cannot be saved by its past,' Djilas concluded his first article. 'The Revolution must find new ideas, new forms. Without creation, the Revolution is only a glorious tradition, but not life. The Revolution must transform itself into democracy and Socialism, into new human relationships, if it is not to be destroyed.'[2]

Another article dealt with the role of the deputies to the National Assembly. Whilst warning against taking any 'steps backwards towards bourgeois parliamentary forms which are anachronistic and untenable', and refraining from admitting that the Assembly had hitherto merely rubber-stamped the decisions taken by the Party and State, Djilas urged that a deputy should be more active in 'protecting and controlling organs, checking arbitrariness on the part of the local [Party and administrative] apparatus' – more, in short, 'of a political personality, active both in parliament and in the field'. Voters should have the right to elect the representatives they really wanted, not just 'people imposed from above'. Deputies had an important part to play in helping to fight current abuses, which Djilas enumerated as various forms of 'favouritism and privilege', by which those without proper qualifications were given jobs, pensions, scholarships, allowances, superior accommodation, special medical treatment, and so on, all thanks to the 'protection' they enjoyed in high places, the result being that 'waste, profligacy and arbitrariness are everywhere rampant. Billions are thus dissipated – and all that in a poor, underdeveloped country.'[3]

In a further article Djilas considered the prevalent assumption that democratic rights should not be accorded to the enemies of Socialism, i.e., to bourgeois reactionaries or to Cominformists, and that only 'the leading and most progressive forces in the country' should enjoy such rights. Without actually disputing this view, he drew attention to the difficulties and inconsistencies involved in it – how to be sure where 'progressive' trends ended and bureaucratic or bourgeois trends began, how to avoid privilege and arbitrary behaviour on the part of the privileged which 'create resistance and dissatisfaction even amongst ordinary working people'. The best he could advise was that a bourgeois should be treated as equal simply as an individual, not as a member of a class; 'the true "Communist democrat" . . . struggles for equality for all before the law, even for the bourgeoisie, whilst at the same time fighting against all bourgeois ideas and against the restoration of Capitalism.'[4]

Two articles of a more philosophical nature were devoted to considering the distinction between 'form' and 'content'. Whilst stressing that the two cannot be wholly separated, he distinguished between the 'content' or specific achievements of the Revolution – 'nationalised industry, workers councils, organised power for defending the established order against illegal overthrow, a steadily-increasing number of democratic social organisations', economic and cultural advances, and the like – and current 'forms' – human relationships, respect for law, the reaching of decisions and application of policies following reasonable discussion and the consideration of other viewpoints – in short, a more humane, civilised and genuinely democratic approach. Before the victory of the Revolution, Communists were rightly concerned chiefly with substance or 'content'; now that this had been secured, more importance should be attached to 'form'. 'We must learn to respect the opinions of others, even if they seem stupid and conservative; we must get used to the idea that our views will remain in the minority even when we are right, and we should not imagine that on that account Socialism, revolutionary achievements, etc. must perish.'[5]

The tone of this first group of articles hardly seems sufficiently provocative to have excited public opinion. Public opinion was excited – but over another issue. The Trieste problem – Zone A, administered by the Western Allies and Italy, and Zone B, administered by Yugoslavia – had been frozen but not solved. Three days before the publication of the first of the Djilas articles, the British and Americans announced that they were withdrawing their troops from the city of Trieste and the rest of Zone A, leaving the Italians in sole possession. Tito, angered at this unilateral decision which put paid to Yugoslav hopes of ever gaining the city, responded by bellicose statements and troop movements, whilst crowds demonstrated in the streets of Belgrade and vented their anger by smashing up the British, French and American reading-rooms. It was a year before Tito reconciled himself to the situation, the loss of Trieste being compensated by Zone B's incorporation within Yugoslavia after some frontier rectification in her favour. Though the Soviet Union had done little to back his claims, the explosion demonstrated the fragility of Tito's rapprochement with the West. Djilas had been as outspoken as anyone in criticising the western powers over their actions in Trieste. The greater freedom and democracy he had been advocating in his articles clearly did not imply any weakening of Yugoslavia's independent and non-aligned stance in foreign policy.

It was during the Trieste crisis, when Djilas was one day with Tito in the White Palace, that he found an opportunity of sounding him out about his *Borba* articles. The Old Man's reaction was guarded: 'Well, the line you're taking seems alright and you write well. But you should write more against the bourgeoisie. It's still strong, psychologically in particular. And you should write more for our young people – the young are the most important. We aren't ready yet for democracy; the dictatorship has to go on.'[6]

Tito's reply left Djilas dissatisfied. He did not agree that the bourgeoisie was still strong. He considered it politically neutralised. Stalinist trends, on the other hand, were dangerous and on the increase. To concentrate fire on an enemy already in full retreat did not make sense. Tito seemed to him to be still living in the past, unaware of the quarter from which the main danger now threatened. Almost without realising it, Djilas had embarked on a path to which he meant to keep, a path which he was beginning to see might lead him away from the man whom he had recognised as his political chief for more than fifteen years.

Djilas resumed his articles – a further group of five – on 29 November, the eleventh anniversary of the founding of the Anti-Fascist Council. The second was entitled *Is there a Goal?* to which he answered 'Yes! – a continuing struggle for democracy – the only real and permanent goal!'[7], and appealed for concrete steps towards it. After its publication he underwent a psychological crisis of which he has left a vivid description:

I remember how it all began – the very day, even the hour, perhaps in the same way that converts and anchorites remember the moment when the godhead was revealed to them.

It was on the night of 7-8 December 1953.

Although I had, as usual, fallen asleep about midnight, I woke up suddenly smitten within by some unfaltering, fateful realisation that I would not be able to abandon my views. At that time I had written a series of articles, said by others to be 'revisionist', for the party newspaper, *Borba*. I knew that my views were bound to lead me into conflict with my comrades on the Central Committee, men with whom I had burned away my youth and half of my mature years in search of an ideal which, after so many hopes and so much blood and toil, had proved unreal and unrealizable. My wife, Štefanija, was sleeping silently on the far side of the room, but I was aware of her presence in the dark, in the interminable silence of the night. I tried to thrust away my forebodings, obstinate in their insistence that something final had come to pass, something within me, or something affecting me, which meant that I would have to subordinate my way of life, my hopes – and, what is worse, subordinate my family or even sacrifice it altogether. I knew that I had no prospect of winning. I recalled Trotsky's fate and said to myself: better Trotsky's fate than Stalin's, better to be defeated and destroyed than to betray one's ideal, one's conscience. Even the probable length of a prison sentence (it was usually seven to nine years for 'slandering' the state or conducting 'hostile propaganda') whirled in my brain, as though it had already been pronounced. I saw myself isolated, with my family terrified and at their wit's end; I saw myself among the so-called little people, who would have no way of knowing whether I was a madman or a sage. But the tussle within me was short-lived; it lasted just a few minutes, until I had time to collect my thoughts from sleep and recover from my intimations. Because I already knew, yes *knew*, that this was my true self, and that I could not renounce it, in spite of the vacillations to which I had succumbed, in spite of the more crucial ordeal that I would have to face. I got up and went to my study, and there I jotted down, in a few sentences, what I now knew; the emergence of my differences with the rulers of the party, the inevitability of my parting company with them, the impending trial of my own strength, or my weakness, in deviating from their path.[8]

After that night of searing illumination, the *Borba* articles took on a still sharper tone. 'In its simplest terms, the problem is whether the interests of any party or group of leaders are always identical with those of the people and of society.' Djilas was thinking aloud, and his thoughts were becoming ever more disturbing, more frankly heretical. 'No one party,' he mused, 'not even a single class, can be the exclusive expression of the objective imperatives of contemporary society. None can claim the exclusive right to administer the development of the forces of production without simultaneously delaying development and exploiting the most important factor in those forces – the people. . . . The times require instead a weakening of this role, a weakening of the monopoly of political parties over the life of society, especially in our country, under Socialism.' What was he saying? Who but his comrades – whether called by the old name of the Communist Party or under the new guise of the League of Communists – claimed such a leading role, such a monopoly of political power? In the columns of the Party's own organ Djilas now invoked the alternative – 'more democracy, more free discussion, more free elections to social, state and economic organs, more strict adherence to the law'. Only thus would it be possible to counter 'those outmoded and reactionary forces which cling to the notion that they represent the whole of social reality, that they are the only legal representatives of society.' It was not, however, for the writer to propose in their place new formulae, new programmes; 'the time for great theoretical and super-theoretical programmes is over – we have had too much of them already.'[9]

In the following article, entitled 'Concretely', Djilas went on to explain that the creative new ideas needed by society would arise spontaneously once the right climate had been created for their free exchange. That was now the urgent need – 'to make possible the espousal of ideas without the persecution of the people who held them. The most important thing at this juncture was not new ideas but freedom of ideas. In particular terms, that means fighting for freedom of discussion everywhere, fighting for strengthening and developing certain democratic forms like workers' councils, people's committees, voters' meetings, etc., in brief, legality, continuing controversy, democracy.' Djilas was speaking out plainly enough now, and the enemy was also plainly indicated. 'Every limitation of thought, even in the name of the most beautiful ideal, only degrades those who perpetuate it.' The greatest crimes and horrors in history – the fires of the Inquisition, Hitler's concentration camps, Stalin's labour camps – stemmed ultimately from a denial of free thought, from the exclusive claims of 'reactionary fanatics who have a political monopoly'.[10]

The *Borba* articles were becoming a national sensation. Never had that cliché-ridden official organ been read with such avid curiosity or aroused such excitement. Most reactions, both from the Party rank and file and from the non-Communist public, were enthusiastic. Some even of the Party elite – members of the Executive Committee – warmly approved. One correspondent hailed the series as life-enhancing 'sunbeams', another, a veteran with twenty-nine years membership of the Party, agreed with the writer that most political meetings were 'obsolete and tedious' and the Party itself 'heading for the museum'.[11]

Only Tito appeared to show no interest; he was vacationing in Slovenia and seemed not to have read the latest instalments. But other leading comrades had been reading them with mounting indignation and alarm which they could no longer suppress. 'It was with Ranković that I first felt an estrangement,' Djilas recalls.

One afternoon in late December 1953 I went to see him. We had been close through all the critical phases of our lives – in the prewar underground, in wartime, and in the anti-Soviet struggle. Nor on this occasion did he show any reserve towards me. He even offered me a hunting rifle as a gift. But in conversation he was ominously reticent. Although I liked the rifle, I did not accept it. What sense is there in my taking it, I thought, when we are obviously going to go our separate ways? When I asked Ranković pointblank what he thought about my *Borba* articles he answered without beating about the bush: 'I hope I'll never have to bother with philosophical ruminations, but let me tell you that what you've been writing is harming the Party!' This came as no surprise to me. Ranković had always made it clear that he opposed reforms which might jeopardise the monolithic structure. On this he was never in two minds, nor was he ever false or double-faced in his dealings with me.[12]

With Kardelj, the case was different. Ranković, Djilas knew, was quite sincere when he disclaimed my interest in ideological controversy; his concern was with the Party, the organisation and exercise of power. For him ideological orthodoxy was simply a cement to ensure the authority of the Party over every nook and cranny of the national life, as did the police apparatus which he controlled. The freedom of ideas, the emphasis on the right to discuss rather than the duty to conform and obey, challenged this authority and had therefore to be resisted. So Ranković had always set his face against reforms, and if they were approved by the leadership, he accepted them only out of Party discipline. But Kardelj was himself a major initiator of reform, at least until mid-1953 when Tito began to apply the brakes. Even after that he had at least gone on discussing them with Djilas, who continued to consult him personally or over the telephone. Kardelj was, after all, recognised to be the regime's leading theoretician, licensed by Tito to propound, with his customary pedantic parade of Marxist learning, the approved tenets of Yugoslavia's emerging 'path to Socialism'. Tito valued his cooperation, knowing that his aptitudes and ambitions lay primarily in the sphere of theory and that his lack of personal charisma posed no implicit challenge to the leader's primacy. But though deeply interested in ideas, Kardelj was reluctant to fight for them. He was too prudent – or could it be too pusillanimous? – ever to stand up for them once he saw them to be in conflict with Tito's autocratic will to power. He had nothing of Djilas's urge to fight for his ideas, to fight even against the ideas held yesterday once he was convinced that they should be superseded by new, truer, more creative ideas. The Montenegrin was prepared to go to any extreme, to make any sacrifice, even that of his past or of his future, for the sake of his beliefs. The circumspect Slovene intellectual drew back when ideas became too dangerous in their implications, impinging too uncomfortably on life and endangering his personal position as number two in the Party hierarchy.

Djilas should not then have been taken aback when, on his observing that they were both still in basic agreement, Kardelj sharply contradicted him: 'No, we are not! I don't agree with you at all! You want to change the whole system!'[13]

In his next *Borba* article Djilas made oblique references to Kardelj's criticisms and gave his reply. They dubbed him a 'philosopher divorced from reality', accused him of writing for a foreign audience, bringing grist to the mill of the reactionaries, and departing from Marxism-Leninism. None of these charges was true. He disclaimed the title of philosopher, though he *was* concerned with the liberating power of free ideas as the best antidote to the 'bureaucratic dogmatism' with which so many people had become infected. Far from being divorced from reality himself, he believed he was voicing the views of ordinary, simple people; it was the leadership of the Party which had been divorcing itself from the masses. If foreigners and reactionaries took comfort from his words he was sorry but not to be blamed; it was the fault of the bureaucrats in power who played into such hands by their arbitrary and unlawful acts. As for the charge that he was departing from Marxism-Leninism, he could only say that he never claimed infallibility for every word he had written; his purpose was rather to stimulate thinking. He believed that truth emerged from the cumulative thought and initiative of the common people; 'every criticism, therefore, every clash of opinion, is a welcome addition to the cause and above all to new democratic practice.'[14]

In his next article Djilas passed over to a hard-hitting attack. Today in Yugoslavia, he declared, 'conscious social forces' existed alongside, and often in opposition to, the official Communist bodies. The latter had no exclusive right to a monopoly of the truth or of social justice or the national interests. Communists – now thus openly named – had separated themselves from the masses, claimed privileged positions, and had turned into 'priests and policemen of Socialism'. They had 'centralised and regulated everything, from ethics to stamp-collecting', with the result that now 'bureaucratism is more dangerous than capitalism.' They nevertheless still concentrated their efforts on ferreting out the few remaining class-enemies. The old forms of Party activity and organisation to which they doggedly adhered had ceased to fulfil any useful purpose and real life went on without them. Most Party meetings had become a waste of time; 'in my opinion they should convene very rarely.' 'Yes, sinful thoughts!' Djilas exclaimed ironically. 'Who will look after the souls, conscience and activity of the people?' Most political workers had no real function any more to perform in society. 'Once men gave everything, even life itself, to become professional revolutionaries. They were indispensible to social progress. But today,' he bluntly concluded, 'they are obstacles to it.'[15]

Tito, still absent in Slovenia, reacted at last to the extraordinary line which his Party's mouthpiece appeared to be taking. Peko Dapčević visited him just before the New Year and on returning to Belgrade told Djilas that he had found the Old Man very angry indeed. The two Montenegrins were close friends; the previous summer Djilas had been best man at the wedding when Belgrade's most eligible bachelor married the twenty-one-year-old Milena Versajkov. His bride, a beautiful young actress, had no Party or Partisan affiliations and was consequently cold-shouldered by the less glamorous wives of 'old fighters' and high officials who formed the cream of the capital's post-war society. Djilas, out of sympathy with his friend – and perhaps for the slighted young lady too, malicious tongues wagged – was at that very time composing a blistering denunciation of the envy and political snobbery which was leading to the young woman's ostracism. He did not foresee – or if he did, seemed not to care – that the attack would rebound on his own head, adding a host of vindictive new enemies to those already alarmed and outraged by his *Borba* articles.

One afternoon in early January, when Djilas and his wife Štefica were at the cinema, Ranković's police agents fetched him out with a message that he was to report immediately to Kardelj. Štefica, who was to stand stoutly by her husband in his coming ordeal, was convinced they had come to arrest him. It was a natural assumption, for on the last day of 1953 *Borba* had carried an article criticising the security service as a law to itself and an instrument for imposing the authority of the Party regardless of the interests and rights of the people. In an article entitled 'The Class Struggle' Djilas had argued that 'the intensification of the class struggle was necessary and correct so long as the struggle for power was necessary;' but to continue it now that the bourgeoisie had been reduced to a harmless vestige was 'to deviate into bureaucratism, in conflict with plain people because they held differing opinions or because of their frequently justified grumbling and objection to artificially imposed tasks. . . . In my opinion, the duty of the state organs (primarily the Courts, UDBA [the Security Service] and the police) cannot be intensification of the class struggle but must instead be the preservation and implementation of the law. These organs must rid themselves of Party interference, otherwise . . . though they may appear to be distinguishing between socialism and capitalism, they are in reality working against the people.'[16]

Bold words, with which most of his readers would heartily agree – but hardly calculated to endear their author to the man who built up and now controlled UDBA! With Kardelj, Djilas found Ranković waiting for him, taciturn as ever, though he fancied he could detect a certain sadness underlying his friend's harsh inflexibility. There was no discussion between them, no attempts at persuasion, no search for a compromise. Their remarks seemed to him 'ambiguous and murky'. The Old Man, they repeated, was furious; things were serious and could not go on as they were. They did not inform him that a special meeting of the Central Committee had been convened for 16 January; this he was to discover only from the newspapers. In a subsequent report to that forum Kardelj would claim that Djilas, in this or a previous conversation with him, maintained that

Comrade Tito was defending bureaucracy, and that he, Djilas, would sooner or later have to fight it out with him. Secondly, that Comrade Ranković and I were in fact in agreement with him, but that we were opportunists and therefore did not want to argue with Tito; thirdly, that whether we wanted it or not, a Socialist left-wing was emerging in our country; and fourthly, that the possibility of two Socialist parties emerging in our country cannot be discounted.[17]

The meeting with Kardelj and Ranković ended without any prospect of reconciliation.

'That's revisionism!' Kardelj exclaimed, brushing aside Djilas's arguments. 'In essence the same as Bernstein!'

'I haven't read Bernstein, except for what I've picked up from Lenin,' Djilas replied.

'I've read him. Here, I've got a copy!' Kardelj said.[18] Djilas noticed that he had been engaged in writing something. Kardelj waved a half-written page in front of him; it was the report he was preparing on Djilas for the plenum of the Central Committee, though he said nothing about it. Kardelj had been specially alarmed by the latest *Borba* article and saw his role as the regime's authorised theoretician threatened. Was not Djilas saying that they had come to an ideological parting of the ways, that Kardelj was defending old discredited ideas whilst he – Djilas – stood for the ideas which would shape the future? If this was indeed what he meant, then he had sealed his own fate as far as the Party was concerned.

Ranković left to attend to other business and the two others remained alone. When Djilas was in the hall about to leave, Kardelj turned to him and said: 'Nothing in my life has been more difficult than this!'[19] There seemed to be a note of genuine anguish in his voice, and he raised his

hands in a gesture of resignation as if to say: 'But what else can I do?'
Then he turned to go upstairs. They were next to meet as enemies;
Kardelj as prosecutor, Djilas as the accused.

CHAPTER TWENTY-EIGHT

The Break with Tito

BELGRADE was making ready for Christmas – the Orthodox Christmas which falls a fortnight later than in the West. For two years now, in the more liberal climate marked by the Sixth Congress, the authorities had permitted the public celebration of the Christian festival. Their relations with the Orthodox Church had improved, though there had been some renewed demonstrations and persecution of priests in Bosnia and Hercegovina in the autumn despite the good impression made by the Patriarch's formal call on President Tito to assure him of the support of the Church in the current crisis over Trieste. Djilas was little affected by such matters. He still considered himself an atheist, and his growing disillusionment with the Communist creed had not caused him to seek consolation in any return to the religion of his ancestors. For believers, this Christmastide might be a season of joy; for him it was rather a Passiontide unlit by any hope of resurrection.

Of the first two weeks of January 1954 he writes: 'During this period I did not get more than an hour's sleep a night. I was exhausted and drained dry, but still in command of my faculties. People looked at me aghast, as though I had come down from the gallows – such horrified expressions I was to encounter for years afterwards.'[1]

His explosive articles still continued to appear in *Borba*, though now he made it clear that they represented his personal views rather than the official Party line. In 'League or Party' he reiterated his plea for the transformation of the latter – but emphatically not its abolition – in order to play its changed role in a society in which the basic aims of the old Communist Party – the triumph of the Revolution – had already been achieved. He saw the present struggle as one 'between life and traditional methods, between reality and dogma'. Now that it was in power, the Party was tending to attract careerists and opportunists; outmoded, coercive methods persisted which were only 'excellent for keeping people backward'. Finally, 'the Leninist form of the Party and state has become obsolete (the dictatorship based on the Party)'; what was now needed was 'less dogmatism and more democratic and humane relations'.[2]

On 7 January *Borba* published his swan song under the simple title of 'Revolution'. The problem, he declared, was no longer how to defend the Revolution, since it was now firmly established, but how to develop

243

it and prevent its perversion by the continued use of old methods which had become positively counter-productive. 'Today Revolution is reform, peaceful progress. Today it is nonsense to struggle for power in a revolutionary form, not only because it is unrealistic, but because it is counter-revolutionary.' 'The soul of the Revolution,' Djilas concluded in words which were at once an apologia for his revolutionary past and the profession of faith by a prophet about to be driven out into the political wilderness, 'the soul of the Revolution can be preserved only in real freedom, because it was carried out by free men, for freedom, and in the name of freedom.'[3]

Nova Misao had in the meantime appeared, somewhat earlier than usual, on the news-stands and was being snapped up by a public eager to read the sensational article entitled 'Anatomy of a Moral'.[4] This was where Djilas described the cruel ostracism of the bride of a famous Partisan general, an opera singer who happened to be younger and more attractive than the wives of other high officials but lacked their previous Party and Partisan background. The article recounted in graphic detail how one of these ladies had snubbed and humiliated the newcomer when she accompanied her husband to watch a match at a football stadium. It was a blistering attack on the vindictiveness, vulgarity and political exclusiveness of Belgrade's post-war high society. No names were mentioned, but it was clear to all that the young victim was none other than Dapčević's bride, the twenty-one year old Milena Versajkov, and her persecutor Milica, wife of General Vukmanović-Tempo. It was a vivid and somewhat melodramatic story written as if with the deliberate intention of causing offence to 'all those exalted women [who] came from semi-peasant backgrounds and were semi-educated' and who seemed to think that their war-time services entitled them to 'grab and hoard de luxe furniture and works of art, tasteless of course, but by means of which they satisfied their primitive instincts of greed and imagined and puffed-up notions of their social status, with all the pretentiousness and omniscience of the ignorant.' The morals of these ex-Partisan parvenues, Djilas went on to declare, were on a par with their social pretensions, and he proceeded to lash them with the moral fervour and indignation of a Jeremiah, thereby arousing the implacable enmity earned by such prophets.

On 10 January *Borba* published a formal disavowal of the preceding series which was branded as 'contrary to the opinions of all other members of the Executive Committee'. The matter would be taken up, it was ominously announced, at the Central Committee's forthcoming Plenum.

244

As soon as Tito returned from Slovenia, Djilas sent him a letter requesting a personal interview. He hoped that some arrangement might be reached which would allow him to withdraw from the Executive Committee (the old Politburo) whilst remaining on the Central Committee and continuing to put forward his opinions in public, but in a moderate and unofficial way.[5] He fondly believed that others could be converted to views which, to those who held the levers of power, now appeared frankly heretical. He still had hopes of Kardelj, who had shared his liberalising views and at one time even suggested that *Borba* might serve as a forum where both Djilas's ideas, and those of his critics, could be freely aired. His greatest miscalculation was over Tito himself. 'I attributed to Tito democratic traits and initiatives,' he admitted later, 'which, in my heart of hearts, it was my hope, rather than my conviction, that he possessed.'[6] Furthermore, he failed to take into account the outside pressure reinforcing Tito's innate distrust of the liberalising tendencies to which he had up to now been obliged to give his support. Stalin's death had opened up the possibility of a reconciliation with Moscow. Djilas, as unrepentant and unrestrained as ever in his condemnation of the Stalinist heritage, would be an undoubted obstacle to any rapprochement. The line he had been taking in *Borba* had been noted by the Soviet Embassy in Belgrade with a displeasure which it made no effort to conceal.

Djilas knew that the forthcoming meeting with Tito was likely to prove the most difficult, and the most momentous in its consequences for his public and private life, of the innumerable exchanges which had taken place between them in the seventeen years they had known each other. The two men had often had brushes before, but never clashes on any major political or personal issue. They had differed over matters of style rather than substance, and their occasional friction had arisen from contrasts of temperament and mentality. There had been something of the father-son relationship in their long association. Djilas had often chafed under the authority of the 'Old Man', but he had never been tempted to challenge it. Nor had he ever questioned the political primacy or the leadership which Tito had assumed over the Party and the personal destinies of its members as if by some natural right. Djilas had never been conscious of committing a single act of disloyalty towards him, still less of organising any faction to fight for the ideas in which he passionately believed – above all, his conviction that the freedom of the human spirit was the supreme and ultimate good, and individual conscience the highest tribunal to which party discipline and the avowed goals of the Revolution must in the final analysis be subordinated. That these things might become incompatible had only latterly become clear. And only now did Djilas begin to see that Tito did not share this faith. They differed in their ultimate view of life and human values. 'I yearned for the power of law, not the law of power,' as Djilas later put it.[7]

It was an unbearable thought that this long and intimate relationship was about to end. 'If someone had asked me five or six months before the rift opened between us whether I could conceive of any force that could separate me from Tito, Kardelj and Ranković, I would have said "No – not even death could separate us!" '[8] The younger man's respect and affection remained undiminished despite his growing realization that the beliefs which now possessed him might not only lead to a break with Tito but cause Tito to break *him*. At one point in their last conversation he said to Tito: 'You I can understand. You created something, and now you defend it. And I too am just beginning something. . . . But these two – ' pointing to Kardelj and Ranković who were also present – 'these two I simply can't understand!' His words seemed to touch a responsive chord, but only for a moment. Tito was not the man to be deflected from his purpose.[9]

No full record survives of that last painful meeting, which took place in Tito's official residence, the White Palace, a few days before the Plenary Session called to settle the 'Djilas affair'. Kardelj repeated his charge that Djilas had fallen into Bernstein's 'revisionist' errors. Tito, as was his wont, eschewed theoretical niceties and summed the matter up by remarking that Djilas was a 'changed man'. That things should have come to such a pass seemed also to have shaken him. When Djilas asked for some coffee to be ordered, as he had not been able to sleep at night, Tito observed pointedly: 'Others are not sleeping either!'[10]

The interview ended inconclusively; the battle lines remained drawn for the decisive encounter due to take place in the Central Committee. Tito knew that Djilas put all his trust in the rightness and force of his ideas; he would at least make no attempt to rally potential supporters, thereby committing the supreme crime against the Party of trying to form a 'faction'. All the same, Tito left nothing to chance. Before the plenary meeting which opened on 16 January, he made a point of speaking personally with those members of the Central Committee whom he suspected of sympathising with Djilas or whose views were known to have been close to the latter's. He shrewdly nominated Bakarić, whose influence had always been firmly, if cautiously, in favour of moderate reform, to head the disciplinary commission charged with recommending appropriate penalties for the offender.

The one hundred and eight members of the Central Committee had been summoned to meet in the marble and bronze splendour of a pre-war Belgrade bank. The proceedings were to be broadcast live – an innovation in keeping with the decision taken at the Sixth Congress for more open Party proceedings, and one which indicated the authorities' confidence that an exemplary discrediting and condemnation of the heresiarch could be expected. The occasion was to serve much the same purpose, though with less blatantly Stalinist savagery and the prospect of milder punishment, as the Moscow show-trials.

In contrast to most of the Committee members, Djilas arrived on foot, looking drawn and haggard, accompanied by Dedijer. He later wrote that 'the ordeal was to be much more frightening and painful than anything I had sensed or could foresee.'[11]

Tito himself opened the proceedings.[12] He spoke more in sorrow than in anger, with almost paternal severity and pathos, referring to Djilas by his party nickname of 'Djido'. He began by admitting that he too was partly to blame for not intervening sooner. He had told the author of the offending *Borba* articles that, though he did not approve of everything in them, he should go on writing. Only towards the end of December, when he had been able to read them more closely, did he realise just what poison they were spreading. The unity of the Party, and indeed of the whole country, was being undermined. Djido had gone too far, brushing aside the justified criticisms and remonstrances of trusted comrades and stubbornly going his own way regardless of the damage and confusion he was causing. By publishing his latest article in *Nova Misao* he had made it clear that he wanted a showdown. How had all this been possible; what had brought it about?

Djilas had drifted away, Tito went on, from the other leaders with whom everything used to be frankly discussed. Ideas had always been expressed and exchanged within the Party leadership with a freedom quite unknown in the Soviet Party. But Djilas had abused this informality and freedom, arrogantly assuming that he alone was always right. Having no administrative duties himself, he had branded those comrades who had to struggle with practical difficulties as 'bureaucrats'. He had lost touch with the rank and file and become a mere irresponsible day-dreamer. 'Detached from present-day life, separated from his comrades, he found another society and made it his milieu,' Tito declared. 'Then the influence of the West, his journeys abroad, and all sorts of other influences from abroad counteracted the influence of our reality, our revolutionary past, and of all revolutionary experience.'

Tito then turned to the heart of the problem; the heresy that the class enemy had been decisively destroyed and that the Party needed to change its character and surrender most of its responsibilities:

I was the first to speak of the withering away of the Party [he reminded them] but I did not say it should happen within six months or one or two years. I said it would be a lengthy process. Before the last class enemy has been neutralised, before Socialist consciousness has permeated all layers of our population, there can be neither a withering away nor a liquidation of the League of Communists, because the League of Communists is responsible for the realisation of the revolutionary achievement, just as it was responsible for victory during the revolution. The League must continue to exist; and not only that, it must be further strengthened ideologically until it is fully conscious of its gigantic tasks. . . .

For Djilas there are no classes – all are now equal. But his case proves precisely how dangerous the class-enemy in our country is. The class-enemy exists, as is clearly shown in Djilas's articles. It exists within the League of Communists and assumes the most varied forms. From now on we shall have to see to it that nobody believes that the problem of the class struggle and its liquidation vanishes with the end of the armed struggle. It is a lengthy process which lasts all through the construction of Socialism, until we arrive at the higher stage, Communism – a very lengthy process indeed, and various hostile forces will oppose and obstruct us in the most varied ways, specially if we take into account how strong Western influence is.

As for the accused's ideological errors, Tito confined himself to remarking that Djilas had been guilty of 'advocating democracy at any price, which is exactly the position of Bernstein'.

Kardelj was left to elaborate the charge. He did so with his customary long-winded pedantry.

'Djilas's conception of democracy is not ours,' Kardelj declared. 'It is not Socialist, but a mixture of anarchism and bourgeois liberalistic forms.'

He went on to explain that Bernstein's heresy consisted in believing that 'the primary goal of the workers' movement is the struggle for democracy, the struggle to transform Germany into a democratic nation,' and quoted with disapproval his well-known remark that 'what is commonly called the ultimate goal of Socialism is nothing to me; the movement is everything.'

Djilas interrupted the orator to exclaim: 'I have not read Bernstein, but I agree with him that the goal is nothing, the movement everything!'

Kardelj resumed his exposition. Djilas's theorising, he said, was a rehash of old errors, a step backwards rather than any new contribution to Socialist thought. It could consequently only harm the ideological unity of the League of Communists. It promoted 'uncontrollable anarchistic forces'. Djilas had arrogantly rejected comradely criticism. Kardelj recalled his own attempt to reason with him the previous December and to open his eyes to the harm he was doing. All had been in vain. But lest his listeners wrongly conclude that anything which was being said at this Plenum might impede the course of development towards 'Socialist democracy' in Yugoslavia, Kardelj wished to reassure them that this was not so. The struggle was being waged on two fronts; against 'bureaucratic tendencies' on the one side, and on the other against the 'anarchist elemental forces' unleashed by Djilas.

Djilas opened his defence with a reasonably worded statement accepting some of the criticisms but clarifying and broadly reaffirming his stand.

When I look back over my past, I cannot claim to have been one of the most disciplined of Communists; but neither have I been one who violated discipline or failed to carry out allotted tasks. I was the kind of Communist who conscientiously performs his duty without thinking too much about discipline. But it is quite true that in recent months I became aware of my increasing ideological disagreement with the accepted theoretical views of our movement on a number of basic questions. That is the true and fundamental cause of my personal alienation from my closest comrades in the Executive Committee. My greatest mistake was in failing to consult with them. Although there was no formal obligation for the leading comrades to submit speeches and articles for checking, it became the practice to do so; my disregard of it may perhaps thus be considered a breach of discipline. I was all the more reluctant to do this as I realised that others might disagree with the views I expressed.

I have never claimed that my views are infallible; it is quite possible that some need to be revised or at least rephrased. I simply regarded them as a useful basis for discussion, and I became convinced that any differences which might exist between us could be ironed out in frank discussion. I was firmly convinced that our movement had reached a stage where its unity could not possibly be jeopardised by such discussion. My criticisms have ranged over many aspects of our system, but I have never called in question the system itself; nor, in the foreseeable future, do I intend to do so.

On questions of foreign policy, and on the fundamental issue of the brotherhood and unity of our peoples, I have always been completely at one with the Party leadership. My election speeches clearly prove that. The different views I have been expressing on philosophical and aesthetic questions have not weakened my basic acceptance of dialectical materialism. The views of Karl Marx have always been, and always will be, the basis for all my personal interpretations.

249

The Progress of a Revolutionary

There are rumours that I am against Comrade Tito. That is absolutely untrue. Tito has always been for me a unique figure of unquestioned authority in our movement and nation.

Before making his statement, Djilas went on to say, he had shown the draft to Tito. This had made it quite clear, Tito had told him, that Djilas had failed to realise the likely consequences of the sort of public discussion he had been calling for in his articles, and how dangerous they would be not only for the unity of the League of Communists but for the whole development of Socialism. He would take this admonition to heart and abide by all Tito's decisions.

I shall go on working to carry out the decisions of the League of Communists and of the government authorities, as I have always done in the past [Djilas continued]. I cannot conceive of Socialism being built in our country in any other way than through the League, the Socialist Alliance and the government authorities. I am ready to stop publishing any ideas of mine which the leadership may consider might be politically harmful. Perhaps the recent article in *Nova Misao* could, in certain circumstances, do such harm. It may have been exaggerated and too sweeping, and anyway it deals with things that are now past. It was not aimed against any specific person or with any actual situation in mind. If anyone feels insulted over it, I am ready to apologise in any way he wants.

The unity of the movement means everything to me. I don't believe it is endangered by freedom of thought, but rather that it is strengthened by it. From my boyhood until now I have been a free man and a Communist, and I hope to remain so until the end of my life. I don't believe these two things are incompatible. I believe that one should both say what one thinks and do what is agreed or ordered. I shall do whatever is required of me without complaining, and I shall speak without preconceived thoughts.

I have admitted that I may have violated party discipline, but I cannot accept some of the criticism levelled against me. On the charge of 'revisionism', let me state clearly what I think. As regards Leninism, I am a 'revisionist'. I believe – and see no reason to disguise it – that such an ideology no longer suits our country. But, comrades, I am no supporter of some bourgeois or Western social-democratic idea. I am not so by reason of my education or way of life, nor have I read about social democracy. If some of my ideas resemble Bernstein's or others, it is not because I have imitated them but because I have come to the same conclusions independently.

Let me make my position regarding the struggle against the bourgeoisie clear. If our Party and government decides that the struggle still needs to be intensified, I accept their decision.

I know that my articles created a great stir within the League of Communists. But I am not in favour of liquidating the League. I am simply

250

advocating certain organisational changes in it.

That is briefly what I wanted to say.

Djilas had wished to be conciliatory; but it was not through conciliation that the Partisans had fought their way to power and were now resolved to keep the fruits of victory. He wanted to reconcile the irreconcilable; to be a free man, as he put it, whilst remaining a Communist. He knew that there were many in the Party and the country at large who approved of the line he had been taking. But he spoke only for himself, not as their representative, and he had neither endeavoured nor wished to organise their support. Now those who could have come to his aid rushed to save their own skins.

Among the Central Committee members were people prepared to stone me in a fit of remorse for their own heresy, which had been 'unmasked' and 'proven' in me [he wrote]. More than that, there were some whose ideas and ideals had become so soft in their lives of power and comfort that they averted their eyes from me, as though I were some dead dog, although they would have gladly been on my side 'if the chips had fallen differently'; if, in short, the balance of forces had somehow or other come down in my favour.[13]

Instead, when the debate was thrown open, Djilas found himself the target of abuse from all sides. The fiercest onslaught of all came from Moša Pijade, only too ready to pay off old scores and give vent to the spleen which, even when their ideas had seemed most in harmony, continued to sour their personal relations. Insult now followed on insult, gibe on gibe. The *Nova Misao* article Pijade dismissed as a piece of 'political pornography' which spelt the author's end as a serious theoretician and political writer. But what else could one expect from such a hypocrite?

Now he has a villa and two cars and so forth; he has far more than those whom he has described as a repulsive caste. He has retained all his posts and privileges while renouncing only the hard work connected with them. While his closest comrades are sweating under the heavy burden of administrative work for state and society, he sits in comfort and writes and writes, and then, as a recreation, shows himself in the streets as a good democrat and drinks in cafes. His articles in *Borba* alone netted him 220,000 dinars. In all this he shows a total lack of a sense of responsibility, an absence of any feeling of obligation towards the movement that has raised him. At forty, a man should mature and enter middle age, but Comrade Djilas evidently has not made this progress; he has rather reverted to the preceding stage of adolescence – to the early days before the war when he wrote his poem: 'I wander whistling through the streets'. It seems this is how he has been promenading through our movement in the last few years;

wandering through the streets and dismissing everything with a whistle – the League of Communists, Marxism, all traditions, and the Revolution.

Lesser figures were each given their say. Blažo Jovanović, his old comrade from the 1941 Montenegrin rising, declared that 'since Djilas has attacked the League of Communists there is no place for him any longer in its ranks.' Tempo branded him a reactionary. Miloš Minić, who as Public Prosecutor had called for the death sentence on Draža Mihailović and was later to become Tito's Foreign Minister, described him as a master of half-truths and denounced him for betraying the working class and attacking the Party leadership. Peter Stambolić repeated the charge that Djilas was falling under the influence of Nye Bevan. Veljko Vlahović, who had run the Free Yugoslavia Radio station during the War and recently passed Djilas's *Borba* articles and even published a Djilas-type article of his own, ate humble pie and appealed for stricter control of the press. Peko Dapčević hastened to disassociate himself from his friend and from the whole *Nova Misao* incident: 'It was all an invention of Djilas,' he declared. 'I myself knew nothing of it!'

Only two voices were raised on behalf of the accused – those of his ex-wife Mitra and his friend Dedijer. Mitra, a prey to strong and conflicting emotions, spoke in such a confused way that it was difficult to make head or tail of what she meant. She appeared to be suggesting that though she did not actually condemn them, she found his articles 'in a certain sense dubious and exaggerated, and that their publication had caused harm and confusion.' Dedijer was not only a close associate of Djilas but, as a sub-editor of *Borba*, bore the responsibility of having published his articles. He explained that he had done so since he believed them to have been written with the authority of the Executive Committee. They expressed very much what other leaders had been thinking and saying. On 25 December he had asked Kardelj whether there were any fundamental differences between his views and those being voiced by Djilas; he had gathered that there were not. A subsequent rereading of articles by Djilas, Kardelj and Comrade Tito confirmed his opinion. In short, until very recently, the articles now under attack were approved by all those now sitting in judgment on their author. Dedijer reminded his listeners of certain embarrassing facts; that at the end of December, when most of the articles had been published, Djilas was unanimously elected President of the National Assembly; and that the charges of 'revisionism' now being made against him had formerly been levelled against the whole of the Party leadership in the anathema pronounced on them all by the Cominform. By throwing mud at Djilas, Dedijer concluded, they were smearing themselves and the Revolution. The whole affair called for a just and sensible settlement. He described his friend as a proud eagle restless for intellectual flight who had broken the cage of dogma and should not now have his wings clipped. 'We have few people of his calibre, Comrades,' he declared, raising some ironic laughter, 'Such men are not born every day! The Party needs his strength and his gifts!'

Dedijer's plea fell on deaf ears. Not even Djilas seemed pleased by it. He intervened to emphasize that, whatever impression his friend may have conveyed, his differences with the Party were not of a personal or emotional origin but political and ideological. He repeated that he accepted ninety per cent of Kardelj's arguments, but was still convinced that the Party needed drastic changes of organisation and direction; in its present form it had become 'the main obstacle to democratic development in Yugoslavia'.

The first day's proceedings left Djilas feeling crushed and embittered. He had hardly expected to carry the meeting with him or to be totally vindicated. But neither had he expected the abuse showered upon him by men who, until a few days before, had called themselves his friends. Meeting Tempo afterwards on the stairs, he reproached him bitterly: 'So you too are one of those who kick a man when he's down!' The ebullient Montenegrin was not in the least abashed. The following day he reported Djilas's remarks to the assembled company as confirmation of the accused's obduracy and 'factionalism'.

Djilas's condemnation was a foregone conclusion. Kardelj drew him aside to confirm that Tito considered the case settled, but that in five or six months' time a more lenient view of his offence might be taken.

Did this hint help to bring about the change of heart, the moral collapse and all but complete capitulation which Djilas underwent between the first and second sessions of the Plenum? He himself could never fully explain it. Physical and moral exhaustion no doubt played their part. For several nights he had been a prey to insomnia. 'My first good night's sleep came at the end of the first day of the session, on the eve of my "recantation",' he recalls. 'I can only conclude that this act was forced upon me in my sleep, unless falling asleep was itself the result of a subconscious decision to take this step.'[14] Subconscious urges of the same sort were commonly experienced by veteran Communists faced with public disgrace and the disavowal of everything they had believed in and worked for. There remained to them then only one recourse, one last service they could render the Party – the public confession of whatever the Party required and the willing acceptance of the penalty it decreed. To refuse to recant would be to negate their whole past, to repudiate a career dedicated to a party whose judgments were infallible. A Communist could not be right *against* the Party. He could only admit his fault – if the Party pronounced it to be a fault – and submit. 'I could not escape paying my debt to the dogma to which I was committed and to the movement that had a claim on me, because my activities until then, my whole way of life, were registered in its records,' he wrote.[15] And later still: 'It took me a long time to discover that, once you are a Communist, it is only a question of time before you are asked to prostrate yourself before the Party and castrate your conscience.'[16]

The decision reached during the night of 16-17 January – the resolve to recant – now seemed as inevitable as that reached in the night of 7-8 December – to publish those views which he knew would precipitate the crisis. On each occasion counter-arguments were powerless. 'There was no one beside me except my wife Štefica,' he recalls. 'She tried to convince me I was wrong when I told her I would have to make a sacrifice of my views to some extent, and though she was sufficiently firm, she was too tender and considerate to succeed in dissuading me.'[17]

The most humiliating thing, perhaps, about the events of the following day was that he made his submission without feeling any humiliation. His final statement, though somewhat confused, was entirely abject. He began by declaring that, since yesterday, 'something had snapped inside him' – 'as though a devil had fallen from his soul'. He now realised that 'either I have to make a definite break with the Communist ideology and practice, or else I have to try, at least as a private citizen, in some way to turn my face towards you, towards your work, towards the League of Communists.' He now saw that he had been wrong and his ideas mistaken. The Central Committee, which he had unjustly suspected of neglecting the struggle against bureaucratism, had been waging it all the time. His obsession with the danger of bureaucratism had blinded him. After taking part in the anti-Cominform campaign, he wrongly imagined that some of the things he was criticising about the Soviet Union were also true of Yugoslavia. Lack of practical administrative duties had led him to indulge in 'abstract theory which, applied concretely, means exactly what the comrades say it means – the mobilisation of the petty bourgeoisie, of social democracy, of the West.'

'This Plenum,' he concluded, 'has convinced me that bureaucratism will not be victorious in Yugoslavia. My faith in the League of Communists is restored – the faith I openly denied yesterday. And with it, my faith in the Central Committee of the League of Communists as the chief anti-bureaucratic force. I will vote for the Resolution with a clear conscience.'

The Resolution was carried unanimously; Dedijer, Mitra and Djilas himself concurred that the views expressed in his articles were in fundamental contradiction to the policy adopted at the Sixth Congress and that they had only confused public opinion and harmed the Party. It was therefore decided that Djilas should be expelled from the Central Committee and given a 'final warning' by the Party.

Tito had won a resounding victory and could afford to appear magnanimous. The Party, he declared in summing up, had demonstrated its monolithic unity. No power on earth could destroy it. Yugoslavia would pursue her own chosen path to Socialism, to Socialist democracy, veering neither to the East nor to the West, as some expected, and having no truck with alien ideas. Djido had been able to convince himself of this, and it was to be hoped that the realisation would console and strengthen him in rectifying his errors. 'And we shall then see,' he added ominously, 'how genuine his self-criticism has been.'[18]

Djilas later described this last remark as 'the acme of callousness and duplicity' but at the same time 'a source of fresh resistance and resentment within me'. But, from the victor's point of view, were not the admonition, and the suspicions which prompted it, fully justified? Tito had triumphantly surmounted the crisis in the Party and disarmed the foe. Djilas had not opposed him in any crude struggle for power. The challenge had stemmed from his ideas, ideas which he might now say he renounced but which Tito, with his quick intuition, sensed still lay rooted within him ready to send forth vigorous new shoots. Djilas was a man in whom an idea, once it had seeded itself, grew irresistibly into action, into a consuming passion. It was not a question of merely disavowing it intellectually; once it had become part of him, he could no more renounce the idea than he could renounce his own nature. Ideas, unlike dogma which serves its possessor as a protective carapace, live and evolve. They are in essence subversive of autocracy. Djilas saw that 'a monopoly of power inevitably imposes a monopoly of ideas'; and Tito knew it too. That is why, once the break between them came, no real reconciliation was ever possible, despite the lure of promised leniency. Tito might crush his challenger but he could not crush the ideas which had settled in him and taken on a life of their own.

The affair was over and Djilas politically dead, Tito assured foreign correspondents. 'When I heard and read about that,' Djilas commented, 'something strong and instinctive came over me – something which had nothing to do with Communism but welled up from the ancient springs of my Montenegrin blood. "No, it won't be quite like that!" I said to myself. "I will never give in; never – as long as I live!"'[19]

CHAPTER TWENTY-NINE

In the Wilderness

DJILAS had fallen – and fallen clumsily between two stools. Some blamed him for not making a defiant stand, for lowering the standard of revolt; others for failing to make a timely and tactical submission until the time was ripe for resuming the struggle from within the Party. Like-minded reformers complained that his reluctant recantation had put the clock back by a dozen years. He himself understood that he could only go forward at the pace set by his inner development. 'I continued to feel that I was a Communist, albeit hesitant about certain dogmas, that I was bound body and soul to the Communist Party,' he explained:

Like the heretics of days gone by, like the sundry oppositionists in the Stalin trials, I proved my loyalty to the ideology and to the Party by recantation. My feelings as I was making my formal 'recantation' were a mixture of disappointment and disgust with myself and with the 'star-chamber' tribunal, and with the ideology and with the fact that it had ever been created. But there was also a certain diabolical delight in this self-humiliation, particularly because it was an illustration and an endorsement of the mutilation of a human being on the wheel of ideology, and even more, because the victim was until recently a comrade and colleague of the persecutors. . . . Nevertheless, I did not burn all my flimsy and unfinished bridges. I did not renounce my philosophical views; nor did I admit that there was anything discreditable in my motives. I knew that I had not submitted, and that I would gather all my strength in the new changed circumstances. I sensed, I was even certain, that people with ideas similar to mine would interpret my 'recantation', at worst, as a bad tactical move and not as a renunciation of my ideas.[1]

On 4 March Djilas took the next step forward. He sent a letter to his local Communist headquarters returning the membership card he had held for nearly a quarter of a century. He explained that he no longer wished to remain a member of the Party as he had ceased to consider himself a Communist. He had already resigned, within a few days of the Plenum, from his government posts, the Vice-Premiership and the Presidency of the National Assembly, a function now taken over by his old enemy Moša Pijade. He continued to draw his pension as an ex-minister and had not yet been evicted from his villa on Dedinje. But no one greeted him in the street or came to visit him. His ostracism by his former comrades was complete. Djilas had become a non-person.

Only Dedijer continued to keep in touch with him, although the strains of their common ordeal had brought on a recurrence of the fever caused by his old head-wound. Milovan and Štefica would walk through the frozen streets to visit him, lonely and tormented, on his sick-bed. One February evening Dedijer confided that, since that fatal Plenum, he had seen Ranković more than half a dozen times and could say that 'they' would be willing to talk with Djilas if he would agree on a meeting. But 'caught in my web of suspicion', as he later put it, Djilas no longer trusted anyone or anything. He even suspected that Dedijer had been sent to spy on him and at once turned down his suggestion. A year later his friend was to return to the charge and suggest that Djilas formulate his ideas and put them to the leadership. Djilas again declined. 'That would only be to criticise Communism,' he declared. The other, abashed, let the matter drop. Dedijer would continue to have his own differences with the Party, but he would also find a way of coming to terms with it.

The 'Djilas affair' created a considerable stir abroad. A fortnight after the Plenum Aneurin Bevan wrote in confidence to Tito to intercede on behalf of Dedijer and Djilas, with both of whom he had become close friends. He also expressed concern over the allegation made at the Plenum that his influence had been partly to blame for setting them at odds with the Party. Whilst disclaiming any wish to interfere in Yugoslavia's internal affairs, he enquired whether there would be any objection to his continuing to write to them. Tito replied in courteous terms that there was no objection and no cause for anxiety. It was unfortunate that Bevan's name should have been dragged in at the Plenum, but it was of no consequence since it was clear that his friendship had been in no way responsible for his friends' unfortunate deviations. Dedijer was receiving 'comradely attention and assistance' in his current illness and Tito had reason to believe that 'he has already altered to a considerable extent his opinion concerning Djilas's actions.' As for Djilas, he had been deprived of his public offices but 'was entitled to material security as a high functionary and our collaborator of long standing'. He was still at liberty and a member of the League of Communists – Tito's reply had been written before Djilas resigned from the League – 'with the possibility to think over and correct his erroneous conceptions, especially with regard to the harmfulness of factionalist activity'. The whole sorry affair, Tito declared, 'has affected you owing to your personal and friendly relations with Dedijer and Djilas, but believe me that Djilas's case has hurt us twice as much, both as friends and collaborators of long standing in a revolutionary cause.

All this has happened owing to the destructive character of his writing about our realities. However, he turned a deaf ear and went ahead so that we had to solve this problem in the mildest and [most] principled manner in order to safeguard the unity of our ranks of our League of Communists and the normal progress of our Socialist democracy.'[2]

In the Soviet bloc the removal of the 'revisionist' Djilas was not welcomed as warmly as Tito had perhaps hoped. At the end of January the Cominform periodical *For a Lasting Peace, for a People's Democracy* (now published in Bucharest) carried an article denouncing in the same breath both the revisionist and the 'Tito clique' which had allegedly been forced to move against him only by the pressure of 'the great masses of toilers'. In the Soviet Union itself, the Yugoslav question figured as an issue in the post-Stalin power struggle between Malenkov, Molotov and Krushchev. Molotov was identified with Stalin's hard-line policy, but Khrushchev saw that reconciliation with Tito would be likely to strengthen the unity of the 'Socialist camp' and create a good impression in the non-Communist world. A committee set up to examine the question reported that, ideologically, Yugoslavia could still be considered 'Socialist'. At the end of the summer Khrushchev suggested in confidence to Belgrade that since the Soviet Party had got rid of Beria and the Yugoslavs had purged Djilas, the chief obstacles to rapprochement had been removed.[3] Tito was not prepared to bury the hatchet on such cheap terms, but other conciliatory gestures from Moscow followed and prepared the way for Khrushchev's dramatic offer of an olive branch in the following year.

In the meantime, steps were taken to purge the League of Communists of 'Djilasites', now classed together with Cominformists, anti-regime Catholics and others as 'enemies of the people'. Djilas had little fear for his personal safety, although there was reason to believe that some of Ranković's subordinates would have welcomed his physical liquidation. Tito, he was sure, would not wish to go to that extreme, if only for the bad effect such a Stalinist solution would have in the West. But he was alarmed for his family and his freedom as a writer. 'I lived for months, even years, obsessed with my plenum "recantation",' he writes, 'and under the fear that pressures were to be used to make me renounce my writings and my ideas. During my first imprisonment (1956-61) I even lived in fear that drugs might be used to destroy my will and make me repent.'[4]

The break with Party and friends left Djilas in a state of emotional and psychological collapse which he described many years later to an American friend as follows:

The Progress of a Revolutionary

The face of my world was transfigured. At first I plunged into an erotic crisis, something that was completely out of character with my normal self. Every other woman in the street seemed attractive to me. I managed gradually to bring this crisis under control. Then I realised I was in an absolute vacuum. People whom I had known for a long time, for whom I had done many favours, did not know me any more. A policeman was placed in front of my home. Those who entered had to show their identification cards. Communism is a closed world. In a sense I didn't exist any more.[5]

This political and social ostracism was accompanied by an acute sense of spiritual alienation:

After the verdict on me had been delivered, mortal fear fanned out around me – the only living being to merge heart and soul with me was my second wife, Štefanija. All that I had learned, all that I believed in, was dissipated into a malign, dehumanized void. I buried myself in books, even those on nuclear physics and biology. I busied myself with sketching out literary ideas and jotting down reminiscences.[6]

Gradually it was borne in upon him that this brutal ending of his political career might be the beginning of something new – the rebirth in him of the creative artist which had been suppressed for more than twenty years and subordinated to his political commitment. It is true that he had served politics with his pen as well as his gun, but the politically motivated writer, disciplined and bounded by dogma, is a different being from the creative artist. Now, silenced and reduced to non-existence politically, he had had the fetters struck off him as a writer. The ousted politician turning for consolidation to literature might succumb to escapism, but for Djilas writing would be the continuation of battle on another and higher plane – the plane of ideas, ideas that were no arid abstractions but born of experience and transmuted by art. The fog which at present enveloped his bruised mind would lift. What was now confused and muddled in the maelstrom of emotions would become clear and reveal both the message and the form – novel, story, essay, autobiography, political philosophy – in which to express it.

But for the present, under the incubus of defeat and humiliation, the writer would not become fully conscious of his renewed vocation, only of a vague urge to discharge in words his bitterness and soul-searching, his recriminations, fears and feeble groping towards the light. Early in 1954 he was to have made a trip to Norway and Sweden, countries which Djilas was eager to see but which, with his fall from power, he could now visit only in the imagination. What he fancied he would have found there, and the reflections it prompted regarding the world and his own destiny, are recorded in a long reverie or dramatic essay written in the course of a single night (29 January 1954) to which he gave the title 'Nordic Dream'.[7] It is of interest less for insights into the nature of those countries, still unknown to him, than as a revelation of the tumultuous transformation taking place in his own thinking and emotions. 'Nordic Dream' is an attempt to analyse and record that inner urge which led him, more than any external pressure, to the decisive break with the movement to which he had devoted all his energies and with the comrades who had shared its perils and joys, its aspirations and its victories. What had driven him to this? Why had he chosen what others saw would only lead to his own destruction? 'I had to follow that road,' he can only answer, 'even if my steps were confused and indecisive. Otherwise I could not remain a man in my own eyes. For if I know something with certainty, if I discover something and I am convinced of its truth, how can I deny it, hide it from my closest friends, from the world and from myself?'[8]

In the silence of that cold January night Djilas relived the trauma of his struggle and the humiliation of his defeat. What made it the more puzzling was that

I knew in advance that the majority would be against me regardless of their personal convictions. True, I had illusions both about people and about the forms of the confrontation. I envisaged two extreme possibilities, a general and academic discussion in the press, or a possibly brutal settling of accounts with me. But neither took place. In the end it turned out worse than they promised me but better than I imagined. This society as a whole is obviously not yet ready for free discussion. I was silenced as an agent of the domestic and foreign bourgeoisie and spat upon as a petty-bourgeois devil – after twenty-two years of membership of the Party and over fifteen years within its highest leadership! Still, I am glad it turned out that way. I have a certain peace of mind, if also a certain bitterness. I don't know how all this will end for me personally – which is not important – or what will happen to the country. Nor how long all this will last – probably a long time – years and years.[9]

Had he acted wisely, honourably, he kept asking himself? Certainly he had had no ulterior motives, no calculations of personal gain. 'I threw myself into the storm, into the dense fog of uncertainty, without heed for the consequences. More by intuition than any conscious process I sensed that truth was on my side. And so I set out.'[10] Why then did he falter, apparently disavowing those ideas which he still really believed in and was ready to sacrifice himself for?

261

I felt as if I were in some kind of religious ecstasy. I should sacrifice everything to avoid hurting the movement as a whole and to avoid harming those who agree with me but who are not organised. The ideas became unreal to me – even if correct for the distant future – precisely because existing practice and authority did not accept them. Perhaps I should not have made my final statement. That will plague me for the rest of my life. At the very moment when I should have been great, I turned out to be small; and this precisely because for all my life I belonged to something I believed was great, because I was part of a church, a believer in dogma. Even though I was not satisfied with the system, I didn't want to change it – only to improve it. If that is possible. . . .[11]

Or was the system, in spite of the Yugoslav leaders' protestations, too rooted in Stalinism to give forth anything but the fruits of totalitarianism? Was this the heart of the matter – that Communism, in the only form the world had known it, the Soviet, Stalinist form – was unsuited to the needs of his country and the genius of its peoples?

Stalinism in Yugoslavia is and will remain something alien, something imposed, which will never bring victory and glory to our country. It is not suited to us because we are already a part of democratic and humanistic Europe, part of democratic and humanistic mankind; or if we are not yet, we will be, we must be to live and to survive. . . . I wanted us to be a part of Europe, a part of democratic socialist Europe, not a part of the Balkans or of Russia. And we shall be Europe, even if I do not live to see it.[12]

His thoughts turned to his family – his wife and his infant son. What would his defiance mean for them? Was it right to put their future, as well as his own, in jeopardy? He was anxious on account of his mother who had been gravely ill.

All the members of this home are crowded into Mother's room. This is the only room that is heated. Once more Mother got the better of death, which almost held her in its embrace during those terrible days when she lay with fixed expression, all skin and bones, for days and nights without speaking, without breathing, without food or even water. During those days, and even earlier while everything was boiling inside of me and around me, I often regretted that she hadn't died earlier. But despite the gravity of her condition and the enormity of her suffering I did not waver. During the war she lost her husband and three children; now she was living to see the destruction and failure not only of her dream about freedom but also of her remaining children. My undeserved troubles are heaviest of all for her. . . .[13]

The dream fades, the reverie ends. 'It is night. How much longer the darkness? Ice and frost attack from all sides. When will the thaw come?

When will the dawn come? Why do the stars fall in the sky and new ones fail to rise?'[14]

For the rest of that year, until the end of December, the world heard little of the 'Djilas affair'. The Party seemed to have withstood its repercussions remarkably well. A good deal of 'Djilasism' no doubt persisted, but as an attitude of mind rather than any articulate creed. As for the 'Djilasites' – their alleged mentor had never aspired or attempted to build up any such following. The Party's Control Commission made sure of the orthodoxy of all Central Committee members by investigating those whose attitude appeared in any way ambivalent. Mitra Mitrović was examined and cleared; so was Peko Dapčević, suspect less for his role as the unnamed General in the *Nova Misao* satire than for the activities of his brother Vlada who had sided with the Cominform. Vlada Dedijer was also summoned by the Control Commission and his unexpected defiance of that body resulted in a reopening of the 'Djilas affair'. In mid-December Dedijer walked out of a meeting of the Commission after declaring that it had no right to investigate him, and then gave an interview to the Belgrade correspondent of the London *Times* complaining that he was being persecuted for refusing to join in the boycott of his friend Djilas. 'I did not agree, and still do not agree, with many of the theoretical theses of Mr Djilas,' he told the *Times* correspondent, 'but I have a great respect for him as an intellectual and a humanitarian. I cannot stop seeing a friend who is now so much alone. In my view, a Communist should be first of all a human being, and every political movement which puts aside ethics and morals carries within it the seeds of its own destruction.'[15]

This was the signal for the principal actor to re-enter the stage. On 25 December the *New York Times* published a dispatch from its Belgrade correspondent in which Djilas was reported as describing the Control Commission's enquiries as 'an attempt to frighten the democratic elements in the Party. Such elements exist but they are unorganized, whereas the Party itself is in the hands of undemocratic elements.' He had no intention, Djilas declared, of leading a revolutionary movement against Tito; the country had had enough revolution. The liberalizing tendencies of the Sixth Party Congress had been halted by the Central Committee Plenum held at Brioni ten months later. If there was to be any real freedom of discussion then a second party, a new democratic Socialist Party, ought to be formed and allowed to compete with the League of Communists. Only then, in perhaps ten years' time, would political democracy become a reality in Yugoslavia.

Tito was at the time away on an official visit to India and Burma, but a letter signed by Dedijer and Djilas and listing the reasons for requesting permission to found a second party based on Socialist principles was handed in to his private office to await his return. Djilas, no longer cowed and apologetic, had raised his voice again with a call for radical, political action. He was aware, he told the correspondent, that he was taking a certain risk in thus nailing his colours to the mast. 'But I think,' he added hopefully, 'that nothing bad will happen. To have a citizen say openly what he thinks will mean a lot for our country.'[16]

He was over-optimistic. Kardelj was Acting President and determined to deal firmly with this new provocation. His many years of collaboration and friendship with Djilas counted for nothing; indeed they made him all the more anxious to dissociate himself from the companion with whom he had travelled so far along the path to reform. First, he trounced Djilas and Dedijer in a speech as 'gentlemen' (a term of abuse amongst Communists) guilty of offering their services to reactionary circles abroad who wanted 'to prevent our progress towards real Socialism'. A similar line was taken by General Dapčević, who hastened to declare, in a letter to *Borba*, that he had nothing whatever to do with the 'dirt intrigues' of his old friends, whom he now regarded as no more than 'u eign agents'. An attempt by Dedijer to put his case to a news conference was frustrated by the secret police and a measure was rushed through the National Assembly stripping him of his parliamentary immunity. Dedijer was also suspended from the Central Committee. Djilas, no longer a member of either Assembly or Party, could have no such sanction applied against him; instead, he was expelled from the Socialist Alliance to which he still theoretically belonged. Then, at the end of December 1954, he and Dedijer were arraigned under Article 118 of the new criminal code for activities calculated 'to damage abroad the most vital interests of our country' through 'hostile and slanderous propaganda'.

Their trial was held in camera. On arriving at the court the accused had to brave some hundred or so hostile spectators who jostled them with much shaking of clenched fists and cries of 'Traitor!' But there were also sympathisers amongst them; one middle-aged man stepped forward to shake Djilas warmly by the hand at the entrance to the court-house. Djilas's old mother, barely recovered from her grave illness, insisted on accompanying them and waited outside the building in a car belonging to a newspaper correspondent. Representatives of the international press were barred from the District Court 'because of the campaign they have been conducting in connection with the case, and because the Court is not persuaded that they will report the proceedings truthfully.' The hearing lasted sixteen hours. It was past midnight before the two exhausted defendants emerged into the bitter cold of the January night.

The Court pronounced the accused guilty and sentenced both to prison – Djilas to eighteen months, Dedijer to six. But the sentences were suspended and both offenders placed 'on probation' and exhorted to refrain from repeating their offence. *Borba*, so long the mouthpiece for their views, declared that it was not for expressing those views that they had been sentenced, but for seeking to enlist foreign support, thus provoking outside interference in Yugoslavia's internal affairs. Otherwise, the paper went on, the defendants had the same rights as any other Yugoslav citizen to express and fight for their opinions, which were their own affair.

The paper did not explain how this might be possible under a one-party system where the media were subject to strict official control. It was clear that the authorities had no intention of relaxing their grip. Nevertheless, though pronounced 'guilty' and deprived of the practical means of putting their case to the public, the heretics remained at liberty. Their conviction in such circumstances was almost tantamount to acquittal. As *The Times* reminded its readers, 'Yugoslav laws are different from British and for a country which is still a one-party State, the sentences are undoubtedly lenient.' The publicity given to such affairs in the international press, *The Times* went on to point out, was not 'interference', but an indication of the legitimate interest taken abroad in a country which had shown independence and originality in evolving its own policies and political institutions.[17]

The affair placed the regime in something of a quandary. Behind the scenes, steps were proceeding for a normalisation of relations with Moscow. Djilas and other rebels were as much of an embarrassment as ever, but they could not be forcibly suppressed without laying the government open to charges of reverting to Stalinist methods. Tito wanted the restoration of inter-state, and ultimately inter-party, relations with the Soviet Union, but he wanted them on his terms. When, a fortnight after the trial, Molotov informed the Supreme Soviet that 'Yugoslavia has apparently departed to some degree from the course she embarked upon during the first years after the Second World War' and that this would have a 'positive' effect on Soviet-Yugoslav relations, Tito angrily dismissed as 'nonsense' the implication that Yugoslavia was coming to recognise her errors and to mend her ways. Malenkov and Molotov were losing out to Khrushchev in the power struggle. The former was relegated to a distant power-station, whilst Molotov's influence had clearly begun the decline which was to end, two years later, in the fall of himself and other members of the 'anti-party group'. The way was being cleared for Khruschev's dramatic gesture of reconciliation. On 26 May 1955, four months after the court passed its suspended sentences on Djilas and Dedijer, he flew into Belgrade at the head of a high-ranking Soviet delegation to extend an olive branch to an impassive but secretly highly gratified Tito.

The interest aroused abroad by the trial was quickly eclipsed by Khrushchev's Canossa and by speculation as to how far and how fast Tito would go in his reconciliation with Moscow. Djilas, like any other private citizen, watched these developments with concern. He was not against 'normalisation' on a state-to-state basis which he regarded as both useful and sooner or later unavoidable. What he feared was the re-establishment of inter-party links which would entail a gradual ideological capitulation to a Moscow which, though it might no longer call itself Stalinist, still took for granted its right to hegemony over the 'Socialist camp'. He could only watch and ponder, for he no longer had any public role to play. He lived in silence and seclusion which the authorities hoped would be guaranteed by the threat implicit in the suspended prison sentence. He had moved from the Dedinje villa to a flat in Palmotićeva, a quiet street shaded by linden trees in the vicinity of the National Assembly of which he had briefly held the Presidency. The neighbouring street-names recalled the exploits of the Partisan war and of the comrades-in-arms, both dead and alive, with whom he had been associated. The great avenue leading to Republic Square naturally bore Tito's name. On the far side of the Assembly was Kardeljeva, and, intersecting Palmotićeva, streets dedicated to the late Lola Ribar and to the Bulgarian Georgi Dimitrov. Not ten minutes walk away had been Djilasova, its name now prudently changed. The flat itself was modest and old fashioned, but roomy enough to house his family, his growing library, and Štefica's pot-flowers and the assortment of nineteenth-century Chinese pottery, ikons and antique oil lamps which she was later to collect.

As Djilas came to terms with his changed circumstances and recovered his peace of mind, his intellectual horizons started to widen and the ideas seething in his mind began to fall into shape. His loneliness was lit by flashes of exhilarating awareness that others too had wrestled with problems similar to those which now obsessed him. Sometimes they illuminated the way he had himself begun to tread. Camus was a particularly significant discovery. 'When I read the *Myth of Sisyphus* in 1954 I felt as if I were reading my own words,' he recalls.[18] He formed the habit of taking long walks through the park on Topčider, and it was then, he tells us, that 'the idea was first born that my thoughts might be of international significance.'[19] In March, only a few weeks after his trial, he began marshalling his ideas in the first draft of what was later to become *The New Class*. He finished it within a month.

The theme had been germinating in his mind for a long time. Ten years before, in an article on the shortcomings of the People's Committees entitled 'Perversion of the People's Power', he had begun to grapple with the problem of why the new bureaucracy was failing to bring democracy. The clash with the Cominform diverted his attention to other things but by the early fifties he had reverted to the subject. In 1952 his article on 'Class or Caste?' marked his first attempt at a Marxist analysis of the question; was Soviet bureaucracy a 'class', in which case a natural development it was pointless to resist, or merely a 'caste' which could legitimately be opposed? Other theorists joined in the debate in the columns of *Komunist*, Djilas reaching the conclusion that, though it enjoyed certain property rights, the bureaucracy was less a class than a caste and should therefore be combatted; the Yugoslav Party must learn the lesson in good time and introduce the reforms necessary to avoid a similar perversion of its ruling cadres. For the next three or four years, whilst the winds of change blew with a certain encouragement from Tito himself, Djilas's conviction deepened that the Soviet bureaucracy constituted a historically new class and that measures were urgently needed to curb the power of its emerging counterpart in Yugoslavia. Already he recognised the rise of professional politicians and administrators obsessed with the maintenance of their own power and he felt morally obliged to speak out against it, however slight the prospects of successful resistance. 'In the spring of 1953,' he recalls, 'sitting in the car in front of the present Secretariat of Foreign Affairs, the thought struck me that Capitalism had not resolved the problem of property and that Socialism had not resolved the problem of freedom. For months I lived under the obsession of those two ideas; it seemed to me that the contemporary world is troubled by those two unresolved questions.'[20] That obsession is reflected in the provisional title which he gave to the draft of *The New Class – Freedom and Property*.

Djilas had intended to follow up his last sensational *Nova Misao* article with another entitled 'The Omniscience of Folly' analysing the working of the Party's top leadership and the rationale for its monopolising of absolute power. This unused draft provided further grist to his mill, as did a later series of three unpublished articles on the Soviet Union designed to open western eyes to what was occurring there. The first draft for *The New Class* was then laid aside whilst he worked on the autobiographical account of his Montenegrin boyhood subsequently issued under the title of *Land without Justice*. In the summer of 1956 he returned again to his earlier manuscript, now definitely given the title under which it became known, but found that his ideas had evolved so radically that much of the material was now unusable. He had just finished thoroughly revising it when, in November, he was arrested and imprisoned.[21]

Much of the book, Djilas tells us, was rewritten with 'the same excitement that one feels when writing poetry. I felt the entire world was opening before me, that with my thought I was modelling its material, uncovering its secrets. While writing it, I had a vision of how thousands of people throughout the world, inspired by it, were fighting. The vision was concrete, sensory, in which there were crowds, in columns, with steel helmets and banners. I am talking about a vision, and not about a real belief that it will happen.'[22]

This apocalyptic vision was triggered off, no doubt, by the extraordinary events occurring in Eastern Europe, for which the ferment of subversive 'Titoist' ideas was held, at least by the Russians, to be in no small part responsible. Khrushchev's visit of reconciliation had ended with the signing of the 'Belgrade Declaration' putting an end to the seven-year-old rift between Belgrade and Moscow and conceding many of the Yugoslav positions about separate roads to Socialism and freedom from commitment to any bloc. It denoted rapprochement on a state-to-state basis. But the first cautious moves in the more delicate area of inter-party relations were not taken until a year later when Tito visited the Soviet capital and signed the 'Moscow Declaration'. The ground for this had been prepared by Khrushchev's 'secret speech' to the Twentieth Conference of the Soviet Communist Party, disclosing Stalin's personal responsibility for the abuses of his regime and placing on him most of the blame for the quarrel with the Yugoslavs. In April, as a further gesture towards the latter, the Cominform was formally abolished. But such signs of liberalisation were taken as an encouragement not only by the Yugoslavs, whom Khrushchev hoped to draw back into the Soviet orbit, but also by the other client states of Eastern Europe who were eager to draw away from it. First in Poland, then in Hungary, there occurred explosions of nationalist fervour and clamorous demands for more democratisation which greatly alarmed the Russians. Djilas was enthusiastic. His hopes for reform, if nipped in the bud in his own country, seemed about to burst into flower amongst the Poles and the Hungarians. On 19 November 1956 *The New Leader* published an article by him beginning: 'With the victory of national Communism in Poland a new chapter began in the history of Communism and of the subjugated countries of Eastern Europe. With the Hungarian people's revolution, a new chapter began in the history of humanity.' He went on to criticise the ambiguous policy towards Hungary followed by the Yugoslav Government which had shown itself 'unable to depart from its narrow ideological and bureaucratic class interests' and had betrayed 'those principles of equality and non-interference in internal affairs on which all its successes in the struggle with Moscow had been based.'[23]

The New Leader article was the most outspoken of a number of contributions which Djilas had been making to the international press, all highly critical of the Soviet leadership with which Tito had been anxious to cultivate a rapprochement and which was now blaming him largely for the unrest in Eastern Europe. The authorities had at first tried to minimise their importance. No action was contemplated against their author, Ranković told reporters, since 'Djilas was not a problem of any significance for us.'[24] But failure to silence him would be seen by Moscow as yet another Yugoslav provocation. Claiming that he had violated his undertaking to refrain from 'hostile propaganda' the authorities revoked the suspension of his prison sentence and let the sword of Damocles fall. On 20 November an investigating judge from the Belgrade District Court appeared at his flat with a squad of plain clothes police and after a four-hour search of the premises placed him under arrest. His wife succeeded in slipping away to give the news to the foreign correspondents. A few days later Dedijer passed them copies of an 'Open Letter to Marshal Tito' stigmatising the detention as unjust and harmful to Yugoslavia's good name and appealing to the President to countermand the order for the arrest.[25]

On 12 December 1956, after a seven-hour trial held once again *in camera*, Milovan Djilas was sentenced to three years strict confinement and re-entered the prison at Sremska Mitrovica where, before the war, he had served a similar sentence for his activities on behalf of the Yugoslav Communist Party.

269

CHAPTER THIRTY

Tito's Prisoner

THE next eleven years of his life were to be spent by Milovan Djilas either in prison or under its immediate threat; a period of four years and two months in the Sremska Mitrovica penitentiary followed by an interlude of fifteen months' conditional liberty, and then nearly five more years behind bars again before being released at the end of 1966. It was a time of physical deprivation, mental anguish, and extraordinary literary creativity. His state of mind on commencing this long period of incarceration is best described in his own words:

All my instincts and energies, my memories and dreams, were still throbbing with the life that I had left outside the prison walls. I had to keep these on a leash and inure myself to loneliness, rejection and slow death. In all this turmoil my thoughts kept their course until, filtered and clarified, they found their release within the steel and concrete walls of a cell in Belgrade's Central Prison. *The New Class* completed, I felt, as things were, a sudden upsurge of yearning for fresh creative work and new visions and themes for it.[1]

The work just completed had been an analysis of the Communist-dominated society in which Djilas lived and which he had helped construct. He now felt the urge to probe and explore further, to suggest alternatives, to speculate on the future. The need for a sequel imposed itself on his mind with a force that continued to obsess him despite the sudden change in his personal circumstances. The obstacles he had first to surmount were not so much external as internal – the psychological block which writers often experience and which, in his case, took the form of uncertainty as to the title for the new work; 'the theme of the book had to crystallise inside me verbally,' he writes, 'in the shape of a title.'[2]

The psychological, if not the material, constriction eased within a few days of his imprisonment:

One day, on my way to the prison yard, a concrete quadrangle surrounded by five-storied blocks where I exercised for an hour in the afternoons, it suddenly occurred to me that the book I was contemplating ought to be called *The Unperfect Society*: it would be an antithesis to the perfect, or classless, society by which Communists justified the continuation of their dictatorship and their own privileged position. Under the dingy canopy of a November sky my footsteps rang out in the concrete void of the yard, hammering into my brain the words 'Unperfect Society', 'Unperfect Society'. . . .[3]

The diary and notes which he kept during his first term in prison (1956-61) were subsequently reworked to form many of the themes of the book published under that title in 1969. The gestation was anything but easy. 'I find it almost impossible,' he wrote, 'to describe the pain and distress I have suffered over the past fifteen years, particularly when I was in prison, as a result of my unsparing efforts to thrash out my ideas – pondering their deeper meaning, their practicability and eventual outcome.'[4]

The difficulties were such as might have deterred the most resolute spirit: a twenty-months' period of solitary confinement; recurrent migraines and other bouts of illness; the deadening winter cold of a prison cell left at times totally unheated; deprivation of writing-paper, forcing the prisoner to scribble down his notes on toilet-paper; petty harassment such as the withholding of letters or the cutting short of the few visits permitted; the absence (in contrast to his previous experience as a political prisoner) 'of anyone with whom I could share my doubts and speculations . . . in a world of iron bars, walls, warders, and small groups of committed felons'; the prying and provocation of fellow-prisoners set to spy on him. Yet the anguish of thinking and rethinking his ideas and of struggling to commit them to paper also induced moods of extraordinary serenity and contentment, even moments of exaltation and liberation, as the featureless succession of prison days brought detachment from the hopes, fears, ambitions and anxieties which had filled his active life. Prison became a purgation rather than a punishment, a unique and precious experience transmuting the miseries of man's inhumanity to man into the raw material for literary creation. Solitary confinement may bring the convict into the company of the rarest spirits; of Boethius, composing his *Consolations of Philosophy* whilst under sentences of death in the sixth century, of Bunyan, contemplating his *Pilgrim's Progress* from behind the walls of Bedford jail, of Solzhenitsyn, raising his prophet's voice above the frozen wastes of the Gulag Archipelago.

A writer, however, feels the urge not only to write but also to publish. This was precisely what Djilas's erstwhile comrades, now his judges, were determined to prevent, at least in their own country; and it was why, for circumventing their prohibition by publishing abroad, they had sent him to prison. But the prisoner would not be silenced; he had found a way of sending the manuscript of *The New Class* to a New York publisher and in August 1957 the book appeared in English translation and achieved instant success. The author was promptly taken from prison and arraigned before the district court of Sremska Mitrovica for attempting 'to compromise the idea of Socialism and the international workers' movement'. The Public Prosecutor read out to the court extracts from the offending publication, waxing particularly indignant over the slanderous assertion that 'the totalitarian tyranny and control of the New Class which came into being during the Revolution has been the yoke under which the blood and sweat of all members of society flow.' Djilas was unrepentant. 'I wrote the truth from the first word to the last!' he defiantly declared. The Judge promptly had the court cleared lest the press should hear and disseminate such blasphemy, and the rest of the trial was held behind locked doors. The defendant's three years' sentence was increased to nine years.

Even by the time of publication, *The New Class* had ceased to express fully its author's current thinking. He had already passed beyond it, discarding many of its assumptions as outmoded, as if resolved to demonstrate the truth of the dictum that the life of an honest man is a 'perpetual infidelity', since in order to remain faithful to truth he must make himself perpetually unfaithful to the lesser, provisional and partial truths so far apprehended. *The New Class* is a Marxist critique of contemporary Communism which it dissects by means of Marxist dialectic. It develops the proposition that 'the society that has arisen as the result of Communist revolutions, or as a result of the military action of the Soviet Union, is torn by the same sort of contradictions as in other societies. The result is that the Communist society has not only failed to develop towards human brotherhood and equality, but that out of its party bureaucracy there arises a privileged social stratum which, in accord with Marxist thinking, I named the New Class.'[5] Djilas, in short, wished to turn one of the sharpest weapons in the Marxist armoury against Marxism itself, not so much so to destroy the latter as to show up the contradictions between Communist theory and practice in terms which an orthodox Communist could understand. But now the very assumptions of Marxism, the 'scientific laws' its founder claimed to have discovered, were under attack in the critic's mind and their potency gradually eroded.

And not always gradually. Sometimes the spell was dissolved in a lightning flash of illumination. The basic dogma of historical materialism, which holds that not only all social institutions but the whole of mankind's intellectual and religious life are determined by the play of the 'productive forces', was dethroned in such a way. Djilas could no longer say exactly when, but he vividly recalls that it occurred during one of the periods of prison exercise:

I remember the change in the weather, with the clouds scudding from west to east, leaving clear patches behind them. It took place behind the former prison chapel which had become the Hall of Culture . . . when all at once it became clear to me, with the incontrovertible certainty of a feeling, rather than of reasoning, that it is not true that society and the individual – and more particularly thought – are dependent exclusively upon material forces.[6]

He no longer accepted the Marxist thesis that the mode of production determined the general process of man's social, political and intellectual life. Did not his own personal experience belie it? What, after all, 'were the material conditions or causes that drove me in particular to hurl myself from the comfortable heights of power into the abyss of desolate alienation and prison humiliations? Why should I have cudgelled my brains over the harshness of totalitarian rule, only to spend my declining years scrubbing floors and carrying slops in prison?'[7]

The daily routine, as noted in the diary entries for 30 and 31 January 1958, when Djilas had completed just over one year in solitary confinement, was as follows:

5.30 – rising (in the summer, an hour later);
6.30 – emptying the chamber-pot;
10.30 – walk (an hour and a half; up to now the walk has been usually at 8.30 and lasted only an hour);
1.30 – dinner;
3.30 – an hour's walk;
7.00 – supper;
9.00 – bedtime, by regulation (the bell rings 15 minutes before that).

I now go to bed around suppertime because I am cold. I seldom take supper, and sometimes not even breakfast (chicory coffee). During the day I lie dressed underneath three blankets and read with gloves on my hands.

During the winter I give some crumbs to the sparrows. They have already got to know me and they are waiting. I want to help them during these cold, snowy days.

The weather remains cold. Every evening around six they turn on the heat for about fifteen minutes. Not much help in that except one can go to bed a little more comfortably.

Fog in the morning. But during the day, beautiful blue skies.

Food – Breakfast – always chicory coffee.

Dinner – Potatoes, beans, cabbage (in winter, sauerkraut – very good), rice. The food is thicker than a chowder. There is little fat or spices, but it is well cooked and clean.

Supper: like dinner. Sometimes, as at dinner, split peas or noodles.

Quantity: always a ladle of a half-litre. Also, half a kilo of bread (very good wheat bread), except for those doing heavy work, who get 700 grams, and those who are on discipline (in solitary confinement), who get only 300 grams.

Meat: three times a week (Tuesday, Thursday, Sunday) cooked in with the food, in very small pieces.

In comparison with the pre-war food here in Sremska Mitrovica Prison the fare is no worse today. There is no less bread; it is even somewhat tastier. Without the addition of lard, sugar and vitamins, the food would be insufficient.

Packages: 10 kilos a month. And the right to buy in the prison store food up to a value of 1,500 dinars (including 1.5 kilograms of lard and a maximum of 1.5 kilograms sugar.)[8]

Cold was one of the prisoner's most implacable enemies and references to it recur frequently in his jail diary. 'As I think back, I have been cold all my life.'[9] he noted after more than a year's imprisonment; cold and poorly clothed at school, cold as a student living in unheated Belgrade attics, cold during his first spell in prison and colder still in the terrible winter campaigns with the Partisans. Even after the war, in his requisitioned villa, when fuel was scarce and expensive, and in his Palmotićeva flat where they would light a fire in one room and only in the afternoons. He had become inured to the cold and liked to think it didn't really bother him any longer. After three years in prison he noted that his right hand had become chapped and bleeding round the finger joints, but that somehow he did not find the winter weather unpleasant since 'in the cold one thinks clearly and precisely.'[10] All the same, he noted wrily, 'I often think that if I save myself from jail and ever have some money, I will spend the rest of my life being warm!'[11]

One night at the beginning of March 1960 the prisoner was seized with acute stomach pains. The next day he was rushed to the Belgrade University Clinic and operated on for appendicitis. Štefica was allowed to spend half an hour with him, but the guards posted outside his room kept other visitors away. The patient made a good recovery and by the end of the month Djilas was back again in his cell at Sremska Mitrovica. There the damp and cold brought on rheumatism and an access of mental depression at the prospect of another winter in prison. All desire to write left him.

Nor could he find much comfort in the company of fellow prisoners with whom he had little in common. During the months when he was in solitary confinement, the exercise periods had made welcome breaks from the solitude of his cell, though he was not permitted to talk with the guards or other prisoners. When the weather was good, he used to sit and sun himself, though this 'privilege' was withdrawn during periods of harassment. His walks did not interrupt the train of his thought, but the prisoner noted that 'there is a difference between the way one thinks when one is walking about and when one is lying down. When I am strolling, my thoughts are scattered and persistent, pressing hard for an answer, even if they are circling around the same topic. When one is lying down, thoughts are lighter and effortless. Lying down seems to be a more natural condition for thinking.'[12]

These prison walks were also valued as a means of bringing him into contact with the life of the natural world, of which, in a new way, he was conscious of forming an organic part. He felt an almost Franciscan respect for life, even in its humblest forms. 'I am careful not to step on any worm I find on my path,' he wrote in his diary. 'In my room I gather them onto a piece of tin and empty them into the waste-paper basket. Only the spider is permitted to roam at will.' Insects were seen as humble links in the life-chain leading up to human beings. 'The differences between myself and the benevolent lady-bird which I meet along the path are really minimal.'[13] Plants, too; he discovered a new pleasure in observing and nurturing them. He tended an apricot which sprouted but then disappointed him by failing to make progress. The violet planted in a tin did better, as did another seedling which he hoped would prove to be a symbolic *arbor vitae*. He kept the tins in the yard where the guards left them undisturbed. They noticed how solicitously he watered them and wondered whether he was losing his wits. The sparrows quickly made friends with him when they found he brought them crumbs. Once he witnessed with concern a drama and rejoiced in its happy outcome. 'Yesterday a small sparrow flew in from somewhere – it can barely fly. I wanted to save it and put it on the *arbor vitae*. It fell again; it is hopping around, and many older sparrows are surrounding it. And there is a spotted cat. The little sparrow hid. The cat did not come out. We are all happy – I, the guard, and the little sparrow. Only the cat is unhappy; but not everyone can be happy.'[14]

On the afternoon of 28 July 1958, in the second year of his incarceration, three prisoners joined Djilas in his cell and in the afternoon they were allowed to take exercise together. Getting to know each other, chatting together as they made up their beds, caused an unaccustomed commotion. Solitary confinement was now over. 'Life will be more pleasant,' Djilas noted hopefully, 'better for my nerves.' The twenty months of isolation had been 'a gradual and mild dying'. He had found the enforced silence trying at first and calling for great self-control; 'probably I would not have succeeded in that so fast had I not had a strong feeling of pride.'[15] There was also the fact that a secluded, if not a totally solitary, life had already been forced upon him some months before his imprisonment with the abrupt cessation of all public duties and ostracism by his friends after his arraignment in the Central Committee. Existence had then been restricted to the company of his family circle and the ruminations of an intense, though tortured, intellectual life. Solitary confinement merely meant a further constriction of the same process, but for that reason it had perhaps proved easier to bear.

The company of other prisoners was not an unmixed blessing. Most were serving prison sentences for murder, though there was amongst them a sprinkling of educated men, civil servants and party members, serving sentences for fraud. The murderers Djilas found to be for the most part

vapouring old men, illiterate or semi-literate; such talk as we could exchange was always about the worries over their homes and their crops and village life, or about the wretched, petty, everlasting and outrageous misfortunes of daily prison life. There were a few honest and sharp-witted ones amongst them; for the rest, they were stupid, mean and treacherous men, and, moreover, lust for evil deeds in some had not been quenched by long years of hard labour and languishment. Yet I did learn something from living among them. While there was little I could learn from what they had to say, or from their conduct, I felt stimulated when I thought about them as human beings with whom, in spite of the differences in our ways of life, I had become identified, and who seemed to set an irrevocable seal upon my life, in the uneventful and lifeless world of prison. They will remain in my memory as long as it endures and in my writing as long as people find any value in it.[16]

In contrast to the political prisoners amongst whom Djilas had served his pre-war prison sentence, there was no sense of solidarity or fund of common beliefs amongst these convicts. Most were more than ready to spy on each other and (with the encouragement of the prison authorities) upon the one prisoner of conscience amongst them. Djilas observed with interest the peculiarities of the criminal mentality. Though eager to curry favour by acting as informers, they were at the same time for ever thinking up new ways of outwitting those in power. Each was prompt to put the blame for his misdeeds on social conditions or to find other excuses to salve his conscience. Forcing a man into recognition of his wrong-doing through 're-education' or other means struck Djilas as 'a terrible form of oppression [which] . . . destroys him as an individual even if he is an evil person'. 'Re-education' generally ended in 'mere verbiage or in deceptive behaviour by the prisoners'.[17]

Crime, he came to the conclusion, was 'part of the nature of man . . . a passion, a thirst for achievement, making up for some insufficiency or inferiority'. Prison conditions seemed to him on the whole more humane than in the old days – less physical brutality and more facilities such as movies and the radio to give prisoners a chance of bettering, or at least of occupying, themselves. Sometimes, he noted in his diary, in response to some inner urge, though without much expectation of success, 'I try to persuade them not to steal or kill in the future.'[18] Even the most depraved of them, he believed, 'had an unwavering faith in something good, unsullied, illimitable, of which they themselves were a part by virtue of that essence or aspect of their being which was also pure, free from offences, and not subject to life's spoiling. . . . And I had a similar ineffable feeling of belonging to some dateless unrevealed reality, a feeling identified with an inexplicable sense of my own, or rather, human invincibility in the clash with the objective world, with the powers and laws governing it.'[19]

In short, the prisoners almost all believed in God, however grievously they had sinned against the precepts of their Christian faith. Some said their prayers in secret, for fear of offending the prison authorities; others, on the contrary, said them quite openly as a defiant affirmation of a faith abhorrent to their captors. The Communist authorities did not prevent such expressions of piety, though they made efforts to wean the younger prisoners away from what they considered superstitious practices. Their attitude was summed up in the reply given by one of the warders when asked by a timid old man whether it was forbidden to make the sign of the cross: 'It is not forbidden; but it is not nice!'[20]

Djilas, though still professing the atheism shared by his former comrades, thought it wrong that they had closed the prison chapel and deprived the prisoners of what many would find a consolation, a means of salving their conscience and perhaps of mending their ways.[21] But did the faith which still glimmered in the hearts of these old convicts reflect any reality more substantial than their own dreams and those of their forebears? Djilas could find no answer to the problem of human existence other than the humanist's belief in the essential brotherhood and ultimate humanising of man.[22]

This 'faith in human thought, in the inevitability of good', persisted despite the bitterness born of personal experience, the occasional moods of depression and despair and a growing preoccupation with the problem of evil. But was it flying in the face of all the evidence? Was it not a wish for what ought to be, the projection of a visionary's ideal world, rather than a reasoned hope? Certainly he recognised himself to be 'one of the visionaries – one of the smallest and least significant ones'.[23] All the same, it was difficult to go on believing in man's capacity for goodness or to retain a keen sense of human brotherhood whilst deprived of contact with the outside world. No more than the scrappiest news of public affairs reached him in prison. Visits were restricted to one a month, when his wife and small son were allowed to see him. Even then, their interviews were conducted in the presence of unsympathetic officials and were frequently cut short. They sat round a table with two warders between them watching their faces to make sure they did not exchange messages. The prisoner was not allowed to embrace his visitors, not even the boy.

Brief and unsatisfying though they were, these rare visits, and the short letters he was allowed to send his wife, were the threads which linked Djilas to the world outside and the company of those dear to him. 'Everything which touches you is of vital concern to me,' he wrote to Štefica. 'I want to know how you live, how you spend your evenings. Do you talk about me sometimes? My heart is brimming over with thoughts of you, my soul goes out to you. I have a feeling that the worst is over. We must have patience. Man's spirit can find its way to the sky, to the light. . . .'

Aleksa was constantly in his father's thoughts. 'Through Aleksa I live in the past, the present, the future,' he wrote to Štefica. 'In him I see the realization, the materialisation of our love. I am happy that you and he live together in harmony; that gives me courage and strength.' On 14 March he noted in his diary: 'Today is Aleksa's birthday. For several days I have been preparing to devote this day in my thoughts to him. Today Štefica and he will mention my name. Today, in the afternoon around five o'clock when he blows out his candles. "Happy Birthday", my son; wishing for your well-being is the only thing I can do for you.'[24] Aleksa, with all the confidence of his five years, was already planning rescue attempts. 'Which is stronger – tanks or aeroplanes?' he asked. His father's reply pleased him, as he reviewed his armoury of toys. 'You know, I have tanks and I could liberate you!'[25]

The prisoner's thoughts turned back to the years when the rescue of captive revolutionaries was planned and sometimes actually carried out. Mitra, herself a prisoner at the time and in danger of execution, had witnessed and later described to him how a band of armed men, acting under the Party's orders, had overpowered the guards and rescued Ranković. Now it was Ranković and his men who, at the Party's command, had arrested him and were holding him under duress! And it was with Ranković's representatives, a high UDBA officer and ex-

Partisan called Slobodan Penezić, whom he knew well from the days of the Užice Republic, that, as the fourth year of his imprisonment ᴜrew to its close, Djilas negotiated the terms of his release. An appeal for clemency addressed to Tito by his family the previous year, following the introduction of a revised penal code, had gone unanswered, but by the autumn of 1960 an end to his ordeal seemed both feasible and imperative. Djilas had already explored the ground in a number of letters to Ranković, Kardelj and other members of the Central Committee. The international situation was favourable; that is to say, relations with Moscow were once again strained, and when the Russians did not have to be placated Tito was inclined to show more toleration of *personae non gratae* such as Djilas. Some accommodation, even some sort of reconciliation, might be possible. Could this be achieved without a betrayal of his principles or the imposition of unacceptable restrictions on his moral and intellectual independence? Djilas believed that it could.

Also, his health was giving cause for alarm. At the beginning of December he began to suffer pains at the back of the neck and around his left ear. One evening he fainted in his cell. A diary entry for mid-December records 'terrible nerve attacks; everything was throbbing – chest, head, stomach, and with such a force that it seemed to me that the back of my skull would explode.' A week or two later he recorded more nervous trouble – 'hot flashes in the brain, of several minutes duration, spreading from the skull into the brain itself'.[26]

The authorities had no wish to see Djilas die in prison. They wanted him silenced, forgotten, not given a martyr's crown. Aneurin Bevan, who had never ceased to intercede on his behalf, died earlier that year but Djilas still had influential friends in the West. Morgan Philips, the Secretary of the Labour Party and a member of the delegation which had been welcomed in Belgrade when Yugoslavia badly needed friends after its expulsion from the Cominform, had also appealed to Tito and drawn a prolix answer in *Borba* from Vlahović, once himself under suspicion as a 'Djilasite'.[27]

Tito continued his delicate balancing act between East and West. At the time of Djilas's arrest in the summer of 1957 Soviet-Yugoslav reconciliation seemed far advanced. Then the League of Communists had held their Seventh Congress and adopted a relatively liberal programme which revived all the Russians' suspicions. Since then, relations had further deteriorated. The Congress of Communist Parties held in Moscow in December 1960 strongly attacked the League for 'revisionism' and 'subversive work against the Socialist camp' – much the same sins for which Djilas had first been denounced. Tito reaffirmed his intention of continuing along the Yugoslav path to Socialism. In the perpetual oscillations of Yugoslavia's foreign policy, the pendulum swung sharply away from reconciliation. Strained relations with Moscow meant milder treatment for Yugoslavia's archheretic. By the end of January 1961 Djilas was again a free man.

But not entirely free. His release was made conditional on his maintaining what the authorities regarded as good behaviour, though Djilas subsequently tended to minimise the scope and specific nature of the undertakings he had been obliged to give. The petition for his release was drawn up by Penezić on the basis of the letters Djilas had previously addressed to Kardelj and Ranković. 'Although penitence is circumvented,' he writes, 'I was led by the desire to meet them half-way. I pointed out to Penezić that I do not renounce *The New Class* and that I have no regrets about the past.'[28]

Elsewhere he admits that

there was one sentence in the request that could have been interpreted as recognition by me that my assertions had been falsified by the facts of real life. Nevertheless, I signed the document. I realized that the state leaders needed it for future blackmail, and this later proved to be the case, but my literary and other plans made it essential for me to get out of prison. I did not find that what I had done lay heavily upon me; in myself I remained unflinching, although tortured by doubts and fears that my action would be misunderstood.[29]

The petition was couched in the stilted language customary in such documents, and ran as follows:

To the Federal Executive Council of the Federal Parliament of Yugoslavia—
    Convinced of your positive decision, I am honoured to present the following statement:
    Bearing in mind that events and our entire post-war development in internal and foreign policy have reversed all that by which I caused an opening of criminal proceedings and passing of sentence upon me, I anticipate that the Federal Executive Council will review my case and decide to permit me to be released from jail. It seems to me that the basis for my release from jail would be my will and firm determination to steer clear of any activity like those which have led to the present relations between myself and the political and governmental organs.
    I am determined to preserve my integrity and to adhere to any solution you propose which is acceptable according to my moral principles: thus, my intentions are sincere and well-intentioned. Therefore, after release from jail I will not undertake any political activity contrary to the laws of the Federal People's Republic of Yugoslavia which would put me in a position of criminal

responsibility, nor will I seek to do my country any damage, and in the future I will permit no one to print anew the book *The New Class*.

I would like to emphasize that this statement is sent in the belief that the decision to release me from jail would, at the same time, abolish the lesser punishments – such as the taking away of my decorations, my pension and other items.

In conclusion, I would like to assure the Federal Executive Council that I will remain true to my statement, expecting that among leading comrades I will find goodwill and understanding. signed: January 14, 1961 Sremska Mitrovica – Milovan Djilas.[30]

On 20 January 1961, after serving four years, two months and twenty days of his sentence, Milovan Djilas was conditionally released from prison.

CHAPTER THIRTY-ONE

Conversations and Consequences

IT was a joyful home-coming. On the evening of his release friends and relatives began to gather at the flat in Palmotićeva Street. There was much hugging and kissing, and no signs of surveillance. Apart from a slight greying of the hair round the temples, Djilas did not seem to have changed much. Few traces remained of the illness and nervous strain of the last weeks, whatever the profounder psychological effects of his prison ordeal. 'I will emerge from this experience strengthened and purer than I was,' he had written confidently from his cell. 'I will suffer; that is true. But I will not go crazy or kill myself or die. It seems to me that it was part of my fate to suffer – in order to affirm myself.'[1] It was his fate too to pass through 'an enormous passionate revolutionary upheaval. Moreover, I have emerged from Communism. . . . Nothing good and pure can remain so if it does not pass through humiliation and suffering.'[2]

Dressed, more formally than was usual with him, in a double-breasted dark blue suit and blue tie, Milovan Djilas lounged in an armchair as he laughed and joked with the foreign correspondents present. His views remained basically unchanged, he told them, though in some respects they had evolved. The views of the government, he added, also seemed to have evolved, from what he had heard, especially in economic matters. *The Times* correspondent, who lunched with him in a Belgrade restaurant a few days later, found him 'relaxed, more confident in his future, more ready to talk dispassionately', remarkably unembittered and cautiously optimistic. Did he expect to resume an active role in politics? Even that, he replied, could not be ruled out. His differences with his former comrades and governmental colleagues had not been over the aims of the Revolution or the broad lines of policy, but arose from the lack of internal democracy and freedom within the Communist Party. In other words, he had wished to work within the system he had helped to create, but under conditions which permitted the free expression of independent views. Perhaps the Yugoslav path to Socialism would broaden out to make this possible.

'I am hoping for much,' he said. 'But so far, the only practical occupation open to me is to devote myself to writing.'[3]

Even this ambition was clearly not to be achieved easily. The authorities had confiscated most of the voluminous notes and manuscripts on which he had been working in prison and would not return them until several years later after he had undergone a further stretch of harsh and humiliating imprisonment. Only then would *The Unperfect Society*, his sequel to *The New Class*, see the light of day and reveal how different was his path from the faltering course towards reform followed by those in power. The evocation of his Montenegrin boyhood, *Land without Justice*, published in English in 1958, had added to his stature as a writer, which would be further enhanced by the subsequent instalments of his extensive autobiographical writing, *Memoir of a Revolutionary* (1973) and *Wartime* (1977). In the euphoria of recovered freedom it seemed that his talents as a writer, and perhaps also as a public figure, would be free to blossom in a more relaxed political atmosphere. A leader in *The Times* hailed his release as 'something that can be welcomed for its humanity and maturity'. Though now 'on probation', the prisoner had not renounced his fundamental views and it looked as if the Government was moving in the direction of greater tolerance.[4] Not long before his release a Commission for Constitutional Questions had been set up under Kardelj to draft the new Constitution which, after further scrutiny and debate, would receive the force of law in 1963 and inject new life into the country's political institutions.

Winter mellowed into spring as Djilas continued to knit together the threads of his personal life. In March he was able to celebrate his son's eighth birthday in his own home. In April, an old friendship was renewed and contact with the Socialists of the West resumed when Jennie Lee visited Belgrade. She brought with her a gift chosen by herself and Nye shortly before the latter's death in the previous July. It was a rare edition of the work of a Dalmatian poet. Djilas wished to honour the memory of his friend by dedicating to him the new book on which he was busy. This was an offshoot of his corpus of autobiographical writings and dealt with the three missions he had made to Moscow in 1944, 1945, and 1948.

In *Conversations with Stalin* Djilas paints an intimate picture of the Soviet dictator and the brutal, sycophantic men allowed to share a portion of his power. The author makes clear in his Foreword that 'there is not much in the book that the well-versed reader will not already know from published memoirs or other literature,' and that he has gone carefully through the draft to make sure that it contains no 'revelations' likely to embarrass or offend the government which he has served. But, as one who has himself been an uncritical admirer, a committed Party militant and a participant in the events he described, he declares that he 'felt driven by an inner compulsion to leave nothing unsaid that might be of significance to those who write history, and especially to those who strive for a freer human existence.'[5] His conclusions are uncompromising and damning. In the eyes of the disillusioned disciple, Stalin 'has the glory of being the greatest criminal in history . . . a monster who, while adhering to abstract, absolute and fundamentally Utopian ideas, in practice had no criterion but success – and that meant violence and physical and spiritual extermination.' For in terms of his own perverted aims Stalin *was* successful – phenomenally and frighteningly successful, since 'he transformed backward Russia into an industrial power and an empire that is more and more resolutely and implacably aspiring to world mastery.' How was it possible that 'such a dark, cunning and cruel man could ever have led one of the greatest and most powerful states not just for a day or a year, but for thirty years?' That is something, Djilas concluded, which has still to be explained by his successors, the oligarchy who may now criticise their dead master a little but kept silent and did nothing in the face of his enormous crimes. The apparatus and the social system which he created still stand intact, though now controlled by others, for 'Stalin still lives in the social and spiritual foundations of Soviet society.'[6]

By November, ten months after his release from prison, Djilas had completed his *Conversations with Stalin.* His book was no indictment of Tito and his former comrades; they appear in it as no less devoted than the author to the Utopian ideals of their movement, and as ready as he was to accept and admire everything about the Soviet Union. They are 'honest revolutionaries' and good patriots shaken by their encounter with Soviet reality, if less ready to draw painful conclusions.

But even whilst he wrote, the political climate round Djilas had begun to change. In September Belgrade played host to the first Summit Conference of non-aligned states; whilst ostensibly holding aloof from any bloc, it was clear from their pronouncements that on nearly every issue the participating governments favoured at least near-alignment to the Soviet view. In November Tito delivered speeches attacking the West for wishing to take advantage of his country's economic difficulties and deploring the effect of 'rotten liberalism' in corrupting Communist manners and morals. The Party set about tightening its grip on the arts and the life style of Yugoslav citizens. The pendulum, despite Khrushchev's remarks at his Party's Twenty-Second Congress that the Yugoslav League of Communists was still infected by 'revisionism', was swinging once more towards détente.

Koča Popović, now Yugoslavia's Foreign Minister, declared in Moscow that 'on fundamental international issues the attitudes of the two countries are either similar or identical.'[7] Rapprochement continued throughout 1962, when Gromyko and then Brezhnev visited Belgrade and Tito went to Moscow 'on vacation'.

This was scarcely the more tolerant and liberal atmosphere for which Milovan Djilas had hoped. No Yugoslav publisher would accept his books, no magazine publish his stories. Once more, as with *The New Class*, he had to choose between seeking an outlet abroad or remaining without readers. He opted for the former and sent the manuscript of *Conversations with Stalin* to his American friend and publisher William Jovanovich. The book was scheduled to appear on 16 May 1962. By the beginning of April the leading dailies in Britain and America had received advance copies and were beginning to publish extracts and comments.

There had already been warning signs of how the Yugoslav authorities were likely to react. Whilst in prison, Djilas had written a short story describing the return from the front of a funeral cortège bearing a coffin containing the body of a conscript; the youth was, in fact, still alive and a would-be deserter, but the officer in charge quickly made a real corpse of him. The campaign on the Srem front, so costly in human lives, was still a delicate subject and no Yugoslav publisher dared accept the story. Djilas then sent it to Ignazio Silone, editor of *Tempo Presente*. This well-known anti-Fascist novelist, eleven years his senior, had once been an ardent revolutionary, a founder member of the Italian Communist Party who had broken with it and carried on the fight against Mussolini as an independent Socialist. He and Djilas had much in common as writers and political thinkers. *Tempo Presente* published the story but the issue containing it was banned in Yugoslavia.

Some weeks before the scheduled publication of *Conversations with Stalin* a new clause was promulgated in the Yugoslav Criminal Code prescribing up to ten years' imprisonment for any person imparting, or making accessible to others, 'confidential documents or information obtained or learned whilst performing his official duty or conducting his state or social functions, that thereby damage, or could damage, political, economic or other interests of the community'.[8] This sweeping prohibition was evidently intended to discourage the publication of political memoirs likely to embarrass the authorities and to provide legal grounds for proceeding against an author who persisted in publishing. On 7 April, the American publishers in New York announced that the publication of *Conversations with Stalin* had been postponed. It was too late. On the same day three detectives and an investigating judge appeared at Djilas's flat and produced a warrant requiring him to accompany them to the District Court. They found him in bed recovering from a sharp attack of 'flu. He got up, dressed and shaved whilst the detectives searched the flat and took away a number of papers and manuscripts. Štefica packed a small suitcase and heated some coffee. After a hurried goodbye to his wife, son and bedridden mother, Djilas accompanied the detectives to a waiting car and was driven away. More than four and a half years were to pass before he returned home.

The news that Djilas had been arrested again caused a stir abroad. In Britain a group of sixteen Labour MPs sent a telegram to President Tito urging clemency and deploring an action that was 'more harmful to Yugoslavia's good name than any critical writings of Milovan Djilas'.[9] A petition couched in similar vein was signed by ninety-nine distinguished British writers. A similar appeal was made from India but met with no better success. William Jovanovich flew in from New York in a vain effort to secure Djilas's release by undertaking to cancel publication of the controversial book altogether. *The Times*, speculating on why Belgrade had chosen to damage the reputation it had been gaining in the West and in the Third World for its relative toleration, surmised: 'It may be that the Yugoslav regime is not anxious, at this moment of new rapprochement with Russia, to reopen old controversies. Or, more simply still, it may be that Mr Djilas, who will not stop writing nor make a recantation nor choose the path of exile, is a man doomed to make the hackles of authority rise.'[10]

It was not until the very eve of his trial that *Borba* informed its readers that the man whose thunder had so often resounded through its columns was making trouble again. The trial of Milovan Djilas opened the following morning, 14 May, in Belgrade's District Court. About sixty people gathered outside – friends, relatives, foreign correspondents. They were allowed in, but only for the beginning of the proceedings. The Public Prosecutor read the indictment alleging that the accused had contravened the recently promulgated article 320 of the Criminal Code dealing with the disclosure of official secrets. It was no defence, he went on, to plead that the information passed on and caused to be published abroad was already known; 'he enlarged upon the information with views of his own, lifting particulars out of context, thus distorting them and giving the semblance of topicality and connecting them with present political events.' He had added an overtone of his own impressions and issued it in a new version, thus giving it topicality to serve reactionary quarters abroad as material for the 'cold war' and as a pretext and means of discrediting Yugoslavia's Socialist social organisations, foreign policy and relations with adjacent and 'non-aligned countries' – and all this too in contravention of the undertakings given on being conditionally released.[11]

Djilas listened with composure but growing indignation as the indictment proceeded. He took a paper from his pocket and began to read a prepared statement, shouting down the prosecutor, the judge, and even the lawyer designated by the court to conduct his defence. Above the hubbub he could be heard declaring that he was innocent of all the charges and that he demanded the right to defend himself in open court, otherwise he would refuse to answer questions or to take any further part in the proceedings. The presiding judge adjourned the court and ordered it to be cleared except for the officials and members of the accused's family. The public was allowed back only six hours later to hear the sentence. The accused was declared guilty and sentenced to five years' imprisonment, to be added to the three years and eight months held over from his previous sentence. Djilas was then hustled from the Court and relegated once more to Sremska Mitrovica with the prospect of spending another nine years in the familiar penitentiary.[12]

Štefica Djilas had remained in Court throughout the proceedings. As the sentence was read out she was seen to sway slightly and close her eyes. Four days later it was announced that she had briefed a lawyer to lodge an appeal; this was permitted to a wife under Yugoslav law, provided her husband did not raise a formal objection. She wanted the case to be carried through the whole legal system and each successive court to re-examine the evidence and the validity of the proceedings, she explained; it was not a question of requesting clemency but of demanding justice.[13] Two months later it was announced that the Serbian Supreme Court had rejected the appeal.[14]

The trial and the return to prison of Yugoslavia's best-known dissident attracted a good deal of sympathetic attention abroad. 'In theory, his offence is to have disclosed official secrets,' concluded *The Times*. 'In fact, his real crime is that, having fallen out with his colleagues in the government, he has gone on writing what he believes to be the truth.'[15] The *New York Times* described the trial as a travesty, the sentence as harsh and the outcome a damaging blow to the good name of the Yugoslav government – a blatant relapse into Stalinism which only went to prove the truth of the accused's assertions.[16]

Conversations with Stalin was published in New York at the end of

May as originally planned. Its success was immediate; 'a brave call for freedom, a denunciation of one-party political and ideological monopoly as the essence of Stalinism', as the *New York Times* put it.[17] A correspondent writing to *The Times Literary Supplement* to rebut a minority view that the book was unbalanced, without historical value, and of doubtful veracity, described its author as 'one of the very few great moral forces of our times that soar high above the spiritual desert of the Communist half of Europe and the materialistic fat-lands of the other half.'[18]

CHAPTER THIRTY-TWO

Back in Jail

FOR the next four and a half years only muted echoes from the world outside reached Djilas behind the walls of the Sremska Mitrovica penitentiary. He scarcely knew how narrowly nuclear war had been averted in October when Khrushchev was forced to pull his missiles out of Cuba and Tito, addressing the Supreme Soviet two months later, hailed his gamble as the act of a far-sighted statesman.[1] Belgrade's reconciliation with Moscow seemed all but complete. But Yugoslavia, however uncertainly, was still committed to her own 'path to Socialism'. In the spring of 1963 the new constitution came into force and promised to bring some reality into parliamentary life. Economic liberalisation of a sort continued, though it was hard to reconcile with the centralised planning and control which Tito was loth to relax, and it would provide a dangerous stimulus to dormant nationalist rivalries. From all these developments Djilas was isolated by his prison walls. He had battles of his own to fight, a course of his own to run.

A turmoil of ideas and emotions still worked within him and clamoured for expression. Yet somehow he could now experience it all with great detachment, analyse and record it more dispassionately; not so much with resignation as with a serene awareness of the conflict and suffering lying at the heart of things and of his personal fate as part of the human condition. The urge to write was still strong, though now its emphasis had shifted. It had become less introspective, less autobiographical. He was working mainly on two novels, one to be called *Lost Battles* and the other *Worlds and Bridges*, in addition to a number of short stories, later published under the title of *The Violet and the Stone*, and a translation of exceptional difficulty – no less a work than Milton's *Paradise Lost*. A Quaker friend from England procured him a text and a useful commentary, and he relied on the dictionary to supplement his still meagre command of English. Later, a Yugoslav with a good knowledge of the language was to help him with the more difficult passages. It was to be the first translation of the English classic into Serbo-Croat; and that by a man who until recently was a Marxist and a Communist militant, and who still declared himself an atheist! Satan appealed to him as the cosmic prototype of the revolutionary hero.

Djilas had experienced no Pauline conversion, received no mystical revelation nor even found a substitute for his lost dogmatism in religious faith – 'unless,' as he writes, 'that word can be applied to my firm attachment to the imperative of the human conscience and the inevitability of struggle against tyranny over human existence.'[2] If sometimes, he admits,

I felt at my wits' end, torn by doubts in my 'faith' and beset by notions of the existence of some higher law which sets everything in motion, including my personal destiny, I reacted at once against such 'culpable' weaknesses and lack of faith. I revelled in the fiendish notion that, if the existence of God should become incontrovertible, I would rebel against His omniscience and immutable order, in the same way that I had revelled in my heretical infection of the party's despotic, inhuman, and contrived unity. Revolt against 'higher powers' was to me a sign of man's creative life-force no less categorical than his propensity to bow to the inevitable.[3]

The harsh lessons of experience had not brought Djilas to a belief in any transcendental God; he recognised only the spark of divinity within each human being and the ceaseless struggle of the dark powers to extinguish it. The crimes and follies of mankind suggested that here below it was the Devil rather than God who had the upper hand. Was not the Dualist explanation of the universe more convincing than that offered by orthodox Christianity? The Bogomils of Bosnia had held this doctrine, which won many converts amongst the mediaeval Slavs and gave their land its national religion. Djilas felt the appeal of this Manichean concept which seemed to explain so many things, both historically and philosophically. It accounted for the legacy of rival fanaticisms disputing possession of that troubled borderland, the militancy of the normally meek Franciscans striving there as missionaries, the avidity with which the heretics embraced Islam rather than submit. The Bogomils rejected the authority of the Church, its hierarchy, its symbols and its sacraments. They held that the Devil had been given dominion over all material things; only a tiny elite, the 'Perfect', denied him earthly allegiance by embracing a life of extreme abstinence and austerity – a hyper-puritanism which appealed to a spiritual minority as strongly as did the sect's uninhibited sensuality to the majority. The idealistic revolutionaries of his youth seemed to Djilas the heirs of the Bogomil 'Perfect'. Were they not fighters in the unending struggle between good and evil? 'The philosophy which holds that in today's world the struggle is between good and evil among men is enormously simple, but it is not completely incorrect,' he had written during his earlier imprisonment. In struggling against evil, was it not sometimes necessary to turn the enemy's weapons against himself – to fight evil with evil? Such, it seemed to him, was in the nature of things; such was man's tragic destiny and such had been his own experience. In rising against the tyranny of foreign occupation and domestic betrayal, his comrades had not held back from crimes and excesses, and once victorious they had imposed a new tyranny of their own. Such actions, born of war and revolution, seemed to him justified because they were inevitable. They had used evil to thwart a greater evil, as a strip of land might be scorched in order to contain the spread of a forest fire. Yet Djilas could still in all sincerity declare: 'I always wanted to be on the side of the good.'[4] Once he had fought in the ranks of the political militants for what he saw as the good; now his vision was clearer and his weapons were those of the thinker and the writer.

There were lessons to be learned, and inspiration to be drawn, from many of the greatest minds of the past. Already, during his earlier imprisonment, Djilas had begun to read the Bible for the first time and had been surprised to note that 'in the first chapters about Job I am finding some views identical to mine about good and evil and the inevitability of human destinies,' hastening to qualify his admiration with an atheist's gloss: 'not because of their religion, but because of its wisdom expressed in purest poetry'.[5]

Dostoevsky, whom he had admired in his youth, spoke to him now with a new force:

Dostoevsky belongs with Shakespeare and Sophocles. He is not only an author of genius and a thinker, but he also creates a new spiritual world. It may be that he is even a new civilisation. Its prophet! And Lenin only the beginning. They are contradictions. But that does not alter the essence. Each is only a different spiritual form of the emerging civilisation. . . . I am surprised at the kinship between some of my ideas and those of Dostoevsky, especially ideas about the senselessness of change and progress among men. I became convinced a long time ago that Dostoevsky was not a reactionary in politics, although he was conservative when it came to dealing with everyday problems; he intimated and saw many truths.[6]

There were native springs too at which a Yugoslav writer might slake his intellectual thirst. First and foremost, for a Montenegrin, there was the great Njegoš, who had been an inspiration to Djilas all his life and the subject of much of his thought and writing during his first post-war term of imprisonment. His short study, *The Legend of Njegoš*, written from a Marxist standpoint, had been published before his break with

Tito, but his monumental literary-historical treatment of the same subject, mostly composed during his first term of imprisonment, found no publisher in Yugoslavia. An English translation was now in the press in America and appeared whilst he was still in Sremska Mitrovica. Another nineteenth-century Montenegrin whom he admired was Marko Miljanov, whose portrait occupied a place of honour in his Belgrade home. A hero of the 1876-8 Balkan wars which won Montenegro her independence, Miljanov subsequently fell out with its authoritarian ruler and the 'New Class' around him and spent eight years in disgrace and isolation. It was then that he became a writer. The parallels between their lives and the force and beauty of Miljanov's fables made a powerful impression on Djilas. He took the life and times of his predecessor as the theme for his new novel, *Lost Battles*.

In his prison reading Djilas ranged far afield. There are references in his diary to such contemporaries as Sartre, Camus, Günther Grass, Bertrand Russell and Mary McCarthy, as well as to Yugoslav authors like the Nobel prize-winner Ivo Andrić – 'our greatest writer' – and the Serbian poetess Isidora Sekulić whose study of his revered Nejgoš had displeased him and been the object of his vehement attacks during his days of power. The prison authorities made little attempt to limit the scope of his reading, but writing was a different matter. Unwilling to forbid it altogether, they tried to make it as difficult as possible by depriving him of the use of writing-paper. The prisoner had recourse to toilet-paper. On 13 September 1964 he noted in his Diary: 'I have finished writing page 3,000 on toilet-paper.' It was a laborious business. The sheets had first to be pasted together, and when one or two had been completed, handed over and locked up in a safe. If the author needed to revise them, the sheets required were returned and then collected from him again.

Towards the end of September the authorities made a welcome concession; Djilas was allowed to buy writing paper at the prison shop. By then, he noted in his diary, he had completed the translation of the ninth chapter of the third part of the second book of *Paradise Lost* on page 3126 of toilet paper.[7] Writing was both stimulus and solace, the antidote to depression, spiritual loneliness and physical inertia, but there were times when the creative urge flagged. 'I am not doing anything; that is, I'm not writing and I feel a gnawing pain because of it,' he recorded at the beginning of 1965.[8]

Did it ever, in some flippant moment, cross the translator's mind that a terrestrial parody of the Miltonic epic was being enacted in his own country? Tito had come under challenge – or so he believed – from the trustiest of his lieges – from Ranković, who stood next to him in power. The liberalising course set by the Party's Sixth Congress, and confirmed at the end of 1964 at its Eighth, was alarming the conservatives, particularly the Serbian centralists who traditionally controlled the Party's 'cadre policy' and the key posts in the administration which permitted them to block the application of the reforms. Permeating and directing all branches of the national life, UDBA formed a state within a state answerable only to the chief who had created and still directed it; and behind Ranković loomed the Soviet Union, distrustful of any changes which might draw Yugoslavia closer to the West.

In the spring of 1966 moves were cautiously begun to curb the power of UDBA and undermine the position of Ranković. Tito, adept at playing off rival organisations against each other, found an instrument to hand in the military intelligence service where Croat rather than Serbian influence happened to be strong. The most sensational piece of evidence produced with its help and turned to good effect by the Party Commission set up to investigate was that UDBA had long been keeping the top Communist leaders themselves under surveillance. Microphones, it was alleged, were even found installed in Tito's own residence. Other revelations followed; UDBA was riddled with corruption, its chiefs were guilty of embezzlement and nepotism; they had enriched themselves through smuggling operations across the Adriatic and carried out the most brutal repression of disaffected groups like the Albanians of Kosovo. Ranković had been left too long to his own devices and his organisation had got thoroughly out of hand. At a meeting of the Central Committee held on Brioni early in July he was stripped of his Party functions and later of the Vice-Presidency of the Republic. The following October he was expelled from the Party and it was reported that he and seventeen of his senior colleagues would face trial.

So Ranković, Djilas's closest comrade in the pre-war revolutionary struggle, the Partisan war and the trial of strength with Moscow, and subsequently his stern opponent and virtually his chief jailor, had fallen! He too had met humiliation and disgrace at Brioni as Djilas had suffered it twelve years before, but not on account of any dangerous thoughts or subversive ideas. Ranković had no thoughts other than for the ruthless extension of UDBA's power over the Party and the nation, and his own absolute control over UDBA. His ideas were merely the received Marxist orthodoxy cementing that power. Though Djilas had once accepted the same ideology, the former friends had long ceased to speak the same language. In attitude and motivation they had moved poles apart.

It was basically a matter of power – the concentration and exercise of a power to which Ranković had devoted all his energies until it reached the point of threatening that of the one man more powerful and more power-hungry than himself. Djilas, on the other hand, could honestly say of himself:

I never wanted to be in power, nor did I seek power, either subconsciously or otherwise. I paid little attention to titles, decorations and the like. I was interested in bringing down the old system and old ideas. Even when I was in power I was full of anxiety, for I realised that one thing was not good, that another should be changed, that still another progressed too slowly, or that something over there was outdated. I could not even comprehend why power, along with property, is the major material motivator of human struggles, desires and passions. Those two are the major levers of social struggles. However, I was not even very interested in material goods. And everything that was made for me and given to me – villas, automobiles and the like – was done mainly against my wishes. . . . When I fell from power, however, not only did I feel all the significance of the fall, but I also realised that power is the most terrible human passion – even within me, despite the fact that I was indifferent towards it while in power. That does not mean that I crave it now, since I was mostly interested in ideas. Yet each struggle contains within itself a struggle for power and influence. Alas, there are no pure ideas – perhaps not even in arts and science![9]

The fall of Ranković was widely welcomed. Only in Serbia, his power-base, did he enjoy enough popularity to elicit some reassuring gesture from Tito. In December a Presidential Decree was issued declaring that 'the strength of self-management, humanism and the past services performed' by Ranković and some of the other accused 'rendered further punitive measures against them undesirable.'[10]

Djilas was not vindictive. He did not gloat over his former comrade's fall nor envy him this gesture of clemency; but if the UDBA chief had been spared trial and imprisonment on account of his 'past services' to the Revolution, had not his own been at least as great? Moreover, much of what Djilas had been condemned for saying was now constantly on the lips of Party spokesmen. The Ranković affair itself was sufficient vindication of his warnings against the abuse of privilege and the bureaucratic monopoly of power. Many other dissident voices too were now being raised against such things, though some of them were far from sharing all the tenets of 'Djilasism'. A group of Marxist intellectuals in Croatia associated with the theoretical journal *Praxis* were attacking even leading reformists within the Party hierarchy. Others wanted to launch a new paper to serve as the forum for a Socialist alternative to the League of Communists – the old heresy propounded by Djilas and Dedijer. This led to the arrest and sentencing of the moving spirit, a young lecturer of Russian emigré origin called Mihailo Mihailov, at the same time as moves were being made against the Ranković hardliners. Certain topics remained taboo; lines were drawn beyond which no would-be reformer might safely venture.

The year had nevertheless seen marked progress towards liberalisation and reform. To crown it Tito announced an amnesty for all but a few prisoners of conscience. On the last day of the year Djilas was summoned by the prison governor and told that he was amongst those to be released. The news was completely unexpected. He had served just over half his nine years sentence and was resigned to the prospect of sitting out the remainder of his term. He had neither made nor received any approaches for a pardon. The only condition attached to his release was a ban on publishing or taking any part in public affairs for five years.

At one o'clock in the afternoon of 31 December 1966 Milovan Djilas walked out of the Sremska Mitrovica penitentiary a free man. His wife and son were waiting for him at the prison gates, with a little knot of foreign correspondents. He had been Tito's prisoner for very nearly nine years.

CHAPTER THIRTY-THREE

Freedom and Frustration

DJILAS was free again; but he was still without the rights of a free citizen, even those theoretically enjoyed under the Constitution of a 'Socialist' state. He could take no part in public affairs, publish nothing in the Yugoslav press. He was not prevented from meeting and talking with foreign correspondents, but forbidden to discuss politics with them. He could travel inside the country, but not abroad. His wartime and post-war decorations had not been restored, nor yet his ministerial pension. He was still considered, outside the circle of his family and friends, a 'non-person'.

For the moment at least, this intimate circle was a world in whose warmth he was content enough to thaw out. There was his wife Štefica, who had stood by him through thick and thin. 'Her face radiates courage, honesty, adoration,' noted an American visitor,[1] and she would sustain him with her calm fortitude in all vicissitudes to come. There was Aleksa, now fourteen and doing well at school, the apple of his father's eye; Mica, more a member of the family than a housekeeper; and his aged mother, now living with his sister Milka in Peć, where he journeyed to see her. He also visited Mitra, with whom he had remained on friendly terms since the dissolution of their marriage. Their daughter Vukica, brought up by her mother and now in her early twenties, accompanied him on expeditions to the Belgrade shops.

The circle of his friends had both shrunk and expanded. Of those who had been closest to him in the Party and throughout the war, hardly one could now be numbered amongst his intimates. Even with Vlada Dedijer his friendship had cooled, though he could never forget that it was Dedijer who, alone of his comrades, had stood by him throughout the ordeal of his disgrace and ostracism. Dedijer too had paid a heavy price. Tragedy had struck his family; one son, goaded by the taunts of his schoolmates, took his own life, another died in a mountaineering accident. Their father, allowed to go abroad for a time to study and write, buried his grief in work, and later, as Tito's biographer and diarist of the Partisan war, made his peace with the regime. Djilas, whilst lamenting the loss of this friendship, was generous in his praise of his old friend's professional work.[2]

But if old friendships had lapsed, new ones had been formed. The talented Belgrade painter Lazar Vozarević presented him with a magnificent picture entitled 'The Victory'. Matija Bećković, son of a Montenegrin Chetnik leader, published his first volume of poems in the year of Djilas's second post-war imprisonment and soon found himself in trouble with officialdom on account of his biting wit and passionate dedication to intellectual freedom. Jovan Barović, a former Partisan and Political Commissar turned lawyer, expelled from the Party for 'Djilasism', won a nationwide reputation for his fearless defence of critics and dissidents of every colour. These, and other young writers, artists and intellectuals, were frequent visitors at the flat in Palmotićeva.

Djilas did not lack for friends or at least sympathisers, but he himself deprecated any claim to a following, still less to that most dangerous of associations, a 'faction'. There was no such thing, he maintained, as 'Djilasism'; it simply did not exist, for what others might term 'Djilasism' was nothing more nor less than democracy. That was what he stood for. Once he had been the most dogmatic of Marxists; now, he would jovially declare, he was a dogmatist dedicated to the dogma that there is no dogma. He considered himself a Socialist, but not a Social Democrat in the Western sense, working to transform a capitalist into a Socialist society. His aim was rather to transform a Communist-dominated society into a Socialist, a truly democratic, society. There were reformers and liberal-minded men within the establishment working for broadly the same ends though with differences of emphasis and ideology. He wished them well, however vehemently they might reject his overtures and deny that there was any common ground between them. As far as they were concerned, Djilas was still a non-person, manifestly less equal than others in a supposedly egalitarian society. He might think, say and write (though not publish) anything he liked, they would airily declare, for he was not important enough to cause more than a ripple on the mainstream of the country's social and political development.

Though he eschewed attempts to build up any organised following or to put forward a specific platform, Djilas had by no means reached the point of renouncing all hope of eventually resuming political activity. He would not actively seek reconciliation with those in power, but neither would he spurn an olive branch if one were proffered. It was whispered in Belgrade, the inexhaustible fount of rumours, that the septuaginarian President had released his former heir-apparent from prison not only in order to heal the breach, but to reinstate him and groom him as his successor. There were absolutely no grounds for such speculation and Djilas sternly discouraged it; but did he nevertheless, in his heart of hearts, hanker after some such dramatic change of fortune? He was loth to admit it. 'However much I may silently crave power,' he wrote about this time, whilst putting the finishing touches to *The Unperfect Society*, 'I hope with all my heart that this cup will pass from me, and that I shall remain safely ensconced in the original, toil-worn innocence of my ideas.'[3]

He would in any case fight on to recover his full rights as a citizen and a writer, to secure his complete moral (and if possible his political) rehabilitation. His financial position too needed regularising. The officials to whom he applied confirmed that he appeared to be entitled to a state pension but explained that a final decision rested with 'higher authority'; for the time being he depended on the monthly remittance sent him on account of royalties by his American publisher. Then there were the questions of the return of his decorations, his demand for a passport, the manuscripts retained by the prison authorities, and a revocation of the ban on publication and political activities.

He decided to take these matters up in person with the Federal Secretary for Internal Affairs, who received him sympathetically, although it was clear that the final decisions would rest with Tito. Before long, the manuscripts were returned – two plastic bags stuffed with several thousand pages of closely written toilet-paper. The pension payments began to arrive, and finally the passport. But the ban on publishing and political activities remained, and permission to wear the decorations was still withheld.

'It's not that they amuse me,' Djilas explained to an American correspondent, 'but if they restore them I know I am fully rehabilitated. Now I am only a second-class citizen!'[4]

With regard to the ban on publication, the same journalist was left with the impression that he would not resign himself to remaining muzzled for five years, even at the risk of another jail sentence. 'I could not remain silent for so long!' Djilas told him. Since he had ceased to be a Marxist, it seemed unlikely that he would ever again be offered high office, but it was clear that once his civil rights were restored, Djilas intended to participate fully in current political discussions, and perhaps even activities, 'putting his thinking and writing to work to support the most liberal elements of the Communist Party working to democratise Yugoslavia.'[5]

It was a curious, indeed a paradoxical, situation. The climate was now one of continuous if cautious change, reassessment and experimentation, but the voice that had been loudest in raising questions and demanding changes was condemned to silence. Djilas had had the misfortune to be right at the wrong moment – a crime which others find hard to forgive. Even now there remained some matters, particularly where they touched the entrenched power of the Party leadership, where the views of the liberalisers fell short of those which had been expressed by Djilas, whilst the latter's had in the meanwhile evolved still further. There was much in the government's present policies of which Djilas fully approved, but much in their implementation which left him dissatisfied. Nor was he alone in his dissatisfaction, for the spectrum of dissent had notably widened. It found its most dramatic expression in the early summer of 1968 in the unrest, culminating in a strike, amongst the students of Belgrade University. Their protest was orderly and, in spite of their efforts, uncoordinated with any corresponding gesture on the part of the workers, but it was sufficiently serious to be settled only after Tito's personal intervention.

Djilas, the moving spirit of student protest thirty years before, followed events with the keenest interest. Amongst the slogans paraded by the demonstrators were some which had long been his own watchwords: 'There is no Socialism without Freedom, nor Freedom without Socialism!', 'Down with the Princes of Socialism!', 'Bureaucrats – hands off the Workers!' A London newspaper carried a report that he had hastened to the university with the intention of addressing the rebellious students but had been greeted with boos and prevented from speaking. He denied the report in a letter to the editor, explaining that he had indeed gone to see for himself what was happening, but only 'as a sympathetic spectator, without any intention to intrude on a purely student movement'.[6] He was still bound by the ban on any political activity and was irritated by the allegation that he had violated it so clumsily and with such humiliating consequences.

The Belgrade student troubles occurred at a time when momentous changes were taking place elsewhere in Eastern Europe. In Czechoslovakia, Dubček and his fellow reformers were trying to democratise the Communist Party and regime and to rebuild society by giving Communism a 'human face'. Their programme included a radical democratization of public life, a free press and guarantees of personal liberty, the rehabilitation of political victims, a guiding rather than a controlling role for the Communist Party, decentralisation of decision-making, the opening up of the country to world markets, honest elections, and equal rights for national groups – all aspirations which many Yugoslavs could warmly applaud. Djilas greeted the

'Prague Spring' with enthusiasm, seeing in it a flowering of his own beliefs, and he fully approved of Belgrade's efforts to support it. In April, a Yugoslav delegation headed by Tito reached Moscow and pressed the Czech case on the Russians who were deeply suspicious, particularly of the trend to play down the 'leading role of the Communist Party', which they saw as a threat to their chief channel of control over the country and to Soviet influence in Eastern Europe in general. Tito tried to dissuade the sceptical Brezhnev from any attempt to restore the old system by force, but in the second half of August the Russians nevertheless opted for military intervention.

Djilas talked freely to the correspondent of *The Guardian* about his reaction to events in Czechoslovakia. The ban on making political statements had been imposed in order to silence criticism of official policies; since he wished only to express approval and endorsement of them, he may have thought that it could safely be disregarded, at least as far as the foreign press was concerned. Djilas told the reporter that he fully supported the line Tito had been taking, and he was agreeably surprised at the firmness with which he had denounced Soviet aggression. He also said:

Dubček and his colleagues have been trying to do precisely what I had myself at one time suggested in Yugoslavia. I have been in complete ideological agreement with the Czech reforms. Their cardinal point is the liberalisation and democratisation of their Communist Party – a real departure from orthodox Communism. I myself have never believed that a multiparty system is essential in order to transform Communism into a humane and democratic system. Once people are free, other political parties may possibly emerge; that is only of secondary importance. I admire the resistance offered by the Czechs and Slovaks; they would have stood no chance in a fight. But I tell you one thing! All the same, I would have fought if I had been in their shoes! Just because I am made that way, I suppose. Most Yugoslavs are. The fact remains that a small nation has been subjugated by Russian Imperialism. But in the long run I'm optimistic. Freedom can never be crushed by tanks. . . . Have any Yugoslav leaders been to consult me? No – nobody! I am kept in complete political isolation and not allowed to make statements for publication inside Yugoslavia.'[7]

On 4 October Milovan and Štefica Djilas arrived in London to spend nine or ten days as the guests of Jennie Lee. Their visit was private, but Djilas took the opportunity of publishing two long articles on Czechoslovakia in *The Times* and giving a television interview. He praised the Yugoslav government's stand in the crisis and declared that Yugoslavia would fight to the last man if attacked. The West, he added, should be prepared to come to his country's aid if required, even at the risk of nuclear war. Wasn't it better to fight on the Adriatic rather than on the Channel? For Tito personally he had words of praise: 'An exceptional man! I say so, though we are opponents. He has an unerring political instinct and saw at once that the Russians' attitude towards Czechoslovakia posed a threat to our country.'[8]

His remarks in the United States, where he arrived nine days later on a six weeks' Fellowship at Princeton's Woodrow Wilson School of Public and International Affairs, were still more explicit: 'We are not far apart,' he said in answer to questions about the possibility of some reconciliation with Tito. 'I don't know what he's thinking. I feel that we are now not against each other as was the case before. I cannot say we are friends, but neither can I say we are enemies!'[9]

The first move would have to come from Tito, and Tito felt absolutely no inclination for any reconciliation. It was not that he was by nature vindictive or vengeful, or even lacking in magnanimity, but the break with 'Djido' had caused him real pain. He looked upon it not only as a defection from the cause but a personal betrayal. It aroused his anger and a deep, persistent resentment. He felt it to be a rejection of his authority, paternal almost as much as political, deeply wounding to his pride. The mere mention of Djilas's name was apt to enrage him. The fact that he, Marshal and President of Yugoslavia and the acknowledged architect of his country's destinies, had reached positions not far removed from those which had caused the defector's downfall, made matters even worse and reconciliation more difficult. He knew Djilas to be a man whose beliefs might honestly evolve, but who would never trim or compromise his principles. If they were now closer in their thinking, this could only mean that he, Tito, had been forced to shift his ground. The thought was humiliating. Besides, Djilas was still anathema to the Russians, and in his eternal balancing act between East and West, Tito would sooner or later need to placate the Russians, in spite of Czechoslovakia.

Tito had gone to Jajce to attend the celebrations of the twenty-fifth anniversary of the founding of the Anti-Fascist Council. He was careful in his speech to refrain from any allusion to Czechoslovakia, the Soviet Union, or the 'Brezhnev Doctrine' claiming the right to intervene in a country whose regime was judged to be threatened by 'forces hostile to Socialism'. In a reply to correspondents' questions he discounted the likelihood of a Russian invasion of Yugoslavia and described the situation as still serious though not to be over-dramatised; in any case, Yugoslavia was quite able to defend herself without the need to turn to

NATO for help. Asked for his reactions to the similar statements Djilas was reported to have been making on this point the Marshal replied testily: 'I don't know what he's been saying! Anyway, he talks too much! We respect Djilas for his literary work, but he's no right to speak for Yugoslavia!'[10]

A curious way of showing 'respect' for an author's work – to ban its publication, even fiction, literary studies and translations of seventeenth-century poetry! Unable to find a publisher in Yugoslavia for his new book, Djilas had taken the manuscript of *The Unperfect Society* with him and arranged for it to be published in New York by William Jovanovich the following spring. The announcement was made when the author was presented with the 1969 Freedom Award – an honour accorded previously to such diverse recipients as Pablo Casals, Jean Monet, Winston Churchill and other prominent figures 'dedicated to the strengthening of free societies'. The award was presented on 9 December on the eve of his return to Yugoslavia where he was determined to continue the struggle. Djilas had never considered exchanging the anonymous life of an 'unperson' in his native country for that of an honoured exile. Circumstances, he knew, sometimes compelled such a course; Svetlana Alliluyeva was living only a few miles away, and the author of *Conversations with Stalin* found it a curious experience to converse with Stalin's daughter in such capitalist surroundings. He encountered exiles too from his own country, many of them survivors and sympathisers from the Ustashe and Nedić regimes, or ex-Chetniks still professing loyalty to the memory of Mihailović. Some demonstrated outside the ballroom of the Roosevelt Hotel in New York where the Freedom Award was made, displaying placards inscribed 'Djilas Executioner!' One of them succeeded in forcing an entry and tried to interrupt the proceedings. Djilas appeared unruffled and dismissed the interruption with the remark: 'These people simply don't understand what's happening in the world!'[11]

He gave his own view of what was happening in a short speech of acceptance. The struggle in Eastern Europe was 'to break out of the closed circle in which national and social communities still live'. The award now made to him would bring encouragement to 'the thousands of free spirits in Eastern Europe who find different ways to express their thoughts'. The path to freedom there had never been easy. It had led through revolutionary changes to the anti-democratic regimes now in power. He praised the examples of Czechoslovakia and his own country. 'Yugoslavia, although it has not yet reached the desirable degree of freedom, is an example not only of national courage, but also of those democratic processes which reactionary bureaucratic forces are no longer able to halt.' He had always been animated by the vision of a freer life for his people in a juster social world; if he had found himself in conflict with his world, it was because he could not reconcile himself to its 'false aspects'. With the moral encouragement of freedom-loving peoples throughout the world he pledged himself to continue the struggle.[12]

The Unperfect Society was published as scheduled in New York at the beginning of May. Its author was technically in breach of the ban forbidding him to publish, but the authorities made no move against him. He was even allowed to make other journeys abroad; to Vienna, at the invitation of his Austrian publisher, and then to Rome, to lecture under the auspices of the *Unione italiana per il progresso della cultura*. The themes of Djilas's new book, and those of his frequent contributions and interviews in the foreign press, were no more to officialdom's liking than before, but their tactics were to ignore the troublesome gadfly and his writings as far as possible and to go on denying him access to the public at home. The crisis over Czechoslovakia passed and international tension diminished; internally, the country continued along its fitful course of liberalisation. The League of Communists' Ninth Congress, held in the spring of 1969, injected new blood into the Party and marked a shift of power from the centre to its regional organisations in the 'republics' which made up the multi-national federal state. It was a trend pregnant with consequences for the country's future.

In October, six months after the publication of *The Unperfect Society*, a decree published in the Official Gazette declared it an offence to import copies of the book from abroad. Issues of foreign newspapers carrying reviews of the book, or articles by Djilas, were confiscated. No reasons were given, but it was clear that a decision to follow a harder line had been taken. Tito himself called for a tightening-up on the cultural and ideological fronts and a stricter control of press, plays and films. The pendulum was swinging again towards 'normalisation' of relations with the Soviet Union. Djilas was quickly made to feel its weight. The passport which had permitted him to travel abroad was withdrawn on the grounds that he had violated the ban on publication. From then on, his life would be that of 'internal exile'.

CHAPTER THIRTY-FOUR

The End of the Tito Era

THE closing years of the Tito era were marked by few outward events of importance in the life of Milovan Djilas. The writing of books; contributions to the international press; conversations with visiting journalists, academics and political observers from abroad; a cautious search for consensus amongst Yugoslavia's varied dissident groups; these things absorbed the energies of the 'internal exile'. His life passed quietly within the circle of his family and friends, but the influence of his thought and personality continued to seep steadily through the barriers imposed by a suspicious officialdom to reach a growing number at home and abroad. With his ex-comrades of the Tito era there had been no reconciliation, no meeting of minds, as he had once hoped. They might indeed have readmitted him to the fold, but only as a docile sheep; and who could expect docility or conformity from Milovan Djilas?

The little seed of self-management which Djilas, Kardelj and Kidrič had implanted in Tito's mind less than a dozen years before had blossomed into the most distinctive feature of Yugoslavia's brand of Socialism. Its growth had also stimulated and complicated the three major inter-related problems which were to dominate that period; the economic, the national, and the political problem. Self-management had come to mean far more than simply 'Factories to the Workers' which had been Tito's first reaction. It brought with it a trend towards decentralised decision-making, concern with profitability, and a demand for Western know-how and Western markets, resulting in a degree of economic liberalisation difficult to reconcile with the centralised planning and control implicit in a Communist system. Djilas was quick to sense these inner contradictions and the curbs they imposed on the country's economic performance. Self-management, he believed, was on the whole justified by the results so far achieved and by its potentialities if practised by 'those who identify Socialism with social justice and human freedom'. But he also saw that in most cases the concept merely served to camouflage the reality of control by a Party barren of all ideas except that of its own perpetuation in power:

The workers' councils and other self-management bodies have been unable, by virtue either of their mandate or their actual position in society, to solve the problems of a free and harmonious development for the economy, or even the problem of equitable distribution (the so-called distribution according to work performed). This is not possible without the statutory guarantees for free and active participation by ordinary people, first and foremost those at work, and also freedom for independent trade unions and other organisations, the right to strike and to demonstrate, and so on. The economy may be regarded as man's war against nature, and as such it demands greater discipline the more complicated the working conditions and the more sophisticated the equipment that has to be handled. In spite of their good intentions, the workers' councils, with their primitiveness and their patriarchal leadership, their merely ostensible democracy, are often a cause of disorder, and inefficiency and illusionism.[1]

Applied to administration and economic organisation on a regional scale, self-management inevitably stimulated local interests and nationalist passions. Of the six 'republics' and two 'autonomous regions' which composed the Yugoslav state, some were considerably more advanced than others. The more developed republics (Slovenia and Croatia) contributed proportionately more than they deemed fair to the less developed, and yet they carried less weight than they believed to be their due at the federal level, in government, the army, etc. The steps taken towards decentralising the administration and the Party were far from satisfying frustrated national sentiment; tension between Belgrade and the regional centres increased dangerously, as the regional Communist Party organisations, theoretically largely independent, became aware that they now, for the first time, enjoyed a real measure of popular support. Tito, alarmed at the threat posed to 'democratic centralism', withdrew the cautious support he had been lending to the decentralisation process and, at the end of 1971, began a drastic purge of the Croat Communist Party and the reimposition of stricter centralised control.

Djilas followed these events with dismay, though without surprise. The League of Communists, in his view, remained an authoritarian, monopolistic body, despite some recent cosmetic changes. The solution of the nationalities problem could only result from greater democratisation. In the war the Partisans had taken amazing strides in the right direction. By rallying Serbs, Croats and others in a struggle against the common enemy they had managed to strike a balance between loyalty to the common Yugoslav cause and local patriotism. Some Communists had, even then, been infected by chauvinism and had had to be disciplined. Djilas recalled the case of Hebrang, removed by Tito at the urging of himself and Kardelj, from his post as Secretary of the Croat Communist Party. Concessions had been made to nationalist aspirations by setting up regional military headquarters and organs of local government, subject to the overall direction of the Supreme Command and Tito's Politburo. After the War, however, the 'independence' allowed the 'republics' had been merely nominal – no more real than was the separate status theoretically accorded to the non-Communist components of the People's Front – whilst effective power remained concentrated in the hands of Tito and the centralised leadership.

'The Kingdom of Yugoslavia was smashed in a few days of war largely due to the dissensions amongst the nationalities,' Djilas writes in *The Unperfect Society*. The Communists, he adds,

for all their fine words, have not gone very far beyond recognising cultural and administrative autonomy in their solution to the nationalities question. Communist Yugoslavia has remained centrist through its single, monolithic political party, which is also propped up by an army and a secret police. The present Yugoslav regime is not, I am convinced, capable of surviving any major crisis any more than the previous regime was. There is no equality amongst nationalities without human freedom, or without the genuine right of each national community to secession, the right to a self-contained economy and independent political organisation and its own armed forces. Only the vision of a new Yugoslavia in which the national communities are associated by agreements as between sovereign states, and in which all citizens have political freedom, offers any prospects for a more stable state community.'[2]

Yet although it seemed to Djilas that 'the forces that maintain Yugoslavia as a central state are weakening internally and the very idea of Yugoslavia is being challenged and evaporating before our eyes,' he did not wish for the destruction of that state nor think it likely to occur. 'I believe in Yugoslavia, and I believe that it will continue to exist,' he declared; but only if it ceased to be bound together on the basis of a single ideology imposed by a single centralised party. The component republics had to be genuinely convinced that it was in their common interest to remain together within the borders of the same multi-national federal state or confederation – a transformation the more easy to achieve the closer Yugoslavia moved towards the European community.[3] As for his own personal position, Djilas considered himself 'a Serb – a Montenegrin Serb' – not a Serb *tout court*, like any inhabitant of Old Serbia. He felt himself to be Montenegrin, a son of the Serbian people, as a Bavarian or Prussian feels himself to be a German, the local and specific identity not excluding loyalty, or the feeling of belonging, to a larger entity. Similarly, being a Serb, he felt himself to be a Yugoslav, linked by blood, language, common interests and the will to statehood with the other branches of the South Slav family, recognising and respecting each other's distinctive identity, rights and interests.

The Serbian Communists had followed developments in the sister republic of Croatia with mixed feelings. The nationalists of the 'Zagreb Spring' maintained that 'Great Serb chauvinism' remained as powerful and baneful a factor in Socialist Yugoslavia as it had been in the old bourgeois state; they welcomed the removal of Ranković as a step in the right direction, and the advent of a new, liberal-minded Serbian leadership headed by Marko Nikezić, a former Secretary for Foreign Affairs and a politician of broad views. During the 1971-2 crisis in Croatia Nikezić and his colleagues were careful to keep a low profile so as to avoid exacerbating nationalist passions. But once the Croats had been brought to heel, Tito nevertheless decided to extend his purge to Serbia where he judged the influence of 'rotten liberalism' to be just as pernicious as nationalist extremism. 'The Great Serb liberals defended the former faction in the Croat Party leadership and demanded that it should not be destroyed,' explained an official spokesman.[4] Liberal-minded Party leaders in Slovenia, Macedonia and elsewhere were likewise eliminated and emphasis was again put on 'democratic centralism' and the tightening up of ideological orthodoxy.

Djilas was made a convenient scapegoat for the spread of these nationalist and 'anarcho-liberal' deviations. The policy had hitherto been to ignore him; now his name became the target of abuse in the press. The leading Belgrade weekly *Nin* launched a series of attacks on current heresies beginning with a four-page article headed 'From Djilas to Liberalism' which argued that most of the present troubles could be traced back to the aberrations of Tito's ex-agit-prop chief.[5] It was maintained that the dangerous innovations of the 1952 Sixth Congress – the 'Djilas Congress' – had been mainly his work and that Tito had never been really happy with them. *Front*, the organ of the armed forces, branded him bluntly as anti-Marxist, anti-Communist and 'a traitor to his country'.[6]

What did officialdom hope to gain by this change of tactic? Why suddenly promote Djilas from non-person to deviationist bogey-man? For two decades he had been sedulously kept out of the public eye, confined either to prison or to the privacy of his home. During all that time the papers had not carried his photograph or published any of his articles or stories. His books were banned from the bookshops. His name could not be totally expunged from the records of the Party and the Partisan war, in which he had figured so prominently, but references to his role in them were played down. This sustained ostracism had not been without its effect. A new generation had grown up which knew little or nothing about Djilas. Foreign correspondents covering the 1968 unrest in Belgrade University and asking the students whether they had been influenced in any way by Djilas were met with blank looks.[7] The sudden publicity – albeit unfavourable – now being given him was a tacit admission that the growing volume of dissent in Yugoslavia *did* owe something to the all-but-forgotten heresiarch. Not that dissidents or opponents of the regime all shared his views – far from it – or if they did, were always conscious of his influence. But by championing the right of others to hold and express their views, however unpalatable to the regime or to himself personally, by refusing to approve a society in which a single monolithic party and one imposed ideology held the field, Djilas was in a sense the ally of every critic and dissident. Apart from those separatists or other fanatics who advocated the use of force, they could all take comfort from the knowledge that in the heart of the nation's capital this man of independent mind and international reputation was bearing his silent witness to the indestructibility of its people's proud and independent spirit.

With every new article and book from his pen, Djilas was steadily adding to his reputation abroad. And not only in the West; in the Socialist countries his writings circulated clandestinely and fed the springs of dissent. In Czechoslovakia, before the fading of the Prague Spring, his books had been widely read, in Czech and other languages. In the Soviet Union too they were known through smuggled copies and *samizdat*. The mathematician Leonid Plyush relates that he had eagerly studied *The New Class* and found that it confirmed many of the conclusions he had reached independently himself.[8] Vladimir Bukovsky borrowed a copy of the same book from the wife of an American correspondent and was in the process of making a photocopy of it when the KGB came to arrest him.[9]

In Yugoslavia, the dissident with whose name that of Djilas was most readily linked, though they differed in some of their beliefs and ideas, was Mihailo Mihailov. Arraigned for the fourth time for maintaining the right to hold and express ideas other than those officially approved, Mihailov was sentenced in February 1975 to a further seven years' imprisonment for disseminating 'hostile propaganda'. Djilas came to his defence in the columns of the international press. The accused man was 'not a worshipper of Capitalism or the consumer society, but rather of human rights and spiritual fulfilment,' he pointed out. 'He could not get a job, his apartment was taken away, and he tried in vain to get a passport so that he could go abroad to lecture at western universities. How democratic is that democracy, how socialist that society,' Djilas asked, which practises such victimisation?'[10]

These were embarrassing questions to be asked at a time when the Conference of European States was meeting at Helsinki in an endeavour to promote détente between East and West. The very convening of such a conference, at which each state figured, at least in theory, as an individual participant rather than an adherent of any bloc, was in accord with the non-aligned stance adopted by the Yugoslav government and promised it the prospect of assuming the role, to a certain extent, of mediator between East and West. The stress laid on human rights by the West, in the Final Act of the Helsinki Conference, was not so welcome. Here Belgrade could speak with less assurance, conscious of its own dubious record and the encouragement the Final Act was likely to give its domestic dissidents. Whilst on a visit to Sweden the following year, Tito admitted, though stoutly justifying its necessity, that his country had probably more political prisoners than any other East European country except the Soviet Union; the Secretary for the Swedish branch of Amnesty estimated their number at a thousand.[11]

Two years after Helsinki, Yugoslavia played host to the delegates who met to review progress on the measures previously agreed. Some months before the opening of the Belgrade Conference on European Peace and Security, Djilas spoke out strongly to foreign correspondents about the still highly unsatisfactory situation in his country with respect to civil rights. The jails, he said, remained full of political prisoners; he put their number at six hundred – a higher proportion than in the Soviet Union. Things had got worse in recent years. In the late 1960s, Yugoslavia could claim to have almost no political prisoners; then, in the early seventies, with the purges in Croatia, followed by those in Serbia and elsewhere, the numbers rose drastically. 'Not that I have any sympathy – let me make that quite clear – for terrorists, spies, or those who advocate the separation of any part of the Yugoslav Federation – no sympathy at all!' he declared. 'But our jails are also full of prisoners of conscience. Never, even in the worst days of repression in pre-war Yugoslavia, were there so many political prisoners as now. On the day Germany invaded Yugoslavia there were only thirty-six Communists in jail!'[12]

The official reaction to these criticisms was sharp; those who made them, charged a spokesman of the Foreign Ministry, were being manipulated from abroad in a campaign designed to put Yugoslavia in the same boat as certain Soviet bloc countries.[13] 'Premeditated provocation on the part of Djilas on behalf of his paymasters!' declared a Belgrade newspaper.[14] An anonymous letter was sent to the flat at Palmotičeva threatening its occupants with assassination; Djilas had little doubt that it was a clumsy manoeuvre by UDBA to silence him.[15] Nor was he the only member of his family to feel the heavy hand of the secret police. His cousin Vitomir, a lawyer living in Montenegro, was arrested on the customary 'hostile propaganda' charge. His offence had been to compose a letter to the Belgrade daily *Politika* asking 'to know whether we too, here in Yugoslavia, can fight for a democratic (a truly democratic!) society – whether there is now the possibility of free speech here, of freedom of the press, or must we still live in fear of arrest and repression?' Officialdom was quickly to provide the answer: police agents burst into the lawyer's home, seized the draft of the letter (which, on second thoughts, its author had deemed wiser not to send) and put him under arrest. He was sentenced to thirty months in jail.[16]

The approach of the Belgrade Conference encouraged hopes that the regime might be more liberal in granting passports to those who, like Djilas, the authorities suspected might cause embarrassment if allowed to travel abroad. A petition to this effect was submitted to the Constitutional Commission but rejected. The very idea that such action might be regarded as an infringement of civil rights called forth an indignant denial from President Tito himself. The government would not bow to any pressure from a handful of dissidents, he declared. Millions of its citizens were free to travel where they liked, but his government was not to be criticised 'because two or three passports were not being issued, and would not be issued'.[17] Bakarić, considered to be one of Tito's more liberal advisers, was asked at a press conference specifically about Djilas. 'I don't know why the police refuse to issue him a passport,' he replied jocularly. 'Maybe they wish to save him from going back to jail. For whenever he is let out of the country he does things which are punishable under our laws!'[18]

But Djilas, unlike some opponents of the regime, had never favoured illegal or violent action against it. In this he was in sharp disagreement with the neo-Ustashe Separatists who organised occasional terrorist acts inside the country and abroad, and the Cominformists who had recently revived their activities through the formation of a clandestine pro-Soviet Communist Party in rivalry with the League of Communists. The group had drawn support mainly from amongst Russophil Montenegrins and in 1974 held an underground 'Congress' which they claimed to be the legitimate alternative to the Communist Party's innovating Sixth ('Djilas') Congress. Amongst the group's leading figures were two former Partisan colonels; Mileta Perović, who followed an unconditional pro-Soviet line, and Vlada Dapčević, brother of the general who was Djilas's former friend, who looked first to Moscow and latterly to Peking. Both had been active in exile and both were abducted by UDBA (Dapčević from Rumania, Perović from Western Europe) to face trial and heavy prison sentences in Yugoslavia. Although their views and aims were totally at variance with his own, Djilas believed that the authorities were wrong to have taken such drastic action against their group. Allowed some freedom of expression, he believed that they would never have attracted more than a harmless handful of supporters; as it was, under present circumstances, they aroused more popular sympathy than they deserved. The real danger, Djilas remained convinced, was still from the deep-rooted, though disguised, Stalinist tendencies in the leadership of the League of Communists.[19]

In November 1977, to mark Yugoslavia's National Day and make a favourable impression on the delegates to the Belgrade Conference, Tito announced an Amnesty under which 723 persons were to benefit, 218 of them political offenders, with remission or shortening of their sentences. Mihailov was amongst those released. But the President's act of clemency did not cause officialdom to look any more kindly on the chief heresiarch. By the spring of 1977 the attacks in *Nin* linking his name with every possible manifestation of anti-regime activity, had grown into a nine-hundred-page, two-volume work which appeared in the bookshops under the title of *Liberalism – from Djilas to the Present.*[20] The wordy indictment did contain a grain of truth. The stand made by Djilas for the right to think and to express one's thought freely had stimulated a variety of currents. As an ex-dogmatist opposed to all imposed dogma, he had done nothing to guide them into any single course, but now circumstances seemed to be channelling them in the same direction. The octogenarian ruler could not dominate the Yugoslav scene much longer, and with his departure the Russians would no doubt redouble their efforts to re-establish their hegemony by exploiting the country's divisions. It was imperative for those who wished at all costs to prevent a return to Stalinism to draw together.

Throughout the spring and summer of 1978 leading dissidents from Croatia and Serbia held a series of talks. They came together not as conspirators plotting a coup against the Government, but as intellectuals interested in an exchange of views. The authorities were suspicious and scornful, but did not prevent them. 'It all boils down to a campaign to ensure freedom of speech for anti-Communists like

Mihailov,' Bakarić told the Croat Communists' Central Committee.[21] Tito himself adopted a more threatening tone. 'We cannot tolerate such people any longer,' he warned. 'We shall have to take the measures which, according to our constitution and laws, we have every right to take. Otherwise they will regard it as a sign of weakness on our part. But we fear nothing and nobody.'[22]

A few weeks later, the dissident movement suffered a cruel loss. Barović was killed in a car crash as he was driving from Belgrade to Zagreb; an 'accident' staged by UDBA, rumour had it. His funeral was made the occasion for an unprecedented display of solidarity. Mourners, many of them his grateful clients, came to Belgrade from Croatia, Bosnia and Macedonia, from the Albanian community on Kosovo, and from many other parts. A former secretary of the banned Zagreb cultural organisation, Matica Hrvatska, delivered a funeral oration and scattered handfuls of earth on the grave in homage from Croatia.

Djilas was deeply affected by the loss of his friend and fellow campaigner; he knew that the struggle would now be still harder and more bitter. The following month he was summoned by the security police and warned that unless he ceased his 'anti-Yugoslav' agitation 'more energetic measures' would be taken against him.[23] The threat left him unmoved. He knew that he was not alone and that others would continue to speak out if he were silenced, but he had no intention of being silenced. Mihailov had gone to the United States, but a group of their friends and younger writers remained in Yugoslavia and were planning to launch a *samizdat* forum for the stories and poems refused publication in the official press. *Časovnik* (The Clock) was a modest mimeographed affair issued in an edition of five hundred copies. Djilas contributed one of his best short stories, published so far only in English – *The Leper*, a brilliant fable of ostracism and slow death at the command of a village tyrant. In October the editor was sentenced to a month's imprisonment for failing to obtain permission to publish *Časovnik*. Djilas, as a major contributor, was fined 10,000 dinars (about £250). He refused to pay on the grounds that the Court had no jurisdiction in literary matters, and he declared his determination of continuing to seek every means possible, whether authorised or not, of publishing his non-political writings.[24]

The Tito era was drawing to a close. Kardelj, its leading theoretician, had fallen silent earlier in the year. His death sent Djilas's thoughts back to the years when they had worked closely together in the heady days of revolutionary change and euphoria. Of the trio Ranković-

Djilas-Kardelj, only the latter had maintained his position to the end, and even he, in the late fifties and early sixties, seemed to have lost something of Tito's favour. But Kardelj had nevertheless survived, subordinating and adjusting himself to the will of the autocrat he shrank from challenging and failed to outlive. He and Djilas had taken different paths.

Djilas had begun work on a new section of his autobiography. It was to be called *Power* and would deal with his period in office and his subsequent fall and imprisonment.[25] He thought it likely to prove the most controversial and explosive of his writings. But at the beginning of the following year he broke off to record his memories of the old President, seemingly so indestructible, who was at last succumbing to an illness which would clearly prove fatal. Djilas completed his short book during the months of March and April and called it *Druženje s Titom – Comradeship with Tito*. It dealt mainly with the years of war and revolution when a common belief in Communist goals and a shared will to power had brought them close together. Even now, twenty-seven years after the political and ideological gulf had opened between them, he felt his life was indissolubly linked to that of the man who had left such an astonishing mark on his country and his times.

Now, in the opening months of the new decade, the old man lay dying in a Slovene clinic, tended by a team of international specialists and surrounded by impersonal attendants and the men whom he had placed in power, his ebbing life sustained only by sophisticated machinery. He died in the afternoon of 4 May.

His body was brought to Belgrade on the special 'blue train' used for his presidential journeys. The coffin lay in state on a flag-decked catafalque in the marble splendour of the National Assembly of which Djilas had once been President. It was little more than a stone's throw from his home in Palmotićeva, but he did not join the crowds which filed past in their thousands to pay homage. Djilas had composed his own personal memorial to his former friend and leader whilst the Marshal was fighting his last battle. He had known him probably better than any of the few whom Tito allowed to see beyond the carefully cultivated public image and to approach the inner sanctum of his extraordinary personality. Their very intimacy and the bitterness of its ending made it impossible perhaps for him to write with full objectivity. Though the memoir which Djilas would soon publish paid tribute to Tito's great qualities, it also dared to note the hero's weaknesses – his vanity, the ruthless pursuit of personal power and prestige, the sedulously concealed mediocrity of the dictator's educational attainments and artistic tastes. In the prevailing atmosphere of apotheosis anything short of the most fulsome panegyric would smack of treason or blasphemy. Whatever the uncertainties of the post-Tito era now emerging, Djilas could confidently expect one thing; the implacable resentment of the new 'collective leadership', the second-rankers who were now stepping uneasily into the dead dictator's shoes.

The kings and presidents, the ministers, party leaders and notables of a hundred nations began to assemble for the funeral. There had been few such gatherings of world leaders ever, and Belgrade had certainly seen nothing like it. Brezhnev was there, his burly presence suggesting that if the heretic had been forgiven, the Fatherland of Socialism had not renounced its claim to his inheritance. The United States had sent only its Vice-President – a blunder which President Carter tried to rectify by a hurriedly arranged visit and courting of the new leadership. From Britain came the Prime Minister and the Duke of Edinburgh; Maclean and Deakin, officers of the former Military Mission, recalled the shared hazards of war and the strange, uneasy comradeship in arms with the western democracies. Germany, the old enemy, was represented by its Chancellor, the Third World by an assortment of despots and democratic leaders anxious to honour the last founder-member of the still vaunted but now distinctly threadbare non-aligned movement. Would Tito's other alleged achievements prove any more solid? Would history endorse the almost unanimous acclaim voiced in the obituaries and the funeral orations?

And what, Djilas mused, would history have to say of his own role? All his life he had felt torn between politics and literature, as if he had two natures warring within him. Politics had claimed his best years; and in politics he saw himself to have been 'something of a dreamer, a corrector of injustices, a seeker after absolute justice.'[26] Moreover, he had fallen from favour, and in politics the vanquished can expect no mercy; 'history nails only a leaden tablet of oblivion over the defeated, as over unpleasant episodes,' he had reflected sadly.[27] In literature too his former comrades had turned on him and done their utmost to deny him a hearing. But the urge to create was still strong within him, and in creating he knew he could overcome all obstacles and difficulties and even draw inspiration from them. In creation the artist can glimpse through the strife and chaos of outward appearances the contours of that hidden order of which his beloved Njegoš wrote:

And all this vast array of things confused
Hath yet some rhythmic Harmony and Law.

By giving literary form to the vicissitudes of his life he had begun to discern more clearly its pattern and significance – the progression from the crude Marxist creed of his revolutionary youth, through the horror and heroism of war, to the intoxication of victory and power and its sour aftertaste of disillusionment and disgrace. Others might dub him a turncoat, but he knew that he had remained true to himself. He had followed what he believed to be the only course honourable for himself and likely to bring greater freedom and justice to his fellows. It was his perception of what those concepts were, and how they were to be attained, that had changed.

Through reflection and literary creation, and through the personal suffering endured as a result of this keener perception, he had penetrated more deeply too into the mystery of good and evil. One night in prison as he lay between waking and sleeping, these words had imprinted themselves on his mind: 'Evil is when someone who is the chief cook in his country is not also the chief taster of what he cooks!' The chief cook was now dead. For a while the people might be content with the dishes served up by lesser men from the master-cook's old recipes, but in time they would demand more nourishing fare and the right to take a hand in its preparation. It was for Djilas and others like him to see that they did not altogether lose the very taste for freedom. Nothing ruins the democratic palate so much as prolonged spoon-feeding by a dictatorship.

The funeral cortège moved off to the grounds of Tito's private villa on Dedinje where his body was to rest. The tomb was covered by a plain stone slab bearing the inscription

JOSIP BROZ TITO

1892 – 1980

In death, Djilas wryly reflected, the Old Man had shown a restraint which, with his passion for palaces, decorations, uniforms, splendid privileges of every kind, had seldom characterised his life.

Though shunned by all but a handful of relatives and friends, Milovan Djilas knew that he was not really alone. Any wish to return to active political life had long since left him, but there were others who, without invoking his example or even calling themselves dissidents, were taking much the same road. They differed only in their starting-points and in the circumstances of their life. His son Aleksa, now studying in Austria and England and beginning to make his own mark as a writer, was of their number. His birthday fell on the anniversary of the death of Karl Marx. Perhaps there was something symbolic in that! Djilas had fought all his life for what he saw as the truth. But truth, like freedom, kept broadening out into ever wider horizons. Lesser and partial truths faded before a new and fuller apprehension of the truth and had to be discarded. Marx had been the first to offer him a creed, but the answers so confidently asserted had in time been found wanting, and he had emerged from Marxism, from Communism. 'I could not have acted other than I did,' he reflected. 'I made my choice in accordance with my vision, my judgment, my conscience. I am still convinced that what I did was right; but I am far from convinced that I shall see victory in my lifetime.'[28]

Truth, it is said, always wins in the end. Djilas believed that, but only in the end; perhaps not, in his corner of the Communist world, so long as he was alive. Yet there would be others to witness its certain triumph. What mattered above all else was to keep on struggling towards the light. 'One must not give in to Evil.'

Sources

THE indispensable source for this book has been the autobiographical writings of Milovan Djilas himself. These are more easily available in English, and the extracts quoted have therefore been taken from the published translations. An exception has been made for *Druženje s Titom* (published in London by his son Aleksa Djilas); there is also an English version by V. Kojić and R. Hayes published under the title *Tito – the Story from Inside* (Weidenfeld and Nicholson, London, 1981). An important source for Tito's life is Vladimir Dedijer's *Prilozi*, and for the War, the same author's *Dnevnik* (Diary), references to which refer to the three-volume 1970 edition published by Prosveta, Belgrade. Another invaluable wartime source is the series of documents published under the title of *Zbornik* . . . by the Institute for the History of the War, Belgrade. The chief newspaper source has been *Borba*, the organ of the Yugoslav Communist Party.

Abbreviations

(a) Milovan Djilas

Land	*Land without Justice*, New York 1958.
Memoir	*Memoir of a Revolutionary*, New York 1973.
Conversations	*Conversations with Stalin*, New York 1962.
Druženje	*Druženje s Titom*,

(b) Other

Prilozi	Vladimir Dedijer, *Josip Broz Tito; Prilozi za biografiju*, Belgrade 1953.
Zbornik	*Zbornik dokumenata i podataka o narodno-oslobodilačkem ratu jugoslovenskih naroda*, Belgrade 1949-65.
Documents	*Yugoslavia and the Soviet Union 1939-1973 – a documentary survey*, (ed. S. Clissold), Oxford, 1975.
PRO	Public Record Office, London.

Notes

Chapter 1: A Montenegrin Boyhood

This chapter is based on Djilas's own account of his boyhood, *Land without Justice*. For an anthropologist's commentary see the essay on Pride, Shame and Guilt in *The Danger of Equality* by Geoffrey Gorer, London 1966.

1 *Land*, p.25.
2 *Ibid.*, p.56.
3 *Ibid.*, p.106.

4 Interview published in *Encounter*, December 1979.

Chapter 2: Student Revolutionary

The material for this and the next three chapters is taken largely from Djilas's *Memoir of a Revolutionary*.

1 *Memoir*, p.92.
2 *Ibid.*, p.103.
3 *Ibid.*, p.31.

4 Stanko Lasić, *Sukob na kniževnoj ljevici, 1928-52*, Zagreb 1970.

Chapter 3: In Jail

1 *Memoir*, p.95.

2 *Ibid.*, p.93.

Chapter 4: On the Eve

1 *Memoir*, p.259.
2 *Ibid.*, p.266.
3 *Ibid.*, p.279.
4 *Ibid.*, p.329.
5 *Ibid.*, p.330.
6 *Ibid.*, p.332.

7 Ivan Supek, *Krivovjernik na Ljevici*, Bristol 1980, p.78.
8 *Memoir*, p.275.
9 *Memoir*, p.354; Vukmanović-Tempo, *Revolucija koja teče*, Belgrade 1971, Vol.1 pp. 149-150.

Chapter 5: To Fight or Not to Fight?

1 *Memoir*, p.385.
2 *Ibid.*, p.388.
3 *Prilozi*, pp.274-5.
4 *Memoir*, p.389.
5 *Ibid.*, pp.388-9.
6 *Documents*, pp.125-6.

7 *Ibid.*, p.127.
8 Phyllis Auty, *Tito – a Biography*, London 1970, p.172.
9 Djilas, *Wartime*, New York 1977, p.8.

Notes

Chapter 6: The Rising in Montenegro

1 *Wartime*, p.18.
2 *Ibid.*, pp.23-4.
3 *Ibid.*, p.37.

4 *Zbornik III*, Vol.1, p.21.
5 *Zbornik III*, Vol.4, pp.20-31:
Wartime, p.63.

Chapter 7: Western Approaches, Eastern Reproaches

1 *Narodna Borba*, 15 September 1941, *Zbornik III*, Vol.1, pp.36-8; *Wartime*, p.87.
2 F.W.D. Deakin, *The Embattled Mountain*, London 1971, p.129; P. Auty and R. Clogg (*eds.*), *British Policy towards wartime Resistance in Yugoslavia and Greece*, London 1975, pp.91-2.
3 *Wartime*, p.70.
4 *Ibid.*, pp.69-70.

5 *Ibid.*, p.38.
6 Auty and Clogg, *op. cit.*, p.91.
7 Julian Amery, *Approach March*, London 1973, pp.259-60.
8 Deakin, *op. cit.*, p.127.
9 *Ibid.*, p.130.
10 *Ibid.*, p.131.
11 *Wartime*, p.70.
12 *Ibid.*, p.72.
13 *Ibid.*, pp.227-231.

Chapter 8: The End of the Red Republic

1 *Wartime*, p.101.
2 F.W.D. Deakin, *op. cit.*, London 1971, p.142.
3 *Ibid.*
4 Gojko Nikoliš, *Korijen, Stablo, Pavetina; memoari*, Zagreb 1981, p.338.

5 *Dnevnik*, Vol.1, p.52.
6 *Prilozi*, p.349.
7 V. Dedijer, *Novi Prilozi za Bio-grafiju J.B. Tita*, Zagreb 1981, pp.717-9.

Chapter 9: Bosnian Interlude

1 *Prilozi*, p.349.
2 *Dnevnik*, 1, p.112.

3 *Wartime*, p.146.

Chapter 10: Montenegro Revisited

1 J. Tomasevich, *The Chetniks*, Stanford 1975, pp.209-11.
2 Author's archives; full text in S. Clissold, *Whirlwind*, London 1948, pp.86-7.
3 Deakin, *op. cit.*, pp.157-177.
4 *Zbornik*, *II*, Vol.3, pp.390-2.
5 *Wartime*, p.149.
6 *Zbornik*, *II*, Vol.3, p.231.
7 *Wartime*, p.149.

8 *Ibid.*
9 V. Dedijer, *The Beloved Land* (London, 1961), p.306. *Dnevnik*, Vol.1, p.176.
10 *Wartime*, p.169.
11 *Ibid.*, pp.164-5.
12 *Zbornik*, *II*, Vol.3, pp.353-7.
13 V. Dedijer, *Novi Prilozi*, p.723.
14 *Wartime*, p.159.
15 *Prilozi*, pp.330-1.

The Progress of a Revolutionary

Chapter 11: The Long March

1 *Wartime*, p.176.
2 *Wartime*, p.296.
3 Walter R. Roberts, *Tito, Mihailović and the Allies*, (Rutgers University Press 1973), p.167.

4 Moša Pijade, *About the legend that the Yugoslav uprising owed its existence to Soviet assistance* (London 1950), p.20.
5 *Prilozi*, p.339.
6 See Chapter 10, Note 3.
7 *Dnevnik*, Vol.11, pp.54-5.

Chapter 12: Operation White

1 *Wartime*, p.220.
2 *Ibid.*, p.224.
3 *Ibid.*, p.231.
4 *Ibid.*, p.232.
5 Fitzroy Maclean, *Disputed Barricade*, London 1957, p.206.
6 *Wartime*, p.231.
7 *Dnevnik*, Vol.2, p.147.
8 *Wartime*, p.237.

9 *Ibid.*, p.240.
10 *Ibid.*, p.242
11 Roberts, *op. cit.*, p.111.
12 Walter Hagen, *Die Geheime Front* (Zurich, 1950) p.268.
13 *Wartime*, p.243.
14 *Dnevnik*, Vol.2, p.25.
15 *Wartime*, p.244.

Chapter 13: Operation Black

1 *Zbornik*, II, Vol.8, pp.359-61.
2 *Wartime*, p.250.
3 *Ibid.*, p.251.
4 *Dnevnik*, Vol.2, p.210.
5 V. Dedijer, *Novi Prilozi*, p.723.
6 Dedijer, *Tito Speaks* (London 1953), pp.197-8.
7 *Wartime*, p.253.

8 Deakin, *op. cit.*, pp.84-5.
9 Deakin, *op. cit.*, p.11.
10 *Dnevnik*, Vol.2, p.275.
11 *Wartime*, p.267.
12 Deakin, *op. cit.*, p.27.
13 *Wartime*, pp.266-7.
14 *Ibid.*, p.280.
15 *Ibid.*, pp.284-5.

Chapter 14: Croat Problems

1 J. Jareb, *Hrvatska Revija* (Buenos Aires 1959) pp. 429-31.
2 *Zbornik*, II, Vol.2, pp.31-2.
3 *Wartime*, p.328.

Chapter 15: Preparing for Power

1 *Wartime*, p.338.
2 William Jones, *Twelve Months with Tito's Partisans*, Bedford 1946, pp.17, 50.
3 *Dnevnik*, Vol.2, p.450.
4 *Wartime*, p.144.
5 *Ibid.*, p.350.

6 *Dnevnik*, Vol.2, pp.528-39.
7 *Wartime*, p.353.
8 *Zbornik*, III, Vol.3, p. 462.
9 *Wartime*, pp.359-60.
10 *Ibid.*, p.362.
11 *Ibid.*, pp.372-3.

Notes

Chapter 16: To the Kremlin

1 *Conversations*, p.18.
2 *Borba*, November 1942.
3 *Conversations*, p.34.
4 *Wartime*, p.357.
5 *Conversations*, p.43.

6 *Ibid.*, p.45.
7 *Borba*, 21 December 1944.
8 *Conversations*, pp.59-60.
9 *Borba*, ibid.
10 *Conversations*, pp.60-4.

Chapter 17: An Evening with Stalin

1 *Wartime*, pp.394-5; M. Pijade, *Izabrani govori i članci*, 11, Belgrade 1950, p.370.

2 *Conversations*, pp.64-79.

Chapter 18: Island Fortress

1 D. Biber (ed.) *Tito-Churchill – strogo tajno*, Belgrade-Zagreb 1981, p.174.
2 Dedijer, *Novi priloz*, p.864.
3 *Wartime*, p.392.
4 *Ibid.*, p.397.

5 Kardelj, in his memoirs, omits to mention that Djilas took part in the talks with Togliatti or that they discussed the Trieste problem. *Borba za Priznanje i Nezavisnost nove Jugoslavije, 1944-57.* Ljubljana 1980.
6 *Naša Reć* (London), No.313, 1980.

Chapter 19: Friendship and Friction

1 *Istoriya Iugoslavii* (Moscow 1963), ii, 241: *Novoya i noveishaya istoriya*, 1960, 126-38.
2 *Borba*, 25 December 1951: *Politika*, 20 October 1951.
3 *Wartime*, p.417.
4 *Conversations*, p.82.
5 *Wartime*, p.419.
6 *Conversations*, p.103.
7 *Ibid.*, pp.82-3.
8 Quoted in letter of 4 May 1948 from the Central Committee of the Soviet Communist Party to the Central Committee of the Yugoslav Communist Party, *Correspondence. . .* , Belgrade 1948.

9 Vukmanović-Tempo, *op. cit.*, Vol. 11, pp.7-17.
10 PRO, FO 371/44395.
11 *Conversations*, pp.86-90; *Wartime*, pp.428-9; Nikoliš, *op. cit.*, pp.636-640, with footnote by Mitra Mitrović.
12 *Druženje*, p.84.
13 *Wartime*, p.429.

The Progress of a Revolutionary
Chapter 20: Return to Moscow

This chapter is based on Djilas's own account of his second visit to Moscow in *Conversations*, pp.90-114.

1 *Khrushchev Remembers*, London 1971, pp.375-6.

2 *Borba*, 16 April 1945.

Chapter 21: The Power and the Glory

1 Quoted in letter of 4 May 1948 from the Soviet Central Committee to the Yugoslav Central Committee: *Correspondence* Belgrade 1948.

2 *Conversations*, p.160. See also *Prilozi*, p.469 and Dedijer, *The Battle which Stalin Lost*, pp.33, 101, 193; Auty, *op. cit.*, p.250, based on information given to the author by Kardelj.

3 *Wartime*, p.449.

4 *Druženje*, p.35.

5 *Wartime*, p.427.

6 PRO, FO 371/48823, Chancery, Belgrade to Foreign Office, 26 July 1945.

7 *Unperfect Society*, London 1969, p.181.

8 *Conversations*, pp.115-6.

9 *Borba*, 8 October 1947.

10 *Ibid.*, 1 July 1946.

11 *Conversations*, p.124.

Chapter 22: The Bear's Hug

The material in this chapter is taken from *Conversations* pp. 238-68 except where otherwise indicated.

1 *Khrushchev Remembers*, pp.259-69.

2 *Ibid.*, p.258.

3 See Note 2 to Chapter 21.

4 Dedijer, *The Battle Stalin Lost*, p.149.

Chapter 23: The Bear's Claws

English versions of the letters exchanged between the Central Committee of the Soviet and Yugoslav Communist Parties will be found in *Correspondence*. . . . (Belgrade, 1948) and *Documents*, pp.166-213.

1 *Prilozi*, p.471.

2 *Druženje*, pp.111-2.

3 F. Maclean, *Disputed Barricade*, p.371, information from Tito to the author.

4 J. Korbel, *Tito's Communism*, Denver, Brown, 1951, pp.336-7.

5 S. Krzavac and D. Marković, *Informbiro*, Belgrade 1976, pp.56-9.

6 *Druženje*, p.76.

7 Maclean, *Disputed Barricade*, p.379, statement of Djilas to author.

8 *Khrushchev Remembers*, Vol.2, p.182.

9 *Ibid.*, Vol.1, p.600.

10 Dedijer, *The Battle Stalin Lost*, p.131.

Notes

Chapter 24: Destination Unknown

1 Text of speeches in *V Kongres KPJ*, Belgrade 1949.
2 *Prilozi*, p.503.
3 *Druženje*, p.71.
4 *Borba*, 4 September 1948.
5 *Khrushchev Remembers*, Vol.2, p.181.
6 *Druženje*, p.112.
7 Letter of 17 May 1948, *Correspondence. . . : Documents*, p.197.
8 *Borba*, 2 October 1948, 4 October 1948.
9 E. Halperin, *The Triumphant Heretic*, London 1958, pp.107-8.
10 *Komunist* (Belgrade) September 1949.
11 Halperin, *op. cit.*, p.108.
12 Vukmanović-Tempo, *op. cit.*, Vol.2, p.110: A. Ross Johnson, *Transformation of Communist Ideology*, Cambridge, Mass., p.96.
13 Halperin, *op. cit.*, pp.112-3.
14 *Borba*, 19 March 1950; Ross Johnson, *op. cit.*, pp.101-2.

15 *Savremene Teme*, Belgrade 1950, p.26.
16 *Ibid.*, pp.4-5: Ross Johnson, *op. cit.*, pp.117: Halperin, *op. cit.*, pp.117-9.
17 *Unperfect Society*, pp.157-8. Kardelj, in his memoirs, plays down Djilas's part in originating the idea of self-management and claims that it was first put to Tito 'some time in the spring of 1949 by some of us in the Politburo' (*op. cit.*, p.136). In his later writings he suggests that self-management evolved more or less spontaneosly 'out of the earliest organs of government created at the very beginning of the national liberation uprising and socialist revolution during World War II'. (*Democracy and Socialism*, London 1978, p.9.)
18 *Druženje*, p.87.
19 *Ibid.*, p.132.

Chapter 25: Windows on the West

1 *Borba*, 29 January 1950.
2 Korbel, *op. cit.*, p.335.
3 Halperin, *op. cit.*, p.147.
4 PRO FO 371/88340, British Embassy to FO, 26 September 1950; Labour Party Archives, Report on visit to Yugoslavia, September 1950.
5 *Ibid.*
6 PRO, FO 371/95539 and 371/95488.
7 Dedijer, *The Battle Stalin Lost*, pp. 63-5.
8 PRO, FO 371/95488 Y 1053/12.

9 Jennie Lee, *My Life with Nye*, London 1980, pp.194-6.
10 *Druženje*, pp.88-9.
11 Michael Foot, *Aneurin Bevan*, Vol.2, London 1973, p.347.
12 *Ibid.*, p.348.
13 *Unperfect Society*, p.30.
14 *New York Times*, 23 July 1950: *Documents*, p.239.
15 Tito, *Govori*, Vol.VI, pp.75-9; *Documents*, pp.239-40.
16 Dedijer, *The Battle Stalin Lost*, pp.285-6.

323

Chapter 26: Reshaping the Party

1 Halperin, *op. cit.*, pp.216-7.
2 *VI Kongres KPJ*, Belgrade 1953.
3 Speech of 18 December 1971 to Trade Unions; Rusinow, *op. cit.*, p.312.
4 *Politika*, 9 November 1952.
5 *Druženje*, p.74.
6 *Ibid.*, p.77.
7 *Ibid.*, p.75.
8 *Ibid.*, p.76.
9 *Ibid.*
10 Dedijer, *The Battle Stalin Lost*, p.322.
11 'Eastern Sky', *Nova Misao*, 10 October 1953; English version, M. and D. Milenkovitch, eds., *Parts of a Lifetime*, New York 1968, pp.183-9.
12 *Parts of a Lifetime*, p.187.
13 *Ibid.*, p.185.
14 *Druženje*, p.119.
15 *Komunist*, July 1953.
16 *Unperfect Society*, p.21.
17 Tito, *Govori*, Vol.VIII, pp.133-9.

Chapter 27: Collision Course

The *Borba* articles referred to in this chapter are given in an English translation by Abraham Rothberg in Paul Willen (ed.), *Anatomy of a Moral*, New York 1959.

1 *New York Times*, 24 November 1953.
2 *Borba*, 11 October 1953: *Anatomy*, pp.35-40.
3 *Borba*, 25 October 1953: *Anatomy*, pp.41-6.
4 *Borba*, 22 November 1953: *Anatomy*, pp.65-9.
5 *Borba*, 1 and 8 November 1953: *Anatomy*, pp.47-57.
6 *Druženje*, p.43.
7 *Borba*, 6 December 1953: *Anatomy*, pp.75-79.
8 *Unperfect Society*, pp.17-18.
9 *Borba*, 20 December 1953: *Anatomy*, pp.87-93.
10 *Borba*, 22 December 1953: *Anatomy*, pp.93-7.
11 Quoted in F.W. Neal, *Titoism in Action*, University of California, 1958, p.70.
12 *Druženje*, p.140.
13 *Ibid.*
14 *Borba*, 24 December 1953: *Anatomy*, pp.99-103.
15 *Borba*, 27 December 1953: *Anatomy*, pp.105-9.
16 *Borba*, 31 December 1953: *Anatomy*, pp.111-115.
17 *Anatomy*, p.xii.
18 *Druženje*, p.141.
19 *Ibid.*

Chapter 28: The Break with Tito

1 *Unperfect Society*, p.174.
2 *Borba*, 4 January 1954: *Anatomy*, pp.123-144.
3 *Borba*, 7 January 1954: *Anatomy*, pp.177-181.
4 *Nova Misao*, January 1954: *Anatomy*, pp.145-176.
5 *Druženje*, p.143.
6 *Ibid.*, p.136.
7 *Ibid.*, p.7.

8 *Ibid.*, p.137.
9 *Ibid.*, p.136.
10 *Ibid.*, p.144.
11 *Unperfect Society*, p.173.
12 The following account is based on the official text published in *Komunist*, January-February 1954 (extracts in *Parts of a Lifetime*, pp.224-237), and the accounts in Hoffman and Neal, *Yugoslavia and the New Communism*, New York 1962, pp.185-95; Halperin, *op. cit.*, chs. 25-6; Rusinow, *op. cit.*, pp.81-7; Vukmanović-Tempo, *op. cit.*, Vol.2, pp.80-95.
13 *Unperfect Society*, p.126.
14 *Ibid.*, 174.
15 *Ibid.*

16 Interview with George Urban, *Encounter*, December 1979, p.34.
17 *Unperfect Society*, p.175.
18 *Ibid.*, p.177; *Druženje*, p.144.
19 *Druženje*, p.144.

Chapter 29: In the Wilderness

1 *Unperfect Society*, pp.176-7.
2 M. Foot, *Aneurin Bevan*, London 1973, pp.420-3.
3 Kardelj, *op. cit.*, p.145.
4 *Unperfect Society*, p.178.
5 Duško Doder, *The Yugoslavs*, London 1979, p.190.
6 *Unperfect Society*, p.127.
7 *Parts of a Lifetime*, pp.238-264.
8 *Ibid.*, p.240.
9 *Ibid.*, p.241.
10 *Ibid.*, p.242.
11 *Ibid.*, pp.243-4.
12 *Ibid.*, pp.244-6.

13 *Ibid.*, pp.246-7.
14 *Ibid.*, p.264.
15 *Times*, 22 December 1954.
16 *New York Times*, 25 December 1954.
17 *Times*, 26 January 1955.
18 *Parts of a Lifetime*, p.120.
19 *Ibid.*, p.332.
20 *Ibid.*
21 *Ibid.*, pp.329-331.
22 *Ibid.*, p.333.
23 *Ibid.*, pp.362-368.
24 *Times*, 20 November 1955.
25 *Ibid.*, 23 November 1955.

Chapter 30: Tito's Prisoner

1 *The Unperfect Society*, p.1.
2 *Ibid.*
3 *Ibid.*, p.2.
4 *Ibid.*, p.15.
5 *Ibid.*, p.5.
6 *Ibid.*, p.97.

7 *Ibid.*, p.68.
8 *Parts of a Lifetime*, 'Jail Diary', pp.266-7.
9 *Ibid.*, p.268.
10 *Ibid.*, p.290.
11 *Ibid.*, p.269.

12 *Ibid.*, p.108.
13 *Ibid.*, pp.272-3.
14 *Ibid.*, p.275.
15 *Ibid.*, pp.276, 284.
16 *Unperfect Society*, p.16.
17 *Parts of a Lifetime*, 'Jail Diary', p.280.
18 *Ibid.*, p.279.
19 *Unperfect Society*, p.17.
20 *Ibid.*
21 *Parts of a Lifetime*, 'Jail Diary', p.268.
22 *Ibid.*, p.183.

23 *Ibid.*, p.289.
24 *Ibid.*, pp.284-5.
25 *Ibid.*, p.268.
26 *Ibid.*, pp.295-6.
27 *Times*, 21.5.56.
28 *Parts of a Lifetime*, 'Jail Diary', p.297.
29 *Unperfect Society*, p.178.
30 *Parts of a Lifetime*, 'Jail diary', pp.296-7.

Chapter 31: Conversations and Consequences

1 *Parts of a Lifetime*, 'Jail Diary', p.289.
2 *Ibid.*, p.116.
3 *The Times*, 23 January 1961.
4 *Ibid.*, 25 January 1961.
5 *Conversations*, pp.9-10.
6 *Ibid.*, pp.169-173.
7 *Review of International Affairs* (Belgrade) 5-20 August 1961.
8 *New York Times*, 8 April 1962.
9 *Times*, 19 April 1962.

10 *Ibid.*, 13 April 1962.
11 *Yugoslav Embassy, London, Press hand-out*, 15 May 1962.
12 *New York Times*, 15 May 1962.
13 *Ibid.*, 19 May 1962.
14 *Times*, 21 July 1962.
15 *Ibid.*, 15 May 1962.
16 *New York Times*, 15 May 1962.
17 *Ibid.*
18 *Times Literary Supplement*, 20 July 1962.

Chapter 32: Back in Jail

1 *Pravda*, 14 December 1962.
2 *Unperfect Society*, p.19.
3 *Ibid.*, pp.24-5.
4 *Parts of a Lifetime*, 'Jail Diary', p.116.
5 *Ibid.*, p.121.

6 *Ibid.*, pp.110-4.
7 *Ibid.*, p.124.
8 *Ibid.*, p.125.
9 *Ibid.*, pp.271-2.
10 Rusinow, *op. cit.*, p.201.

Chapter 33: Freedom and Frustration

1 *New York Times*, 9 June 1968.
2 *Parts of a Lifetime*, 'Jail Diary', p.126.
3 *Unperfect Society*, pp.171-2.
4 *New York Times*, 2 April 1967.
5 *Ibid.*
6 *Observer*, 9 and 23 June 1968.
7 *Guardian*, 14 September 1968.

8 *Times*, 5 October 1968.
9 *New York Times*, 27 November 1968.
10 *Sunday Times*, 1 December 1968.
11 *Christian Science Monitor*, 12 December 1968.
12 *Freedom House Press Release*, December 1968.

Chapter 34: The End of the Tito Era

1 *Unperfect Society*, pp.159-160.

2 *Ibid.*, pp.152-3.

3 Interview in *Weltwoche*, June 1978.

4 *Politika*, 10 February 1974, quoted in Duncan Wilson, *op. cit.*, pp.212-3.

5 *Nin*, 17 June and 12 August 1973.

6 *Observer*, 18 March 1973.

7 *New York Times*, 21 June 1973.

8 Leonid Plyusch, *History's Carnival*, London 1979, pp.148-9.

9 Vladimir Bukovsky, *To Build a Castle*, London 1978, pp.136-7.

10 *International Herald Tribune*, 20 November 1975.

11 *Keesing's Contemporary Archives*, Vol.xxii, 1976, p.27754.

12 *New York Times*, 9 February 1977; *Times*, 9 and 10 February 1977.

13 *Financial Times*, 11 February 1977.

14 *Večernje Novosti*, 11 April 1977.

15 *Frankfurter Allgemeine Zeitung*, 7 March and 13 April 1977.

16 *New York Times*, 24 March and 13 April 1977.

17 *Times*, 17 April 1977.

18 *Süddeutsche Zeitung*, 18 April 1977.

19 Djilas interview, *Die Welt*, 27 March 1979.

20 M. Mihailov, *Washington Quarterly*, Autumn 1979, pp.64-73.

21 *Guardian*, 22 December 1978.

22 *New York Herald Tribune*, 26 December 1978.

23 *New York Times, Daily Telegraph*, 23 March 1979.

24 *Guardian*, 16 October 1979.

25 *International Herald Tribune*, 23 August 1979.

26 *Parts of a Lifetime*, 'Jail Diary', p.114.

27 *Ibid.*, p.115.

28 *Diary of Thoughts, 1953-54: Parts of a Lifetime*, p.224.

INDEX